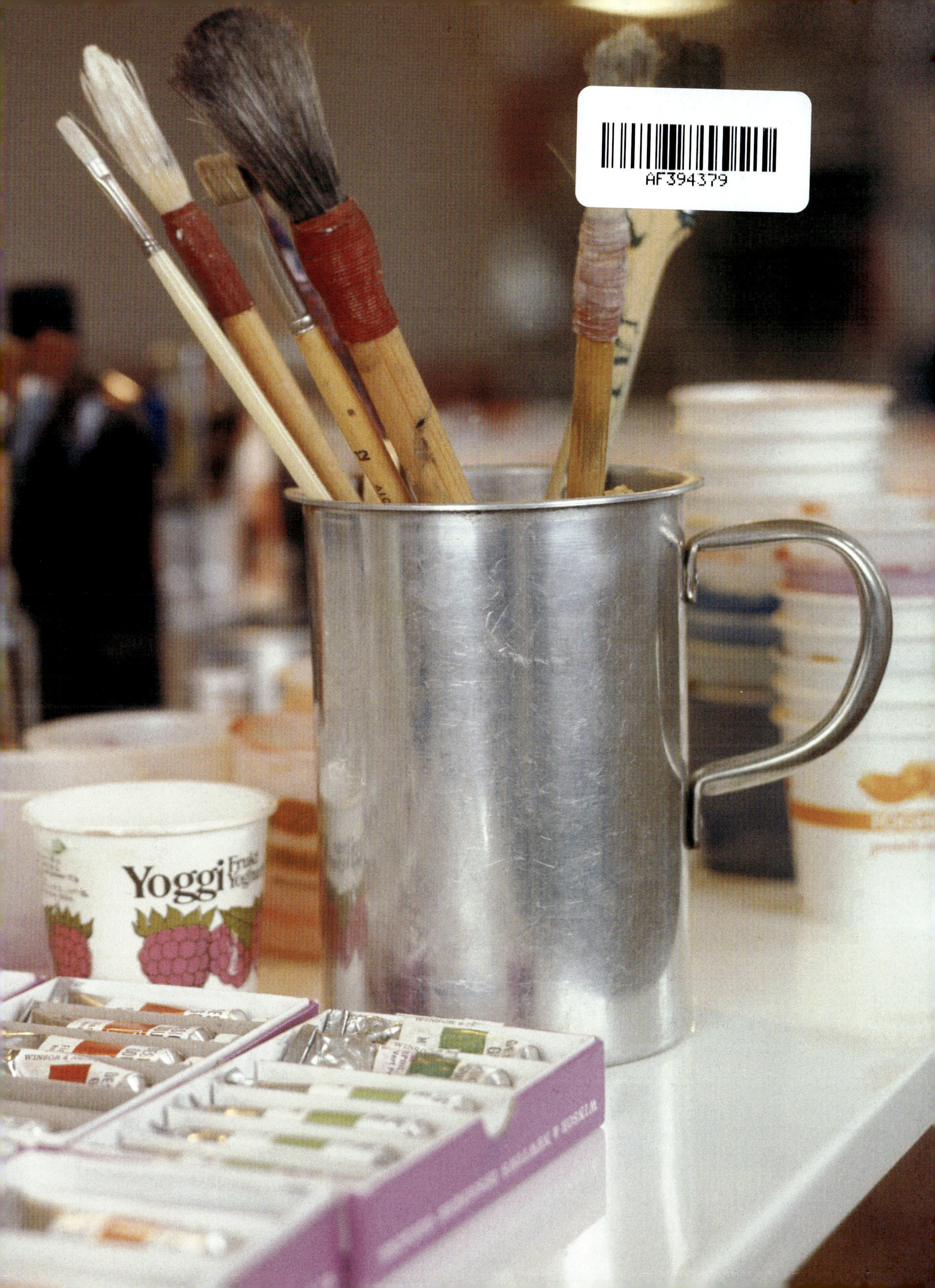
AF394379
Yoggi
WINSOR

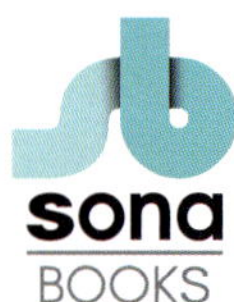

**First published in 2022 by Sona Books
an imprint 0f Danann Publishing Limited.**

© 2022 Danann Publishing Limited

WARNING: For private domestic use only, any unauthorised copying,
hiring, lending or public performance of this book is illegal.

Published under licence from Future Publishing Limited a Future PLC
group company. All rights reserved. No part of this publication may be
reproduced or stored in a retrieval system or transmitted in any form or
by any means without the prior written permission of the publisher.

Copy Editor Carolyn McHugh

CAT NO: SON0528
ISBN: 978-1-912918-83-6

Made in EU.

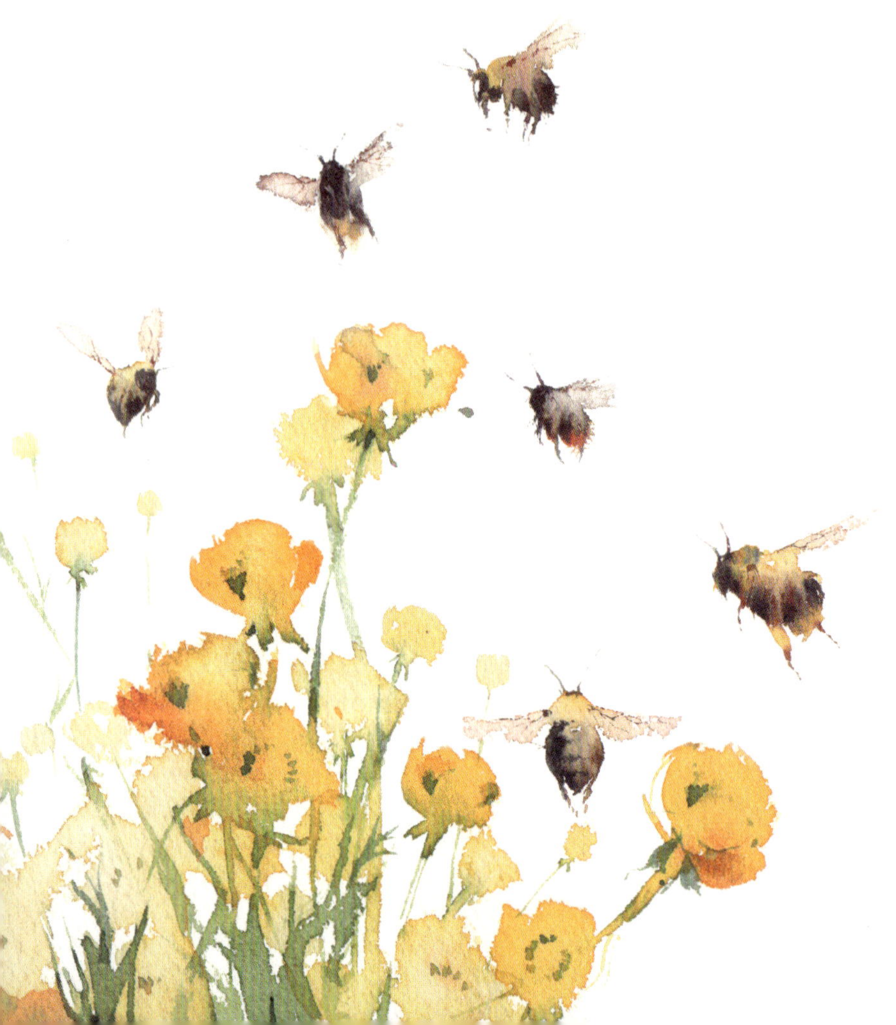

Watercolours

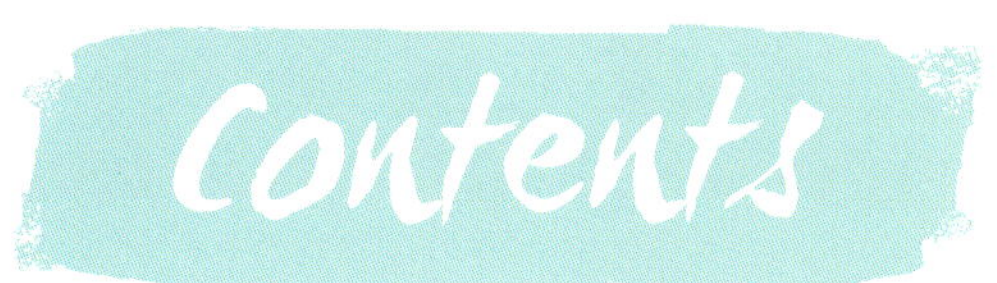

Contents

Kitbag essentials

Skills & techniques

Projects

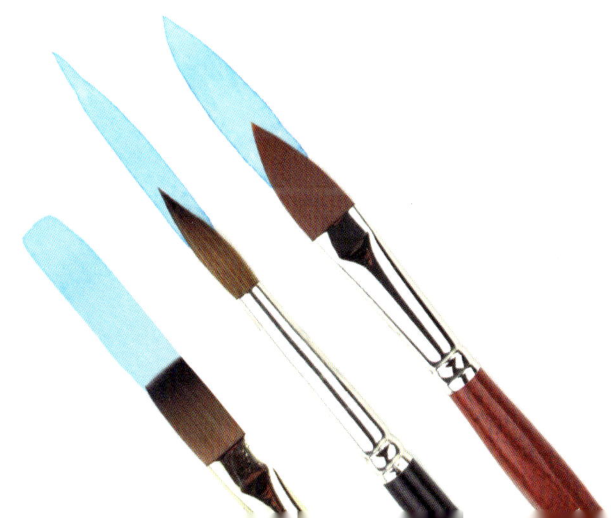

Essential kit for watercolour

This guide from **Lancelot Richardson** introduces common watercolour materials, explains what they are and gives suggestions for building your own watercolour kit

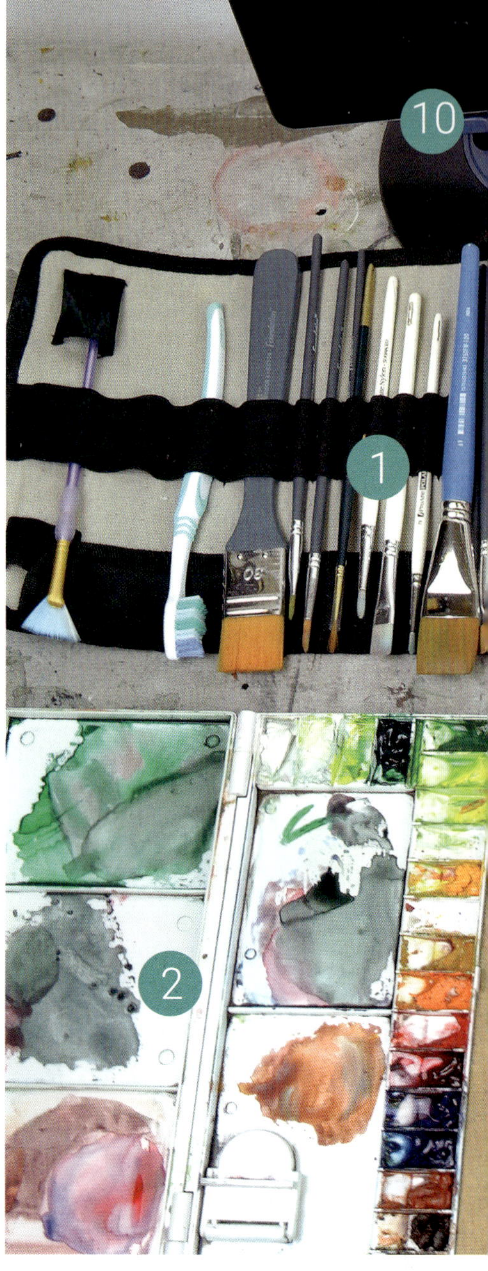

Watercolour is a diverse medium, with lots of different options for paints, brushes and papers, as well as extra tools for applying and manipulating colour. This introduction covers a range of materials available on the market, highlighting what they are used for and how they may fit into certain working processes.

There is an awful lot to choose from, and most artists won't need everything shown in this guide. Focus on picking materials that suit your process and sensibilities. For instance, if you are interested in producing large-scale work, consider choosing paint that offers wide coverage and brushes that make larger marks. If you are interested in tight details, however, it might be better to select materials more suited for producing fine brushstrokes. If you are unsure, consider selecting a few versatile materials instead of specialist ones, and expand your kit over time.

Quality of materials wins out over quantity, more so for watercolour than almost any other medium; a few tubes of good paint will create a better result than an entire set of cheap ones, and a single good brush will serve you better than a vast kit that cannot hold a point.

Below I've listed my go-to tools for painting watercolour, but bear in mind that you'll want to start small.

1 Brush roll
A selection of brushes in a roll covering a range of shapes and sizes useful for day-to-day painting. Keeping them in a roll protects them and keeps them together.

2 Palette with paints
I prefer to paint from tube paints squeezed into a palette, since it is convenient and suitable for the sizes I work at. Tube paints are allowed to dry in the palette – if fresh paint is needed, I can squeeze out more.

3 Watercolour paper and board
Here I use a board as a support for the watercolour paper and hold it down with masking tape so the paper doesn't buckle while I'm painting. If I'm working with more washes, I'll use stronger, gummed tape instead.

4 Pipette
Pipettes are handy tools to have around. I use them for squirting water into mixtures to help thin out washes, and they are also useful for dripping a little water onto dry paints in order to reactivate them.

5 Watercolour pencils
Often I use watercolour pencils for the initial sketch of a painting I am working on, as they add a little colour to the initial stages, and the lines melt away to something softer.

6 Watercolour tube paints
I like to store my tube paints in a jar to keep them fresher for longer. It also keeps them from getting lost! I keep a tube of gouache handy for occasional opaque highlights, too.

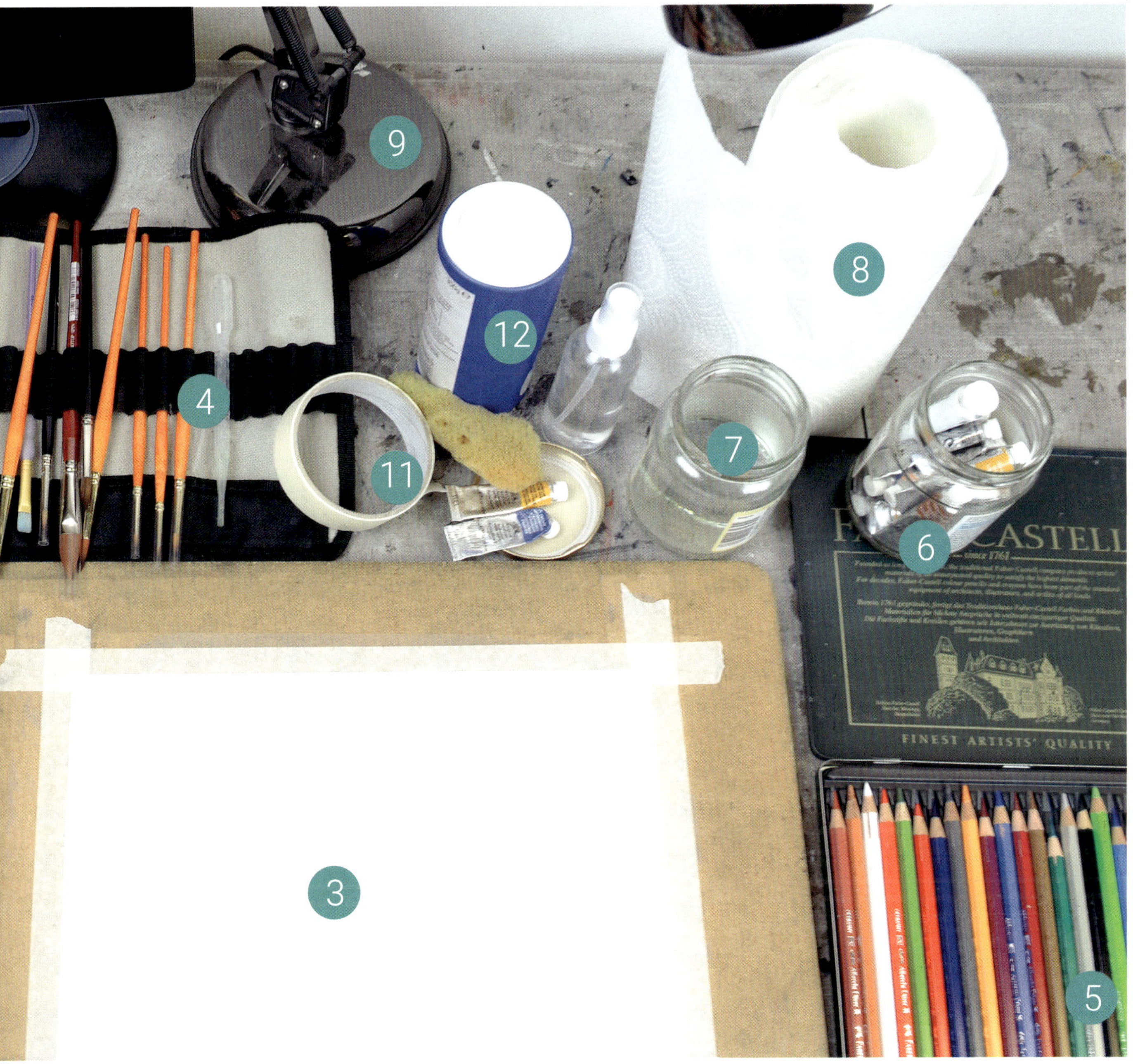

7 Jar of water

I always try to keep my water fresh, as dirty water can contaminate paint. I prefer old jars – they are clean and heavy enough to not knock over easily, or be mistaken for a cup of tea!

8 Paper towels

Paper towels are useful for mopping up excess water, cleaning palettes quickly and soaking water out of overloaded brushes. They can also leave interesting 'daubed' textures in wet areas. Cloths can also be used like this.

9 Lamp

I tend to have plenty of natural light in my space, but during evenings or cloudy weather it is useful to have extra lighting to top up any overhead lights, especially when avoiding cast shadows whilst working.

10 Tablet

When working from reference, I use a tablet or screen rather than paper printouts. This is partly for convenience, though I do find that the picture colour on a screen is better than on printouts.

11 Masking tape

Masking tape is useful for holding paper down if you haven't stretched it, and it can deal with a little cockling (wrinkling). Try to pick a fairly low-tack tape to avoid damaging the paper. And most importantly, when removing it, always peel away from the page!

12 Extra kit

These items tend to change depending on what I am working on. The salt and sponge are used for creating textures and gradients, while the spray bottle is useful for creating wet areas to work into.

Picking your paints

Watercolours can come in a variety of different forms that make them suitable for many working styles

Different forms of watercolour play different key roles in any working process due to their individual strengths and limitations. Are vibrant colours an essential requirement? Is it important to have a portable set-up for plein air sketching? Or is tight detail a high priority? Some paints will serve these needs better than others.

Watercolour paint comes in many forms, including tube paints, pans and as water-soluble pencils. There are many different brands that produce each of these, often with their own traditional formulations that provide slightly different results. Some provide cheaper options aimed at students, too.

Pigments are an ingredient that gives paint its colour, and good brands usually list the pigment numbers on their products. These are recognisable as a P plus a letter for the colour (such as R for red) and number for the pigment – for instance, PR108 is Cadmium Red. Look these up when buying paints, as different brands often give similar pigments different names, and may pad out paints with cheap pigments. Even expensive ranges may include the occasional poor-quality pigment that fades quickly – watercolour washes are particularly vulnerable to this, so be sure to select paints with excellent or very good lightfastness. It is usually better to pick paints with single pigments, as they mix more predictably.

Student versus artist quality

Paint is made of a formulation of ingredients including pigment to give it colour, flow enhancers, and binders to stabilise it. Many brands offer student-quality ranges of paint, which are cheaper for various reasons; they have more fillers to pad them out, they lack more expensive pigments, or they lack ingredients that help the paint perform better – or sometimes a combination of all three.

Overall, student paints are fine for sketching and learning, but will disappoint when intense colours and longevity is required. More expensive artist-quality paints will typically produce brighter colours, perform more consistently, and are less likely to fade over time. One mid-ground between the two is to swap out student paints that perform poorly or have bad pigments with artist-quality ones, such as replacing cadmium hues with real cadmium. Some cheaper pigments are perfectly good, such as earths like Yellow Ochre, so the student paint may work well enough.

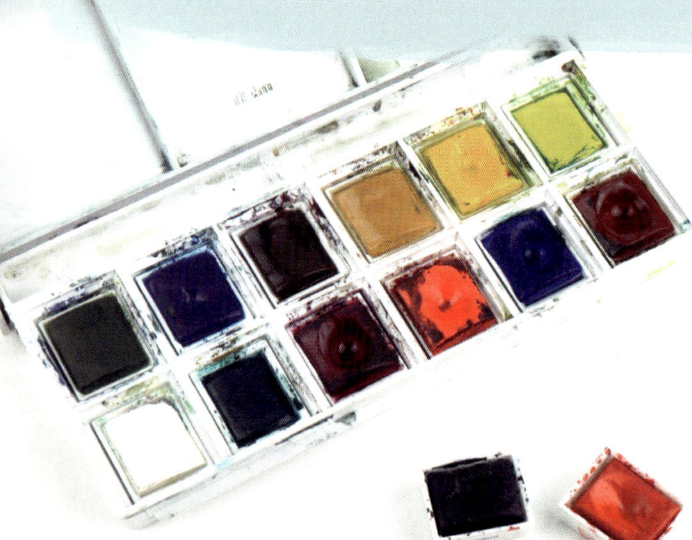

Watercolour Pans

Watercolour pans are small containers of solid paint that are activated with water. Usually they come in rectangular full or half pans, though some sets use circular ones.

The big advantage of pans is that they can be held in a portable set. Small sets are easily held in one hand, making them useful for sketching on the move. They also last a long time compared to tube paints.

The downside is pans are not as vivid as tube paints, and it is more difficult to get large amounts of colour out of them for washes. Always keep a lid on them when they are not in use to keep dust off.

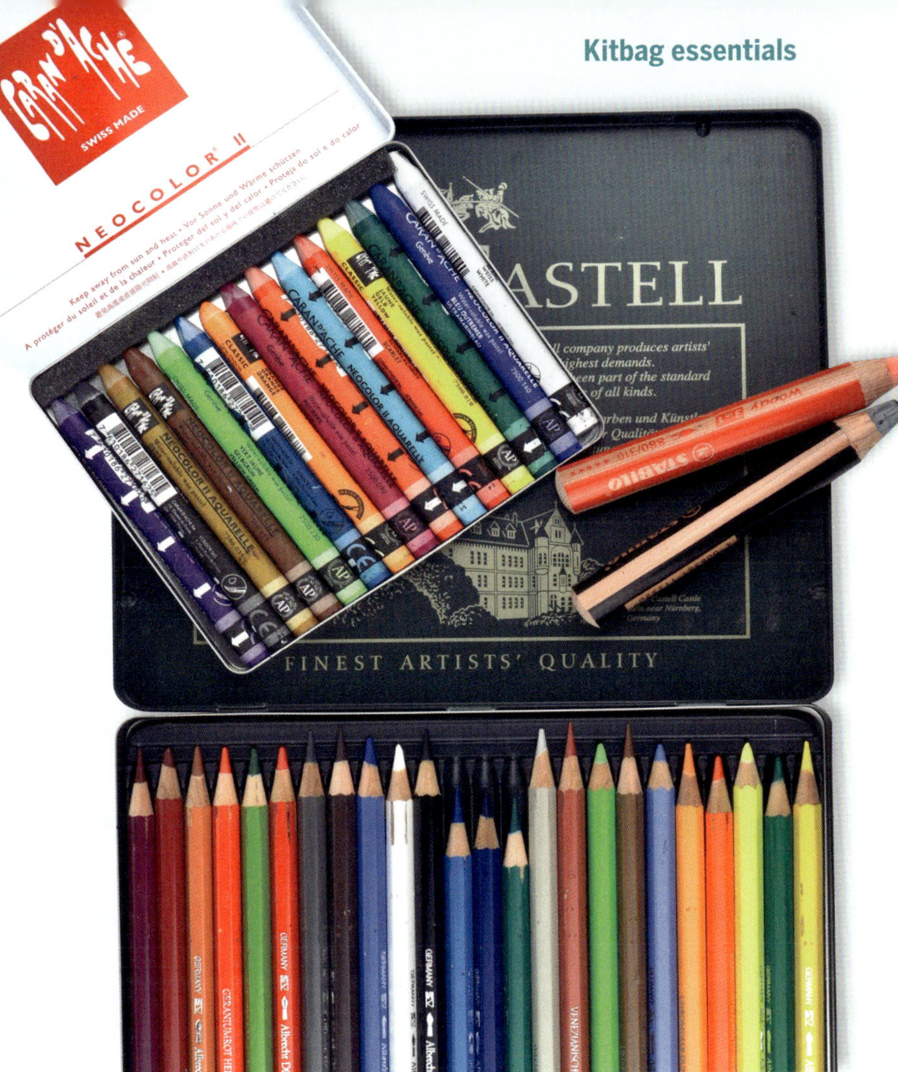

Watercolour pencils

Watercolour pencils comprise a variety of pencils and crayons that use a water-soluble binder. These work like normal crayons, but once the marks get wet they dissolve and behave like watercolour paint. If used on a wet surface, they leave marks of intensely coloured pigment.

This form of watercolour is excellent for handling details, textures and small areas of intense colour. Their solubility and colour also make them useful for sketching under watercolour washes.

Because of their fine points, they are generally not suitable for producing washes, although the pigment can be pushed around using excess water. Water-soluble crayons can cover large areas if used on their side, forming unique textures in the process.

Get the most from watercolour pencils

Follow these steps...

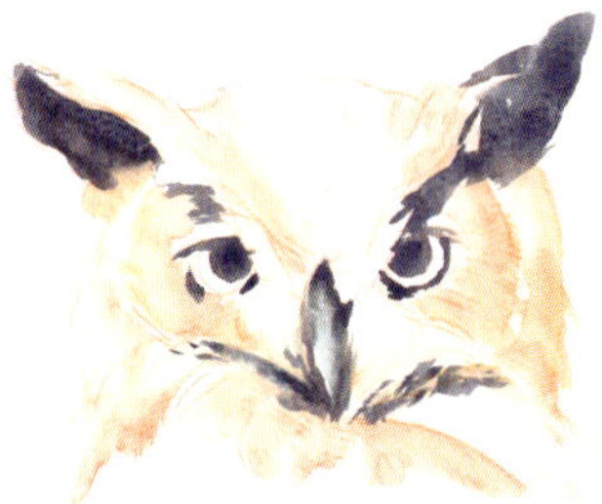

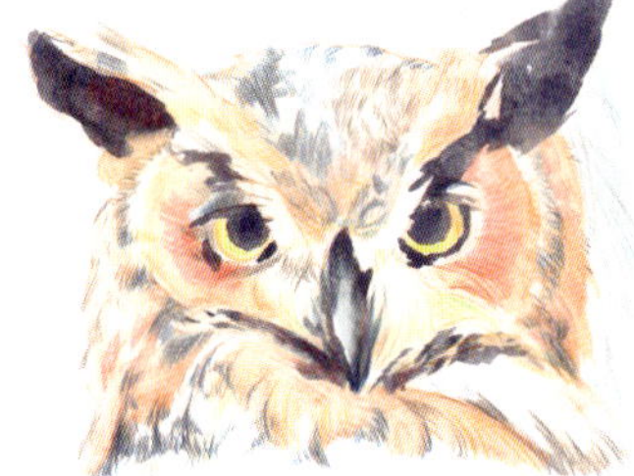

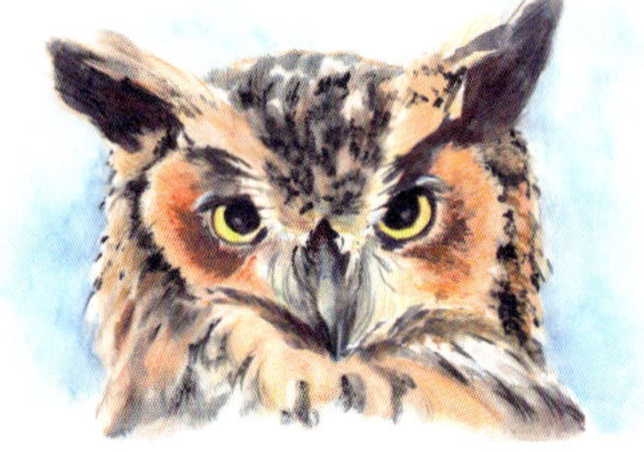

1 ⬤ Under drawing
Watercolour pencils are great for sketching out an image, as they don't muddy watercolours and dissolve readily without leaving harsh lines. Here I sketched an outline of the owl's head with a bit of hatching for shading, then wetted it with a brush and clean water to create a simple wash.

2 ⬤ Building colour
One way to 'mix' watercolour pencils is by layering them on top of each other and wetting them with clean water. Here some of the black feathers are sketched in with the brown and black pencils, while different combinations of browns, reds and oranges build up the other plumage.

3 ⬤ Add texture and detail
Most of these final details were added by dipping the pencil tip into water, or by lightly brushing water into an area before drawing on it. When wet, watercolour pencils leave more richly pigmented marks. A white watercolour pencil is used for the final touches.

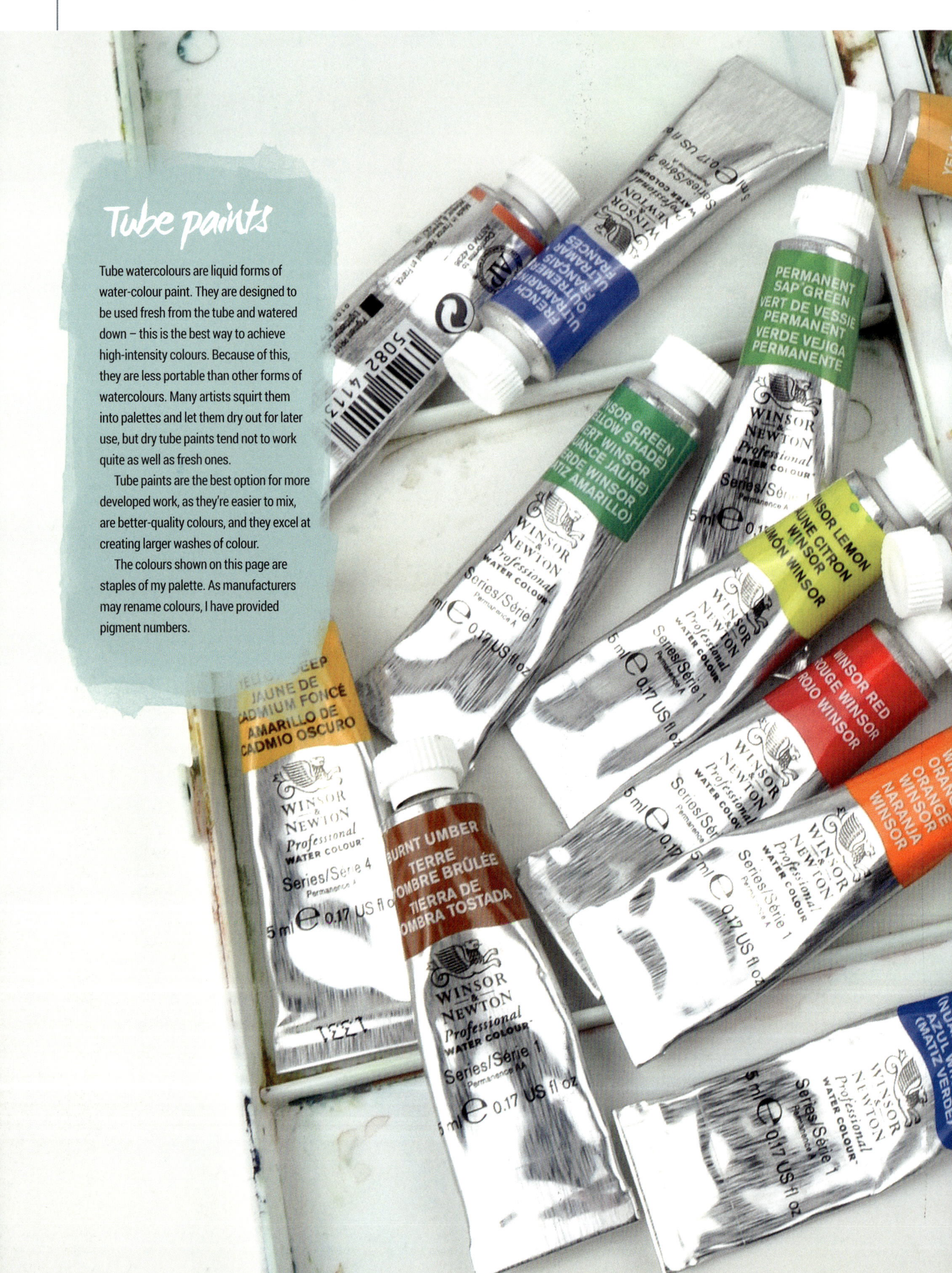

Tube paints

Tube watercolours are liquid forms of water-colour paint. They are designed to be used fresh from the tube and watered down – this is the best way to achieve high-intensity colours. Because of this, they are less portable than other forms of watercolours. Many artists squirt them into palettes and let them dry out for later use, but dry tube paints tend not to work quite as well as fresh ones.

Tube paints are the best option for more developed work, as they're easier to mix, are better-quality colours, and they excel at creating larger washes of colour.

The colours shown on this page are staples of my palette. As manufacturers may rename colours, I have provided pigment numbers.

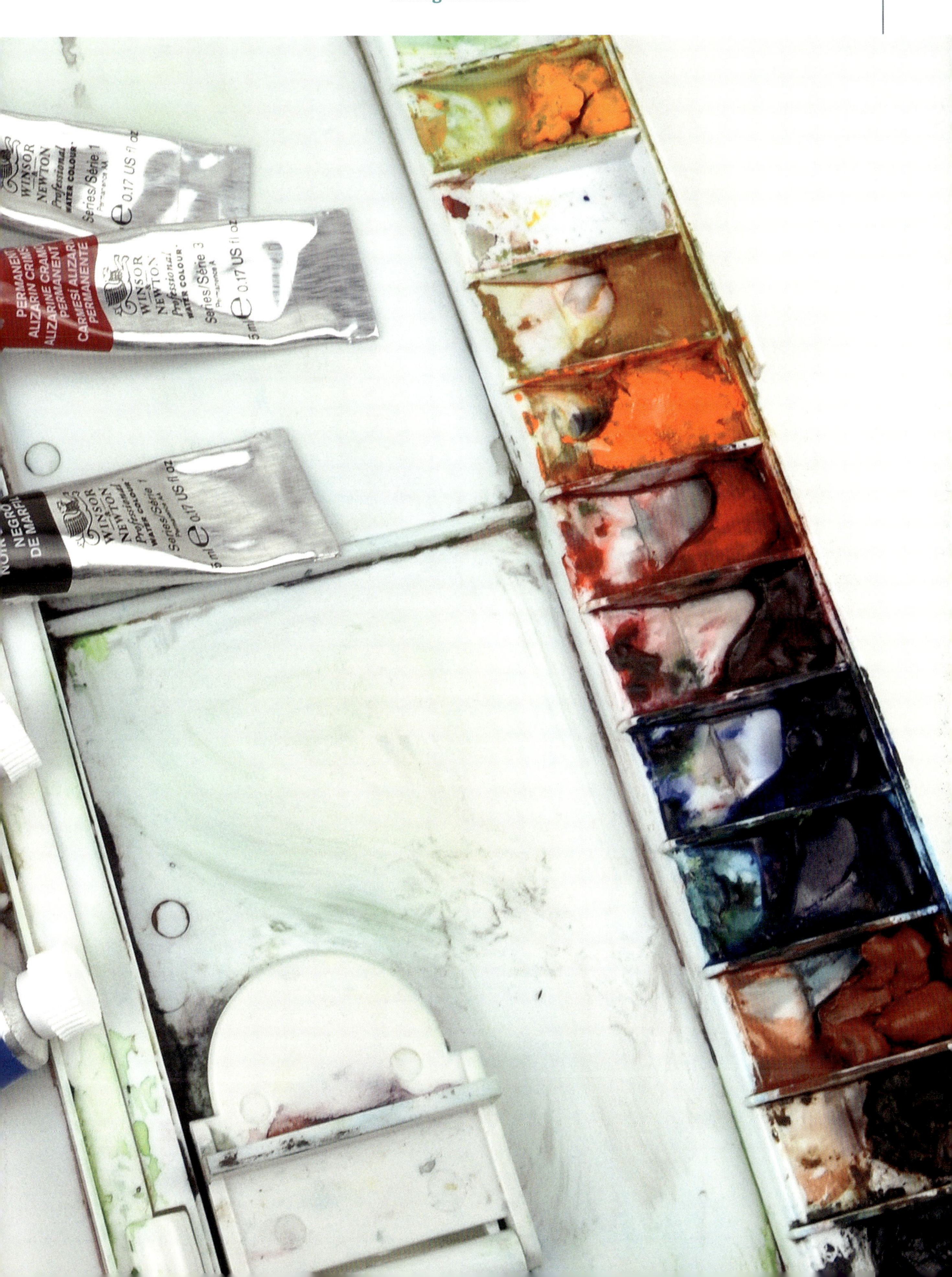

Essential colours

1 Lemon Yellow (PY175)
An excellent green-leaning yellow that is especially useful in landscape painting. It quite translucent and mixes vivid greens. It is also suitable for glazing, and combines well with phthalo colours. It's less effective for mixing with reds, but still retains some luminescence.

2 Cadmium Yellow (PY35)
Comes in varying shades. This is a versatile red-leaning yellow with a lot of uses – if you pick just one yellow, make it this one. It is quite opaque and mixes excellent warm lights as well as oranges, making it useful for colourful subjects and skin tones.

3 Yellow Ochre (PY43)
Yellow ochre, a warm yellow, is a useful earth pigment, used for skin tones, dull greens and a wide variety of neutral colours. It is very opaque, like most earth pigments – this means it isn't very good in glazes, but it does mix well into light colours.

4 Pyrrole Red (PR254)
Also known as Ferrari red. A modern alternative to Cadmium Red with good light fastness and high intensity – a little goes a long way. It is very versatile, mixing well into skin tones, oranges, shadows and lights. If you buy just one red, go with this one.

5 Permanent Alizarin Crimson (PR206)
A more lightfast alternative to Alizarin Crimson, which can fade quite quickly. Permanent Alizarin Crimson is very translucent, making it a great colour to mix into shadows. It mixes an excellent chromatic black with Phthalo Green, and is also useful for painting cool shadows in skin tones.

6 French Ultramarine (PB29)
A staple of artists' palettes, this is a slightly red-leaning blue with a dark tone. It mixes a good chromatic black with Venetian Red – these two colours can form a limited palette together. It is versatile, mixing into shadows and neutrals well. If you only have one blue, this is the one you need.

7 Phthalo Blue (green) (PB15)
An intense blue – handle this with care as it goes a long way (this also makes it excellent value for money!). Some artists don't like phthalos as they can overwhelm colour mixes, but when handled with care they are excellent for mixing greys and greens.

8 Phthalo Green (yellow) (PG36)
Like Phthalo Blue, this is a really strong colour. It's useful for landscapes, though it is also handy for mixing greys and cool neutrals, as it behaves a lot like Phthalo Blue. Phthalo paints are very translucent, making them useful for glazing and mixing shadows.

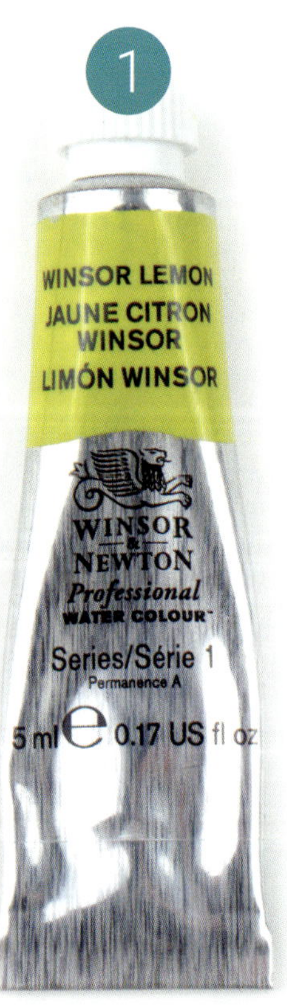

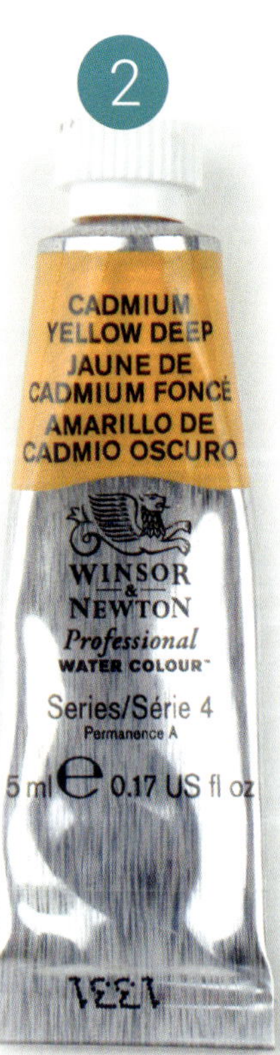

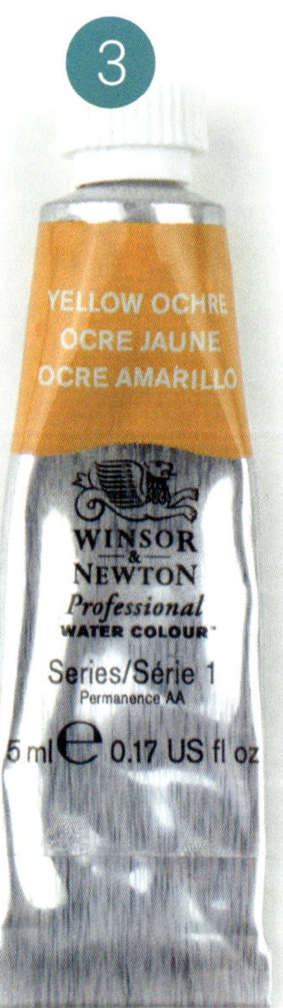

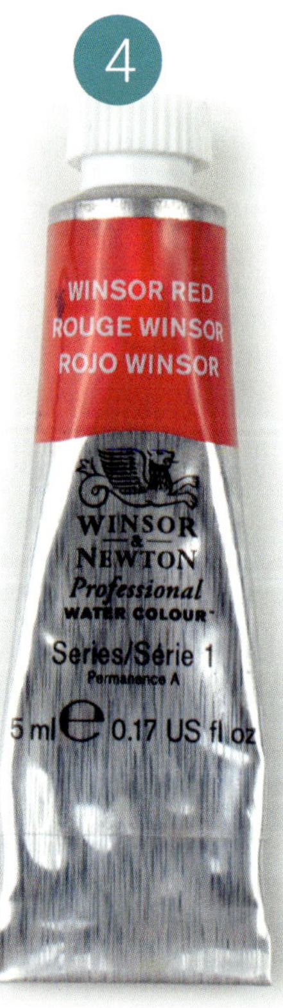

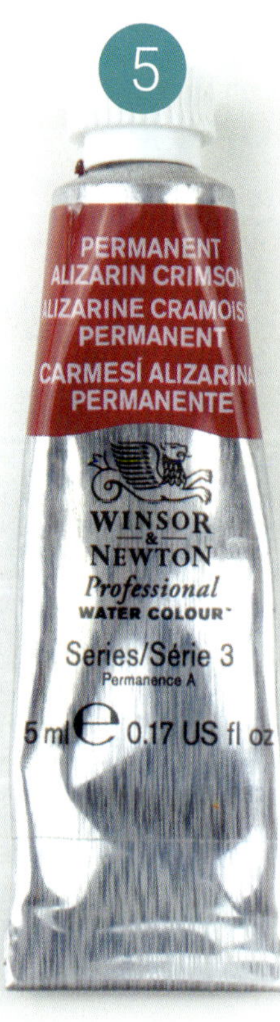

9 Venetian Red (PR101)

There are lots of names for this pigment and it varies between manufacturers. It is a strong, reddish-brown earth pigment and is fairly opaque. It is very useful for mixing lots of brown and neutral colours. If you pick only one brown, go with this one.

10 Burnt Umber (PBr7 and others)

This colour varies between manufacturers, but should be a dark, slightly yellow-leaning, opaque brown made from earth pigments. It is handy for mixing neutrals, skin tones and warm shadows, generally being more useful with natural subjects. It is less versatile than Venetian Red, but more suited to subtle shifts in colour.

11 Ivory Black (Pbk9)

This is a traditional black (thankfully no longer made with ivory!), which is fairly opaque. It's useful for dulling colours and is especially good for mixing dull greens. Generally, it doesn't mix great shadows, as it tends to look a bit flat, but it's occasionally handy for deep, opaque blacks.

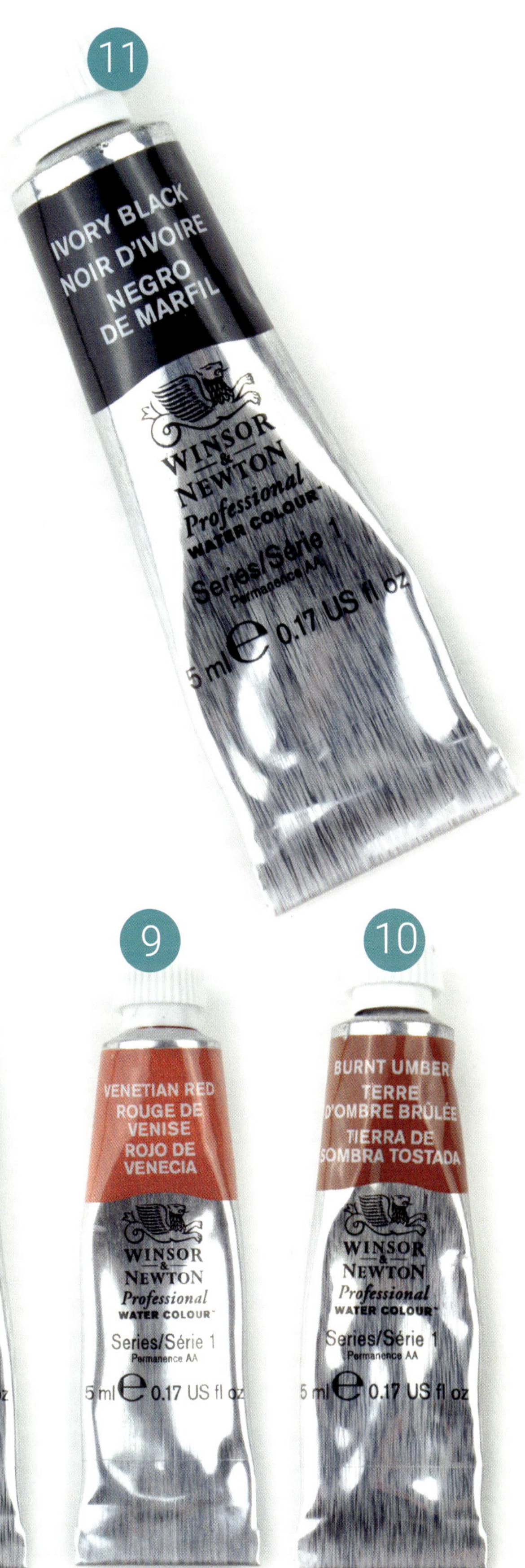

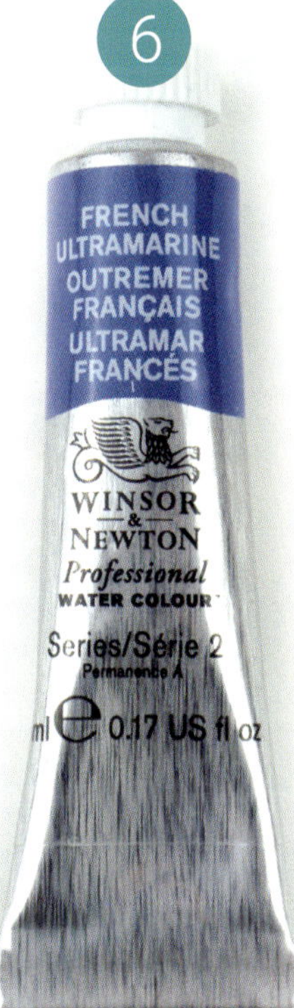

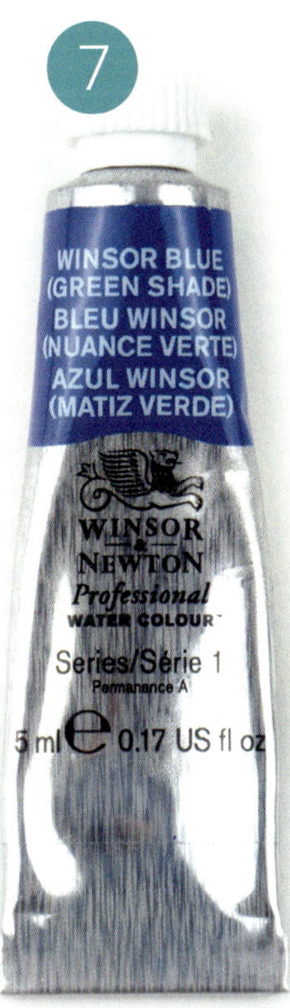

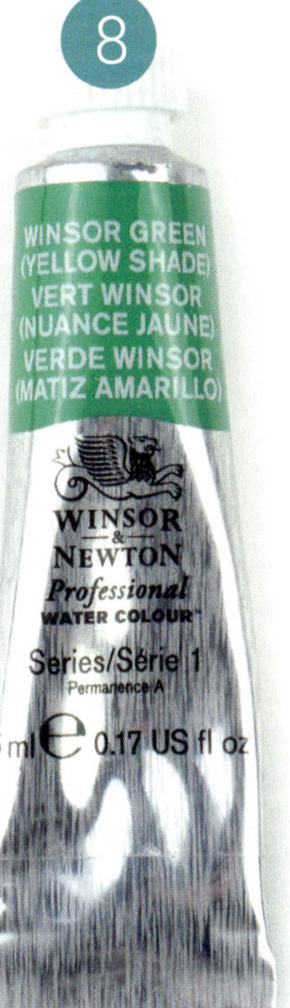

Brush up on brushes

Brushes are an essential element of your kit. This guide introduces some common brush types and explains their different uses

There are many brushes to use with watercolour, and picking suitable ones will make painting significantly more enjoyable. A big part of this is personal inclination – the brushes should suit our working processes and individual styles. Different brush shapes make unique sets of marks, making them more or less suitable for different jobs.

With watercolour it is best opt for quality over quantity in brushes. Brushes should hold their point when wet and not 'split' or deform, and should not drop bristles when used – cheaper brushes tend to do both of these things. Good brushes often look 'denser', as they have more bristles.

It is usually best to have some bigger brushes, as they can make a wider range of marks and hold more water – try to avoid starter packs padded out with cheap, tiny brushes! A good starting point for your kit is a large flat for washes, a medium-large round, another medium-sized flat, and possibly a small round or rigger for details. Add brushes as needed – for instance, a hake brush for big washes, or a fan for textures.

Good brushes aren't cheap, but will last for years when well cared for. Don't let paint dry in them, as it will damage the shape – be sure to wash them thoroughly with a mild soap after use.

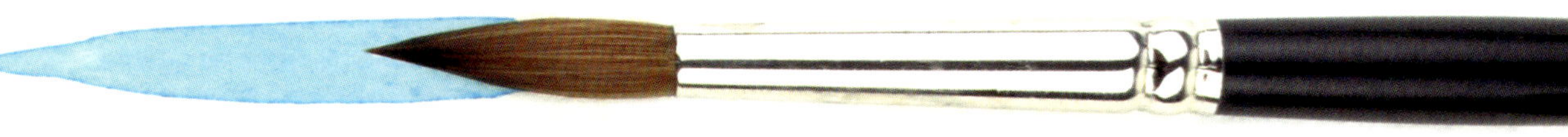

Round

Round brushes are a versatile option, capable of doing a lot of different jobs. A good round will hold its point, and make thin enough lines to draw with, but with increased pressure creates a wide variety of thicker marks. Bigger sizes hold water well and can make small washes. Round brushes tend to make more 'organic' feeling marks.

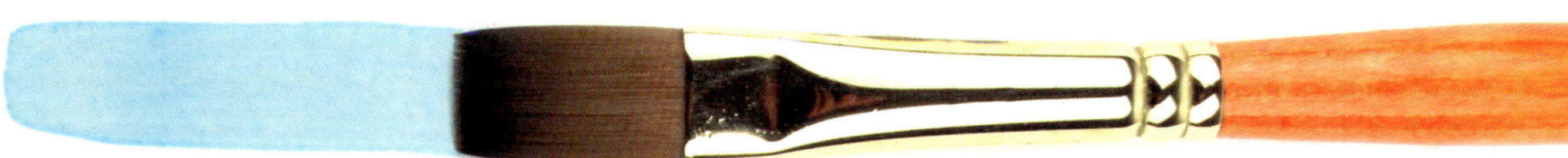

Flat

Flat brushes are good for laying down even areas of colour, but are also very versatile. When turned on their edge, they can make thin, straight lines, making them useful for details. The body of the brush can also be dragged along at a shallow angle for dry-brush effects that work well on cold and rough papers. They are good for small-medium washes, painting man-made structures and adding rough, random textures.

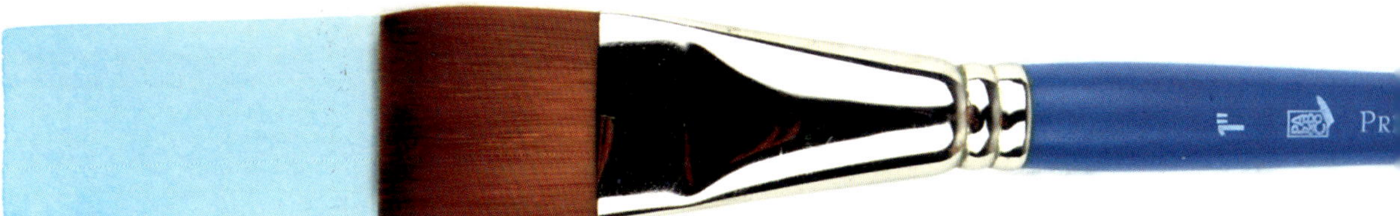

Flat Wash

🔺 Flat wash brushes tend to be larger, thicker flat brushes – ones that are an inch or more wide are most useful. They are used for laying in large areas of colour, applying water and creating broad brush strokes. By using large brushes like this, washes don't get streaky from drying part way through.

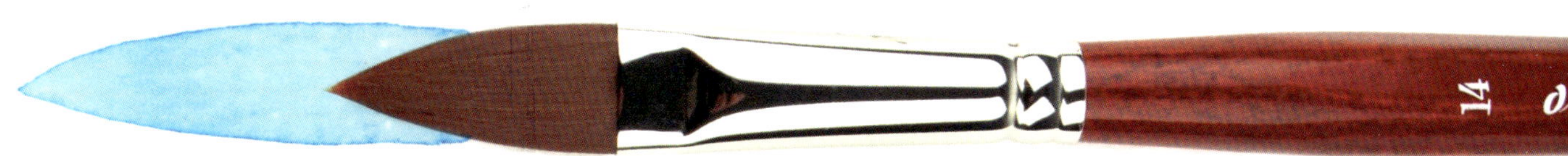

Cat's Tongue

🔺 Also sometimes referred to as an oval brush. This a more unusual brush shape with a pointed tip that can produce fine lines and a flat belly for holding lots of liquid to produce thick marks and washes. Changing the pressure means it can go from thin to thick and back again within one brush stroke, opening up a wide variety of different marks.

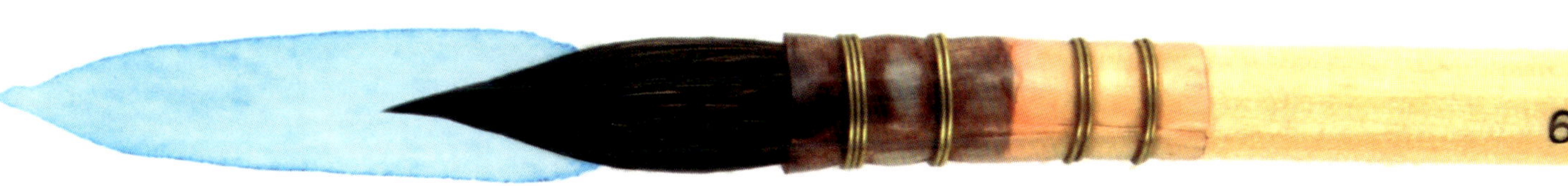

Mop

🔺 Often used interchangeably with quill brushes. Mop brushes have a bigger belly than a round that is great for holding lots of water, and are good for working wet-in-wet in particular. They are very soft and tend to be far less 'springy' than round brushes, so while they can make thin lines, they are not as good at it as a round and can be harder to control.

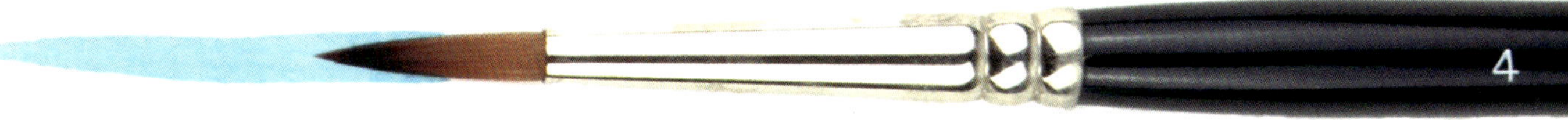

Small Round

🔺 Small rounds are used in different ways to larger round brushes. They tend not to hold much water, so are not suitable for any kind of coverage or long line. However, they are useful for fine, isolated details, especially if extra precision is needed, and for painting very tiny things. Another unique use of this brush is stippling, a type of painting that involves creating many closely packed dots of colour.

Rigger

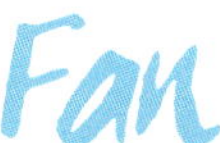 Rigger brushes are a specialised brush used for painting long, thin lines of a consistent width. The clue is in the name – they were used to paint ships' rigging! However, they can be useful in many situations; they hold more liquid than a small round brush and make longer lines. Ensure the hairs are filled up with paint to achieve this. The brush length can accommodate a slight tremor, as the hair cushions movement.

Fan

Fan brushes are fairly specialised brushes that are good at generating random textures. Dragging or flicking the brush creates lots of thin, stringy marks, pulling it sideways creates thin, slightly uneven lines, using the edge creates random organic textures, and tapping it generates a stippled effect. The unusual shape means changes in direction, angle and application can produce a wide variety of marks, which is especially useful for landscape work.

Chinese Brushes

Chinese brushes are typically used with ink in calligraphy, but work well with watercolour too. They tend to be medium to large round brushes made with a variety of different natural hairs, and sometimes combine two different types. This means they are quite soft, but generally good at holding a point. These are a great option for big, loose brushstrokes.

Types of brush hair

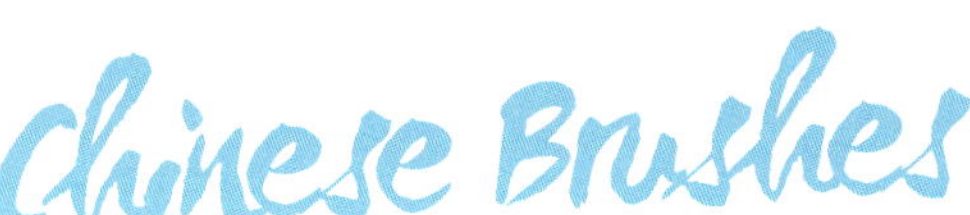

There are many different kinds of brush hair in use that can be broadly categorised as synthetic or natural.

Natural bristles are made with hair from a variety of different animals, such as sable, squirrel, goat and many others. Typically, natural brushes are softer and more flexible than synthetics, hold more water, and form better points.

Synthetic brushes have become very diverse, ranging from quite firm to almost as soft as the hair they are trying to emulate. They tend to be more hard-wearing, though they can lose their shape faster than natural brushes. It is better to go with more expensive synthetics – their firmness is particularly good for flats.

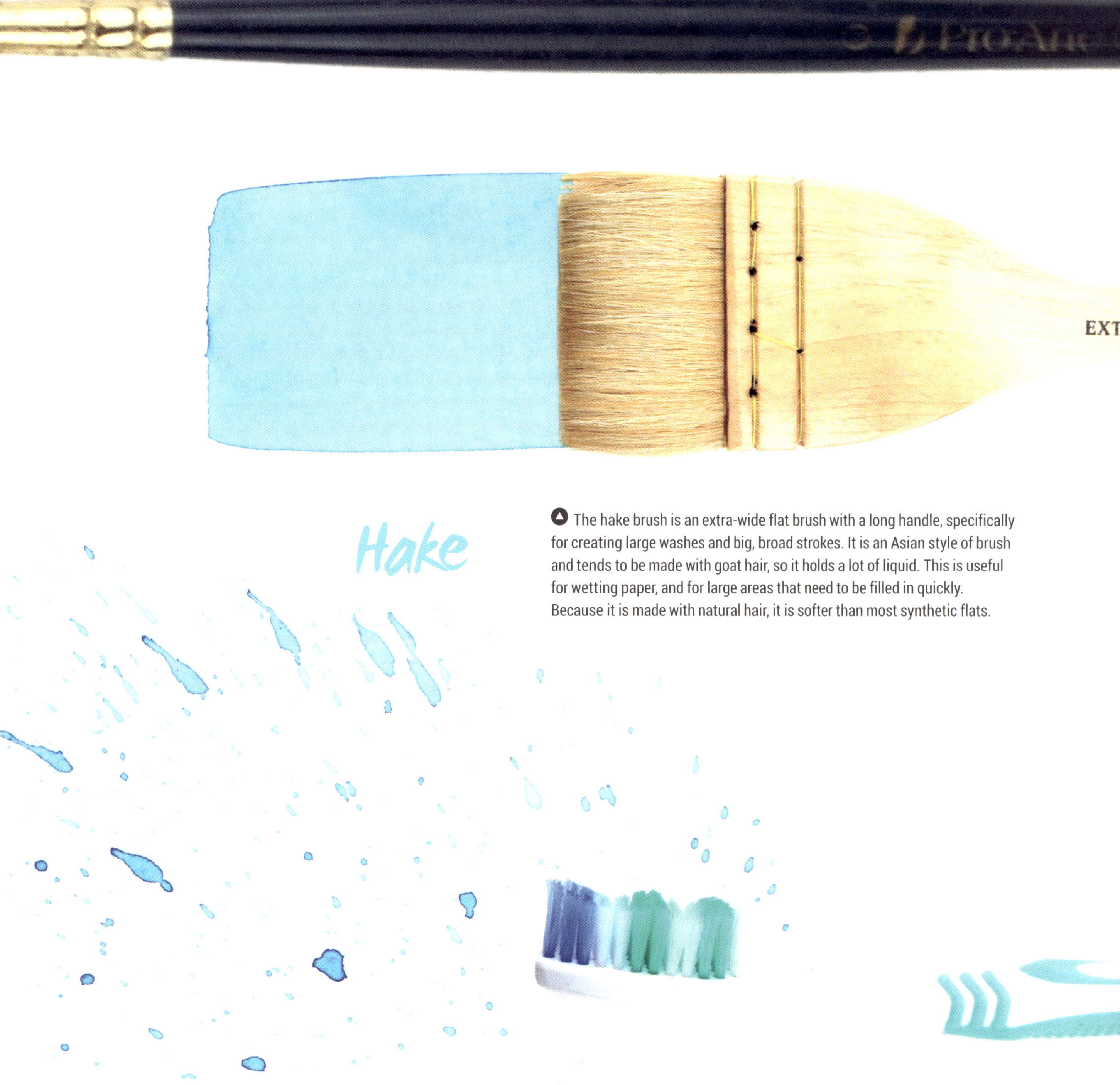

Hake

The hake brush is an extra-wide flat brush with a long handle, specifically for creating large washes and big, broad strokes. It is an Asian style of brush and tends to be made with goat hair, so it holds a lot of liquid. This is useful for wetting paper, and for large areas that need to be filled in quickly. Because it is made with natural hair, it is softer than most synthetic flats.

Toothbrush

Toothbrushes are useful to keep around for creating splatter effects. Simply dip a toothbrush into a pool of watercolour wash and flick the bristles with your thumb or a piece of stiff card to create a spray of droplets. This is effective for creating random textures. It can be hard to control, so use loose sheets of scrap paper or card to guard other areas from this effect.

Paper choices

The surface we work on plays a pivotal role in the process and end result of our artwork

Choosing the right paper depends on preference and working style, so it is important to consider what is needed of the paper before buying it. Watercolour paper is broadly split into three main types: hot press, cold press and rough. Each type of paper performs differently, resulting in different marks and textures, but they can all be good quality. Different types of paper have their own strengths and limitations; for instance, a rough paper would make detailed botanical illustration very difficult, whereas textured effects would not show up well on a hot press paper.

Paper is usually made from wood pulp (also labelled 'woodfree') or cotton. Cotton papers are considerably more hard wearing and longer lasting, but also more expensive. Mould-made papers tend to be of superior quality to machine-made papers, as they come in heavier weights and have a stronger surface, but machine-made papers may have a more uniform surface. It is worth testing out a selection of papers with watercolours if possible, as many brands have their own formulations and may behave differently despite being a similar type of paper.

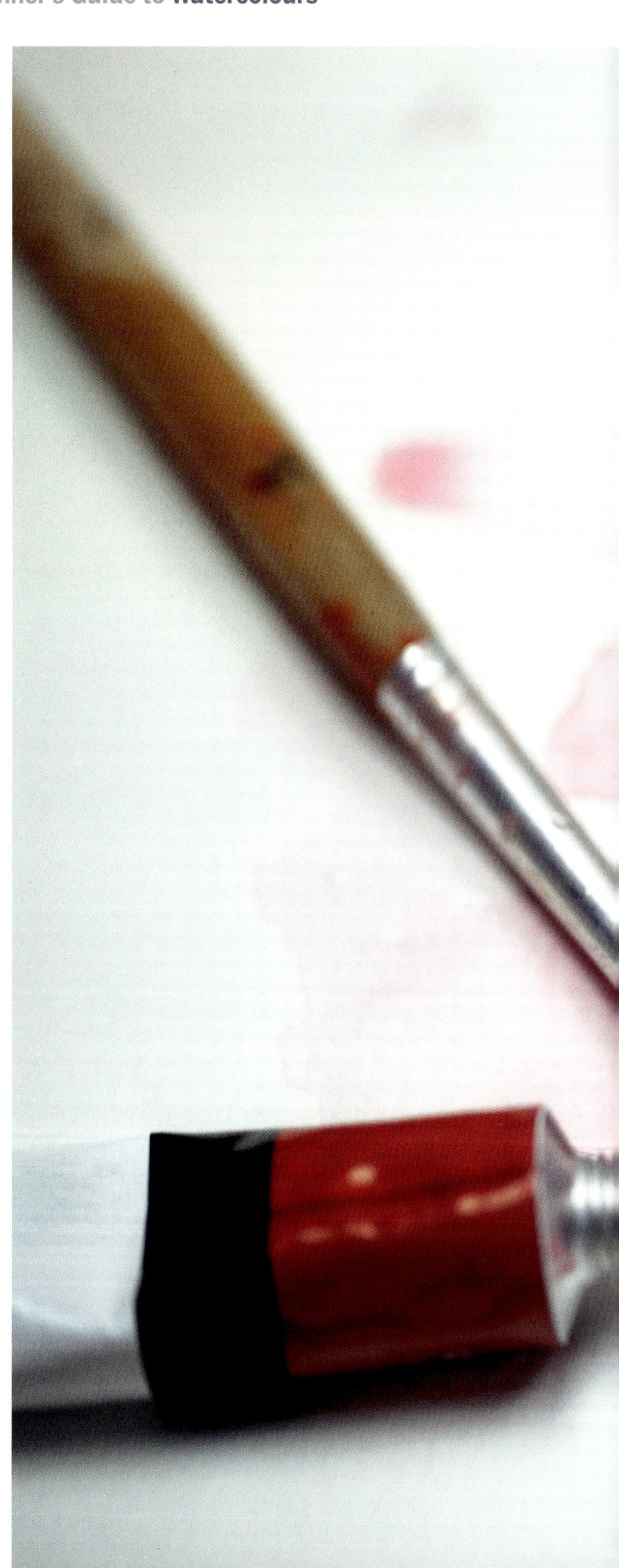

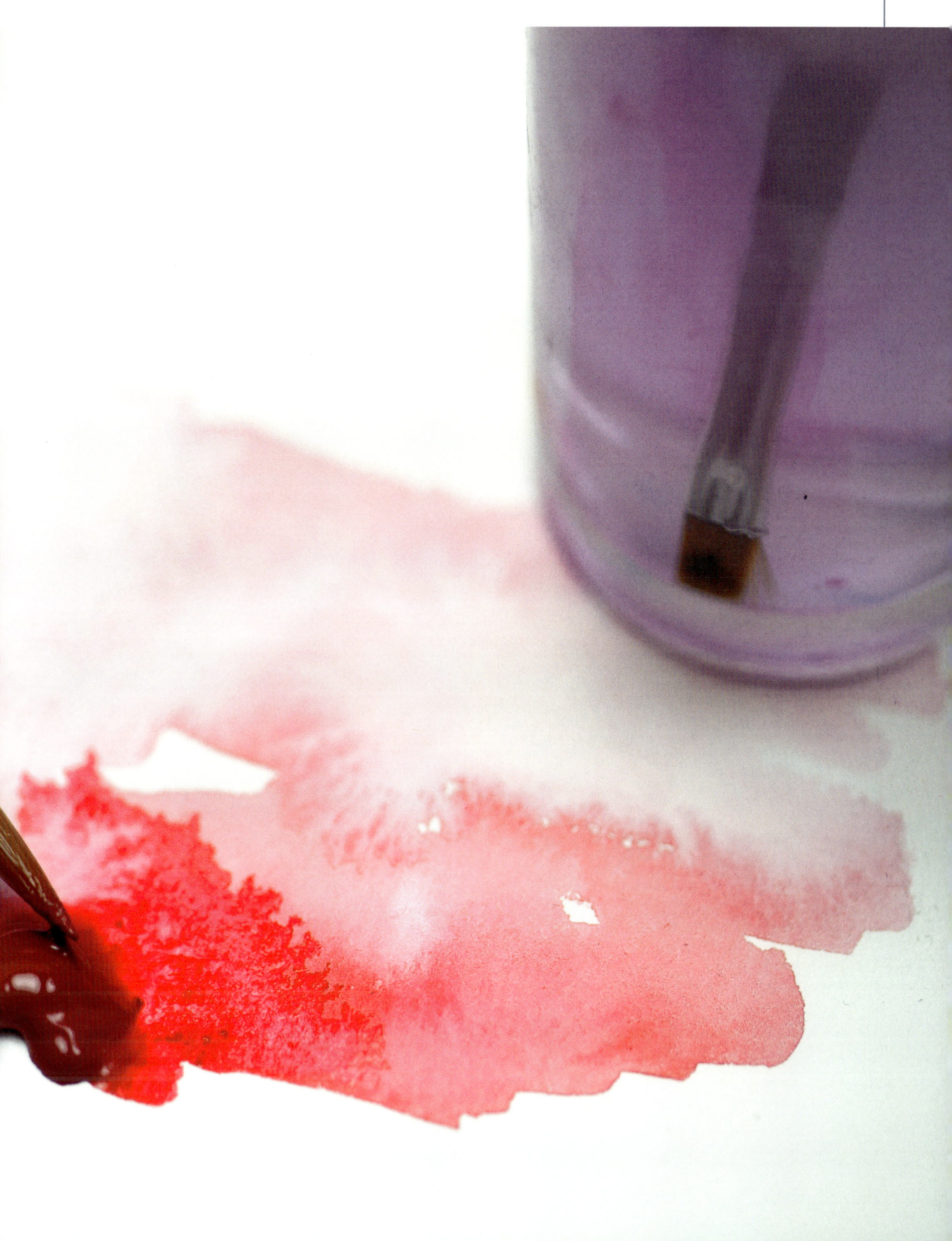

Hot press paper

Hot press paper refers to the process of making paper by flattening it between two hot rollers, resulting in a flatter, less-textured surface. This smooth surface is better suited to detailed work, and lacks the granulating behaviour of more textured papers, making it less suitable for unusual effects. This type of paper also works better with pens and pencils. Hot press paper is often made with a lot of size (a substance used to control absorbency), which means it can handle large washes well and let them dry uniformly.

Cold press paper

Also called 'NOT' paper. Cold press paper is made in a similar way to hot press, but is pressed between two cold rollers instead, resulting in a rougher surface texture. This is the most commonly used watercolour paper as it is versatile – the texture is enough to add interest but doesn't interfere with detailed work too much. Watercolour can be used with a dry brush on this type of paper to produce gritty textures, and in washes the pigment sinks between the teeth of the paper, forming a granulated effect.

Rough paper

Rough papers have the most highly textured surfaces, as the name suggests. This is great for dry brush effects, creating granulated textures within washes, and adding a naturalistic feel to paintings, though it's unsuitable for detailed work as the texture can interfere. Sometimes they also produce interesting 'bleed' effects, which are unpredictable. These papers can vary in how paint behaves on them, due to differences in textures and absorbency. Another quality of rough papers is that they tend to be tough, allowing for wetter washes and for paint to be 'lifted' out without too much damage to the surface.

"Cold press paper is versatile – the texture is enough to add interest but it doesn't interfere with detailed work too much"

Stretching watercolour paper

Stretching watercolour paper is done to prevent it from going bumpy – 'cockling' – when it gets wet. This is important when using lighter-weight papers under about 425gsm, or if your painting approach involves a lot of wet washes.

The key is to prepare everything before starting, so all the equipment is to hand. It's also a good idea to cut the tape ahead of time.

Afterwards, artists usually paint on the paper while it's taped down. Completed paintings can then be cut away, leaving the tape around the edges and covering it with a mountboard when framing. Pulling the tape off will likely damage the artwork.

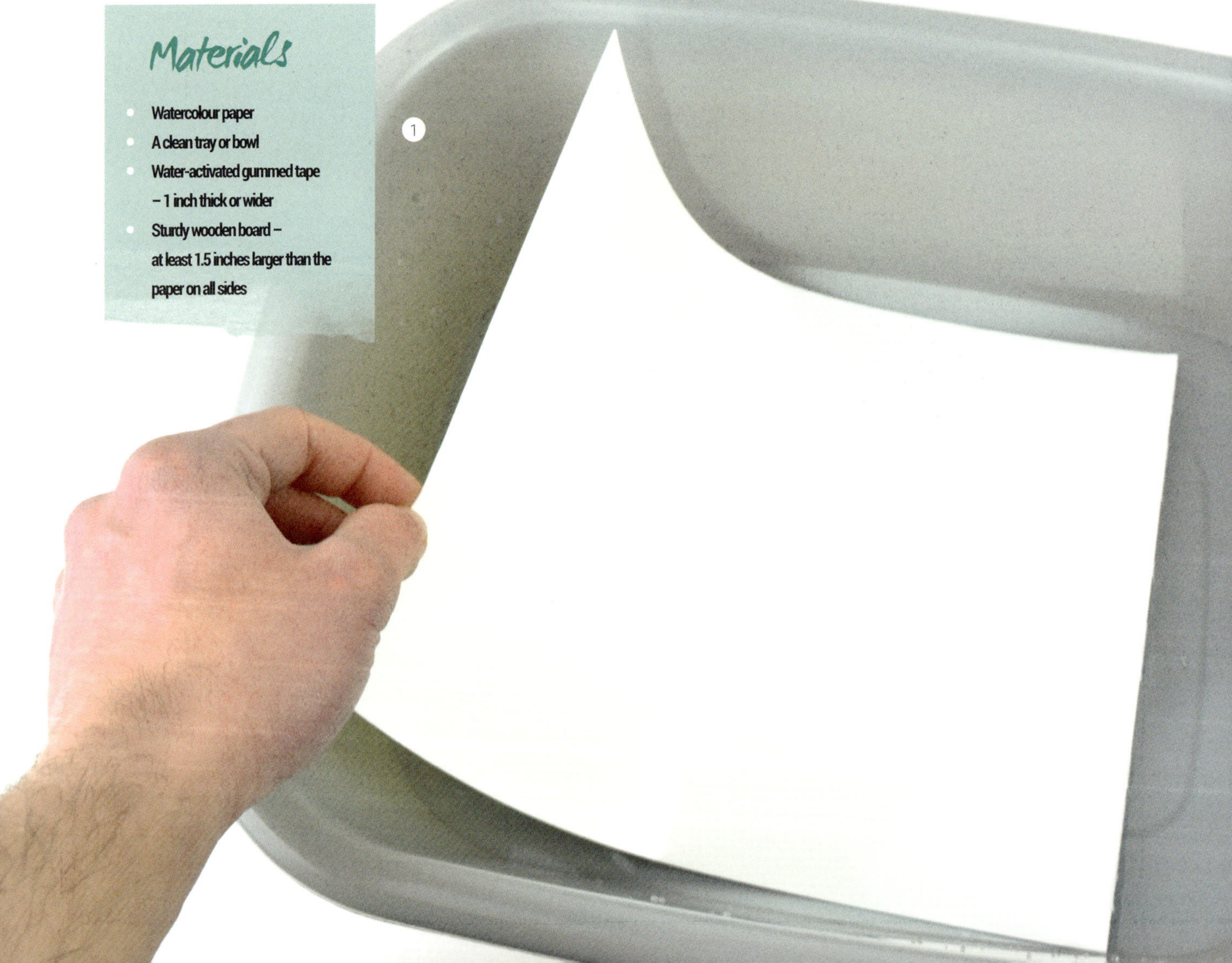

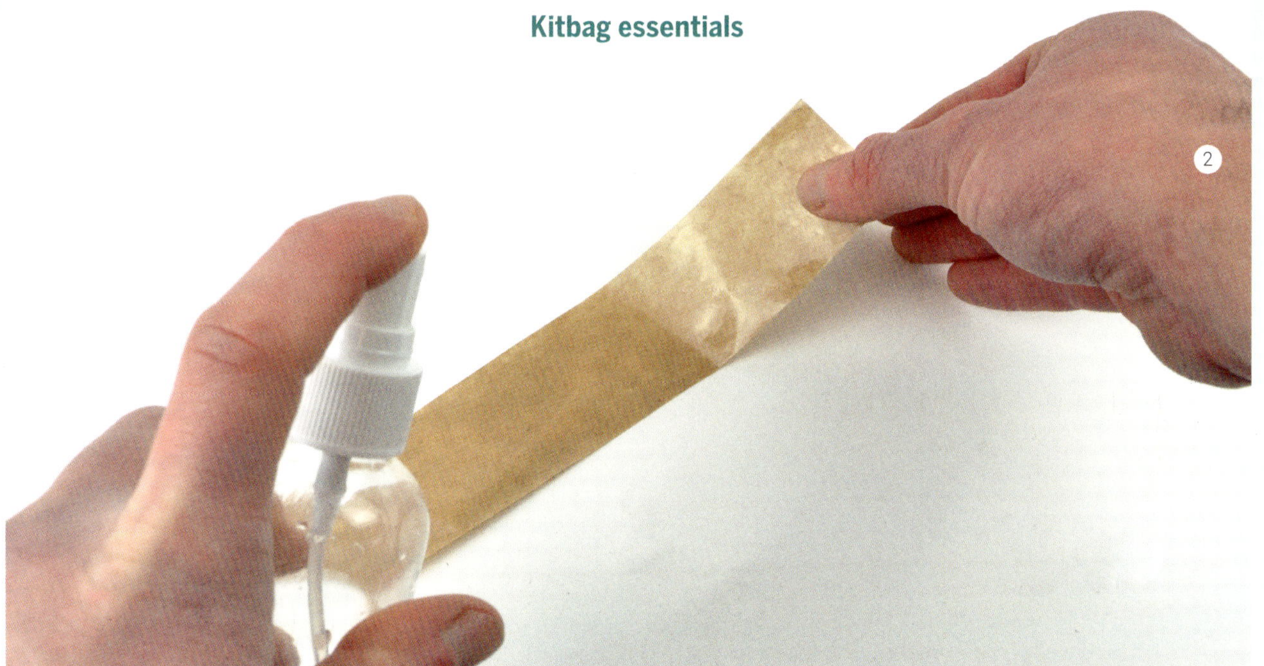

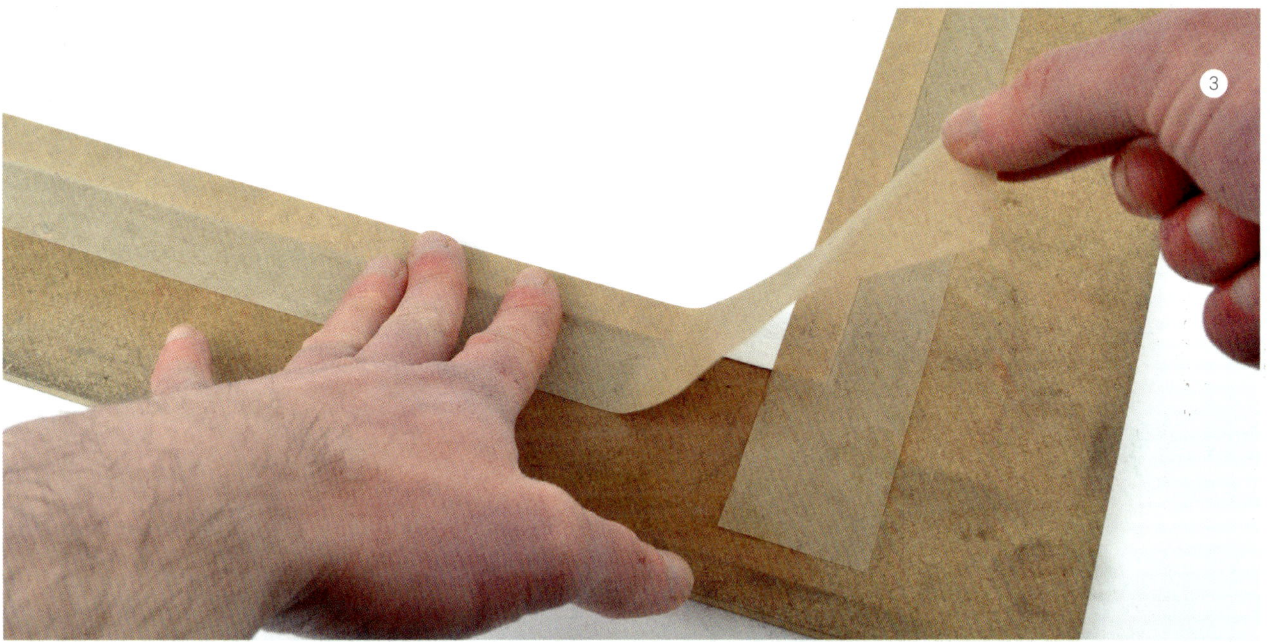

Follow these steps...

1 Soak the paper
Start by soaking the watercolour paper in clean water, in a tray or flat-bottomed basin. It should be wet enough to be saturated and 'floppy'. Try not to leave it in too long, as this can remove too much size from the paper, making it too absorbent and causing paint to 'sink'. Take it out, letting any excess water drip off, and lay it flat on the board. When picking up paper, pick it up by the corners so the oils on your hands don't affect the surface that will be painted on later.

2 Wet the tape
Cut the tape into strips, making sure there is plenty of excess at each end. The adhesive on the tape is activated by water, so here I'm spraying it with a spray bottle to wet it evenly. Another way to do this is to run a damp sponge over it. It only needs enough water to activate, so try not to saturate it or it will fail. It's very strong, so hold it at each end and avoid letting it stick to itself.

3 Tape down the paper
Tape down the paper with the gummed tape – for extra security, the tape can be long enough to wrap around the edges of the board. Try not to get the upper side of the tape wet as this can cause it to fail. Now leave the paper to dry completely, ideally overnight. Don't get tempted to use a hairdryer or heater, as this can cause the tape to fail and the paper to buckle. I find it works best when the paper is flat while drying.

Additional tools

While paint, brushes and paper are the core of our kit, other equipment can be useful or open up avenues to experimentation

Outside of paints, paper and brushes, there are a number of other tools and materials that can help with painting in watercolour. Some tools are purely practical, such as palettes and spray bottles. These are worth having on hand (for instance, spray bottles are useful for reactivating dry paint) but may also change depending on your work process, such as selecting deeper palettes if you use washes.

There are also lots of other materials that can combine well with watercolours, often to create unique effects. This is not an exhaustive list, and it is worth experimenting by combining watercolour with other materials. Anything that interacts with water, either by dissolving, absorbing or repelling it is worth considering.

When selecting other equipment, try to pick items that suit your working process and the outcomes you'd like to achieve. Watercolour has a lot of versatility as a medium and suits a wide range of artistic styles because of this.

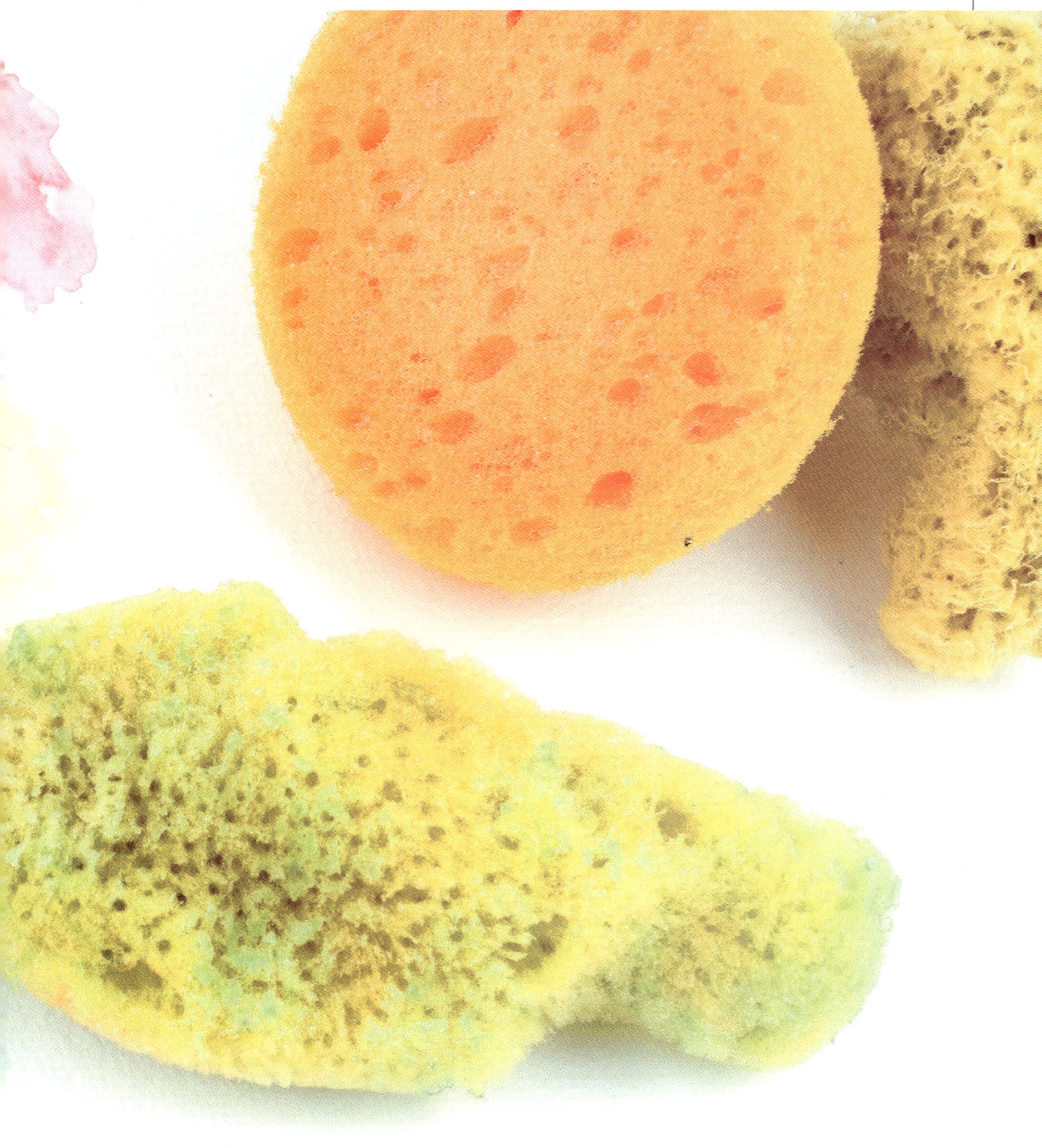

Sponges

SPONGES COME IN many forms and shapes, and work much as expected – they can suck up large amounts of wet pigment.

This is useful for two purposes; firstly, they can be used to lift out excess paint, creating a subtractive texture as they remove pigment from washes. The other way of using them is to make up a watercolour wash by mixing paint and water, and using the sponge to apply it.

Both methods are an effective way to create naturalistic, random textures, and applying paint with a sponge works well for blending two colours together, both wet-in-wet and wet-on-dry. Try experimenting with how saturated the sponge is – it tends to create grittier textures the less water it holds.

Usually, sponges work best when wetted and wrung out before use, so they are slightly damp all the way through.

Palettes

PALETTES ARE AN essential piece of kit and come in many different shapes and sizes. Typically, watercolour palettes are made from plastic, ceramics or metal, though sometimes other materials are used, such as enamel. They may have large areas to mix on, or deeper wells for holding lots of water for large washes.

For tube paints, plastic or ceramic palettes are usually used – plastic palettes are inexpensive and come in a huge range of styles, but tend to stain and can be harder to clean. Ceramic palettes have more durable surfaces and are still quite diverse in style, but can be heavy and are more fragile, making them a less portable option.

Pans tend to be held in metal or plastic palettes with a folding lid – this keeps them free of dust. Both come in lots of styles, so consider how much mixing area you need, and how many pans you want in your set. Metal palettes are more hard-wearing, but cost more. Some of these palettes are very portable, as they hold fewer paints and fold down to pocket size.

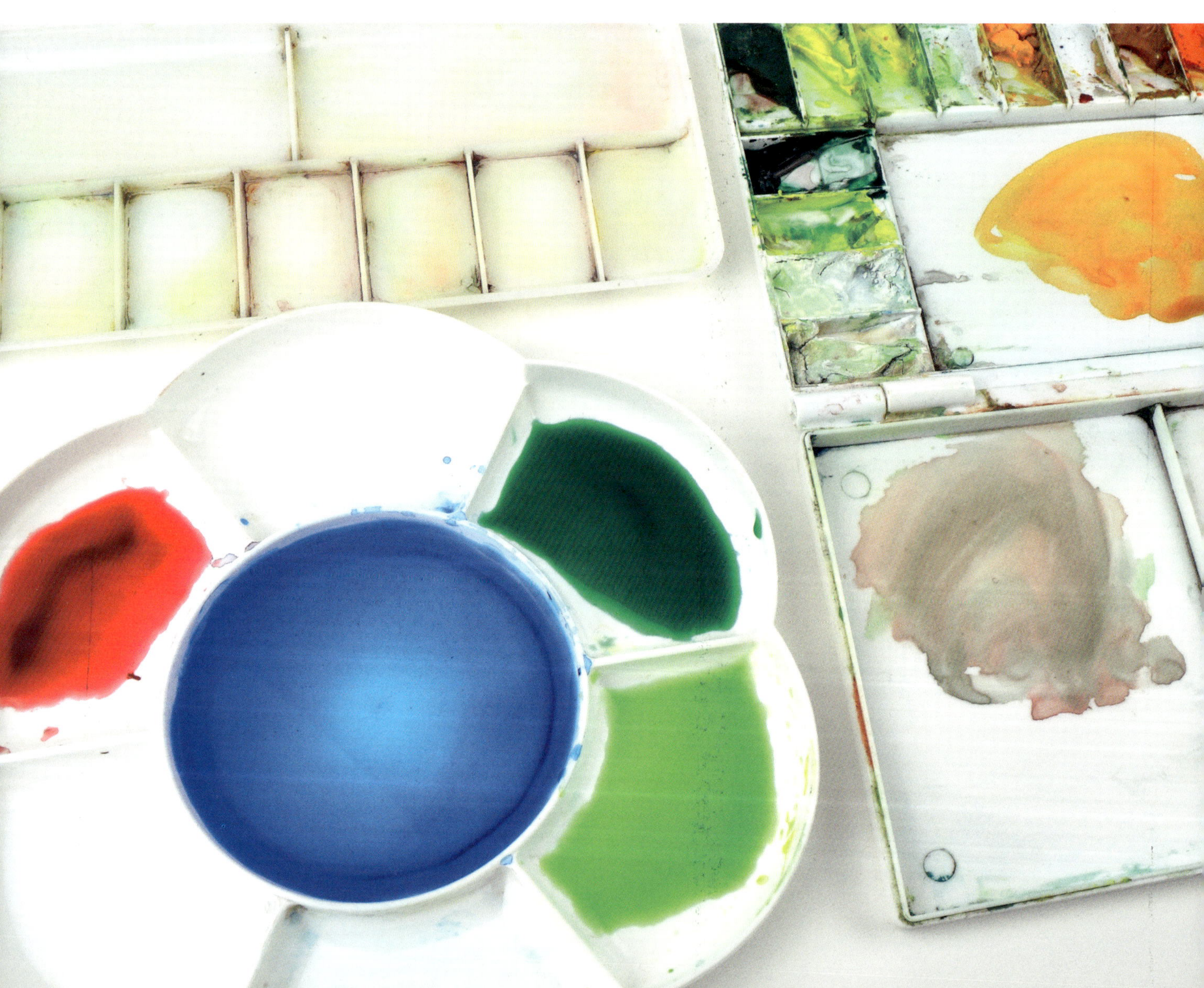

Spray bottles

A SPRAY BOTTLE is a useful and inexpensive item that is well worth including in your kit. It can be part of a working process, as it can wet paper quickly and evenly, which is handy for wet-in-wet work and laying down even washes of paint. Using watercolour pencils on wet paper like this can also produce interesting effects and more highly pigmented marks. Spraying water around applied paint can also create misty patterns and soften hard edges whilst avoiding leaving brush strokes.

More practical uses include spraying water to clean dry paint from palettes (especially when out and about), activating dry watercolour pans, and wetting gummed tape.

If you are keen on working wet-in-wet, consider trying different spray bottles. Different nozzles can produce bigger or smaller water droplets, deposit more or less water, or cover different-sized areas.

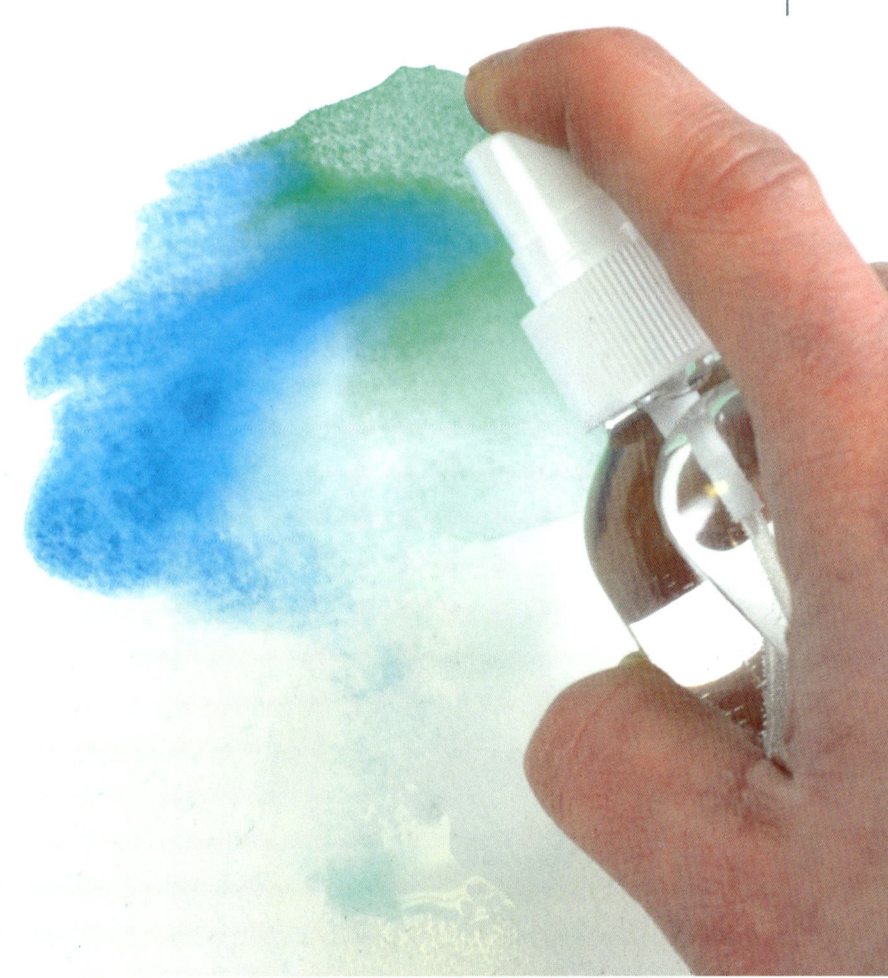

Salt

COMBINING SALT WITH watercolour washes can create interesting textures and patterns. The salt needs to be applied to a wet area of paint, where it absorbs the wet paint and leaves a pale, random, crystalline pattern. Using more pigmented paint washes tends to result in a more defined pattern due to contrast. This technique is particularly useful for abstract and landscape work, but can be incorporated into other subjects, especially when creating an underpainting in a layered approach.

All you need for this technique is regular kitchen salt or sea salt (they work the same but may produce different patterns). The random textures and patterns they produce can be controlled by the placement and quantity of the crystals, with large concentrations able to produce gradients. Be patient with this technique – the watercolour needs to dry completely before the salt is removed for the full effect.

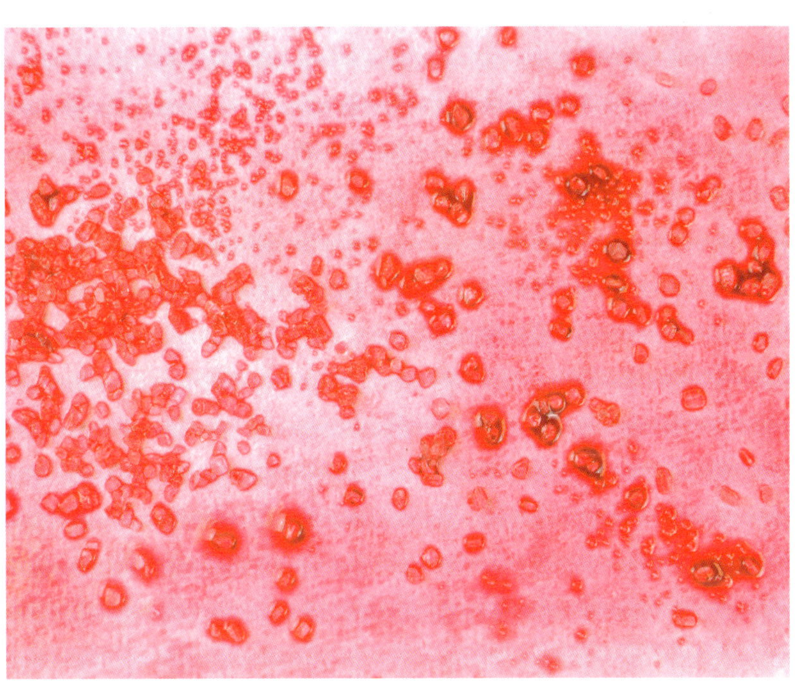

How to use salt

Follow these steps...

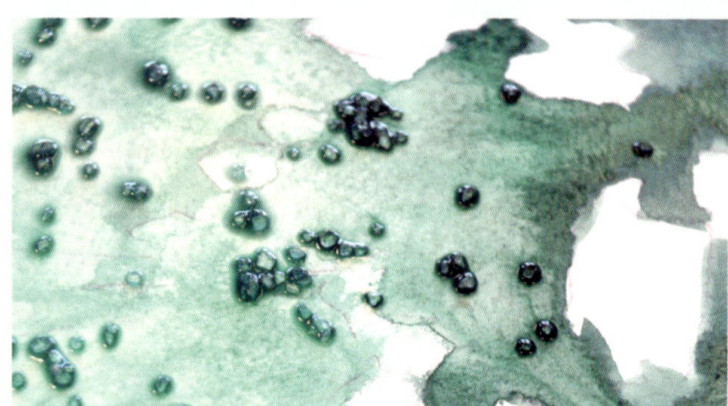

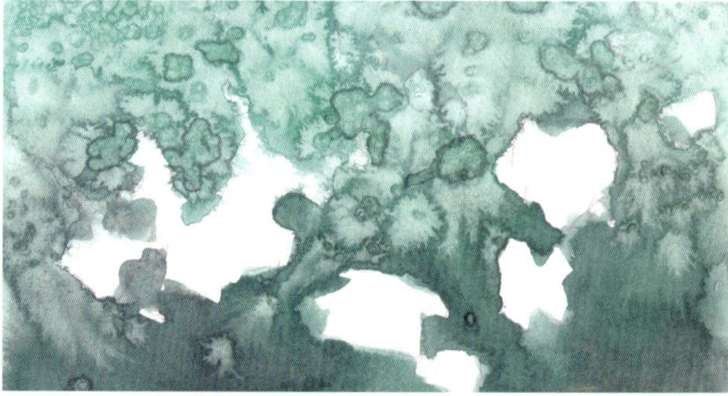

1 ⬤ The initial wash

To start, I sketch out the rough placement of the major elements of the roses and greenery, then fill the green areas with a wash. Immediately after this, the sea salt crystals are applied, with concentrations at the top of the image.

The idea is to create a random texture to imply the leaves in the distance and suck some of the pigment from the wash to lighten the area, forming a gradient. The salt needs to be applied as quickly as possible for the maximum effect, before the water starts to sink into the paper.

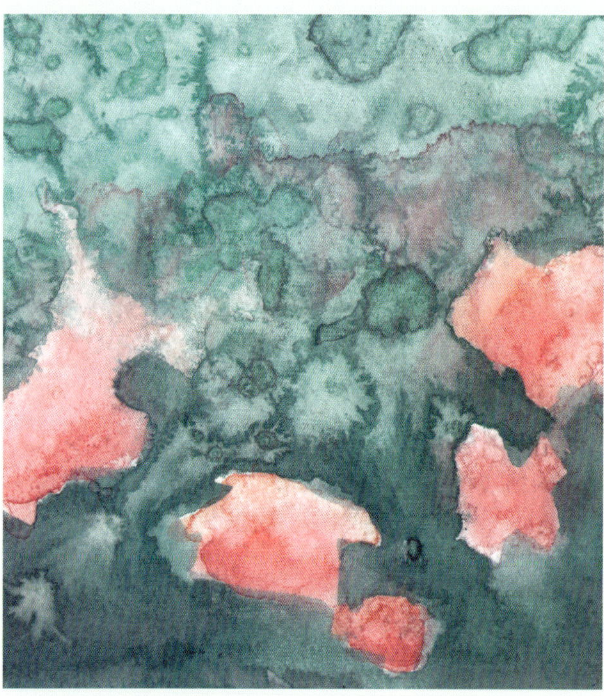

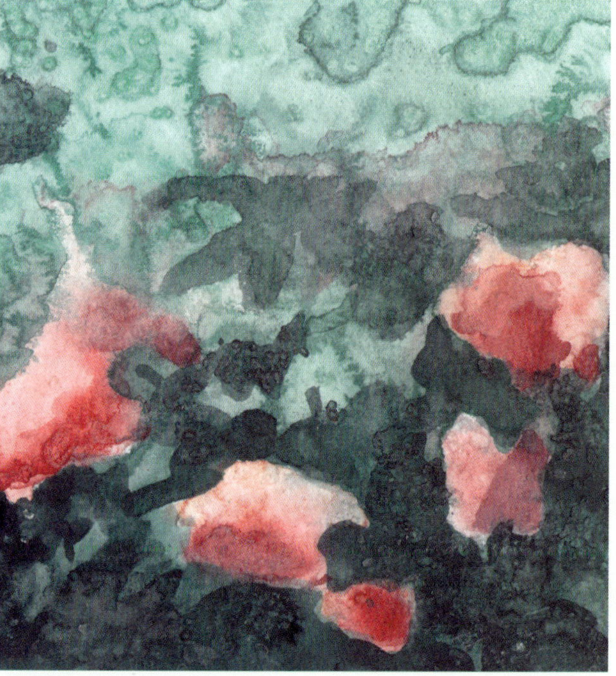

2 ⬤ Building colour

In this step I follow a similar process with the roses, applying a pinkish wash with a round brush after letting the first one dry. The salt is carefully scattered in the areas I want to lighten, to create a gradient that mimics the overall light and shadow on the roses.

In some places, the paint isn't as intense as I would like, so to remedy this I mix a stronger colour and apply it to the wet areas away from the salt with the round brush.

3 ⬤ Add shadow & detail

After letting everything dry, I add another layer of green for the foliage, paying more attention to the leaf shapes and working with the pre-existing patterns. I let it sit for a bit before adding salt; this allows a decent amount of pigment to sink into the paper, but produces a random, gritty texture. Once the shadows dry, I use the round brush to add extra leaves and branches, and extra detail to the roses. Salt textures are fine to paint on, though take care to remove all the salt first.

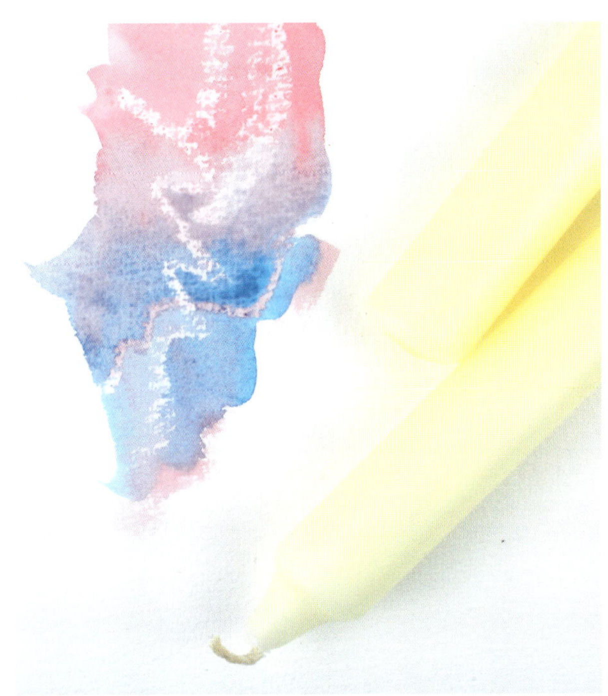

Wax

WAX NATURALLY REPELS water, which makes it a useful tool. When wax is applied to paper, the watercolour cannot adhere to it – this technique is sometimes called 'wax resist'. Regular wax candles can be used for this effect, as can wax crayons if colour is wanted. Oil pastels interact in a similar way, but tend to be a bit unpredictable and may bleed into watercolour paint.

This technique is especially useful for producing gritty natural textures such as stone, especially when done on cold press or rough papers. A wax candle can be cut into a chunk and rubbed over the paper so the grain picks it up and leaves gaps the paint can get into. Wax can also be drawn with, either to create under-drawings that repel paint, or, in the case of white wax, preserve highlights early on in a painting process.

Pens

PENS ARE GREAT to have around for sketching with watercolour. One popular way of working is by creating a pen sketch and painting it with watercolours.

A common challenge is selecting the right kind of pen, as many have inks that run when they get wet – whilst this is sometimes desirable, it can also be a nuisance. Ink is often labelled as waterproof, water-resistant and water-soluble. Water-soluble ink will, of course, run into watercolour paint and muddy it. However, water-resistant ones will also do this; the difference is that they maintain their lines whilst water-soluble inks will fade or may dissolve completely. Waterproof pens are the only ones that shouldn't do this (depending on their quality!) and can be painted over with watercolour.

This also applies to bottled inks that you may want to use with refillable pens, brushes and nibs.

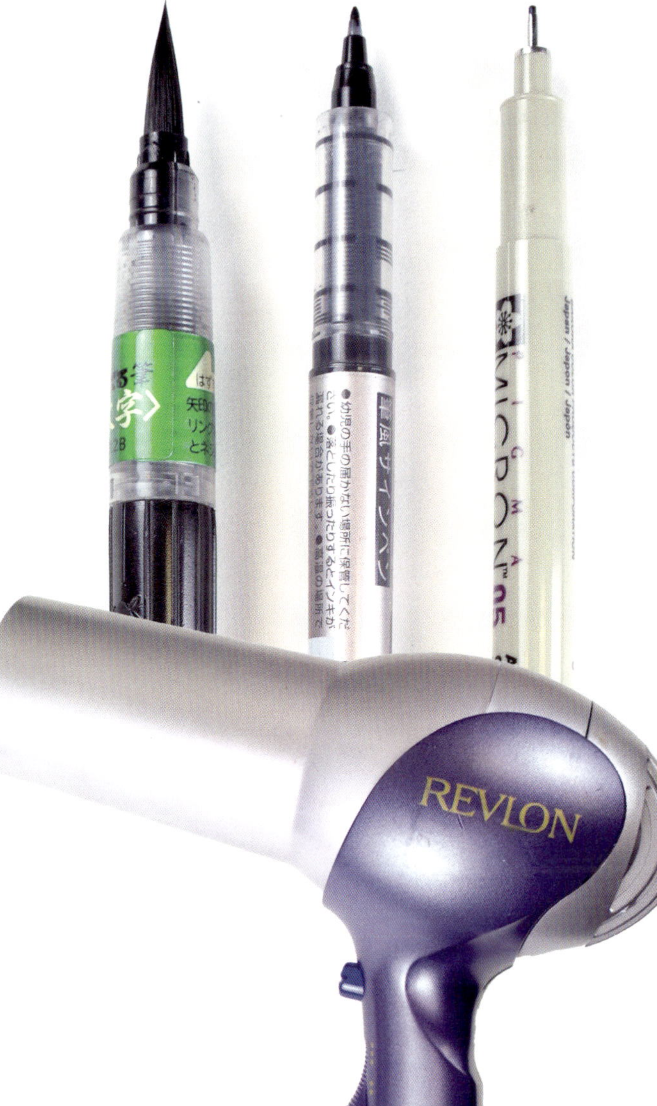

Hairdryer

A HAIRDRYER IS worth having on hand for speeding up drying times, especially if you work in a layered fashion with less water.

Do take care when you do this, as the heat can also interfere with other processes – such as melting wax and reducing the effect of salt. It may also cause tapes to become unstuck and paper to buckle more easily – this is especially true with thinner paper. To avoid disturbing wet paint, direct the hairdryer vertically down at the page.

Another use for the hairdryer is pushing around washes – turn it onto the lowest heat setting possible and use the air to direct water over the paper. This is handy for getting a little control over gradients, and can also be used to create drip effects by pushing the paint around.

clean your brushes

Watercolour brushes are more delicate than brushes designed for acrylic and oils, and should be treated accordingly, explains **Rob Lunn**

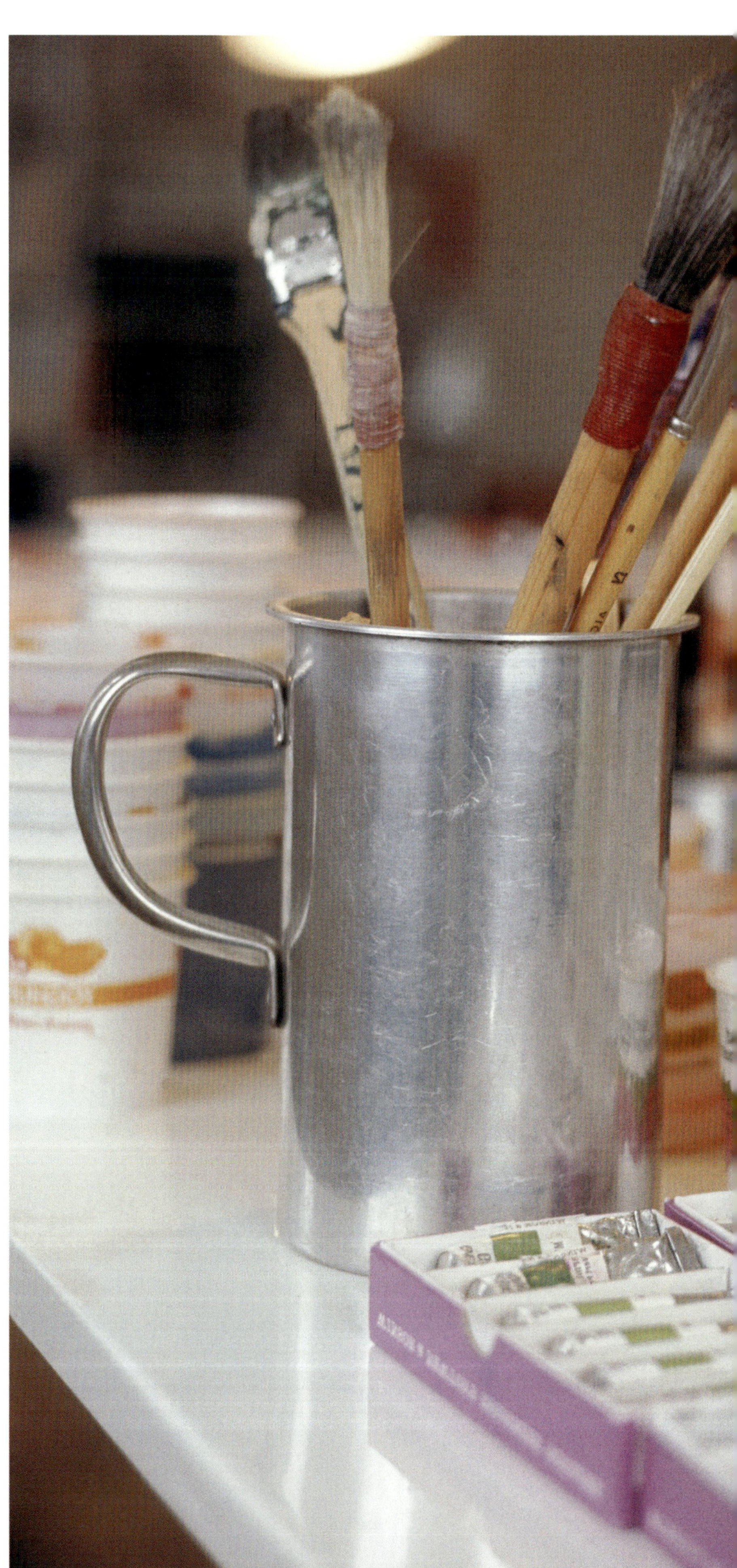

Learning how to clean your paintbrushes properly is an important skill. As the old saying goes: If you look after your tools, your tools will look after you. When you start painting, a good set of brushes is one of the most important investments you will make – and they can set you back a fair amount of money, too. So it makes sense to give them a bit of TLC.

The golden rule when it comes to looking after paintbrushes is to keep them wet while in use and give them a good clean when they're not. This approach will keep help keep your brushes in good nick for a long time. But cleaning paintbrushes is easier said than done – there are some techniques you need to know if you're going to get the paint out effectively.

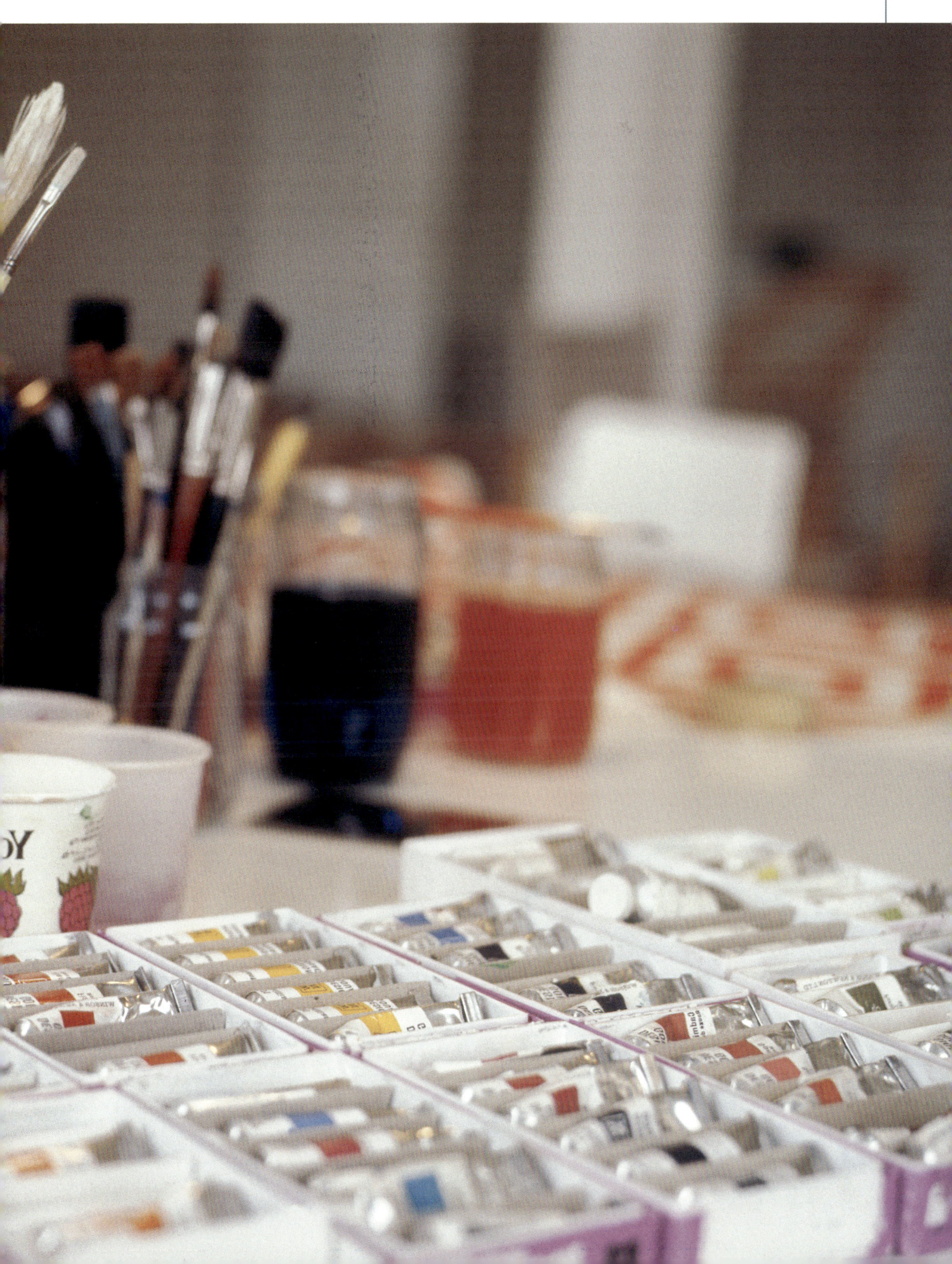

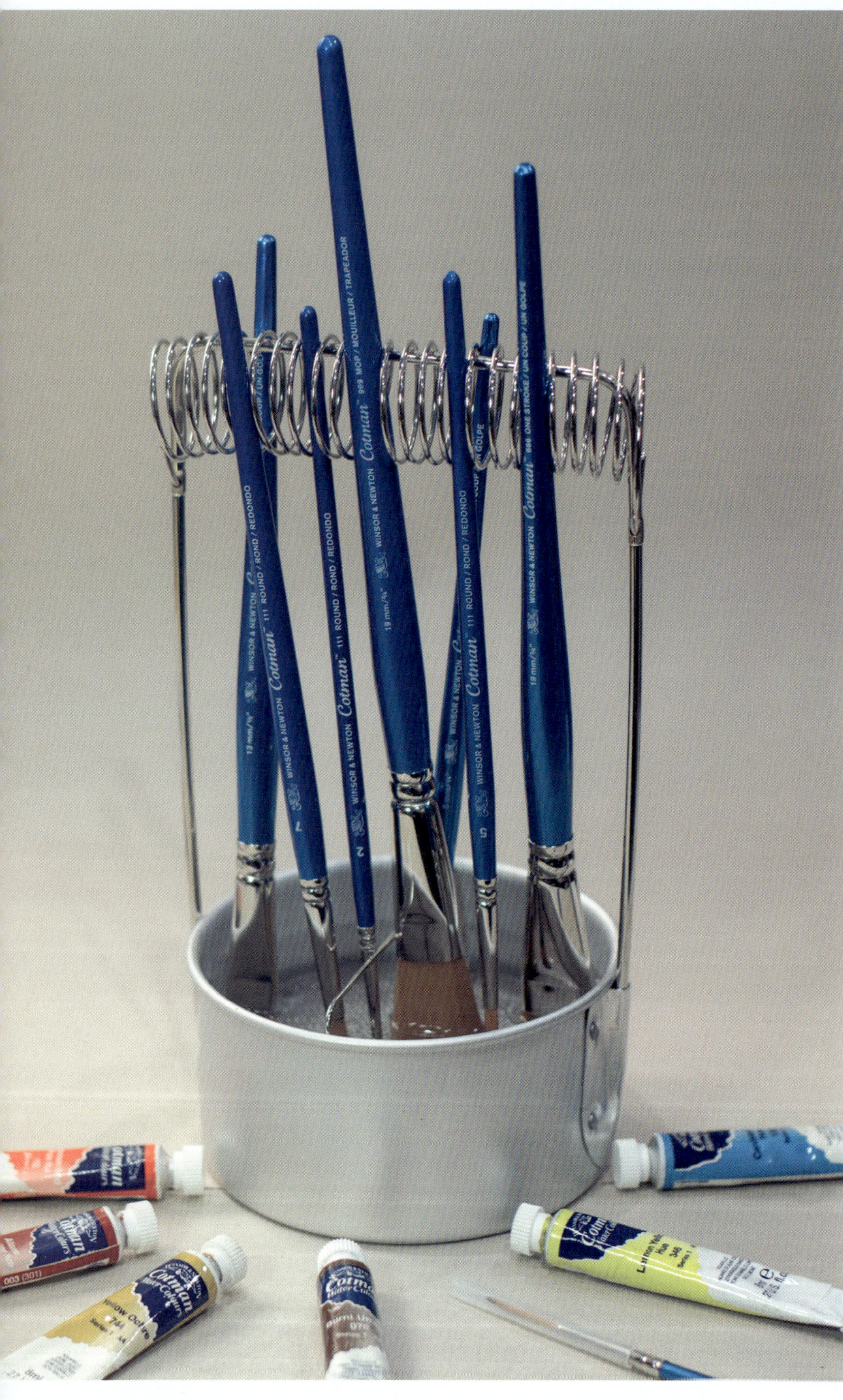

1 ▶ Clean with water as you go

As a lot of watercolour paint is used in highly diluted 'washes', it should take less work to remove the pigment from the bristles. Instead of cleaning with a cloth, keep a vessel of water close to hand at all times, swilling the brushes between washes. One tip is to use a brush washer with a holder so you can suspend the bristles in water when not in use.

2 ◀ Dry with a cloth and store

Using water in a jar or brush washer, clean as much paint as you can from your bristles. Use a clean cloth to make sure you've removed the paint. Repeat if necessary.

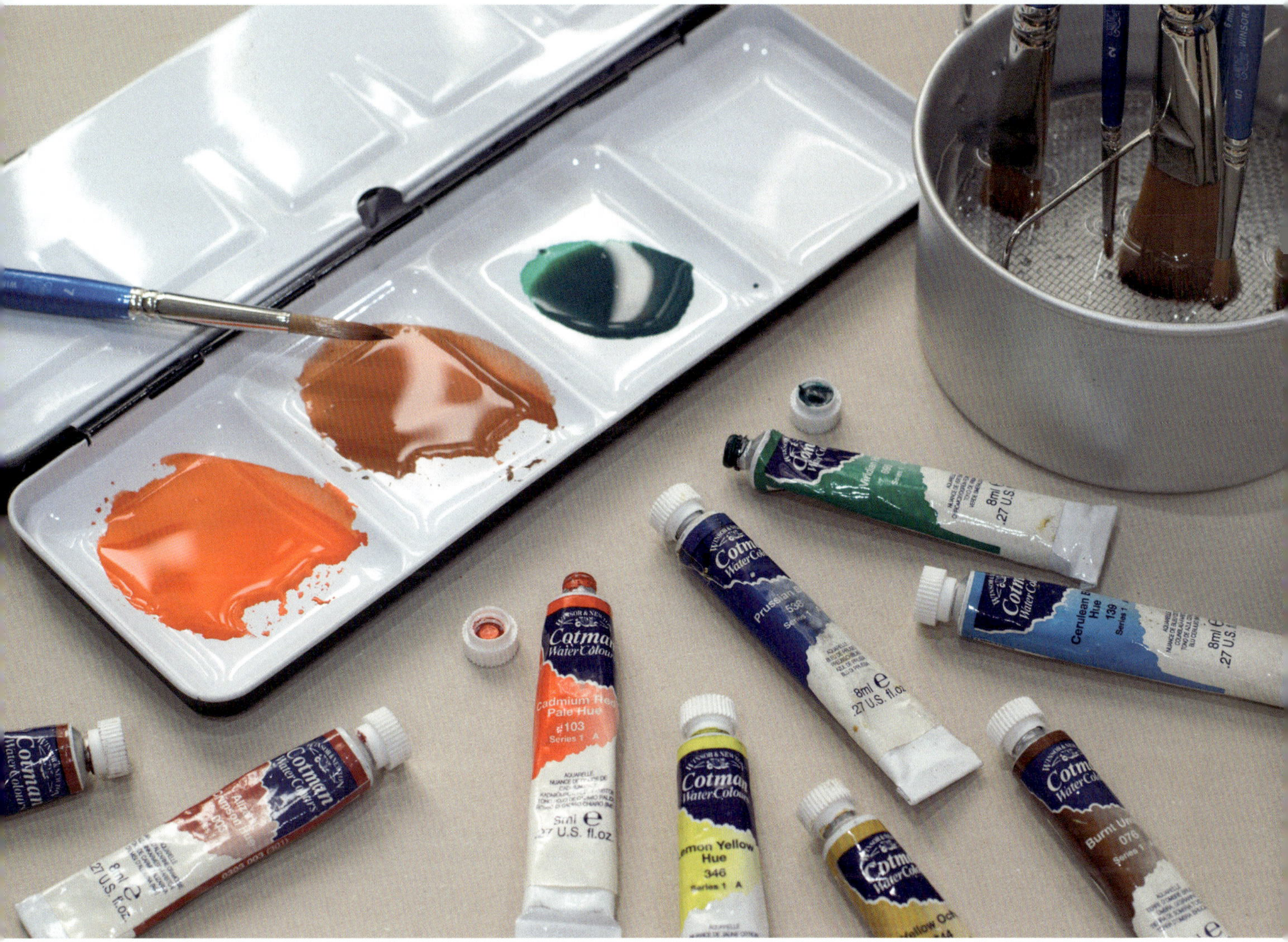

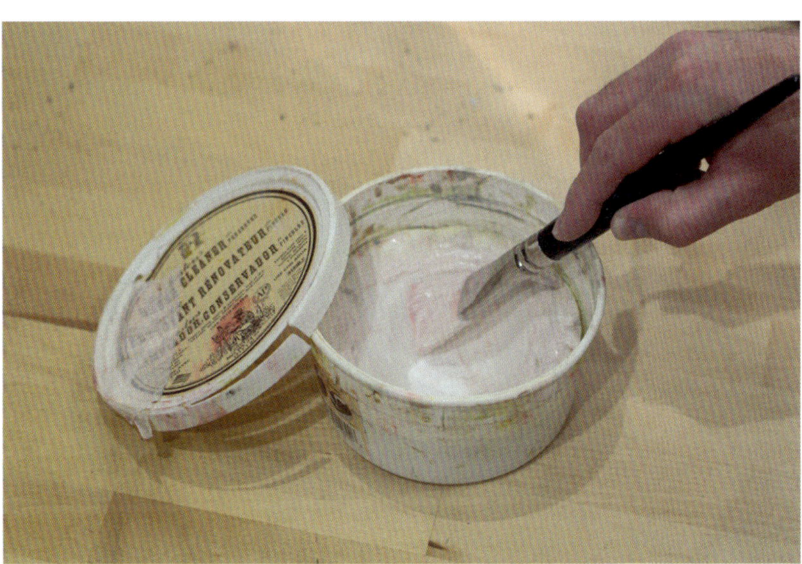

3 ◖ Reshape the bristles

For a final clean, consider using a paintbrush cleaning soap. We recommend The Masters Brush Cleaner and Preserver (available in 2.4oz pots or industrial-sized pots). Using a little water, work up a lather with your brush in the centre of the soap. Work the lather through the bristles with your thumb and forefinger, always working from the ferrule out towards the ends of the bristles. Continue until no pigment can be seen in the lather. Note that some pigments will stain bristles permanently.

Dirty 'wash' water should be collected and disposed of responsibly. It is also possible to allow dirty wash water from watercolour paint to settle naturally in larger containers. The golden rule is: never chuck it down the sink!

How to paint with watercolours

Watercolour painting can be tricky to master, but can produce wonderful results. **Brynn Metheney** walks you through the basics, with some expert tips

Watercolour is a versatile and flexible medium that can yield a variety of results. Also known as aquarelle, it's a painting method in which the paints are made of pigments suspended in a water-soluble vehicle.

Dating back thousands of years, watercolour is a tricky medium to master, but it's certainly one worth pursuing. When you create a painting in watercolours, light reflects off the white of the paper and bounces up through the colours, giving it a luminosity that can be truly magical.

Professional children's book illustrator Alina Chau (alinachau. com) has a whimsical style that's highly sought after for various art exhibitions worldwide. Chau's lyrical watercolours have garnered her a devoted fan base and the accolades of her peers.

"To achieve a desirable result with watercolour it's important to have the right tools," she recommends. "While you don't have to invest in an expensive set of supplies, you don't want to use paint or paper that turns out not to be suitable for watercolours."

Here's her advice for people

starting out: "A common misunderstanding is that you have to use the same palette that you used for the colour study when creating your final painting.

"While it's true that you'll recreate the look of the colour sketch, you should always start a new painting with a clean set of tools and a clean palette.

"This will stop the colour on your painting getting too muddy and hard to control. Also, wash your tools regularly whenever they start to get dirty. This will keep the purity and accuracy of the colour."

One final tip to beginners: "While you don't need to worry about paper getting buckled in a sketchbook, you do need to watch for this in your final painting. To prepare the paper you can either stretch your paper or get a watercolour block, which is pre-stretched."

But first things first: across these pages, we'll walk you through some of the basic techniques of painting with watercolours.

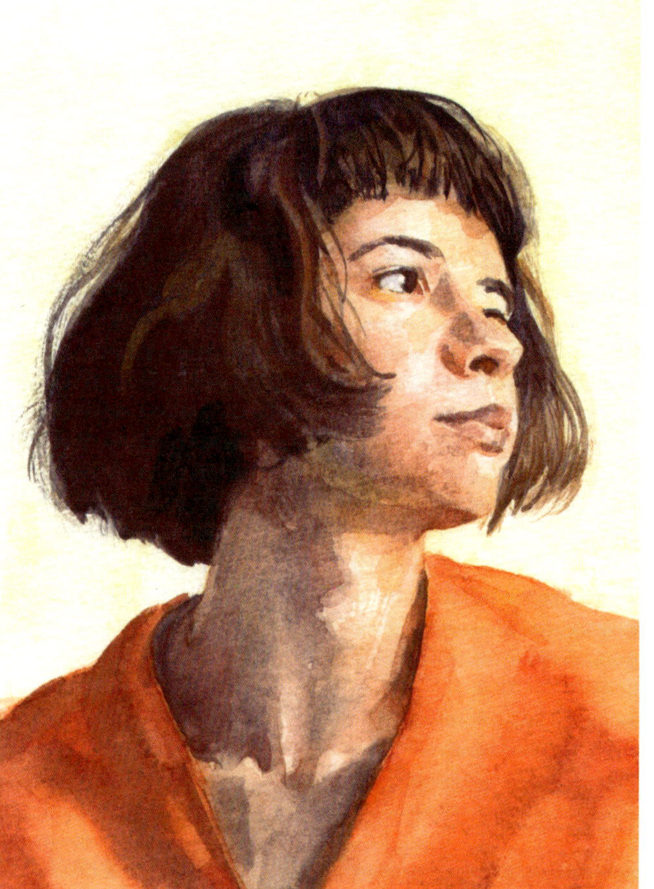

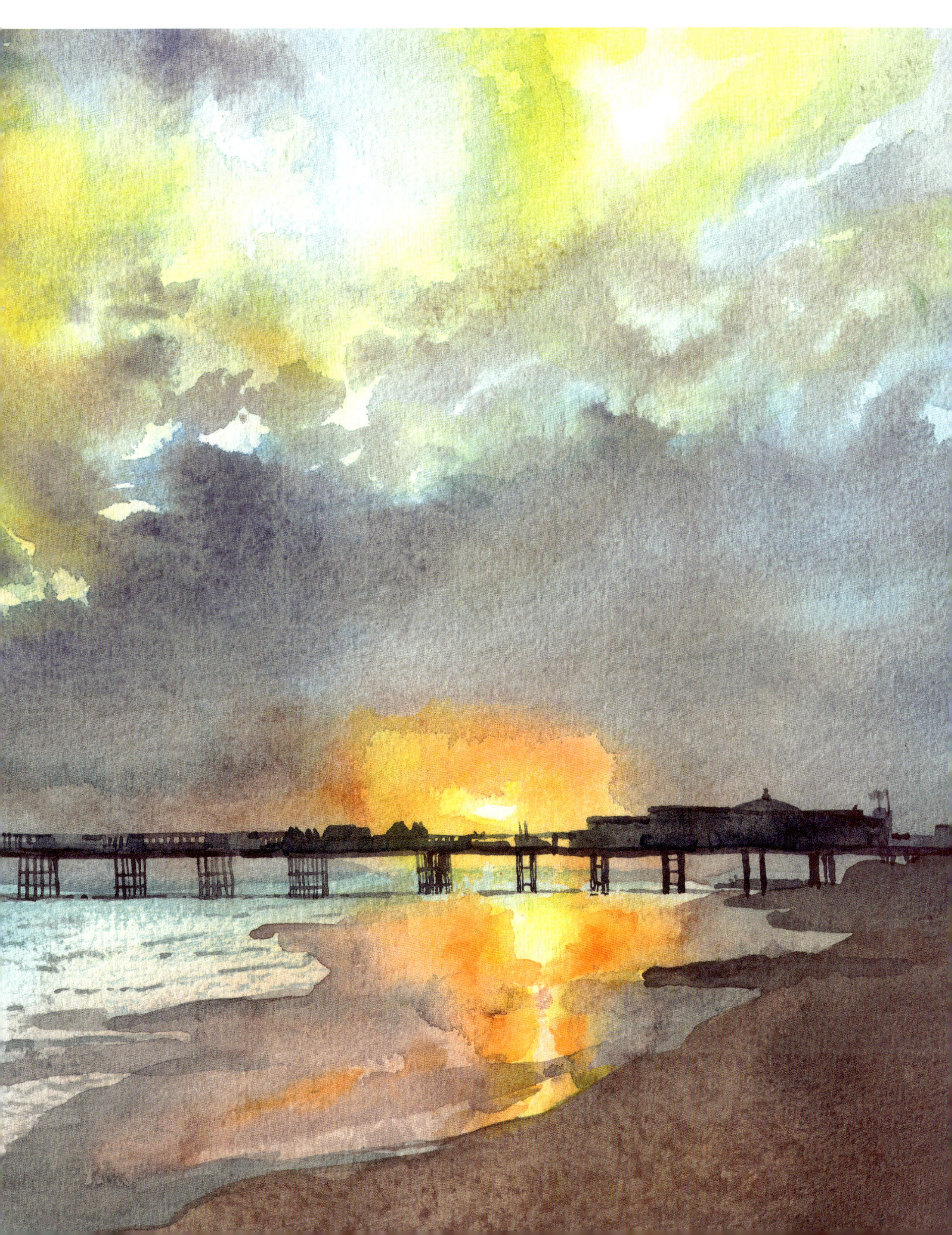

The basics

Watercolour painting is all about layering and texture. We explain how to get it right

Materials

- Holbien Artists Watercolour
- Winsor & Newton Watercolour
- Arches Hot Press Watercolour Paper, 140 lb
- Watercolour Brushes sizes: 6, 3, 0.8, 000
- Kneaded Eraser
- 2H Caran D'Ache Pencil, Paper Towels, Masking Tape, Salt, Sponge

Follow these steps...

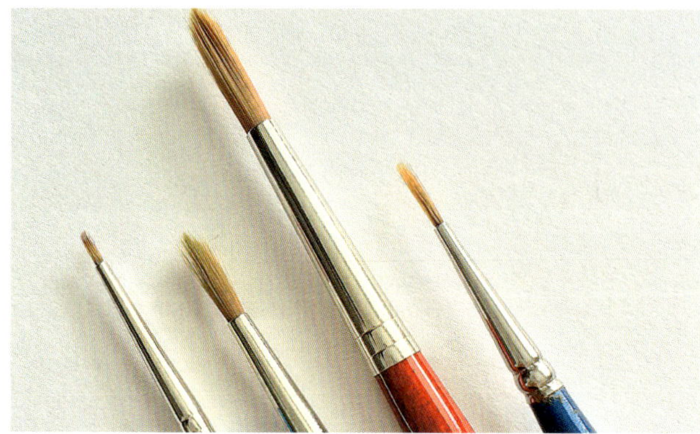

1 ○ Buy a range of brushes

It's important to have a range of brushes. This will depend on how large or small you work. I tend to work on the smaller side so my brushes range from 000 to 6. Experiment with different sizes to work out what your favourites are. But I'd also recommend getting hold of brushes that are smaller than what you think you'll use. These will come in handy for those small details you don't anticipate.

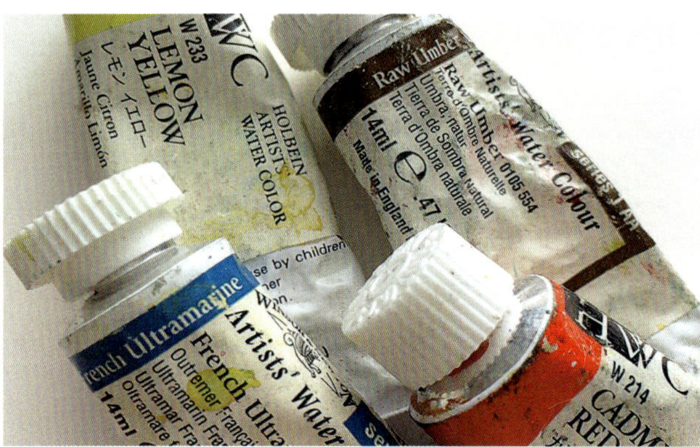

2 ○ Get some good quality paints

It's important to invest in good-quality watercolour. It will last longer and won't yellow or degrade as much over time. There are lots of different brands and levels available in stores and online. I use a variety, from Holbien and Winsor & Newton. Buy a few colours from different brands and find out which you prefer. Start small: you can mix a variety of colours using a limited pallete.

3 ○ It's all about dry vs wet

There are two major factors when painting with watercolours: wet and dry. As the name suggests, watercolour is a water-based medium. We can manipulate the darkness and saturation of the pigment depending on how much water we add. There are many ways to paint in watercolour and as you try them, you'll find the ones that work best for you. I've found working dry to wet helps me achieve more control.

3 Grades of watercolours

Artist grade watercolours contain a full pigment load, suspended in a binder, usually natural gum arabic. They're usually made with fewer fillers like kaolin or chalk, which results in richer colour and more vibrant mixes. They're normally sold in moist form, in a tube, and are thinned and mixed on a dish or palette.

Student grade watercolours have less pigment, and often are made using two or more less expensive pigments. They're generally cheaper and come in a smaller range of colours.

Scholastic watercolours are made with cheap pigments and dyes suspended in a synthetic binder. Good for teaching purposes, they're usually non-staining, easy to wash out and suitable for use even by young children under supervision.

4 ⬤ Work from light to dark

Another important rule to remember when working with watercolours is that we're working from light to dark. This means that anything we're keeping white or light in our painting needs to stay that way for the whole duration of the work. We'll build our values up; layer-by-layer to arrive at the effect we want. This does take a lot of planning but the results will be worth it.

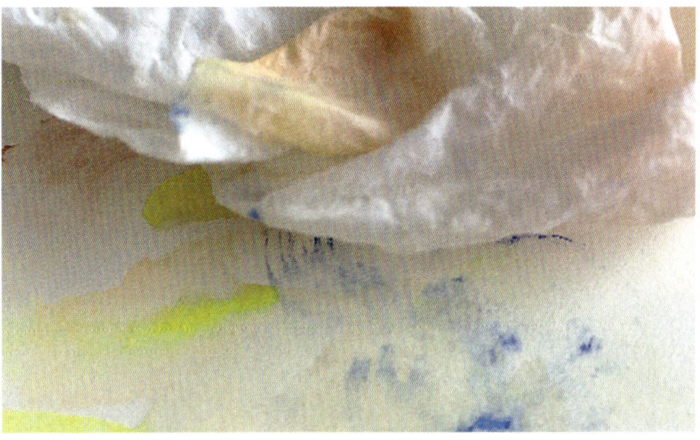

5 ⬤ You'll need paper towels

One very important tool to have in your tool kit when working with watercolours is a paper towel. The paper towel almost acts as a kneaded eraser for your watercolours. Laying down a wash of colour and then lifting parts of it up is a great way to add layers of detail gradually. Paper towels are also very useful for correcting mistakes or directing the paint in different direction.

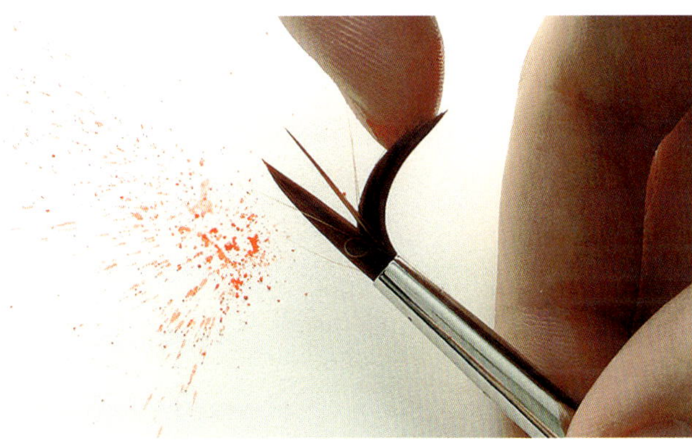

6 ⬤ The splatter technique

One handy trick to add some action to your watercolour painting, such as water spray or floating dust, is to use a splatter technique. Hold your paintbrush between your thumb and middle fingers. Using your index finger, pull back on the bristles and let them snap forward. This method is a bit random, but can yield some very fun results, so I'd urge you to give it a try.

7 ⬤ How to use blooming

A good way to bleed colours into one another is through "blooming". Take a good amount of water to pigment in your brush and apply it to the paper. When the stroke is still wet, add in another colour with the same amount of water. You can manipulate the colours to where they need to be at this point. Allow this to dry and you'll notice that there are subtle gradients throughout the stroke.

Six expert tips

Here are some more ways to get more out of watercolours

- Mixing bleach into your paint will produce a blotchy effect, as it fights with the pigment.

- Use a toothbrush to create a spray/splatter effect. Try varying the distance from the paper for different effects.

- Adding water to dry watercolours lifts and redistributes pigment, creating contours.

- Apply tape and liquid masking products to retain lightness. Remove when paint's dry.

- Try scraping painted areas away to introduce gritty marks and lines.

- Use the brush's butt end to spread thick lines of wet paint in an unusual way.

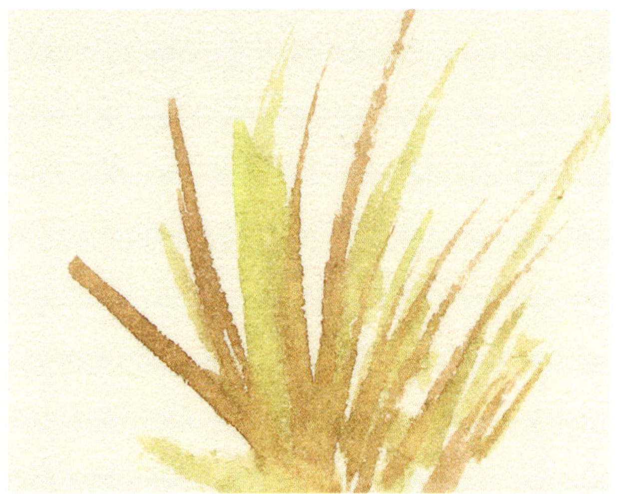

8 ⬓ Getting textures right

You'll notice that working in watercolours on a rougher paper does have its advantages. One of the obvious ones is that you don't have to work too hard to achieve a nice texture. This said, it's important to try to depict objects and materials with their textures included. This means using lights and darks as well as wets and drys.

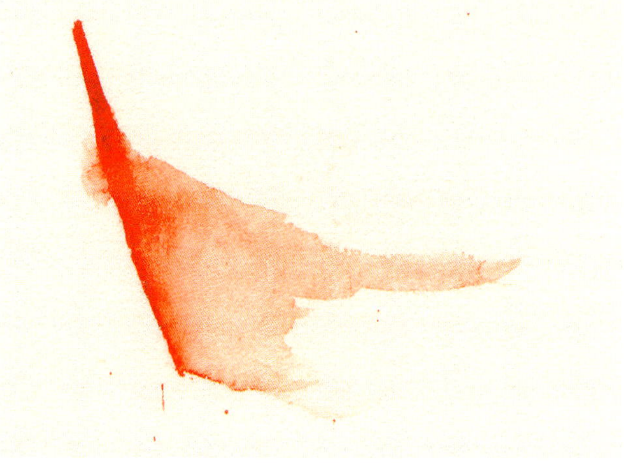

9 ⬓ Pulling in colour

When you apply a dry, more saturated stroke, you can pull from that stroke with just water. This is a great way to show form and indicate a light source or edge. Apply a stroke using very little water and more pigment. Before the stroke is dry, take a moderately wet brush and pull the colour out from the darker stroke. You can pull the colour quite far depending on how dry that initial stroke is.

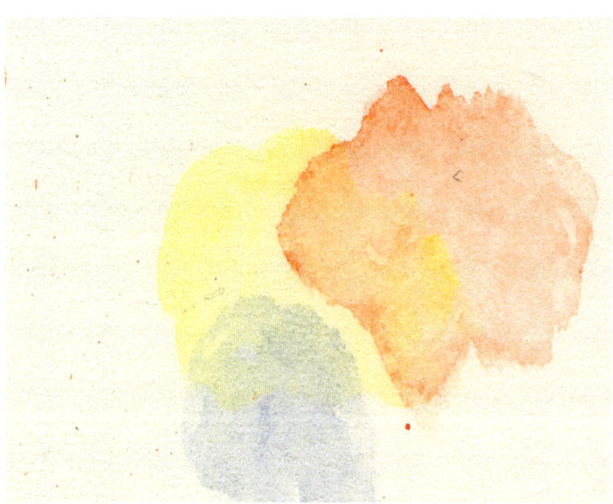

10 ⬓ Layering colour

Because watercolour is a thin medium, you'll need to build up colour gradually. This is another advantage to the medium as you can do some color mixing right on the paper. Take one colour and lay it down. Allow it to dry and then revisit with another shade. You'll notice where they overlap, the pigment mixes and you're left with a different colour. This is great for building up flesh tones.

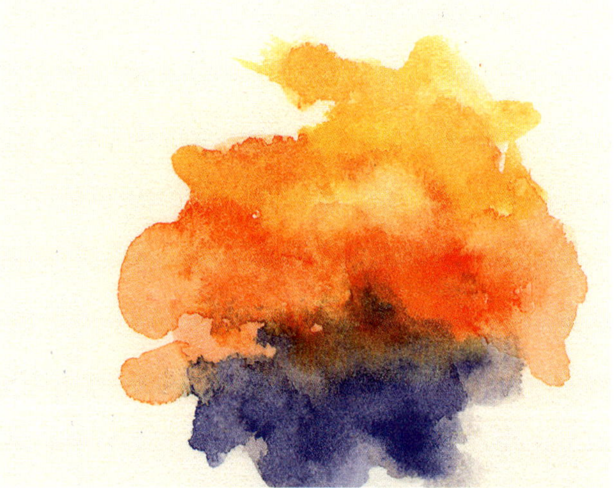

11 ⬓ The scumbling technique

Scumbling is a technique used by many oil painters to create soft hues of layered pigment and light. You're essentially layering the colour in soft, indirect layers to create the hue and look you want. Simply lay in semi-wet strokes of paint in watercolour. As I apply more colour, I'm careful to keep adding water so the colours blend and stay soft. It's easy to overwork and produce a muddy look, so less is more.

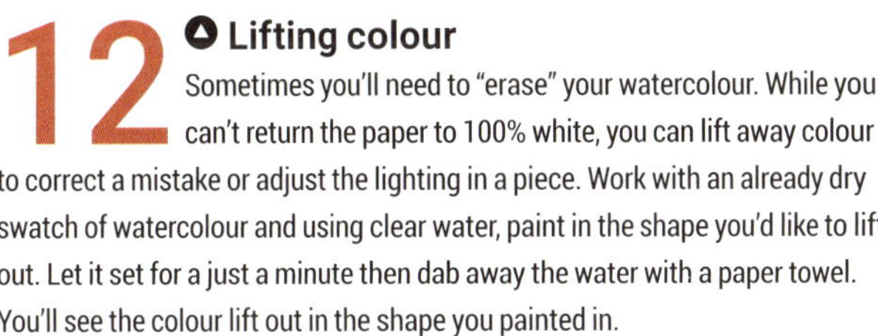

12 ⬤ Lifting colour

Sometimes you'll need to "erase" your watercolour. While you can't return the paper to 100% white, you can lift away colour to correct a mistake or adjust the lighting in a piece. Work with an already dry swatch of watercolour and using clear water, paint in the shape you'd like to lift out. Let it set for a just a minute then dab away the water with a paper towel. You'll see the colour lift out in the shape you painted in.

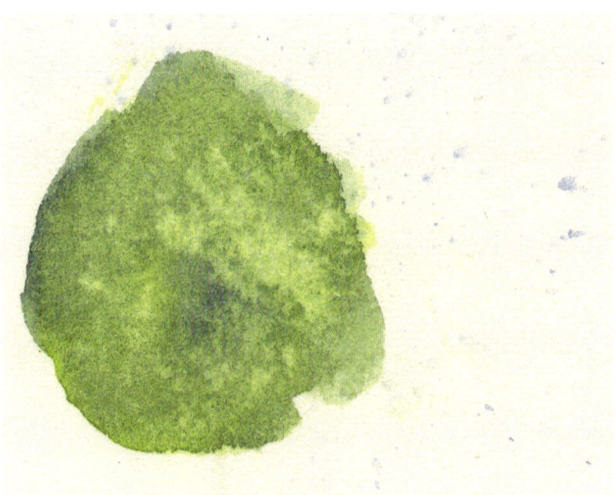

13 ⬤ Using salt

Watercolour is all about layering and texture. Salt can provide an interesting texture with little effort as the salt crystals absorb the water, leaving a unique pattern in the pigment. Lay down a swatch of watercolour and while the paint is still wet, sprinkle over salt. Let this sit until dry and simply wipe or blow away the salt. This technique is useful for adding texture to natural surfaces like rocks or tree bark.

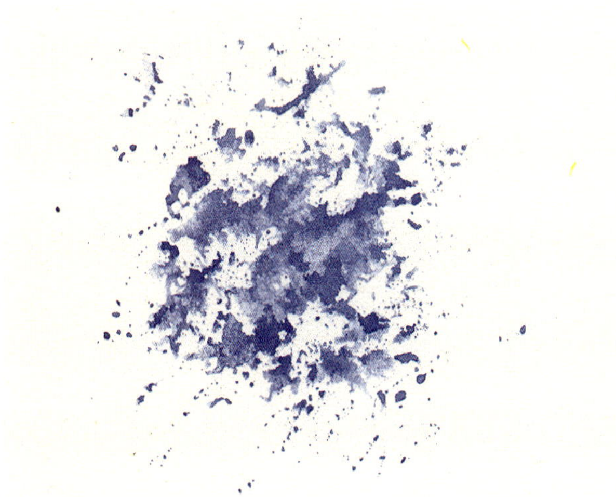

14 ⬤ Sponging

Another household item you can use to apply watercolours is a sponge. Simply mix your pigment in a small dish or tray, dip the sponge into the paint and blot onto your paper. You can alter the wetness of your paint and achieve different effects. A drier look would be suited for plant life or scaly skin while a wet application might be more suited for waterscapes or clouds.

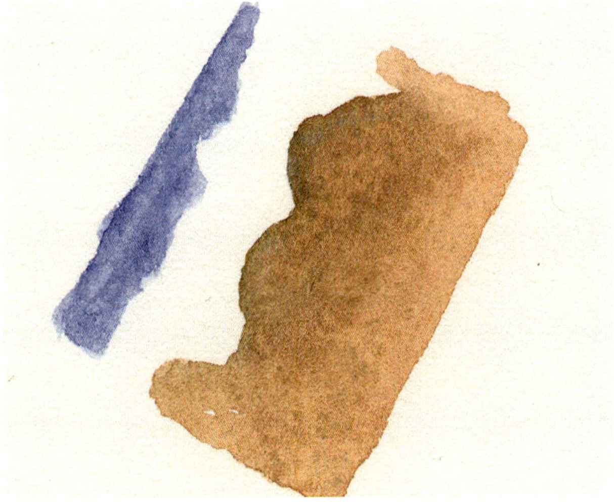

15 ⬤ Negative painting

Watercolour is about planning. Think about where you'd like your whites and lights before you apply paint. It's vital to keep control of your brush as you paint in the edge of where you'd like your negative space to begin. Load it with semi-wet pigment and paint along the edge of where you'd like your negative space to begin. Then pull the color away from the edge of the stroke to fill in where you'd like pigment.

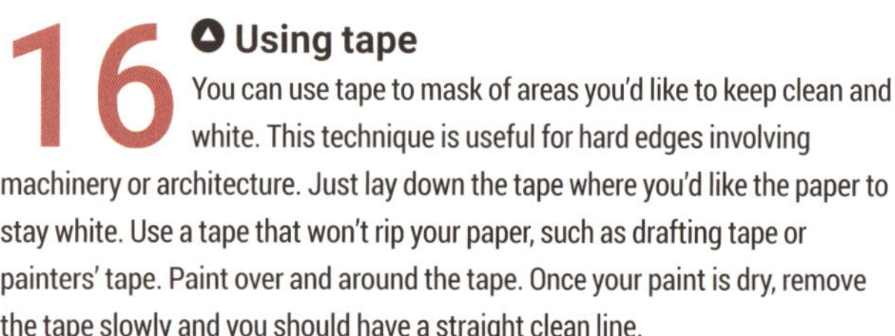

16 ▲ Using tape

You can use tape to mask of areas you'd like to keep clean and white. This technique is useful for hard edges involving machinery or architecture. Just lay down the tape where you'd like the paper to stay white. Use a tape that won't rip your paper, such as drafting tape or painters' tape. Paint over and around the tape. Once your paint is dry, remove the tape slowly and you should have a straight clean line.

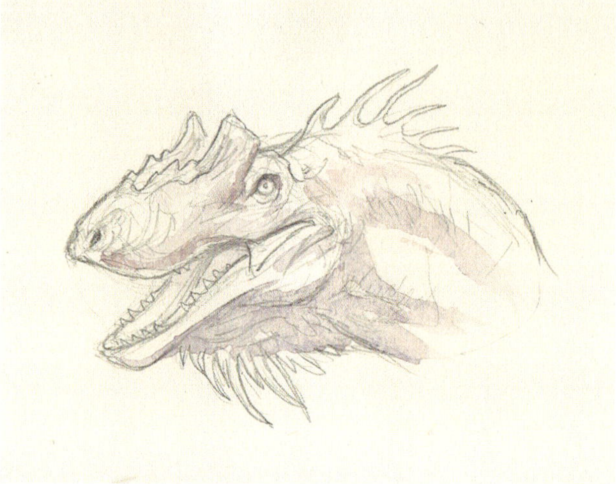

17 ▲ Find a light source

I've used a pencil with 2H lead to keep my drawing able to withstand the water from painting. First, I lay in some light paint strokes with a medium sized brush. My paint is very watery so won't stain the paper right away. Using a paper towel, I blot away most of it. Now I have an idea of where my light source might be, I add in more opaque strokes; this will be the basis for the form of the dinosaur, shadows and darks.

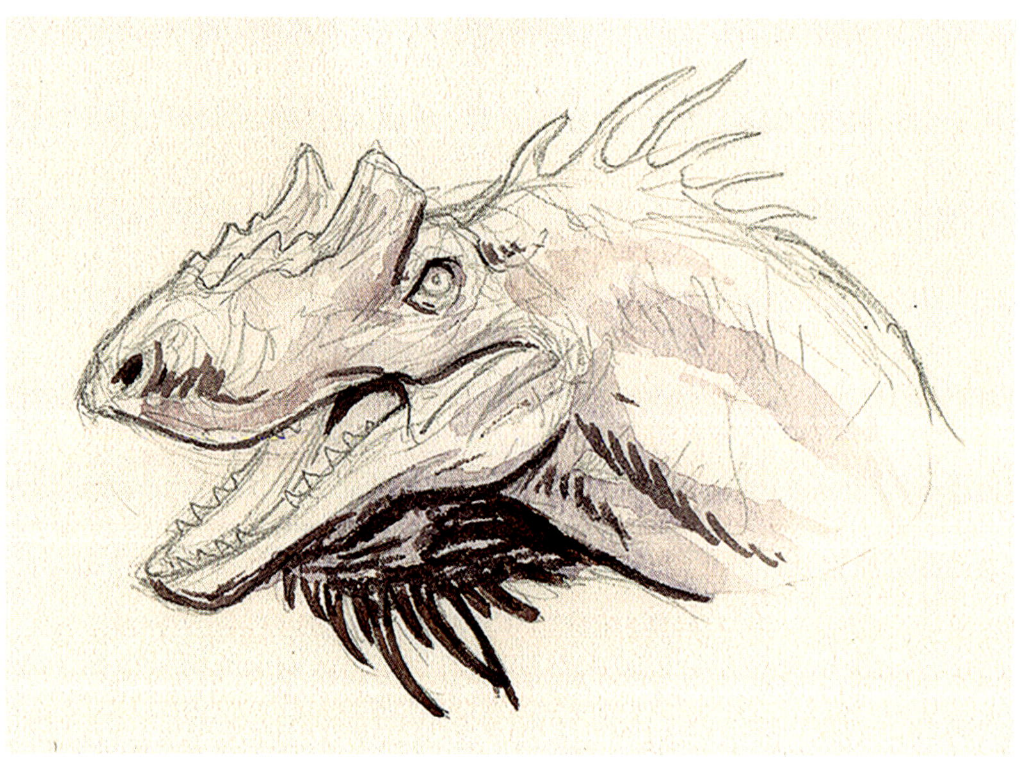

18 ◀ Pull colour and layer tones

Now you can use what we learned earlier about pulling colour from a dark stroke using just water. Using a wetter paintbrush, I am able to push and pull the pigment around out of the strokes I've just laid down. This technique helps me further to find my light source and it also makes it easier to layer in more tones and colour.

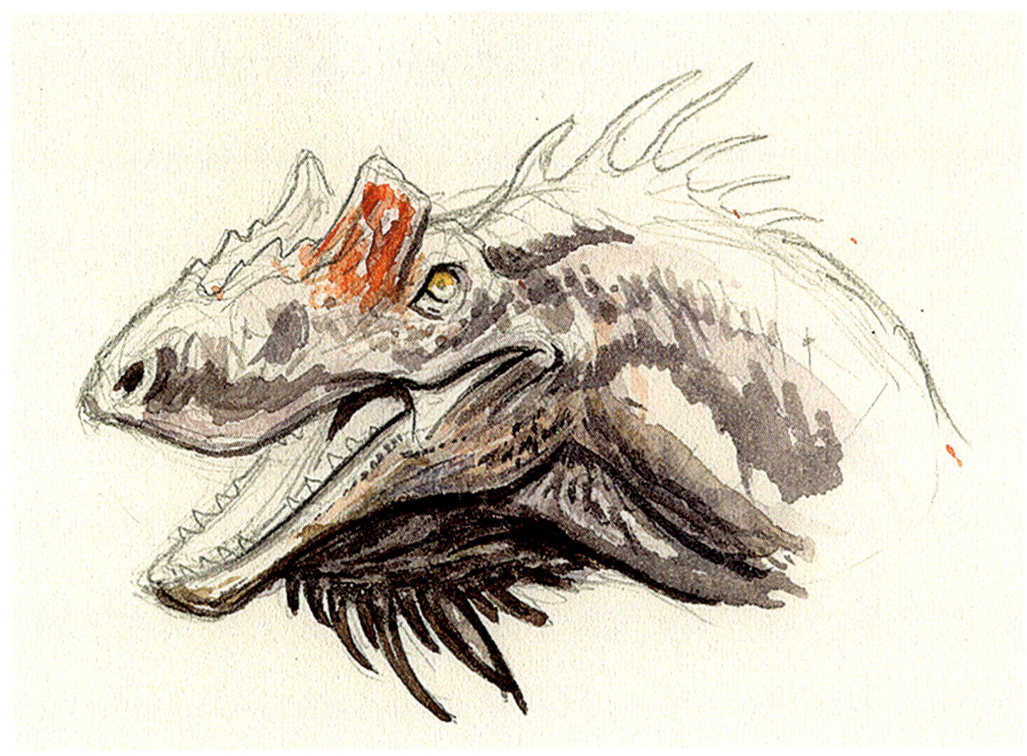

19

◄ **Keep layering**

Using my paper towel, I begin to lay in colour and take it away to get a more layered look to my piece. I am careful to let areas dry before I apply more colour. This allows me to move around the whole study. I'm also paying more attention to what colour goes where. Again, I'm using techniques I described earlier – Light to Dark, Wet and Dry, as well as Colour Pulling – to achieve the look I'm wanting.

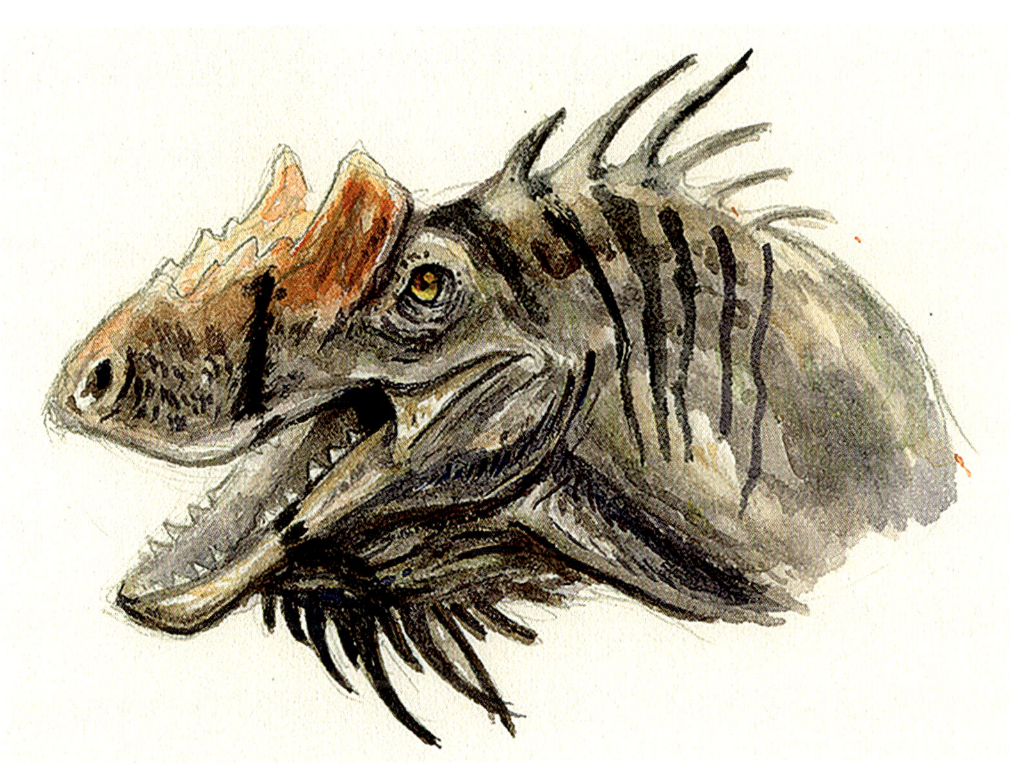

20

◄ **Add finer detail**

I'm nearly finished with my dinosaur – I'm now at the stage where I can begin to lay in markings, final dark brush strokes and skin texture. It's important to resist the temptation to use your darkest darks until you reach this step. Because watercolour painting is a transparent medium, you'll need to make sure you keep your lights light, and save the darks and details until the end.

Use masks in your watercolour art

Kelly McKernan demystifies the process in preserving your paper with masking materials

O ne of the most vexing and intimidating elements to working with watercolour involves preserving the white of the paper while painting with the amorphous media.

Watercolour purists will insist that using white watercolour or white ink no longer makes your painting exclusively watercolour. My opinion is that this is silly. What matters in the end is a solid image; however, masking materials exist for those who wish to work traditionally with watercolour. I don't believe that masking materials should ever be a crutch for your art, but they can be a time-saver nevertheless.

As you develop your skills, you'll also become more efficient with your process. I'm frequently asked if I use masking fluid on the Art Nouveau-esque hair in my paintings. It's very rare that I do, because it takes more time to apply the masking fluid than it does to just carefully paint around the hair. However, if I'm doing a wash over a large area and I don't want the flow interrupted when avoiding an area, so I'll just mask that off.

Truth be told, I really don't enjoy masking in my watercolour paintings since it can often be frustrating and have a steep learning curve. Many of the masking fluid techniques that I use have been discovered through trial and error. I ended up further developing my painting skills in lieu of depending on masking materials unless they'd save me considerable time. But it might be different for you, so let's have a look at these masking materials and methods – read on to learn how to mask!

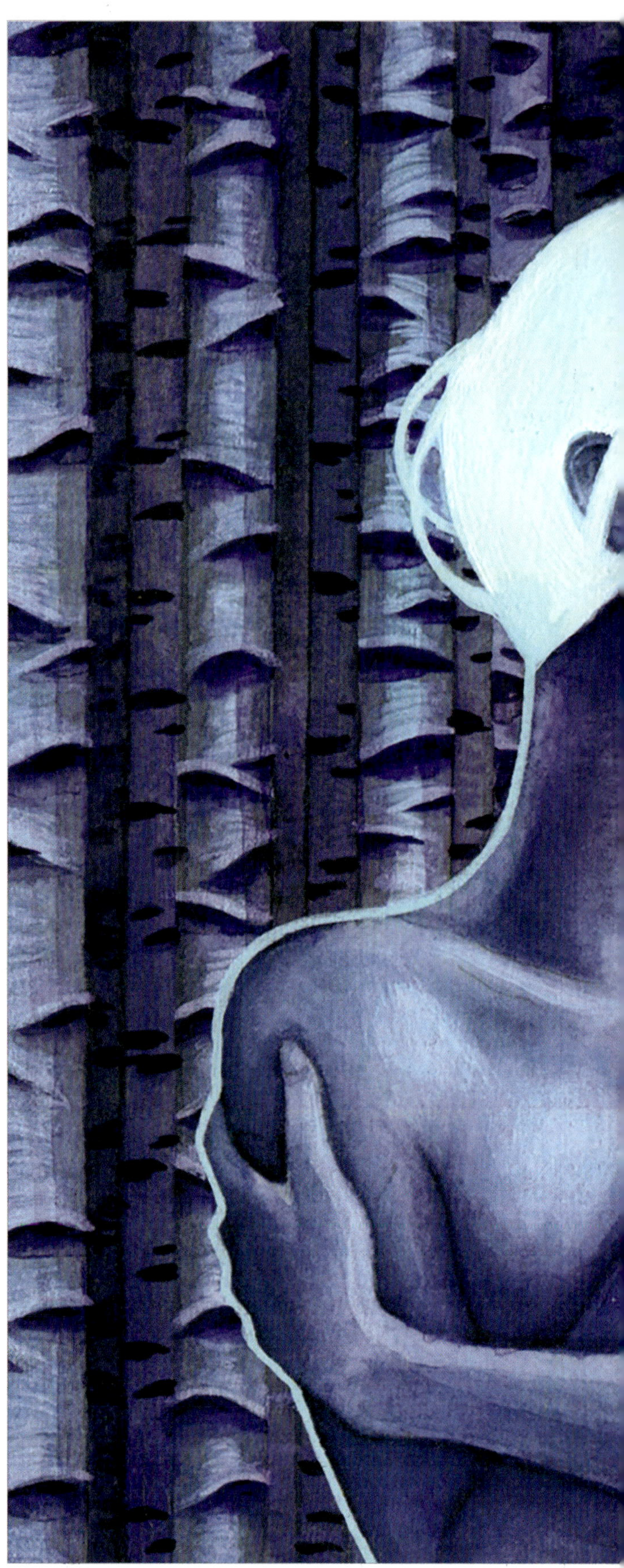

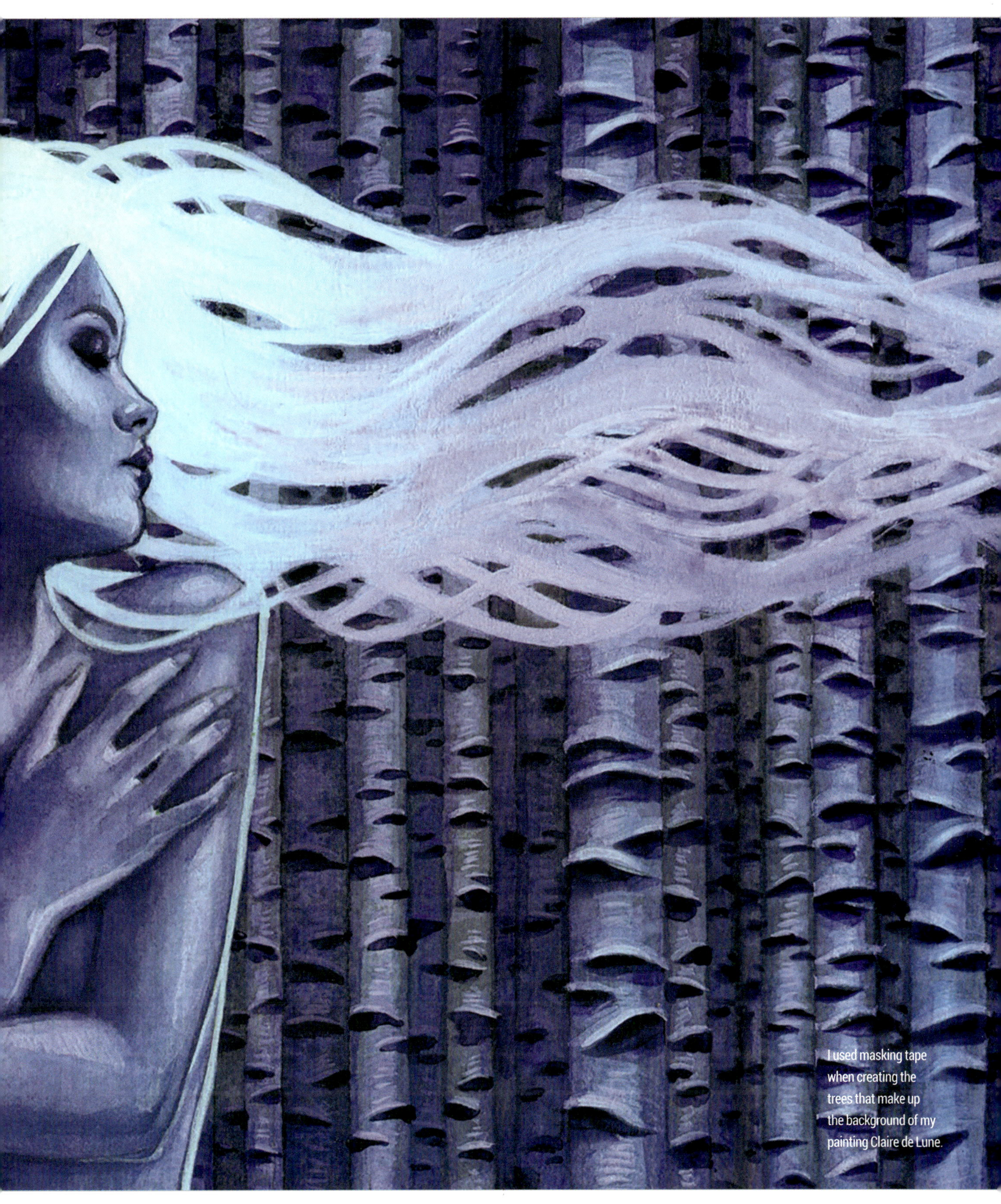

I used masking tape when creating the trees that make up the background of my painting Claire de Lune.

An introduction to masking materials

Masking to preserve an area in watercolour is just science. These materials repel water and protect whatever's underneath them, whether it's white paper or an area already painted. The tricky part is learning which materials are appropriate for the job and how to use them.

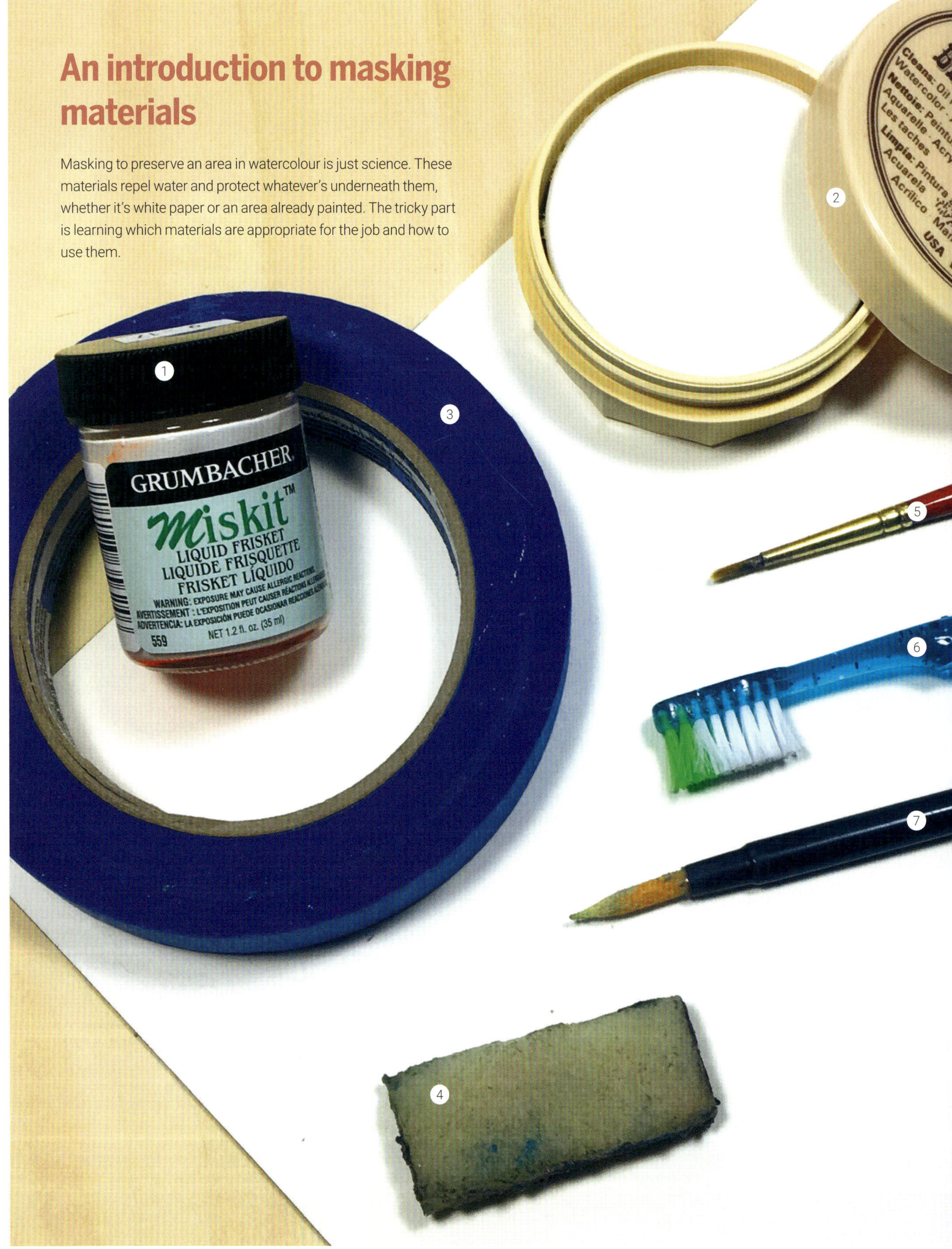

1 **Grumbacher Miskit Liquid Frisket**

My preferred brand of masking fluid. I'll never forget opening a jar in high school and the appalling odour that came forth! Over the years, I've tried a handful of brands and kept returning to this one because it's the most reliable and easy to work with. Stir, don't shake! Air bubbles will affect the consistency of your application.

2 **Brush cleaning soap**

I'll use this to coat a brush in a protective layer before using it with masking fluid. Brushes can be easily destroyed by masking fluid if not cared for properly, so I typically use brushes that are already in rough shape for this job.

3 **3M Blue Painter's Tape**

My go-to for masking tape. I have it in several sizes, and use it for many things in addition to masking.

4 **Rubber cement Pik-Up eraser**

This is ideal for removing masking fluid. It gets gunky pretty fast, so I cut it up into smaller pieces for extra edges.

5 **Size 2 Round brush**

Already a bit beaten up. Coating the bristles with brush cleaner will help to protect it from being further damaged by the masking fluid.

6 **A toothbrush**

Handy for splattering tiny dots of masking fluid (and other media, including watercolour, rubbing alcohol and water). I recommend also distributing brush soap into your toothbrush to help preserve it.

7 **Grafix Original Incredible Nib**

This is a tool with a pointed end and a chiselled end. This is my preferred tool for distributing masking fluid because it clogs up less, although thin lines are difficult to achieve with it.

Each tool has a purpose – get to know them!

Of course, a lot of experimentation will need to occur in order to get a comfortable handle on masking materials. Many of your first attempts may not go well, so be sure to practise before applying your masking knowledge to a final painting for the first time.

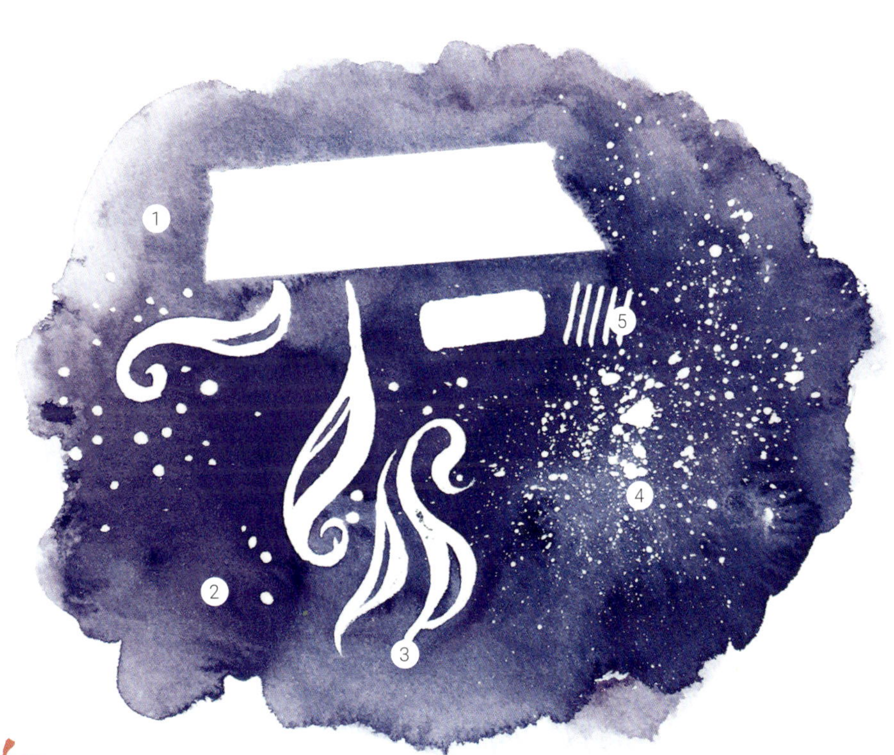

Follow these steps...

1 Masking tape is regularly used for preserving edges of a painting, but it can also be used for masking large areas of a piece by layering in strips, then cutting to a precise shape with a blade. This is not a preferred method for me, but when precise, sharp edges are necessary, the masking tape is my go-to. To help avoid tearing when removing the tape, heat it with a hair dryer as you peel away. I've found that masking tape works best on hot press paper.

2 The pointed end of the Original Incredible Nib is excellent for consistently sized dots or making long strokes, since it holds the masking fluid slightly better than a brush.

3 This shape is created with a size 2 Round brush with brush soap and masking fluid. Precise lines are a lot easier to achieve, but the consistency of masking fluid can make it challenging to produce smooth lines.

4 This splattering is created with a toothbrush and masking fluid. It's fairly unpredictable, but can be used to produce really neat effects.

5 This is the chiselled end of Grafix's Original Incredible Nib tool.

Best practices with masking fluid

When making a decision about what you'd like to preserve in your painting, you'll also need to identify when to apply it. If using masking fluid will save you time in your painting, the next step is to work out when to use it. Writing down steps can help! Let's look at an example of a complicated layering sequence.

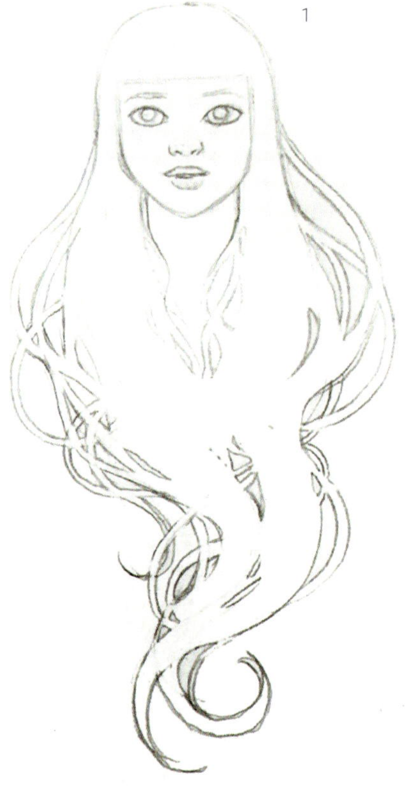

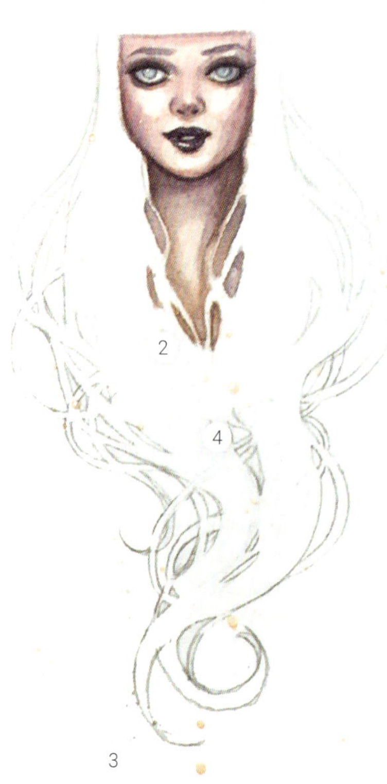

Follow these steps...

1 For this example, I'm beginning with a simple drawing. I want the hair to have a galaxy effect. Because I know that the hair will be darker than the skin tone, I've decided to paint the skin first.

2 To keep consistency with a limited palette, I'm using only a few colours: Opera pink, Indigo and Lemon yellow. This is on Arches hot press 140lb watercolour paper.

3 I know that when I apply the masking fluid with the toothbrush for a splatter effect, it will get on the face, but the dried masking fluid won't harm the painting underneath.

Don't attempt to speed up the drying time of the masking fluid with a hair dryer or any heat, because this will make the latex bond to your paper.

4 I want to preserve some of the white paper as stars, so I've splattered just a little with the toothbrush and added a few more spots with my Original Incredible Nib tool in selected areas of the image.

Layering with masking fluid

We know that masking fluid is usually used to preserve the white of the paper, but it can also be applied to areas you've already painted. This preserves the colour and texture underneath while you put a wash over it, and is a great technique for creating depth or a layering of colour.

Follow these steps...

1 To produce the splatter effect, brush your thumb against the bristles away from the paper. If you do the opposite, it'll just get in your face – not a good look.

2 I'm not being terribly precise with the hair because I plan to paint around it later.

3 I've now added the first layer of colour – a dusty pink – over the outline of the hair after the first layer of masking fluid spots have dried.

4 Don't add masking fluid to paper that's anything but bone dry. This makes it a long process of waiting for everything to dry, but adding masking fluid to damp or wet paper will cause it to disperse into the fibres and then become all-but impossible to remove.

5 Once the first layer of colour is dry, I add a second layer of masking fluid splatters with the toothbrush. In between these layers, I rinse the masking fluid out of the toothbrush and wipe it dry.

Patience is key

Working with masking materials requires patience, but since you're working with watercolour anyway, you're familiar with waiting for things to dry. Rushing the process of working with masking fluid can result in torn paper, misplaced blobs and permanent adhesion. However, when things go as planned, removing your masking materials is like opening up a present!

1 In this example, I've added three layers of colour, creating four preserved colour variants of splatters – including the white paper underneath.

2 After allowing each layer to dry naturally, carefully removing the masking fluid with my rubber cement Pik-Up eraser is incredibly satisfying! Don't use your fingers, because any oils on them can discolour or damage your painting.

3 If the masking fluid isn't coming up easily, you can apply more on top, allow it to dry, and then try lifting again. For masking fluid that's dried on to a brush, lighter fluid will remove it.

4 Experiment with your application for different effects. Sticks, a palette knife, sponges and other tools can be used to apply masking fluid to a painting. You could even use an atomiser!

Remember, the most important thing in the end is that your painting is a good image. It doesn't matter how "pure" your watercolour technique is if the painting can be improved with the use of mixed media. Adding additional white dots with ink or iridescent acrylic paint would make this painting better. Keep experimenting!

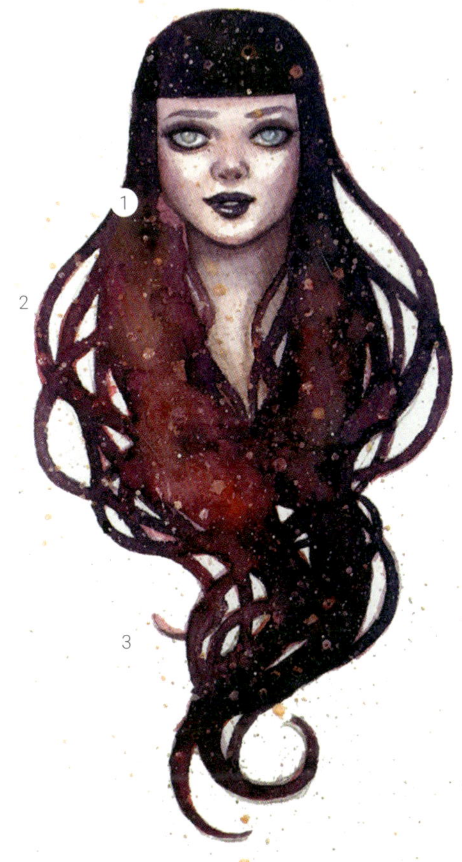
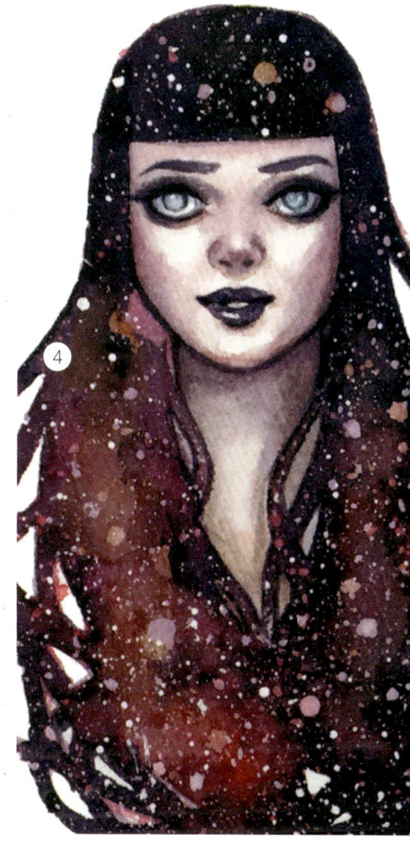
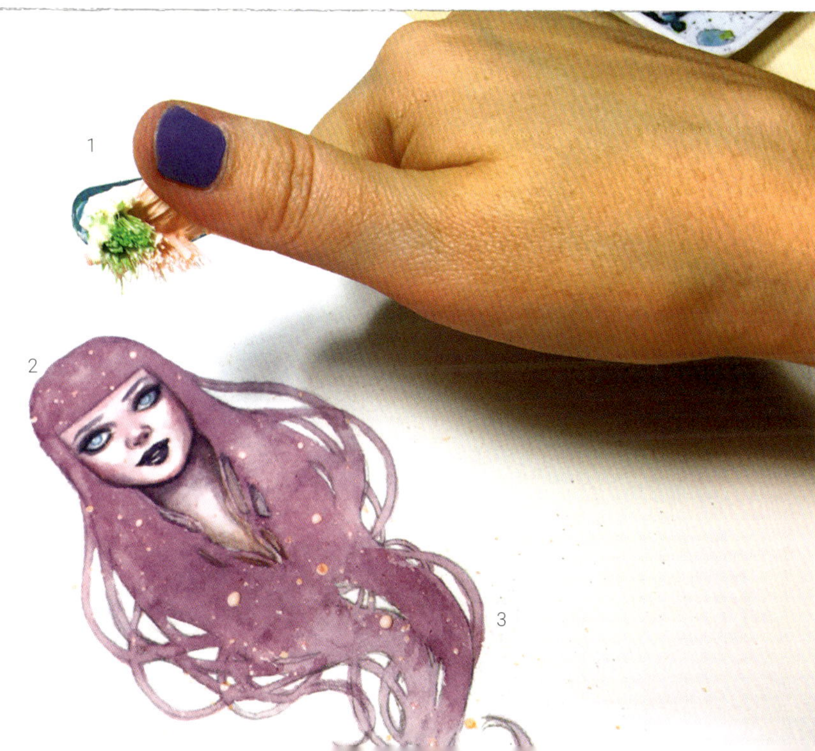
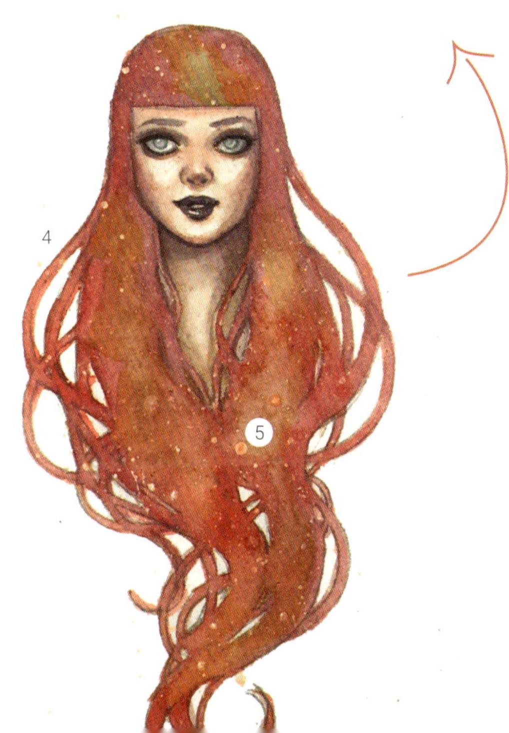

colour theory for watercolour

Lancelot Richardson introduces the fundamentals of colour theory, and shows how it can be applied to a watercolour painting process

The relationships between different colours are broken down using colour theory. This guide will look at how colours are arranged on a spectrum around a colour wheel and how they form groups depending on their relative positions on it. It also looks at how colours are made up of the fundamental elements of hue, saturation and tone, and shows how to use these ideas to assist in the painting process.

Colour theory is especially useful when composing images and mixing colour. Different colour combinations can form compositions with different moods and harmonies. There are many ways to achieve harmonious colour compositions; certain placements of colours on a colour wheel and their combinations is one way to do this. The balance of light and dark in an image – its key – is also important.

Mixing colour can feel rather like a shot in the dark when you don't know how different colours behave and interact. When mixing colour, the colour wheel can guide us to mixing better neutral colours or understand what paints are needed to make more intense mixes.

These ideas are a guideline with which to get started. Colour is a diverse and subjective topic, with multiple interpretations that may vary depending on how it is used, the science of colour and light, and the language we use. This guide focuses on how painters typically use colour, but it is well worth digging deeper into this topic and learning more about the science of colour, and how it is used in other settings, such as printed media.

Understanding the colour wheel

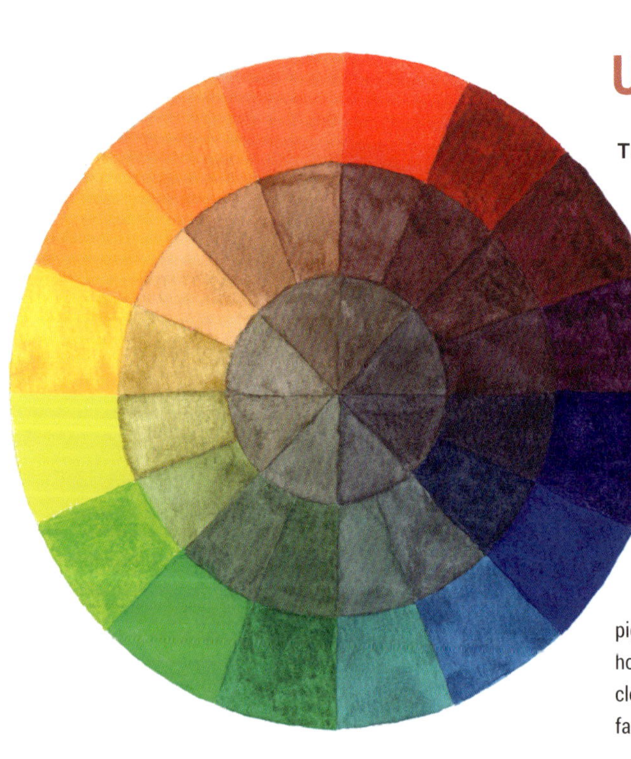

THE COLOUR WHEEL is an essential part of understanding the spectrum of colours we see . Even though colours exist on a continuous spectrum, artists typically break them down into individual blocks that can be named. This forms the outermost ring of the colour wheel.

In painting, the conventional primary colours are red, yellow and blue. These form the basis of an artists' colour wheel and are evenly spaced around it. Secondary colours are created by mixing two primary colours – if red, blue and yellow are the primary colours, the secondary colours are green, orange and violet. Tertiary colours are created by mixing a primary with a secondary colour – for instance, vermilion is an orange-red.

Using red, yellow and blue as primary colours is not entirely accurate, as greens and blues take up more of the colour spectrum than this covers. Sometimes alternative colour wheels are used, such as red, blue and green, or cyan, magenta and yellow. It is possible to mix traditional primary colours with these alternative colour wheels, though they will not be as intense as pure pigments. The idea of primary colours is that any colour can be mixed from them – however, again, these secondary mixtures are less vivid than pure pigments. The closer two colours are on the colour wheel, the more intense their mixture is. The farther apart two colours are, the duller the mixture.

Colour groups

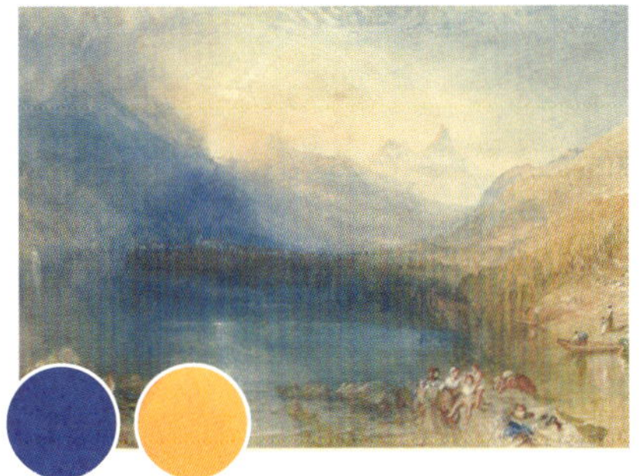

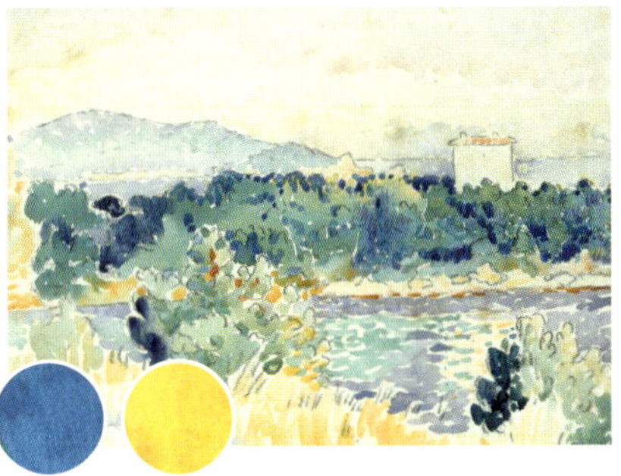

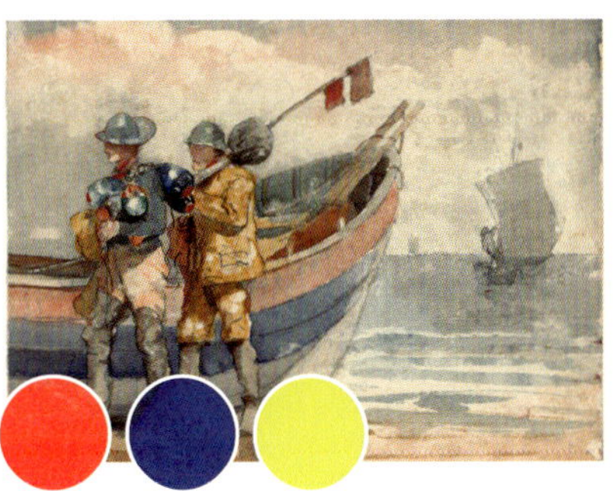

1 ◐ Complementary colours

Complementary colours sit opposite each other on the wheel. They have the highest colour contrast, often looking very intense when placed next to each other in a composition. Two saturated complementary colours may clash and strain a viewer's eyes, especially in close proximity. One way to use them effectively is to ensure one colour is more neutral – in this example by Turner, the oranges are pushed into lighter, more neutral browns to balance the saturated blues. Mixing two complementary colours together produces a neutral grey, or even a black, as they cancel each other out – the greys in the centre of the colour wheel can be made this way.

2 ◐ Analogous colours

Analogous colours are neighbours on the colour wheel. They can span a very narrow portion of the colour wheel, or a wider section.

Because these colours neighbour each other, they have less colour contrast and harmonise easily – almost too easily. To add contrast in these sorts of colour schemes, one option is to push the tonal or saturation contrasts (or both) instead – this example by Henri-Edmond Cross uses darker blues to contrast lighter yellows.

When mixed, analogous colours produce bright intermediary hues. The closer two colours are on the colour wheel, the more saturated their mixture.

3 ◐ Triadic colours

Triadic colours schemes are comprised of three colours evenly spaced around the colour wheel.

This can be challenging with saturated colours, as a large area of the wheel is included in these schemes, making colour contrast hard to manage. One option is to pick a dominant colour and let the other two support it as more subdued tones. Another strategy, used in this example by Winslow Homer, is to tie a triad of saturated colours together with whites, which give the eye a break, and reflects subtle indications of the triad, tying the composition together. Alternatively, triad colours can be used in small amounts to 'spice up' neutral arrangements.

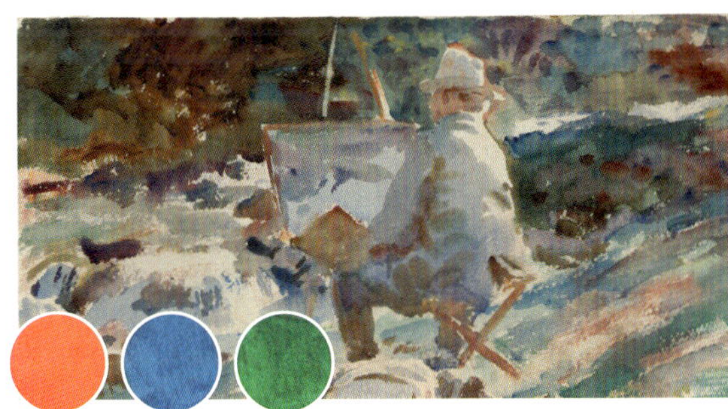

4 ◐ Split complementary colours

Split complementary colour schemes are like complementary schemes, but one colour is split into two. The other colour sits opposite the centre point of this pair. The separation between the split pair can be narrow, like in this example by Sargent that splits across the blue-green colours, or can expand until it transforms into a triadic scheme. This is a great set-up for a limited palette, as it has the harmony of a complementary colour scheme, but covers more ground on the colour wheel and includes a wider range of colours in the composition. Some complementary schemes split both colours – sometimes called a tetradic scheme. They work especially well if the range of each pair is limited.

The emotions of colour

COLOUR CAN PLAY a key role in the mood of an image, depending on the dominant hues and how they are used, such as how grey or saturated they are, or the key of the image.

Colour can be associated with certain emotions. There are many complex reasons why a colour creates a psychological reaction in a viewer, and this depends on context, societal influences and other colour interactions as much as a colour's inherent properties. A field of yellow flowers would be a bright, uplifting scene, but yellow is also associated with danger as it appears on warning signs and wasps. Therefore, some of these associations may seem contradictory.

RED = excitement, aggression, romance
YELLOW = warmth, friendliness, danger
GREEN = nature, sickliness, envy
BLUE = relaxation, coldness, grief
WHITE = cleanliness, innocence, emptiness
BLACK = oppressive, calm, powerful

Tonal value

TONAL VALUE is how light or dark a colour is on a scale that ranges from white to black.

Monochrome colour schemes are purely tonal – they only use one colour, and only change its tonal value. As colours get lighter or darker, their saturation changes as well. Different colours have different tonal values – yellow is very light, red and green are in the middle, and blues and purples are quite dark.

Tints and shades are light and dark forms of a colour. Lightening a colour creates tints, whilst darkening it creates shades. This can be done by adding white or black paint, though this may give 'flat' results. In watercolour, lightening colours can be done by diluting them so the white of the paper shows more. Darkening colours is best done by mixing them with a chromatic black – a black made from mixing colours.

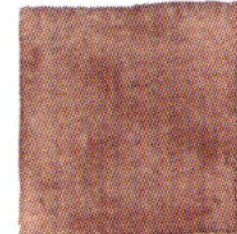

Saturation

SATURATION is how intense or 'vivid' a colour is, on a scale that ranges from grey to a pure colour. This is also called chroma, or purity.

It is tempting to use saturated colours exclusively – after all, they look colourful! However, if all the colours in a composition are saturated, none of them look especially vivid. To use saturation effectively, employ its full range and use some duller colours – a saturated red will stand out dramatically on a dull green background. Most of what surrounds us is made of duller colours – human skin, for instance, is largely comprised of warm greys.

The farther apart two colours are on the colour wheel, the less saturated their mixture is. This is why if you mix an orange-ish yellow with a blue, the resulting green will look dull.

Hue

HUE IS A COLOUR'S place on the outer ring of the colour wheel, or on a spectrum of colours. Though we often identify certain hues with specific names – such as red or blue – it is actually a continuous spectrum resulting from the wavelengths of light reflected off a subject.

Hue is often used as synonym for colour, but is a little different as it refers purely to a colour's position around the colour wheel or in the light spectrum. It is combined with saturation and tonal value to create individual colours. For instance, brown colours are often oranges with a lower saturation and darker tonal value.

Colour schemes in painting tend to look at hue contrasts. Because hue loops back on itself in a circle (unlike saturation or tonal value), these relationships are easier to visualise on a wheel.

High key versus low key

THE KEY OF an image is the dominant tonal value it has overall, and how it limits its tonal values to a certain range.

High key compositions are dominated by light tonal values, and omit or minimally use dark tonal values. This creates a dominance of more pastel colours, and allows saturated colours to act as colourful shadows. In the example by Rosa Bonheur below, whites and light colours dominate, and a lot of the shadows are limited to middle greys. High key compositions often have a light, airy feel – here, it helps showcase the movement of the horses.

Low key compositions have a predominance of dark tonal values, and omit or minimally use light tones. This is good for showing atmospheric and weather effects, as well as night scenes. The addition of small touches of light values creates dramatic tonal contrast. This example by Whistler (right) is full of atmosphere. The tonal contrast draws immediate attention up to the sitter's face.

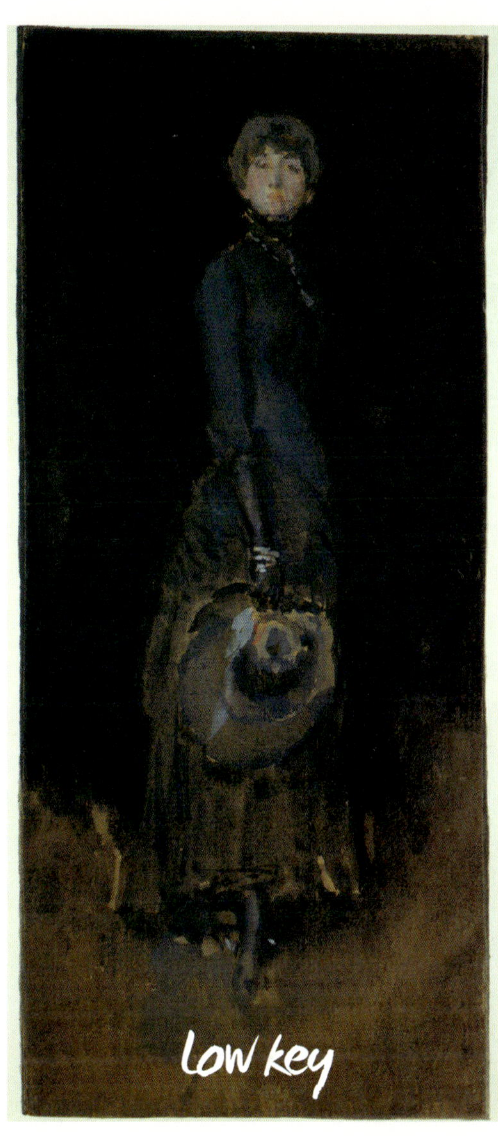

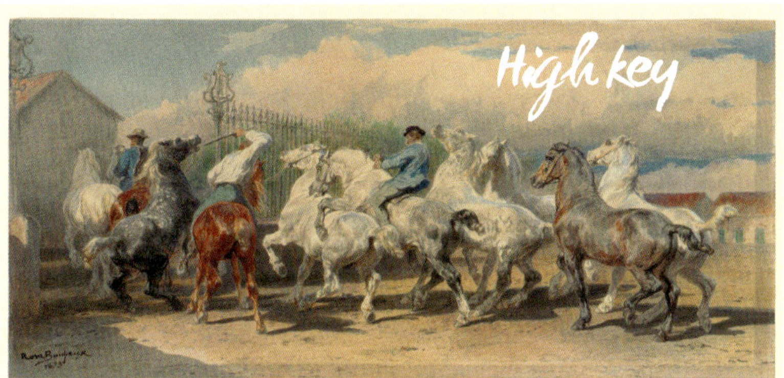

Warm, neutral & cool tones

COLOUR TEMPERATE is how 'warm' or 'cool' a colour is perceived to be. Blues, greens and violets are typically considered cool colours, whilst reds, oranges and yellows are considered warms. Neutral colours are less saturated colours that don't show colour temperature as strongly, with greys being completely neutral. Neutrals can lean towards being warm or cool.

Temperature is a relative property that is used to compare hue – for instance, magenta is near red on the colour wheel, but is a comparatively cooler hue, whilst orange has a warmer hue than red. It is also used specificity variants on a colour – for instance, a warm-leaning red would be approaching orange – like vermilion – whilst a cool-leaning red would approach purple – such as crimson.

Like many aspects of colour, temperature can be quite subjective. It can be tricky to decide what the coolest and warmest colours are precisely, or where warm colours stop and cool ones start.

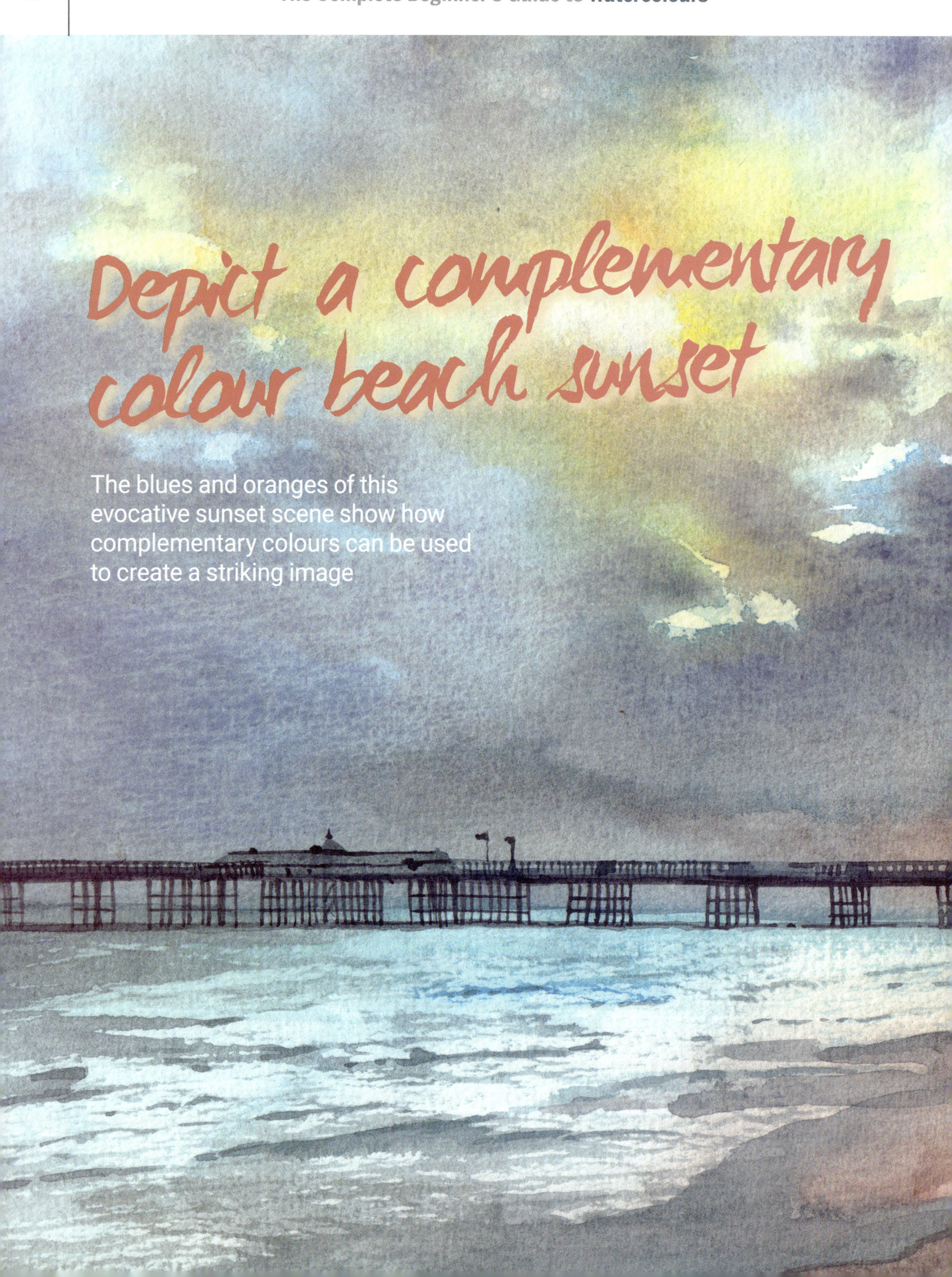

Depict a complementary colour beach sunset

The blues and oranges of this evocative sunset scene show how complementary colours can be used to create a striking image

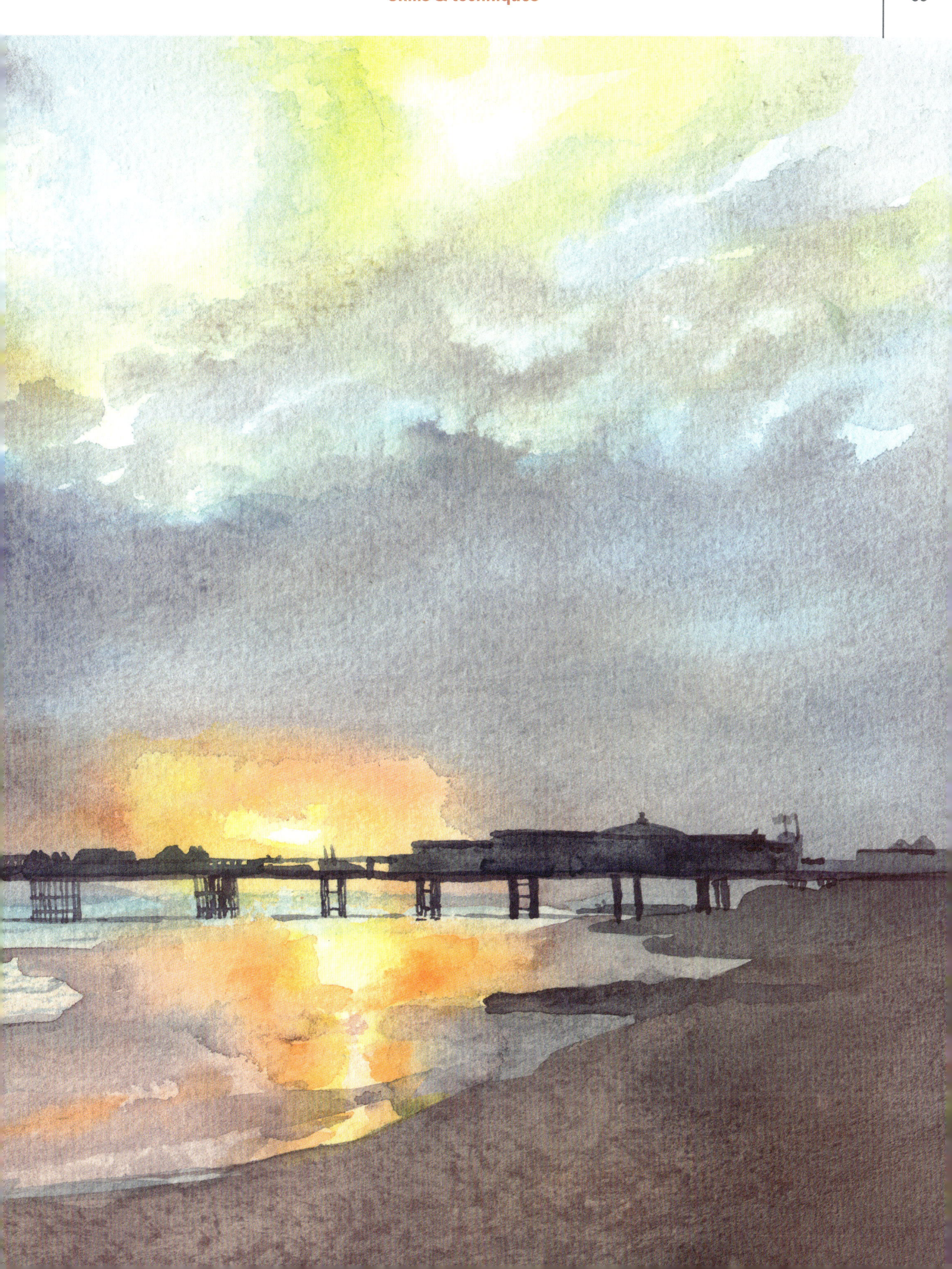

Materials

- Winsor and Newton Artists tube watercolours: Lemon (Winsor) Yellow, Cadmium Yellow, Pyrrole (Winsor) Red, Permanent Alizarin Crimson, French Ultramarine, Phthalo Blue, Venetian Red
- Brushes: 1 inch flat wash, 3/8 inch medium flat, round sable #8
- Seawhites cold press watercolour paper
- 2H graphite pencil
- Spray bottle

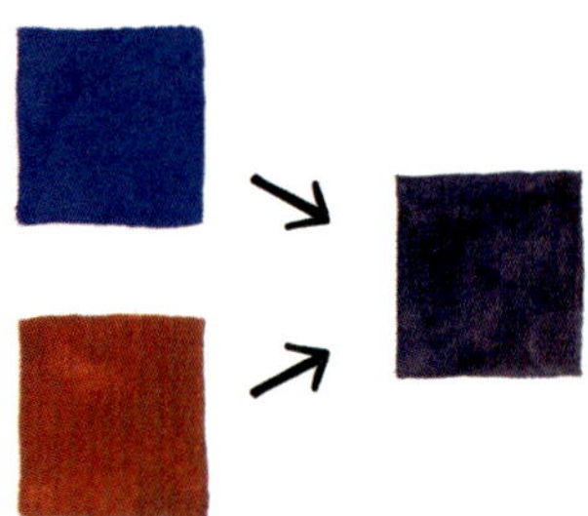

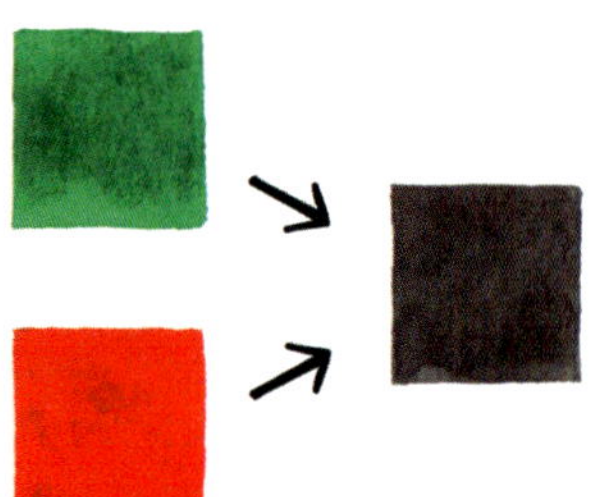

Mixing shadows

It is tempting to use black when mixing shadows. However, tube black can result in 'flat' shadows, so it is best to use chromatic blacks. Chromatic blacks are shadows mixed using colours, such as red and green, or blue and brown. These are usually complementary, though mixing a triad of colours can work too. Add these to colour mixes to make richer shadows.

Follow these steps...

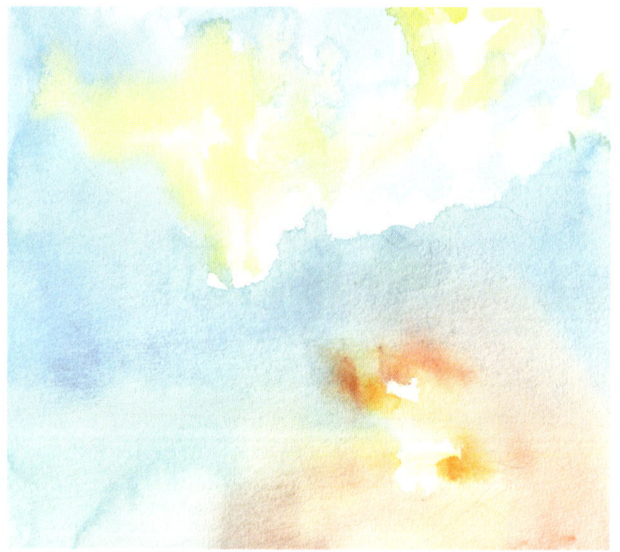

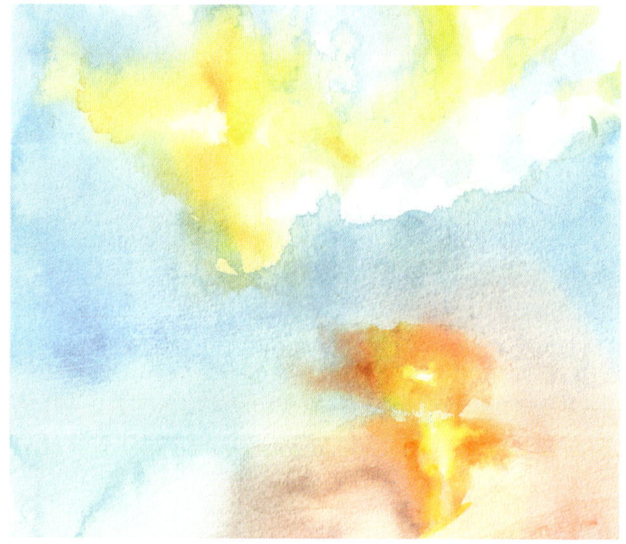

1 ▲ Wet-in-Wet: initial wash

To start, I create a loose sketch in pencil and apply broad washes using the flat wash brush.

The colour scheme for this image is going to be a roughly split complementary of blue with a yellow and orange pair, so I start with these colours. After laying in the blue wash first, I add the oranges and yellows while it is still wet to create soft edges as they bleed together.

The paint in this stage is very watered down to keep things light, and the very lightest areas still keep the white of the paper.

2 ▲ Intensify colour

In this image, the yellow and orange are going to be the most saturated colours, while the blues are going to be duller and darker, and other colours will be much more neutral.

After allowing the blues to dry completely, I add more intense yellows and oranges to push the saturation of these areas up. To achieve the soft blooms of colour, I gently brush a little water onto the paper and let the paint bleed into it as I apply it – this is a bit easier to control than a spray.

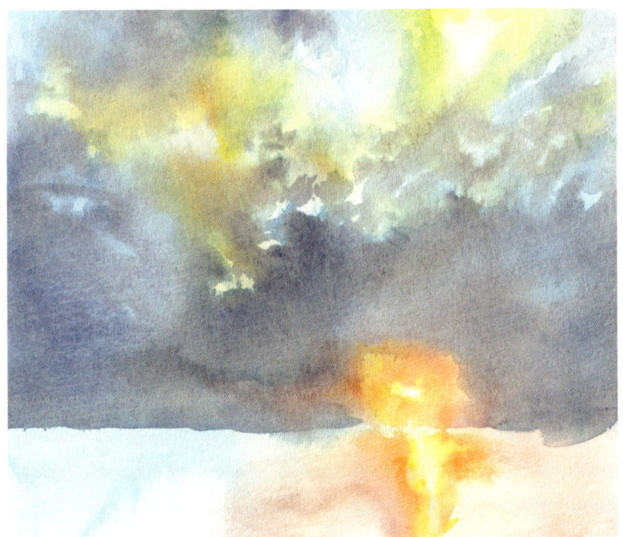

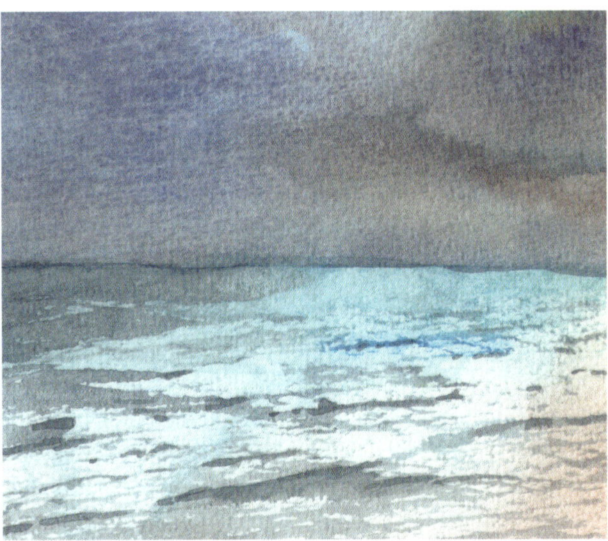

3 ⏺ Add clouds

The clouds cover a large area with fairly neutral blues. This colour may not seem exciting, but it provides a backdrop for the vivid sunset colours.

For the neutral blue, I mix Ultramarine with a tiny bit of Phthalo Blue and some Venetian Red to dull it. The mixture is kept quite diluted to keep it pale enough, and around the sunset I add extra Alizarin Crimson where the red light glows through the clouds. To soften the clouds, some parts of the sky were wetted with a spray bottle to allow the paint to run.

4 ⏺ Add sea texture

The sea is in a couple of layers. It is more saturated and slightly green-leaning near the horizon line and sun, so I use a little wash of Phthalo Blue with a tiny bit of Lemon Yellow to push it greener and with Ultramarine to dull the saturation a touch.

For the second layer, there is a bit more Ultramarine and touch of Venetian Red in the mixture to make a more neutral grey-blue colour. This is applied with a fairly dry brush, dragged over the grain of the paper to make the broken-up texture of the waves.

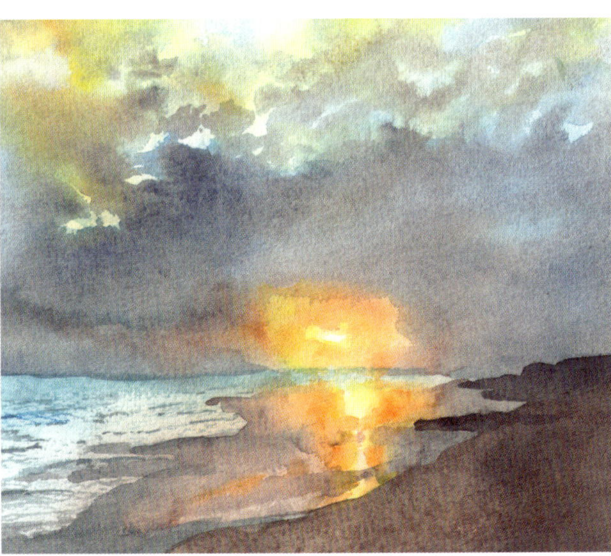

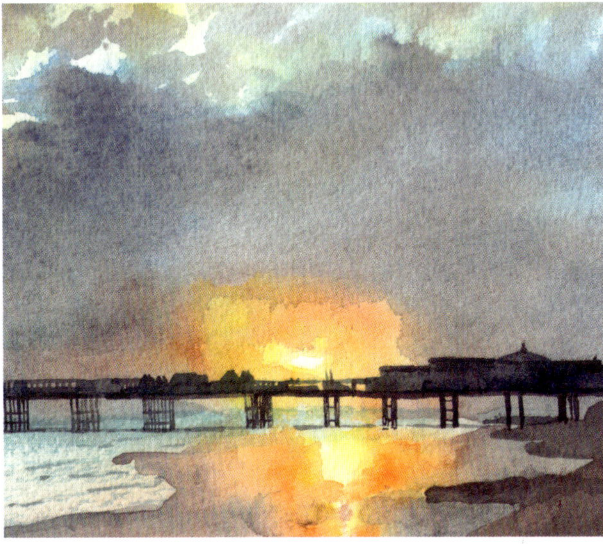

5 ⏺ Dark neutral tones

The sand and beach seem almost purple due to contrast from the blues and yellows, even though these areas are dark, neutral colours. Dull blues are used for the wet sand – these are blended into the reflection of the sunset with a little Alizarin Crimson. I brush water on the paper first so the paint will bleed.

To get the colour of the shadowy beach, I mix Ultramarine Blue and Venetian Red to get a dark neutral colour, then add a little Alizarin Crimson to warm it up. The texture of the beach is scumbled in using a dry, round brush, making twisting motions.

6 ⏺ Add the pier

The colour for the pier is Venetian Red and Ultramarine Blue – using a little water this time – with a touch of Phthalo Blue to cool it down. Because a lot of the other elements have been painted with more water, they are relatively light in tone and allow the pier to stand out.

The pier is added using a medium round sable brush – a good natural hair brush should hold a fine point well. I draw the boardwalk first, then add the structures on top and below. The reflection around the struts is added at the end using a more dilute shadow colour.

Portraits in watercolour

This portrait demonstration shows an analogous colour scheme at work and looks at mixing warm neutral skin tones

Materials

- Winsor and Newton tube paints: Cadmium Yellow, Winsor Orange, Pyrrole (Winsor) Red, Permanent Alizarin Crimson, French Ultramarine, Yellow Ochre, Venetian Red
- Faber Castel watercolour pencils – Yellow Ochre
- Brushes: 1 inch flat wash, 3/8 inch medium flat, round sable #8, round synthetic #7, fan
- Seawhites cold press watercolour paper

Mixing skin tones

In most situations, skin is largely made up of warm, neutral tones. When mixing colour for darker skin, I'd use a similar palette to this demonstration, but may incorporate more reds, blues and browns to mixtures to warm and darken it. Lighter skin uses more dilute paint and is sometimes more red-leaning.

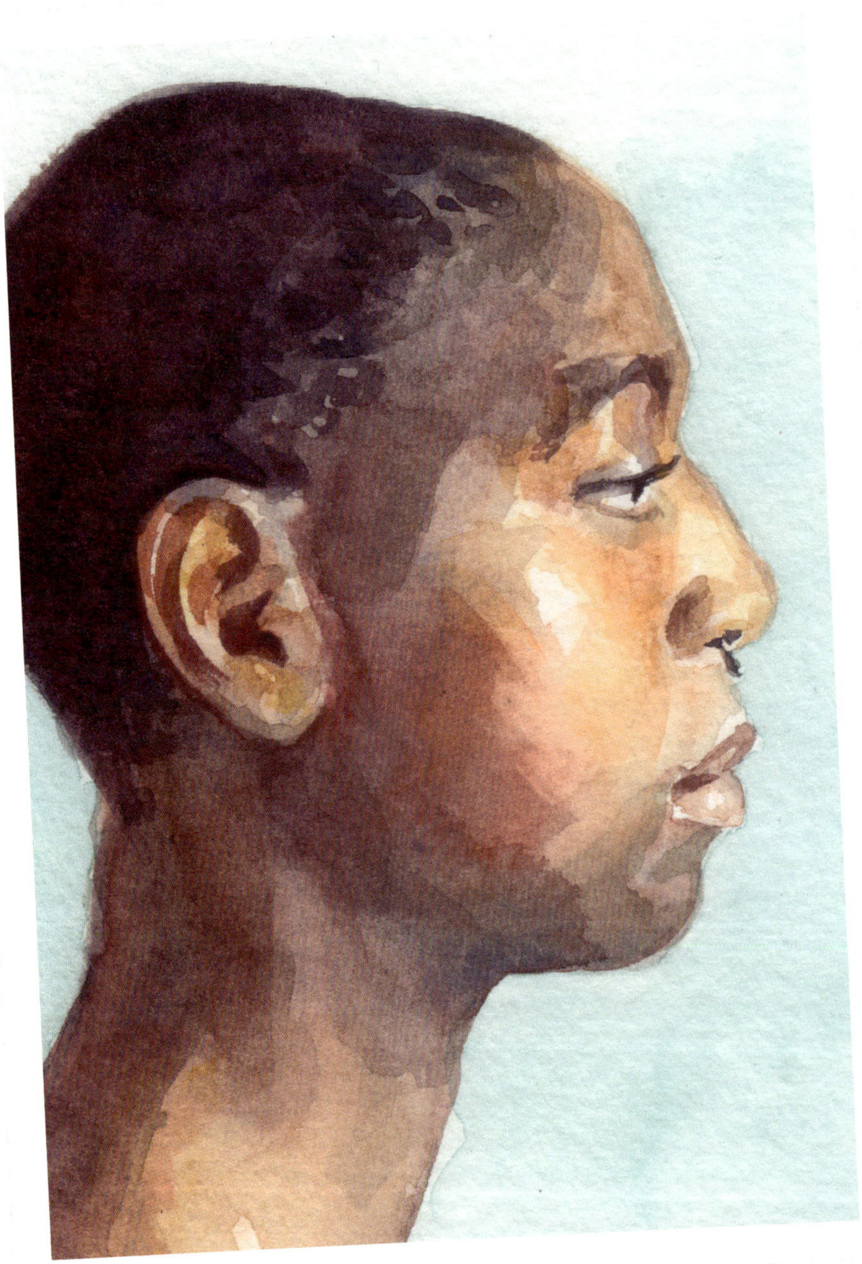

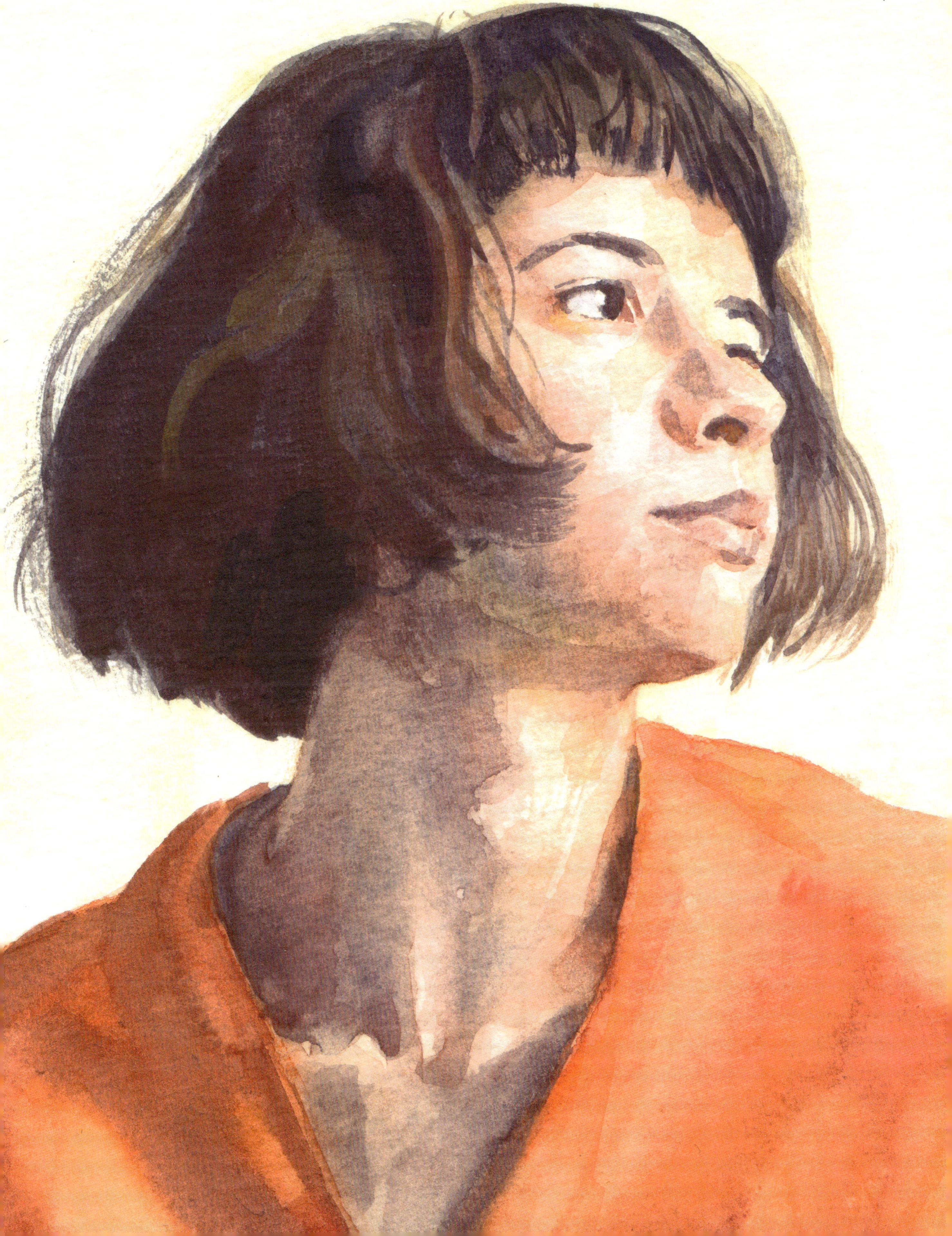

Follow these steps...

1 ⬇ Lay in base colours

To start this portrait, I sketch out the face as a simple line drawing in water-soluble pencil. Then, using fairly dilute paint, I apply some warm neutrals to the skin and background. The colour scheme for this portrait is going to be analogous, with the warmest yellows and oranges for the lighter areas, and cooler reds and purples for the darker areas.

The sketch is done in a Yellow Ochre pencil to complement the colour scheme. When selecting paints, I need a lot of freedom in mixing warm colours here, so my palette has multiple reds and yellows.

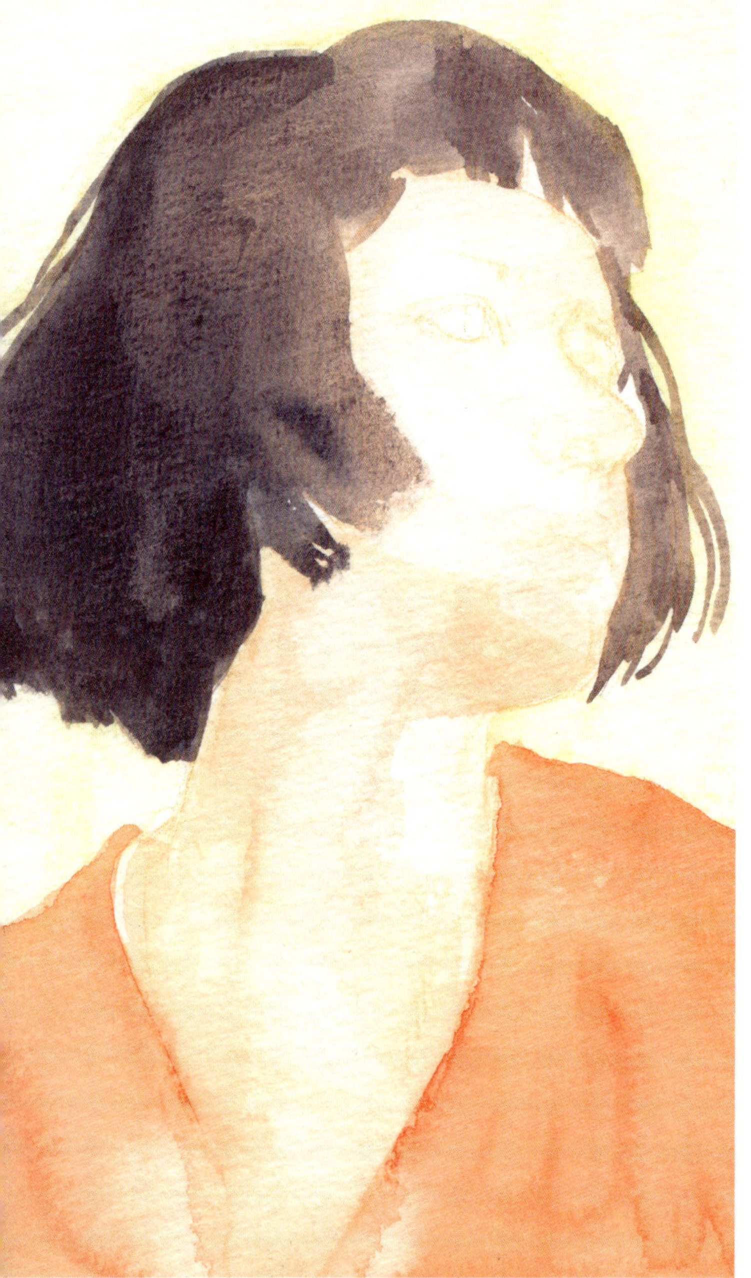

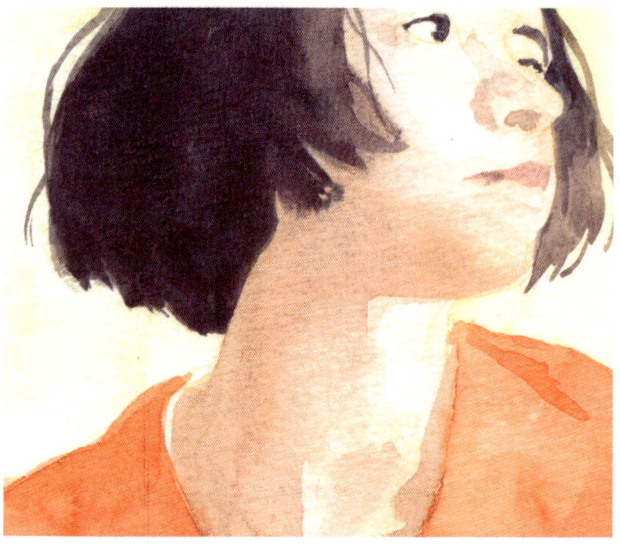

2 ⬆ Establish shadows

Using broad areas of colour, I establish the major shadow shapes. For the skin, I place a roughly average, warm neutral that is starting to lean towards purples in the cooler places. Typically this is done by mixing skin tones from Cadmium Yellow and Pyrrole Red, then neutralising them by adding Ultramarine Blue and a little Venetian Red, and nudging the hue with other colours. Try to avoid saturated colours for now, and instead keep the colours fairly neutral at this stage.

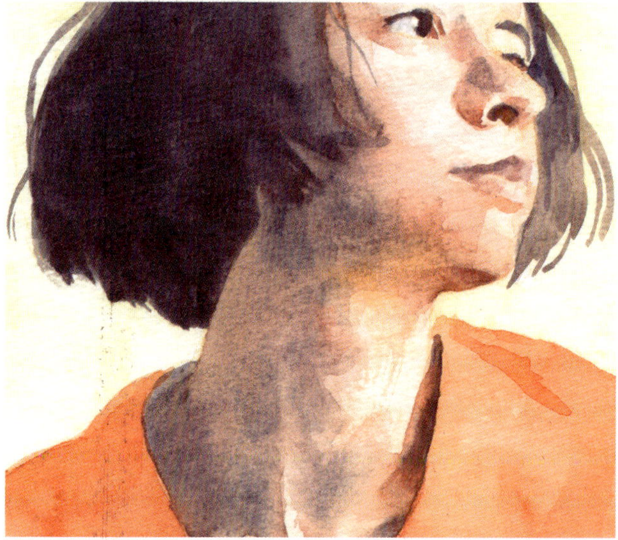

3 ⬆ Shadow variations

Skin has subtle variations, leaning warmer or cooler in different areas. Here, I've intensified the shadows. Under the chin, the reflection of light from the dress nudges them warmer – these are mixed with Winsor Orange and Pyrrole Red. On the other side of the neck and the cheek, cool tones are added – Ultramarine Blue and sometimes Alizarin Crimson. Some of the deepest shadow areas (e.g. the nostril) are rendered with more red. They tend to have warm shadows and this avoids making them too dark.

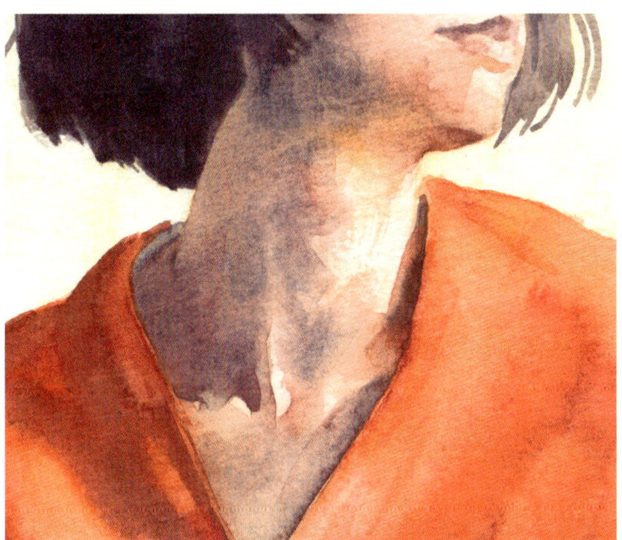

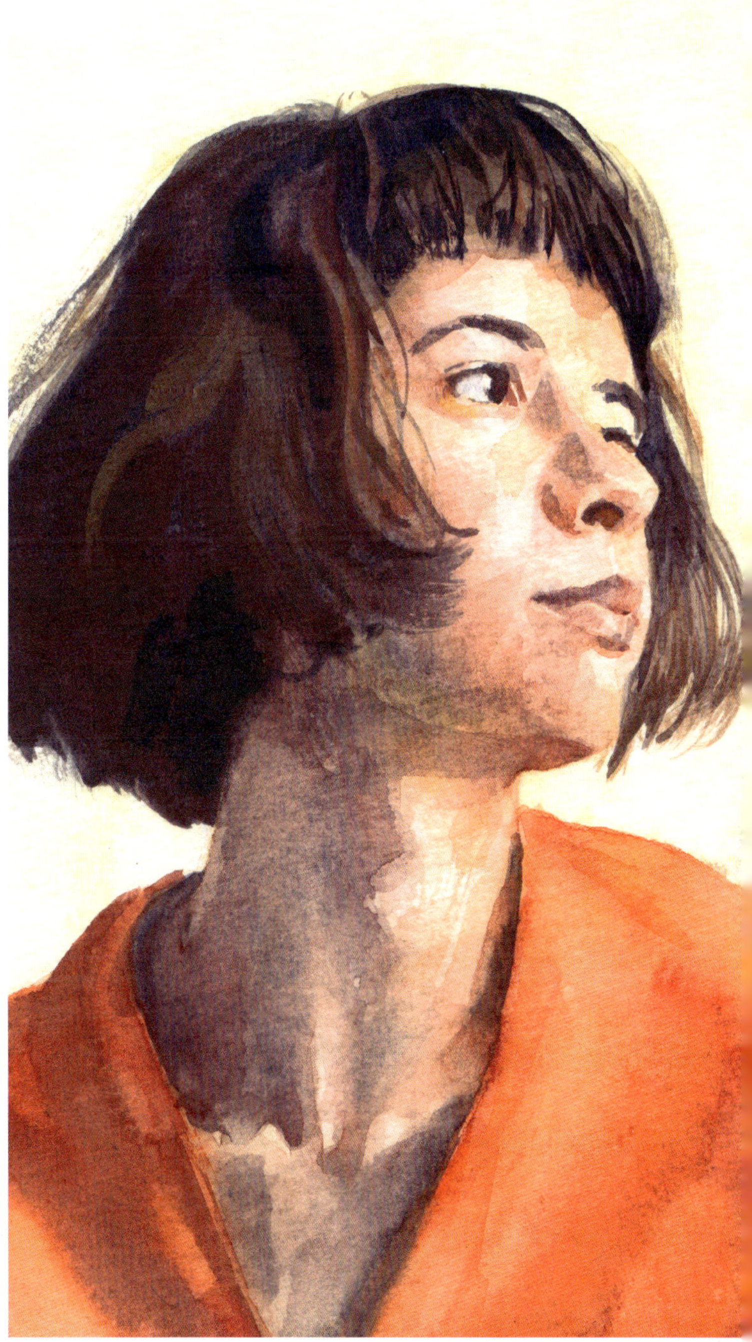

4 ◐ Mix bright colours

The dress is the most saturated part of this portrait. To produce a such a vivid colour, I mix Winsor Orange and Pyrrole Red, close neighbours on the wheel. I then add some Alizarin and Ultramarine to the cooler shadow areas.

Another thing that helps the dress colour 'pop' is the contrast in saturation it has with its surroundings – the skin tones are fairly neutral, making it appear more vivid in comparison. The best way to make a colour appear bright and saturated is to surround it by less-saturated neighbours.

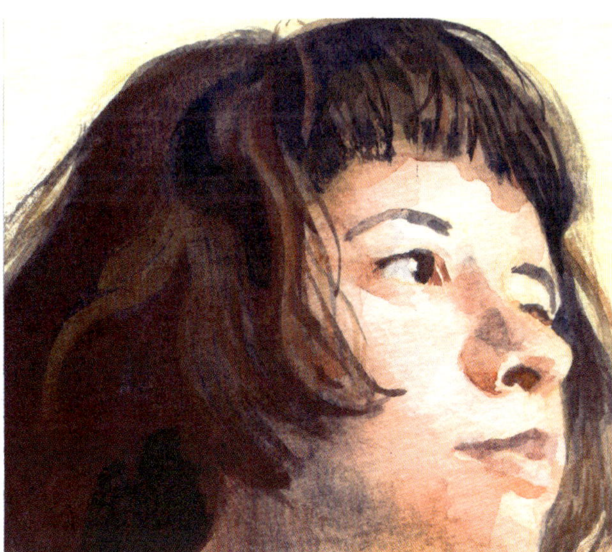

5 ◐ Build darks for the hair

The initial layer for the hair is mixed using Ultramarine Blue and Venetian Red to make a chromatic black, with some Permanent Alizarin Crimson to warm it up.

Here, I add another layer, working with more highly pigmented paint to make it darker. The shadows are more of the same, with a lean towards Venetian Red to warm them up at the back of the head. In the light locks, a few colours peek out – these were created using thinner mixtures based around Yellow Ochre, which is opaque and can sit 'on top' of darker colours somewhat.

6 ◐ Finish the face

In this stage I tighten up the details around the facial features and warm up the light colours on the face. Typically, if the shadows are relatively cool, the light is warmer (and vice versa – warm shadows have relatively cool light) so I clarify this by warming the lit skin tones with thin washes of Cadmium Yellow mixed with Pyrrole Red or Alizarin Crimson. These are very translucent, as I do not want to darken these areas.

I add a reddish neutral to the shadow shapes around the cheek and neck, and use thin washes to soften the cheek.

Simplify painting with a strong composition

Margaret Merry demonstrates how to use watercolour to capture the charm of a summer garden, with its ephemeral light, shade and colour

Since ancient times, gardens have been a source of inspiration for artists. However, they can be tricky subjects to tackle because when the eye is confronted by a confusing array of tone, form and colour, it's difficult to know where to begin.

The answer is good composition, and the best way to compose a garden painting is to find a point of focus, such as an ornament, a chair or a fountain. Old, weathered walls are a favourite of mine. For my demonstration, I chose this quirky, painted sewing machine table, set against the plain background of a white wall. The dappled light that shines through the trees casts some interesting shadows.

For all my work, I use a limited palette comprising: Ultramarine Blue; Cobalt Blue; Yellow Ochre; Raw Sienna; Burnt Sienna; Burnt Umber; Lemon Yellow; Alizarin Crimson; Cadmium Red. However, when painting flowers or similarly colourful subjects, it's useful to have one or two extra pigments, such as the Brilliant Opera Rose and Cobalt Turquoise I've used in my painting. Transparent pigments, not opaque ones, are best for painting flowers.

Light is an important consideration when painting gardens because it is constantly changing. I painted this watercolour in strong afternoon light, shaded by trees. For a more romantic effect, early morning is the best time because all the colours are softened.

Green is the predominant colour in a garden and to maintain colour harmony, I mix my own using my basic pigments.

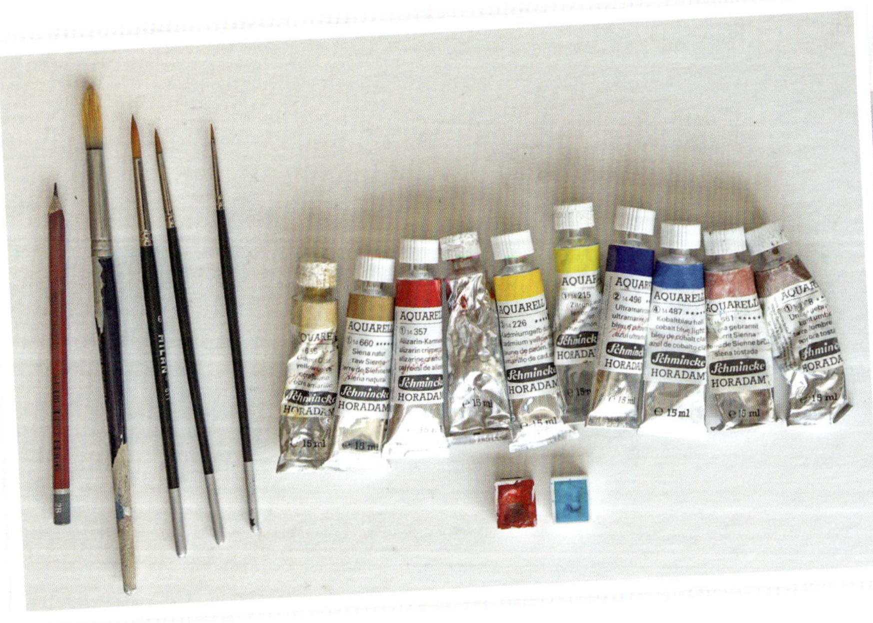

Materials

Margaret uses tubes of Schmincke watercolour paints. She likes to paint on Arches 300gsm paper, approximately 11x15in with a fine surface stretched onto a board. This is her preferred paper because the surface has just the right amount of resistance to enhance the inherent transparency and brilliance of the medium. Margaret uses synthetic round brushes.

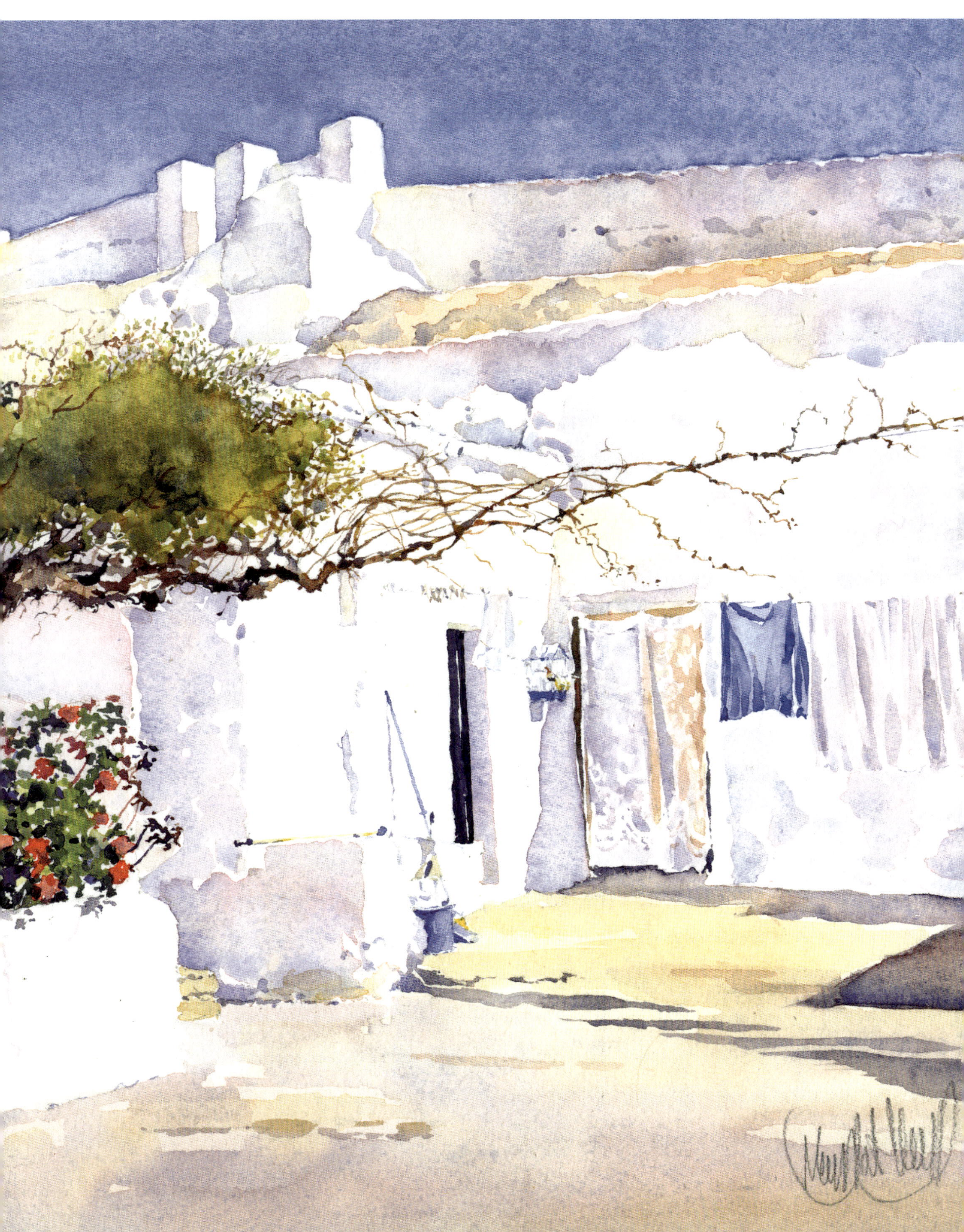

Follow these steps...

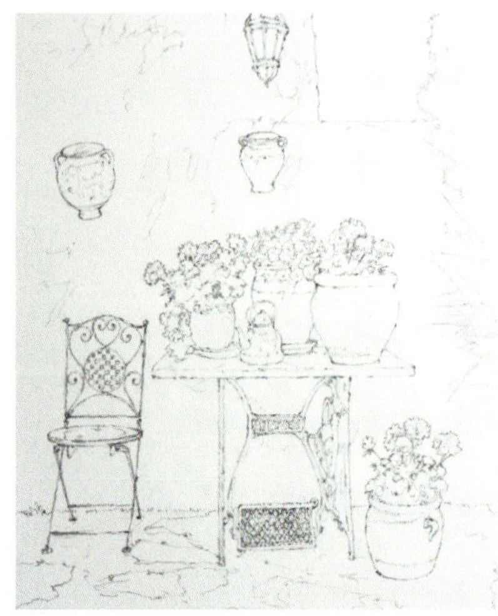

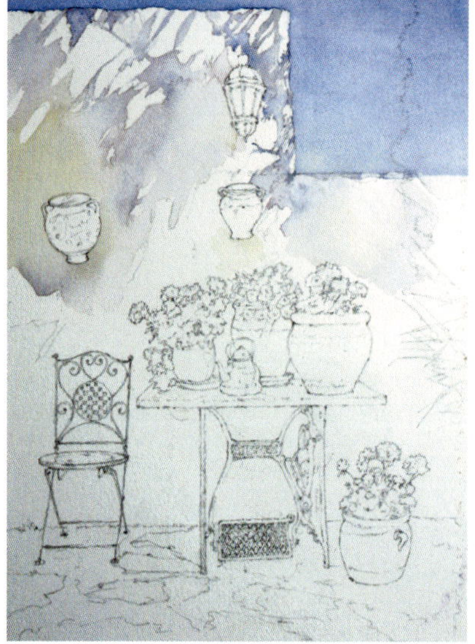

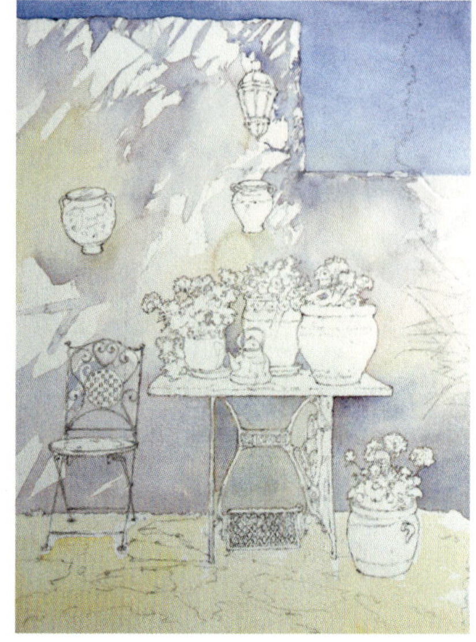

1 ⬤ Do a preliminary drawing

With well-sharpened 2B pencils, I make a fairly detailed drawing of the composition, altering things I don't like, such as the position of the chair. I have included the cypress tree on the right and a few fronds of palm leaves because I like the sense of enclosure they create. Use soft strokes for drawing and don't be tempted to use an eraser because this will mar the surface of the paper.

2 ⬤ Begin painting

I apply a transparent wash of Cobalt Blue for the sky, using a synthetic size 12 brush, extending it over the tree. With a mix of Cobalt Blue, Yellow Ochre and Rose Madder, I paint the shadows in quick, bold strokes, softening hard lines with the brush loaded with clean water. I allow the water to separate the pigments to prevent the background from being too uniform.

3 ⬤ Continue to apply background shadows

I continue painting the shadowed areas with my Cobalt mix and with a smaller synthetic brush (size 6) I carefully work around all the various objects so that the paper remains white. I paint rapidly because I want to finish this stage before the pigments dry. Lastly, I lay a transparent wash of Raw Sienna on the ground.

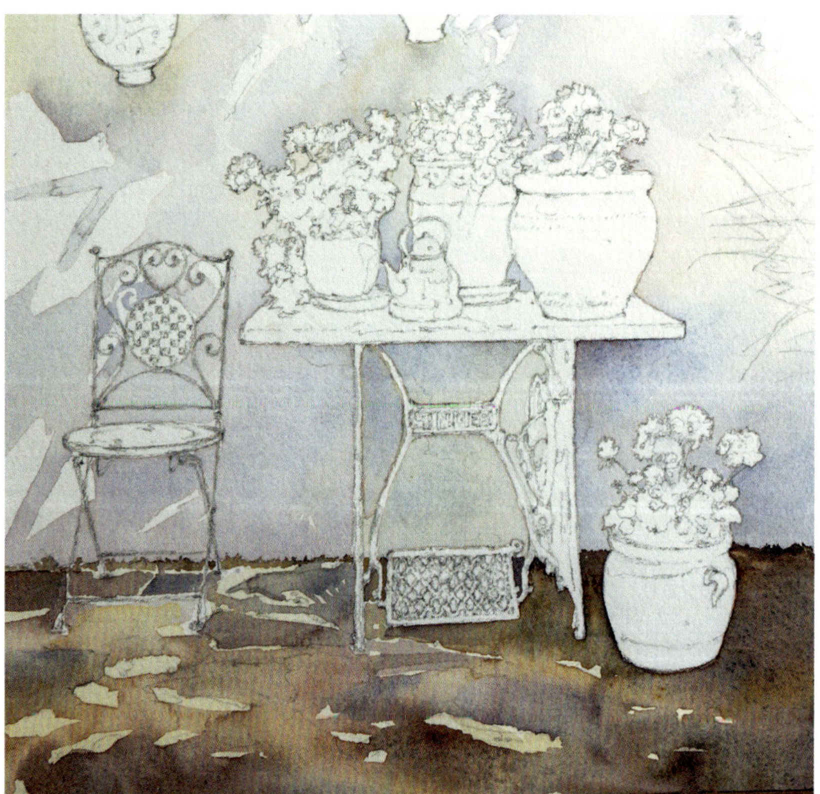

4 ◀ Finish the background

When the Raw Sienna has dried, over-paint it with a mix of Ultramarine Blue, Raw Sienna and Alizarin Crimson. While the paper is still wet, allow some touches of Burnt Sienna to flow into the grey, giving warmth to the foreground. Again, I let the pigments separate and I use my size 2 brush to quickly draw around the various objects before the paint dries.

Know your tools

When I first began to paint with watercolour, I used it mainly to lay flat washes over pen and ink drawings or pencil sketches. In this way, I familiarised myself with the medium and developed my technique from there.

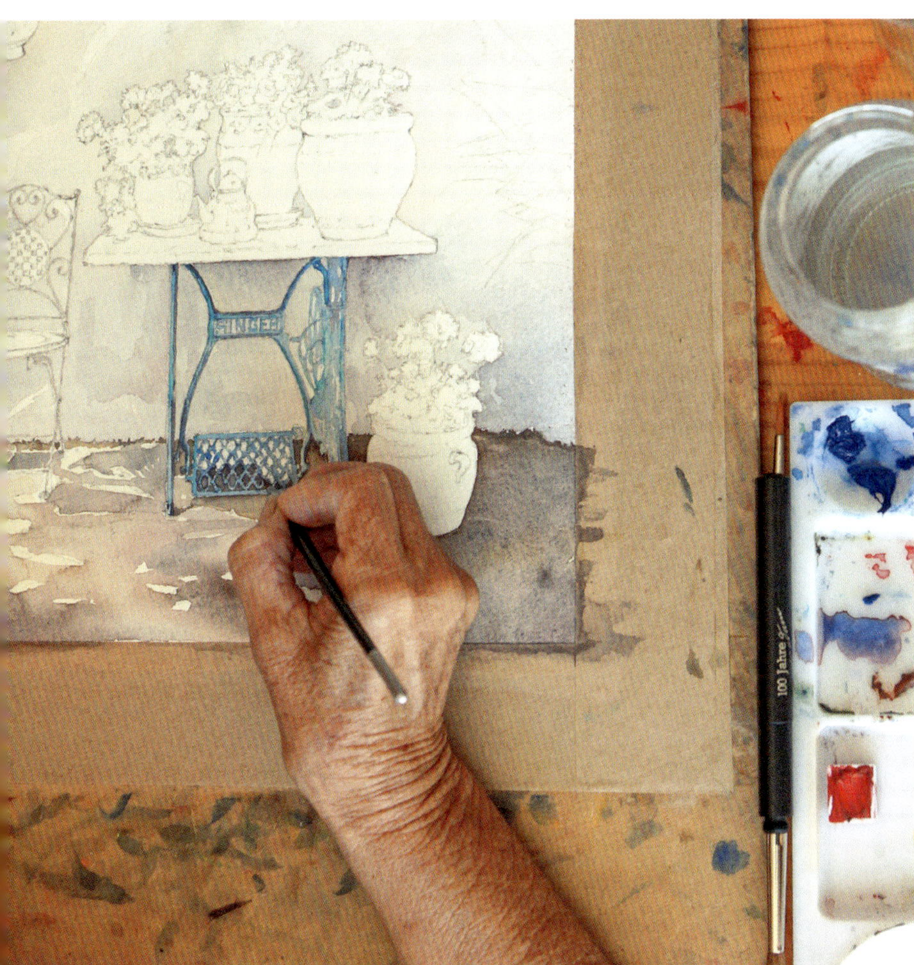

5 Draw with the brush
Now that all the unnecessary white has been eliminated, I can begin working on the main feature: the sewing machine table. This involves detail, so I continue using my size 2 brush, which has a fine point yet is large enough to hold a reasonable amount of water. I use Cobalt Blue with a touch of Cobalt Turquoise and I vary the tones by diluting the lighter parts with water.

6 Add more detail
Now that the table has been painted, it looks as though it's floating, so more shadow is needed. I use my dark grey Ultramarine mixture to paint around and below the table and add more definition where the blue tends to merge into the background. The marble top is painted with a very diluted grey and I add some dabs of Yellow Ochre to the wet paint.

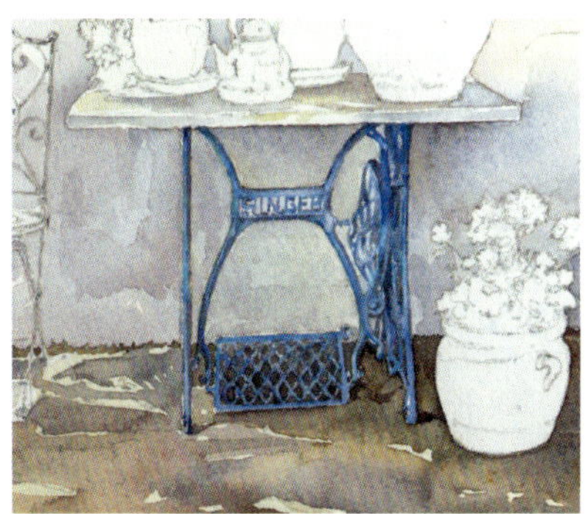

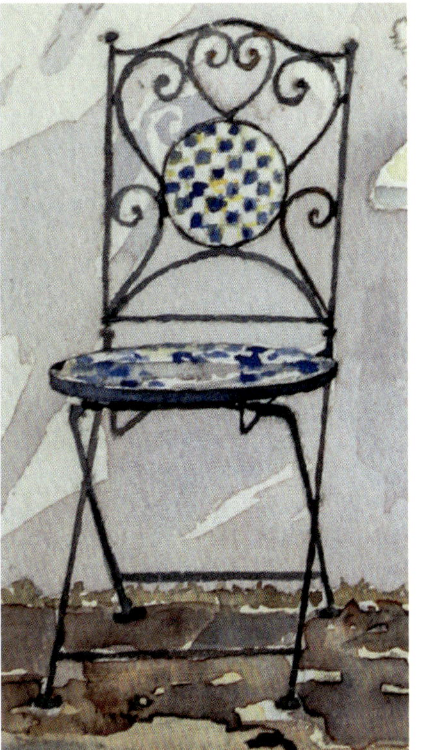

7 Draw with a fine brush
The little metalwork chair is relatively simple to paint as it involves mostly drawing. For this I use my finest synthetic brush, size 0. The chair is painted black but I never use black pigment because it contaminates other pigments. I mix, as an alternative, Ultramarine Blue with Burnt Umber. I use less water than before and with a steady hand, draw the details. With the Ultramarine grey mix, I add more shadow around and below the chair.

8 Paint the flowerpots and lamp
I return to my size 2 brush to paint the lamp and the flowerpots on the wall. In order to avoid overworking them, I use plenty of clean water to soften the outlines and give just an impression of detail. I introduce more colour by adding Burnt Sienna and Cadmium Orange for the terracotta pot and the lamp, and Cadmium Red for the decoration on the ceramic pot. I paint the shadows on the pots with a watery grey, using circular brushstrokes for a rounded effect.

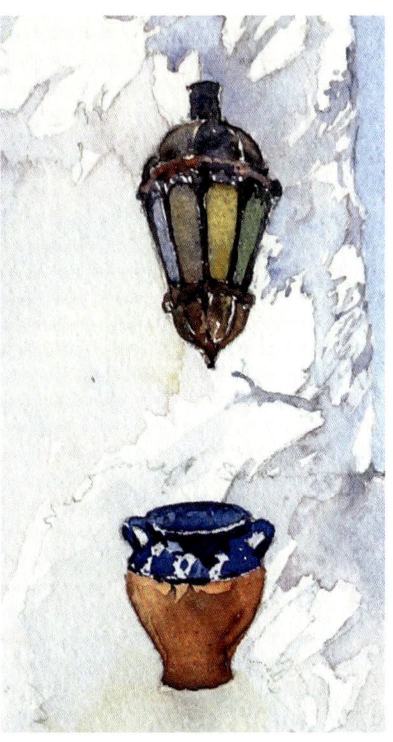

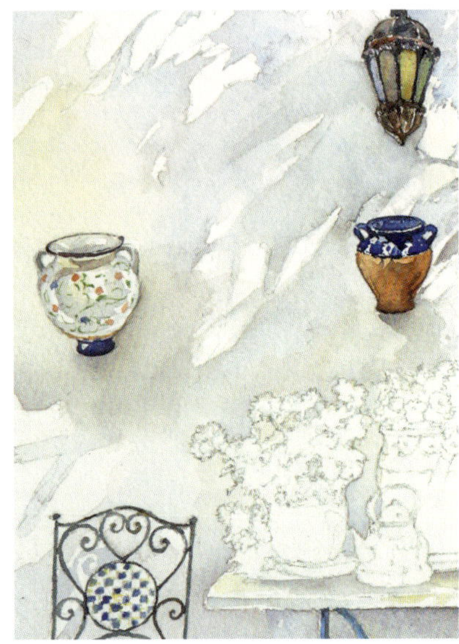

9 ⬥ Embed with shadows

As was initially the case with the table, the lamp and the pots look as though they're floating. This is fixed by adding shadows around and underneath them. For this, I use the subtle Cobalt Blue mix with which I began painting the background. Again, I soften some of the hard lines with a brush loaded with clean water.

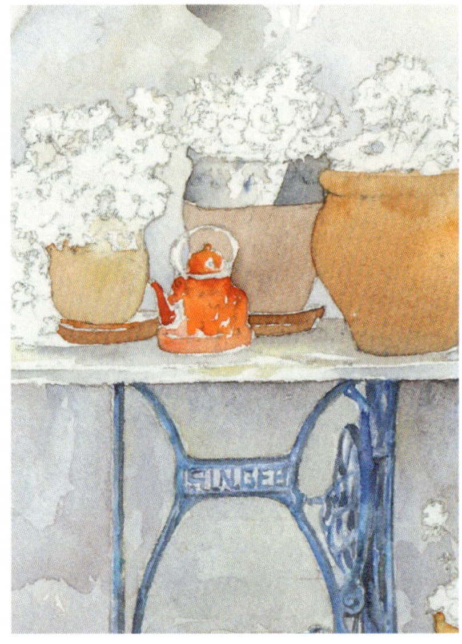

10 ⬥ Work on the terracotta pots

My method for tackling terracotta flowerpots is to paint a transparent base coat using Cadmium Orange, Burnt Sienna and Raw Sienna. The shiny kettle has a transparent coat of Cadmium Red and where the light falls, I've left white patches. Before I continue with the second stage, I make sure the base coat is completely dry.

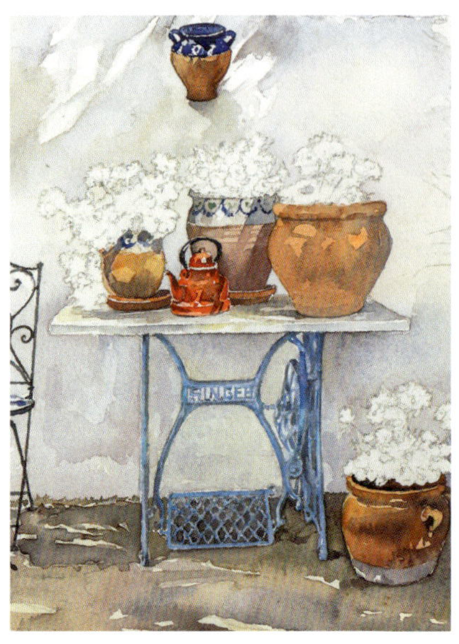

11 ⬥ Create form

To create form, I paint a second coat using my Ultramarine mix and, as before, my brushstrokes are curved to follow the shape of the pots. I like the patterns cast by the shadows and so I make a feature of these, but still keeping the paint very fluid to maintain transparency. I apply the same technique to the red kettle and finish by painting the decoration on the pots.

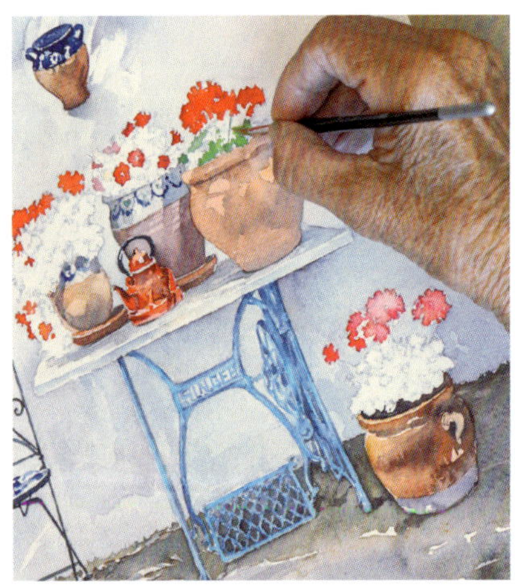

12 ⬥ Paint flowers

I give the flowers and the leaves the same treatment as the pots. The first task is applying a base coat. I use Cadmium Red, well-diluted, for the flowers and a mix of Lemon Yellow and Ultramarine Blue for the leaves. The pink geraniums in the foreground are painted with Brilliant Opera Rose mixed with Cadmium Orange. I use two brushes, size 2 and size 4.

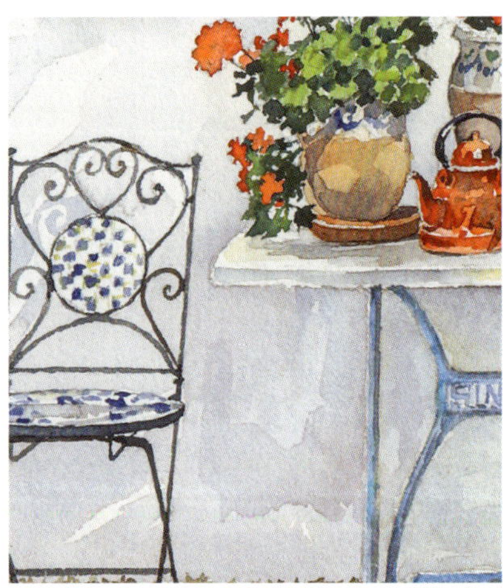

13 ⬥ Add definition

I begin with the leaves, adding a touch of Raw Sienna to the green mixture to make it darker. I have to take care not to paint too much detail, but, at the same time, I want to make a feature of the leaves. Knowing what to paint and what to leave out comes with experience! Again, the hard lines are softened with water and it's the latter, rather than the brush, that works to blend the greens into each other.

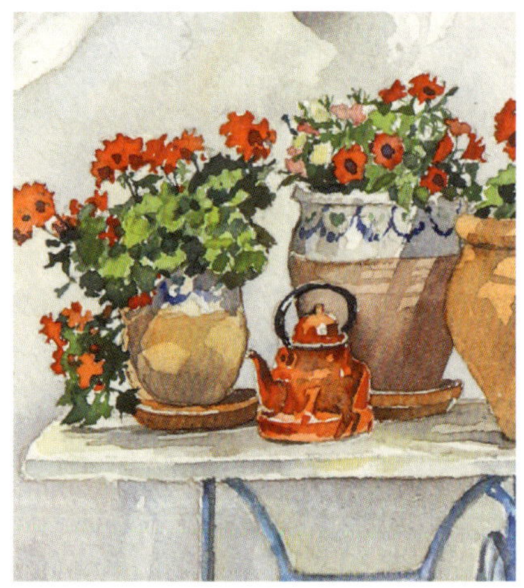

14 ⬥ Finish the flowers

I paint the darker tones on the flowers as I did with the leaves, using just a hint of Ultramarine to define the shaded parts. When painting flowers, it can be very easy to lose the freshness and transparency of the medium if they are overworked and for this reason, I keep the pigments as pure as possible, bearing in mind that it is difficult to rectify mistakes when painting flowers in watercolour.

15 ● Complete it

As the painting nears completion, it's time to paint the cypress tree and the palm fronds to form a frame. For these, I use my basic green mixture (Ultramarine Blue and Lemon Yellow) darkened with Raw Sienna and Burnt Sienna. For the lightest areas, I drop pure Lemon Yellow into the wet paint and with a fine brush, I draw the pointed leaves, from base to tip, using a flicking movement. A few last touches of shadow complete the painting.

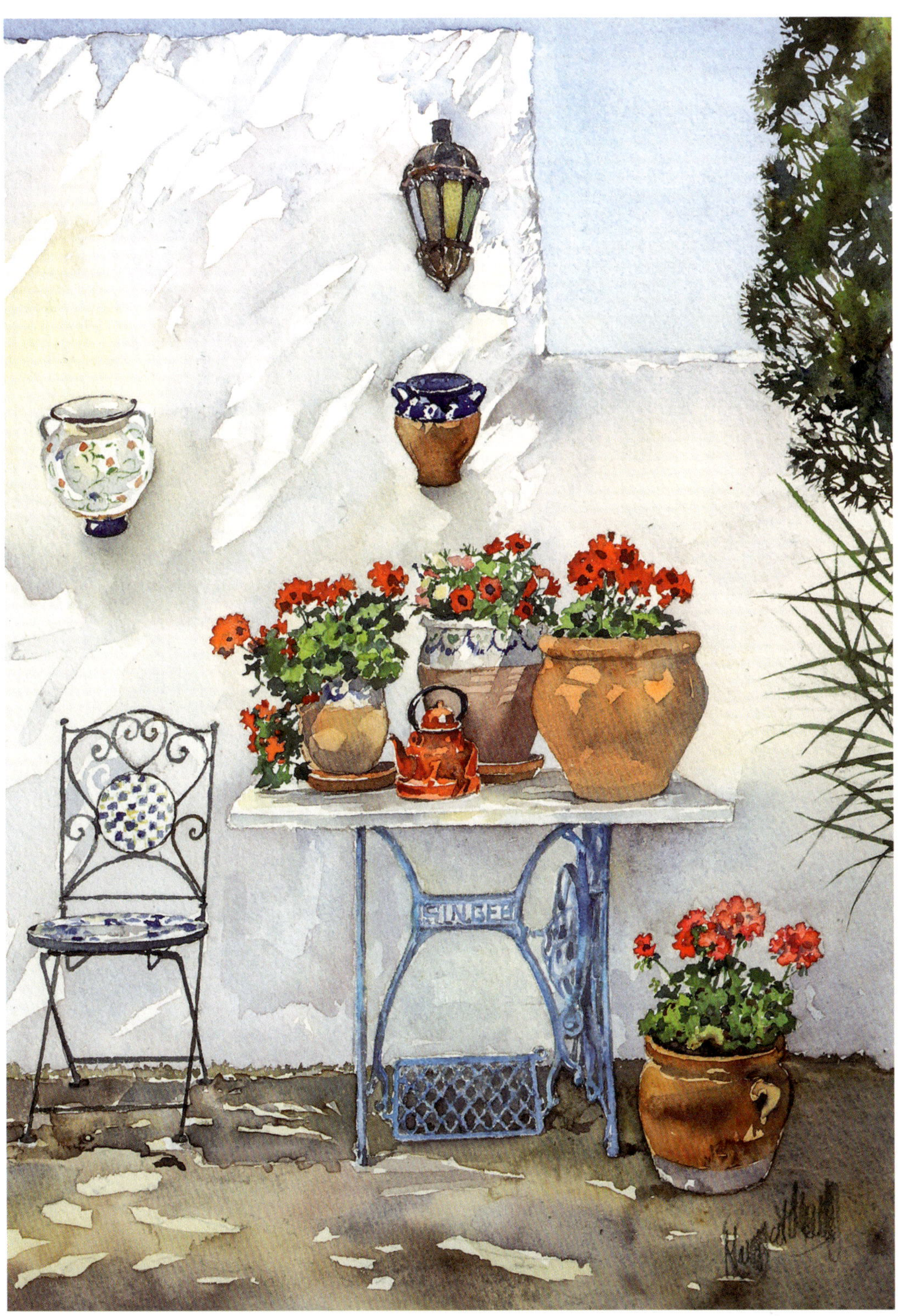

Speed painting

Watercolour is a medium best suited to rapid, spontaneous painting. I find that if I spend too long on a work, inspiration wanes and I'm invariably dissatisfied with the result.

lesson learned!

When I was an art student, we once spent an entire session painting vertical stripes in oils, using just Cobalt Blue, Yellow Ochre and Alizarin Crimson. The point was to demonstrate the wide range of greys that were possible using just these colours – and it's a lesson I've never forgotten.

capture a winter farm

Using his unique '5 Cs of Painting', **Robert Newcombe** demonstrates how to paint a snow scene in watercolour from a sketch

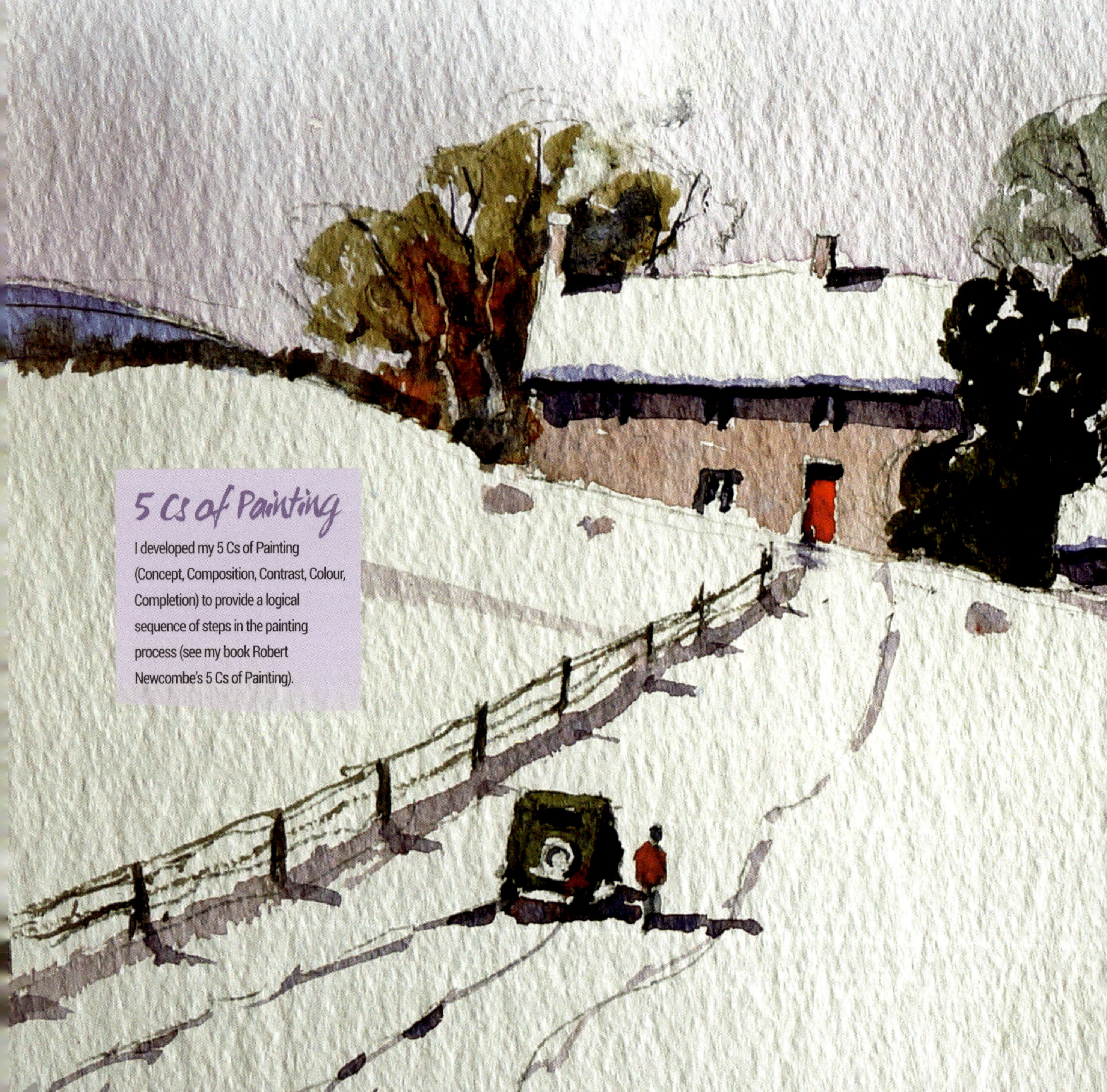

was in the English Lake District in the early 1980s just after I had taken up watercolour painting as a hobby. It was late November and there had been a fresh fall of snow. Taking the road towards Derwent Water I came across this magnificent view of Skelgill Farm; it was too cold to paint but I did a ten-minute sketch of the scene shown in step 1 with a felt-tip pen, using a soft pencil to shade in the reddish-grey stone walls of the farmhouse and assortment of barns. I added some colour notes. I didn't realise until many years later that Skelgill Farm is mentioned in Beatrix Potter's *The Tale of Mrs Tiggy-Winkle*, with a drawing of part of the farm by the author as an illustration.

I will now use my '5 Cs of Painting' to show you how I develop a unique interpretation of this subject.

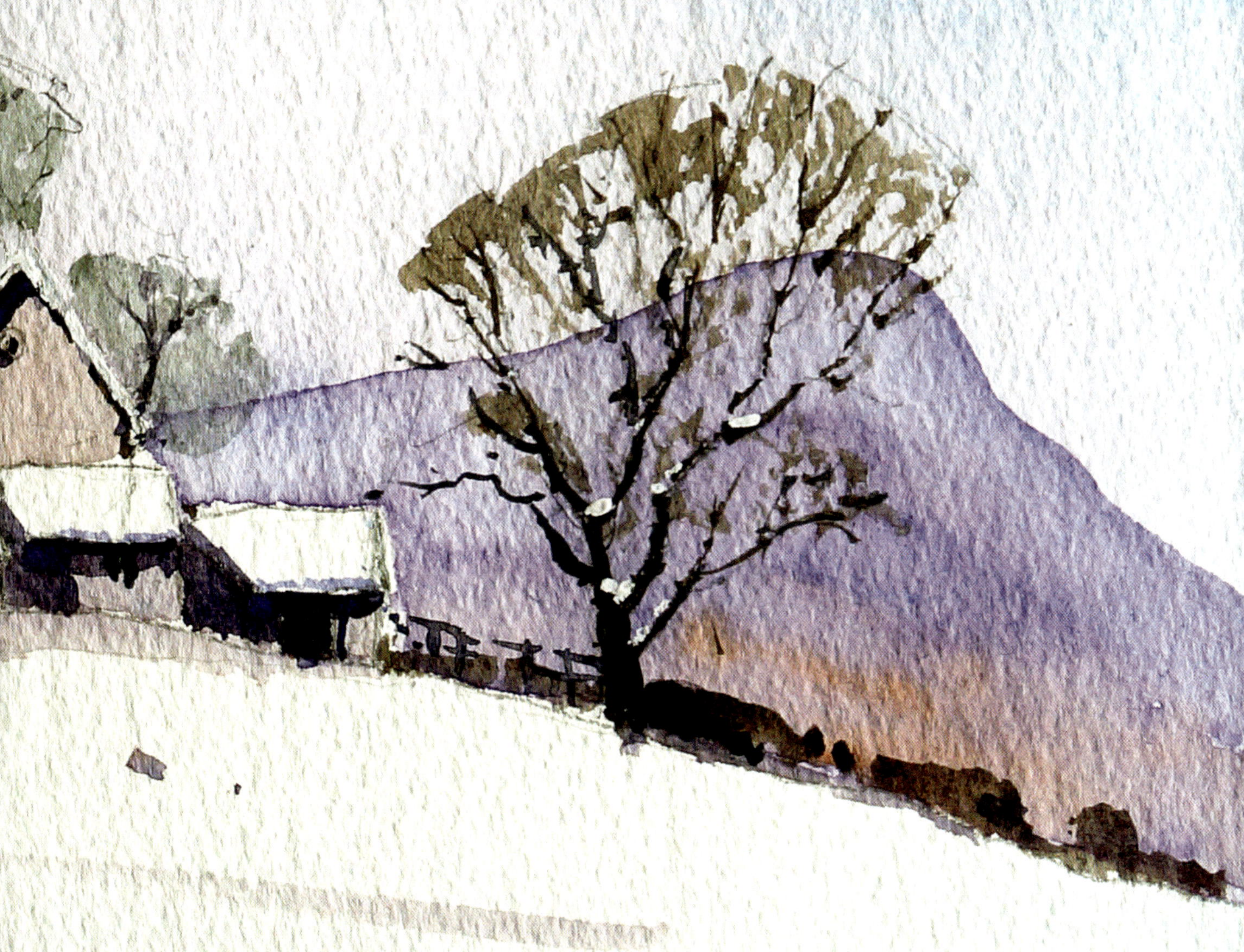

Materials

- Winsor and Newton (Professional Watercolour range): Burnt Sienna, Burnt Umber, Cobalt Blue, Ultramarine Blue, Brown Madder, Light Red, Indian Red, Cadmium Red, Permanent Magenta or Alizarin Crimson and Winsor Blue (green shade)
- Brushes – a one-inch Hake brush for the broad washes and Escoda Perla (8 and 12) for the architectural details and a rigger brush for the trees
- Paper – Whatman Not 140lb (300gsm), size one-quarter Imperial (11 x 15 inches) – Whatman is whiter than some watercolour paper and is ideal for snow scenes
- 2B pencil
- Putty rubber

Snow paint

Snow paintings are a gift for watercolourists as the white of the paper represents the snow (no white paint) but the critical skill is to preserve the white paper.

Follow these steps...

1 ● The sketch

The concept (the first C) is a Lake District farm under snow. The subject is predominantly cool with a brilliant winter sun coming from the front-left, which lights up the front of the farmhouse and barns creating strong shadows.

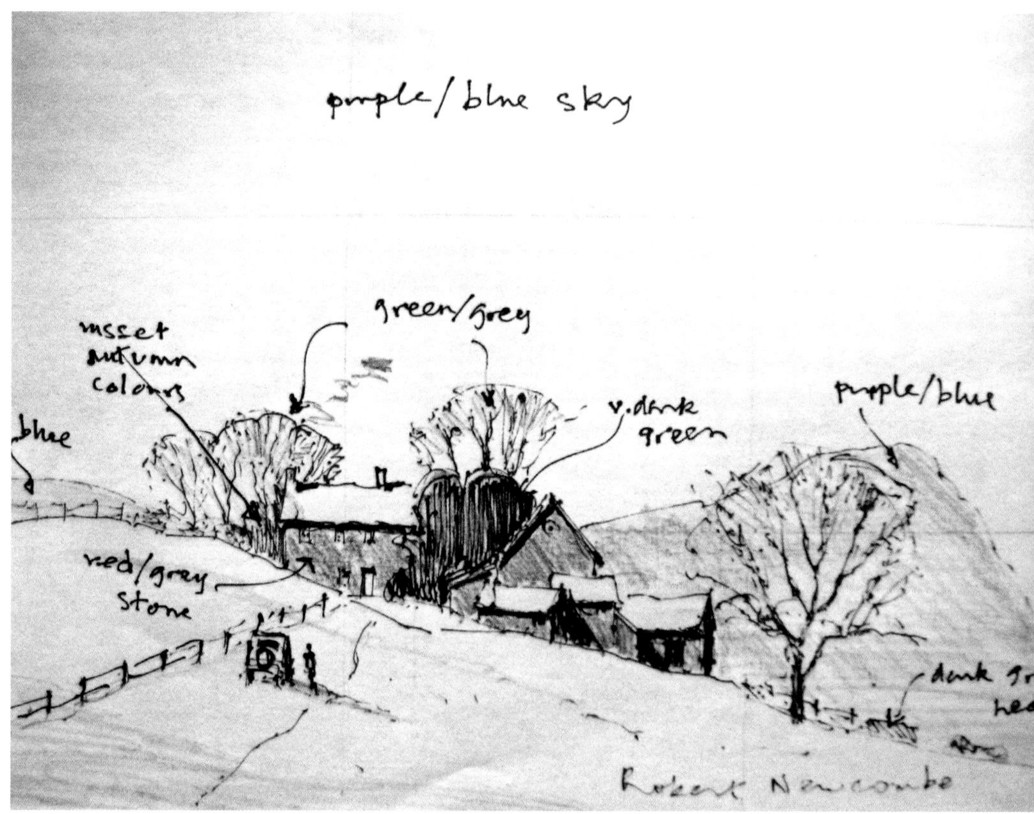

2 ● The pencil drawing

Composition is the next C and refers to the design of the painting. I felt it was a perfect composition. The snow-covered roof of the farmhouse contrasts with the dark yew tree at the centre of interest, there are some lovely autumn/winter trees and the sloping ground adds to the character of the subject. The mountain (Catbells), which gives distance and depth, will be put in directly with the brush. I raise the horizon in the drawing to give more prominence to the foreground snow.

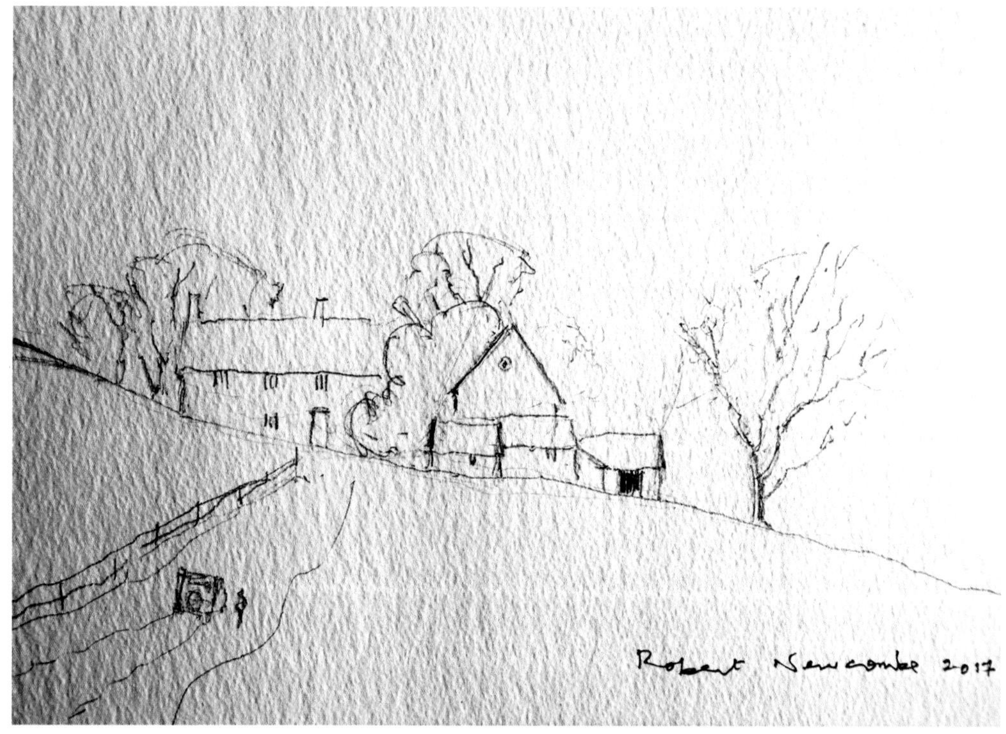

3 ❖ The tonal scale

The next C is 'contrast' or tone values. On the left of a fresh sheet of watercolour paper I create a five-value tonal scale using squares, numbering the squares from 1 to 5. Tone 1 is the white of the paper; Tone 5 is the darkest tone I can get with Ultramarine Blue. I add water to achieve tone 4 and more water again to achieve tones 3 and 2, creating a gradual transition from the dark to light. The space to the right is for checking the tones of the colours I'll use in the painting.

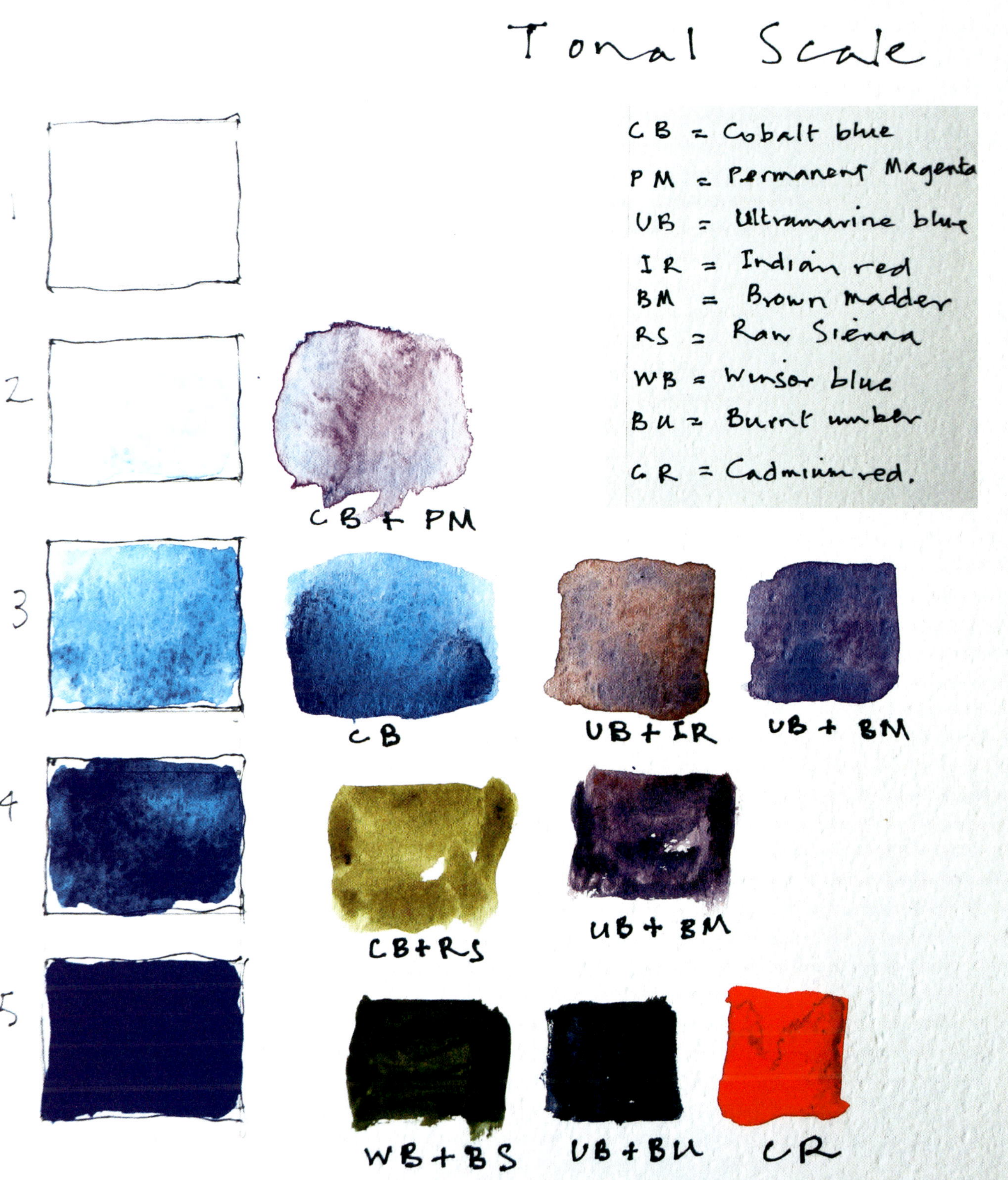

4 ▶ The tonal plan

Referring to my five-value tonal scale and using Ultramarine Blue again I produce a small tonal plan for the painting to enable me to see colours as tones. The white of the paper is the lightest tone (Tone 1 – the snow) with almost neat ultramarine blue for the darkest tone (Tone 5 – the yew tree) and the intermediate tones shown as per numbers on the tonal plan. As we paint from light to dark in watercolour this tonal plan will also give me my painting sequence.

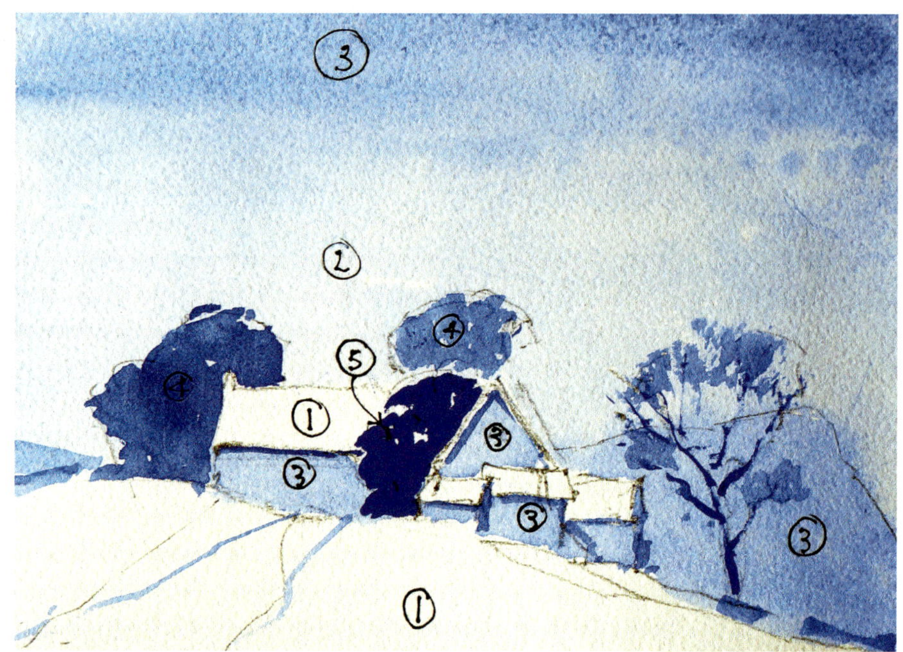

5 ▶ Paint the sky (tones 2 and 3)

I turn the paper upside down to paint the sky to prevent dribbles running down the white paper representing the snow. After checking my colours on my tonal scale sheet I use my Hake brush to paint a tone 2 purple wash (Ultramarine Blue and Permanent Magenta) starting at the snow-covered roof of the farmhouse and barns and taking the wash down to ground level elsewhere, then gradually changing this to a Tone 3 wash of Cobalt Blue at the zenith of the sky. The paper cockles slightly at this stage but will dry flat.

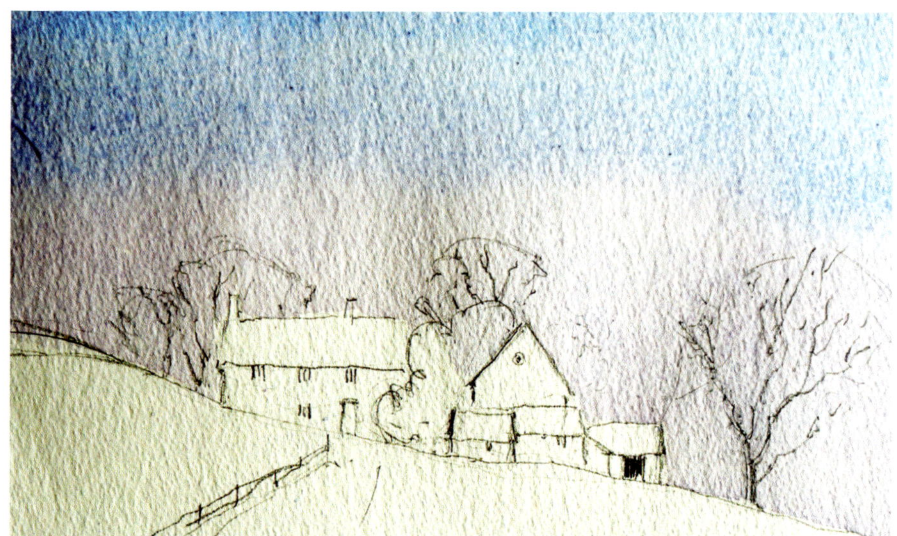

6 ▶ Paint buildings (tone 3)

Following my tonal painting sequence I paint the stone walls of the farmhouse and barns with a tone 3 mix of Ultramarine Blue and a little Indian Red to achieve the warm colour of Cumbrian stone. I use my Escoda Perla 12 brush having checked the mix on my tonal scale.

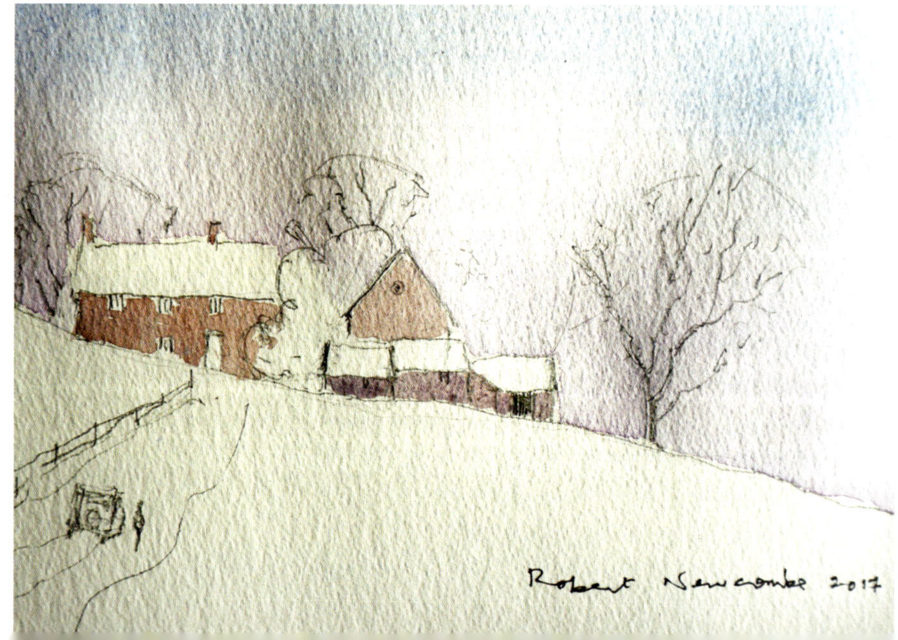

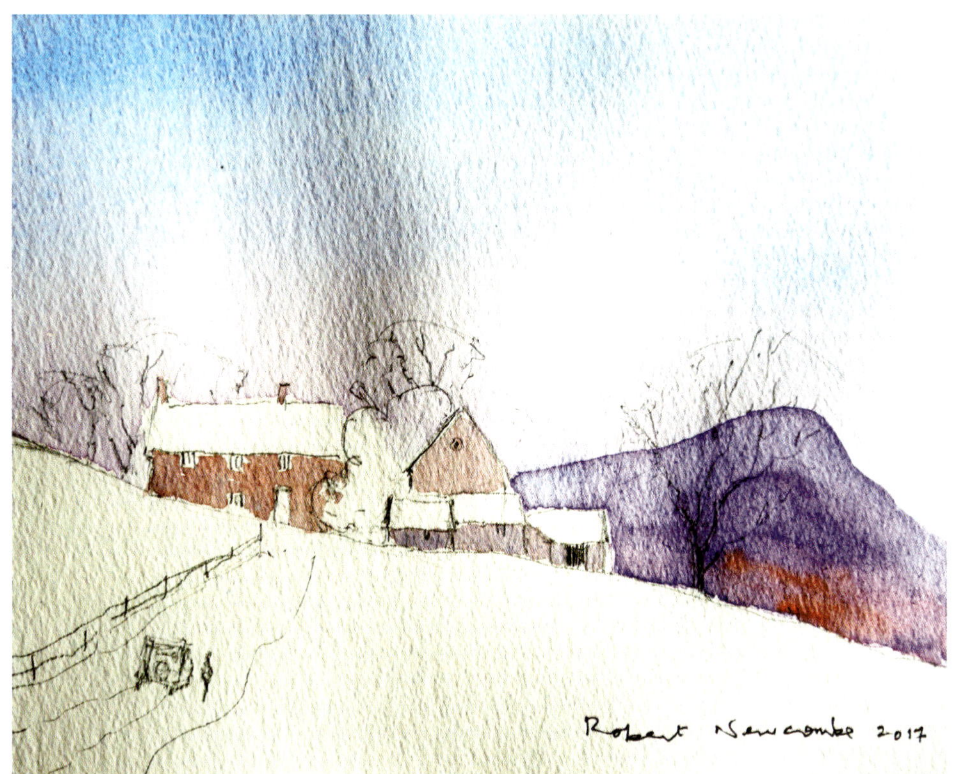

7 ◖ Paint the mountain (tone 3)

The simple mountain shape is now painted in directly with the same brush with a mix of Ultramarine Blue plus a little Permanent Magenta to give a purplish tinge. I check the tone against my tonal scale. It may look too dark at this stage but watercolour dries lighter and I know the tone 5 oak tree I'll be adding later will push it back into the distance of the scene.

8 ◗ The background trees (tone 4)

The tone 4 winter trees to the left of the farmhouse still had some warm autumn colours so are painted a cool green-grey with Burnt Sienna dropped in at the base. The trees behind yew tree and the big barn are painted with the same cool green-grey wash. While the washes are still damp I paint in the trunks and branches with a dark brown mix of Ultramarine Blue and Burnt Sienna, then scrape out some lighter tree trunks with my pen knife.

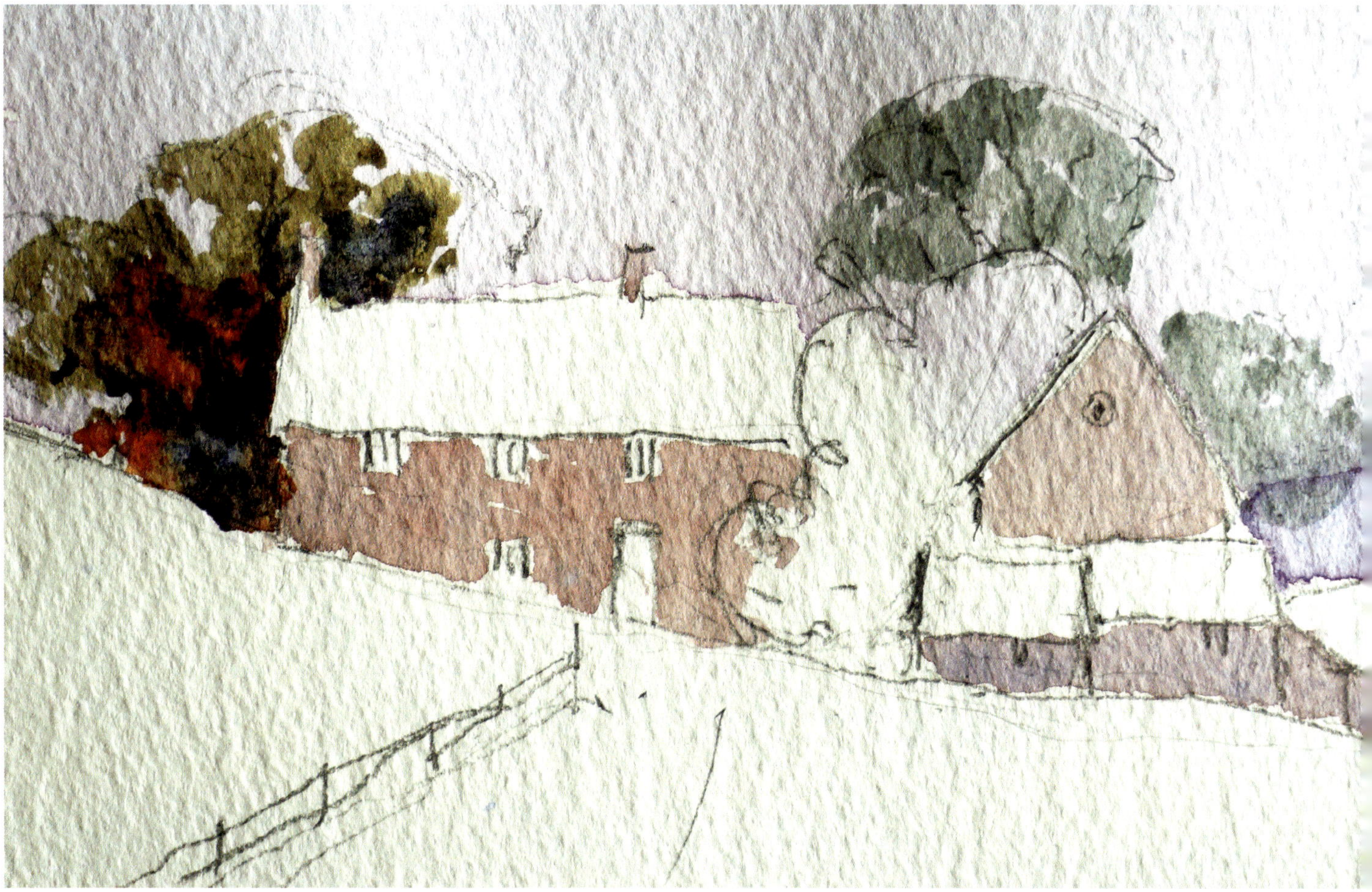

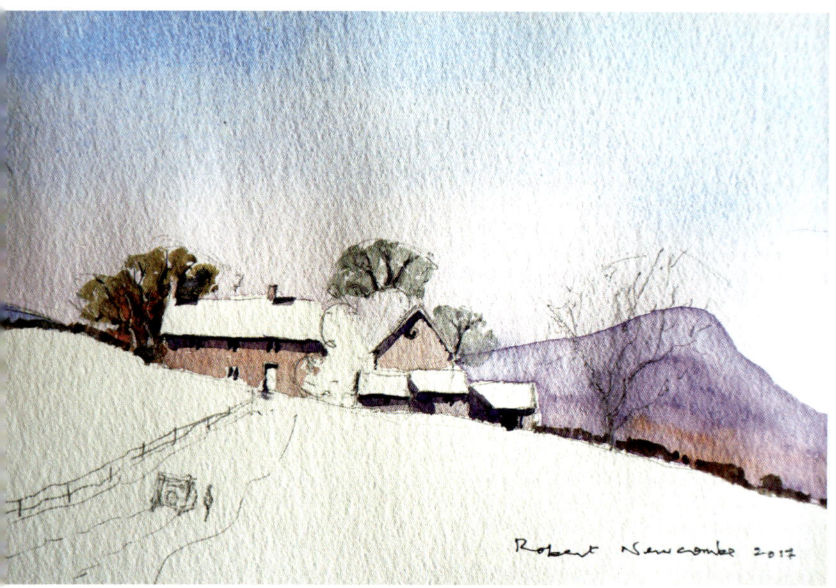

9 ◒ The shadow wash (tone 4)

Switching to my Escoda Perla 8 brush, I use a transparent mix of Ultramarine Blue and Brown Madder to paint the shadows on the buildings. The sun is coming from the front-left so there will be shadows under the eaves of the farmhouse and barns where the roofs overhang and the barns will cast some attractive raking shadows on other barns.

10 ◒ The yew tree and the oak tree (tone 5)

Next the darkest tones in the picture using tone 5 mixes. The dark-green yew tree is painted with Winsor Blue (green shade) and Burnt Sienna to create the impact of the darkest dark against the lightest light at the centre of interest. The oak tree in front of the mountain is a mix of Ultramarine Blue and Burnt Umber painted with my rigger brush. I then establish the outline of the tree with quick downward strokes of diluted Burnt Umber.

importance of contrast

I had a major painting breakthrough when I realised the importance of tone values (contrast) in creating paintings with impact. I spent three months painting only monochrome paintings using different dark colours that enabled me to capture a full tonal range, e.g. Ultramarine Blue, Burnt Sienna, Light Red, Indigo etc (see steps 3 and 4), after which I was able to see colour in terms of tone. Try it.

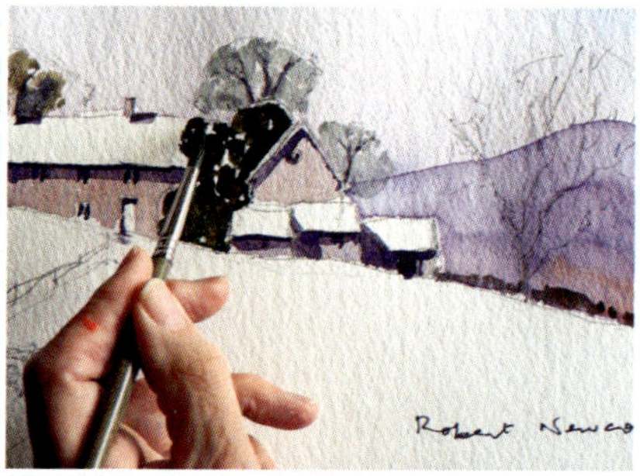

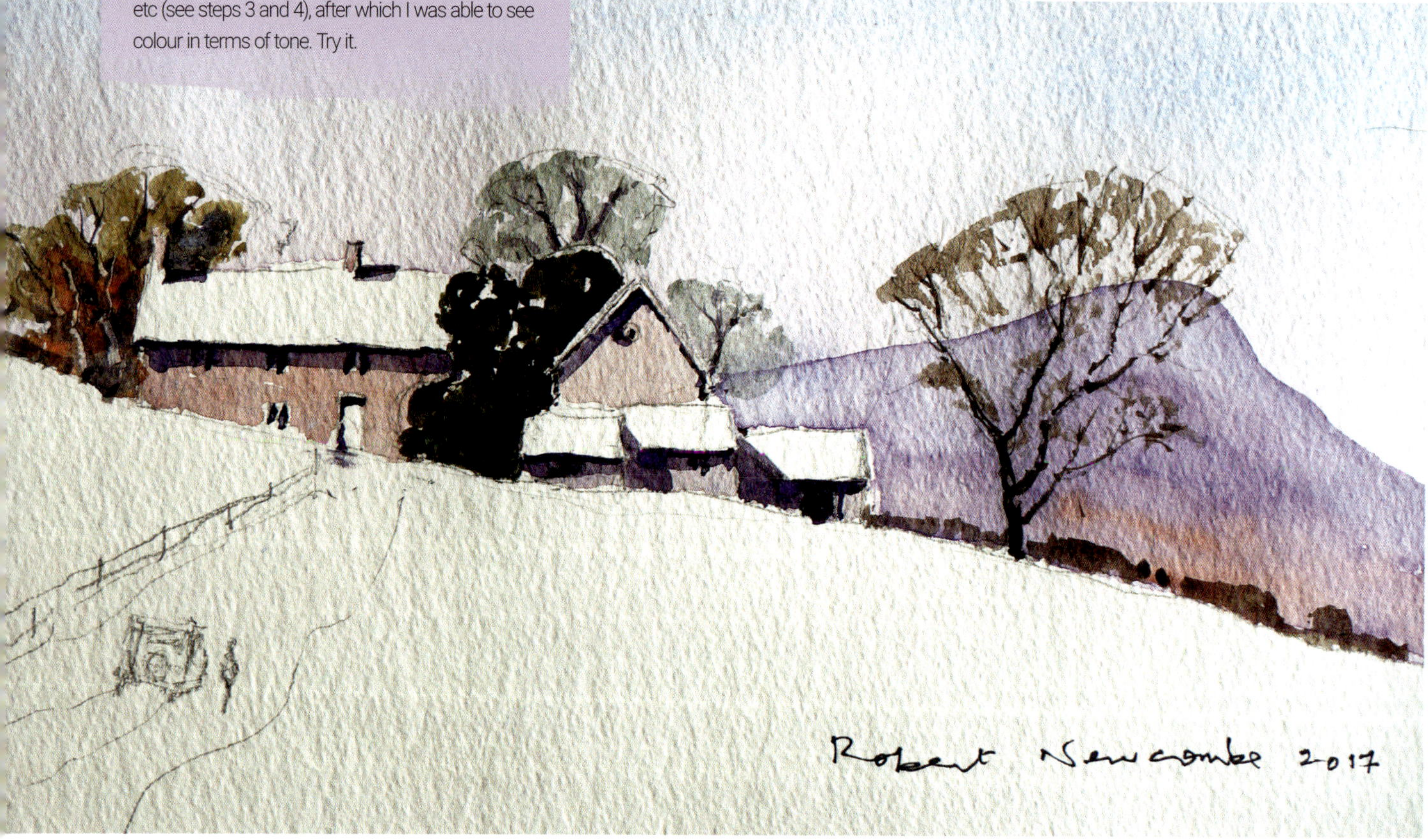

11 ▶ Make the final touches (tone 5)

I'm nearing the Completion stage of the painting where there is a danger of adding too much. Using the same mix as for the oak tree I paint the fence leading the eye to the centre of interest together with its attendant shadows, then the Land Rover and the figure talking to the driver. The last touch is to paint the front door of the farmhouse in bold Cadmium Red to attract the viewer's eye to the centre of interest.

12 ▼ The finished painting

At this point I refer back to my concept, Lake District farm under snow. Have I achieved my concept? I feel like turning up my coat collar so I think I have and the painting is finished.

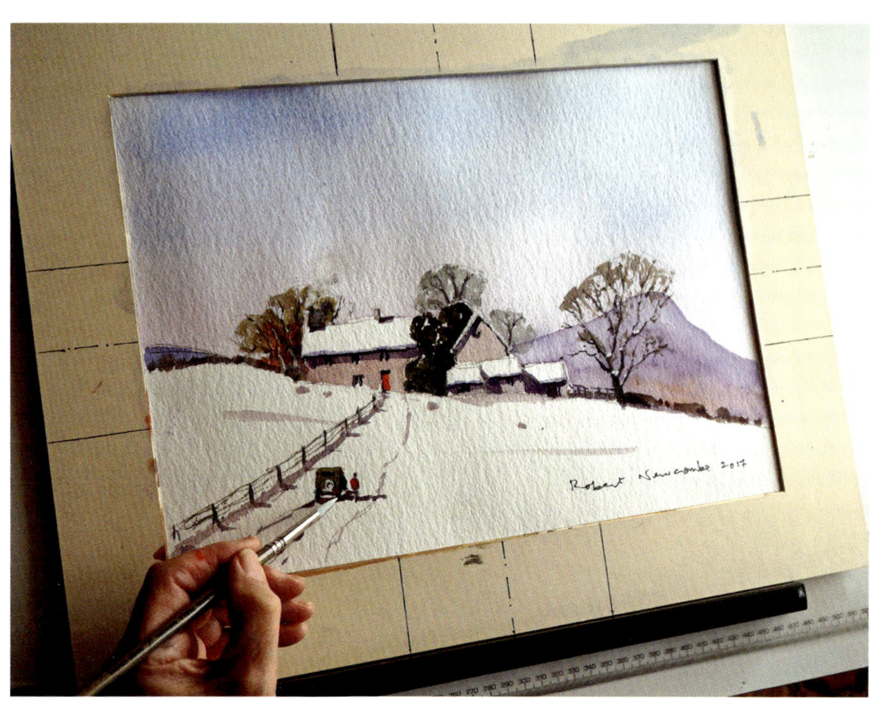

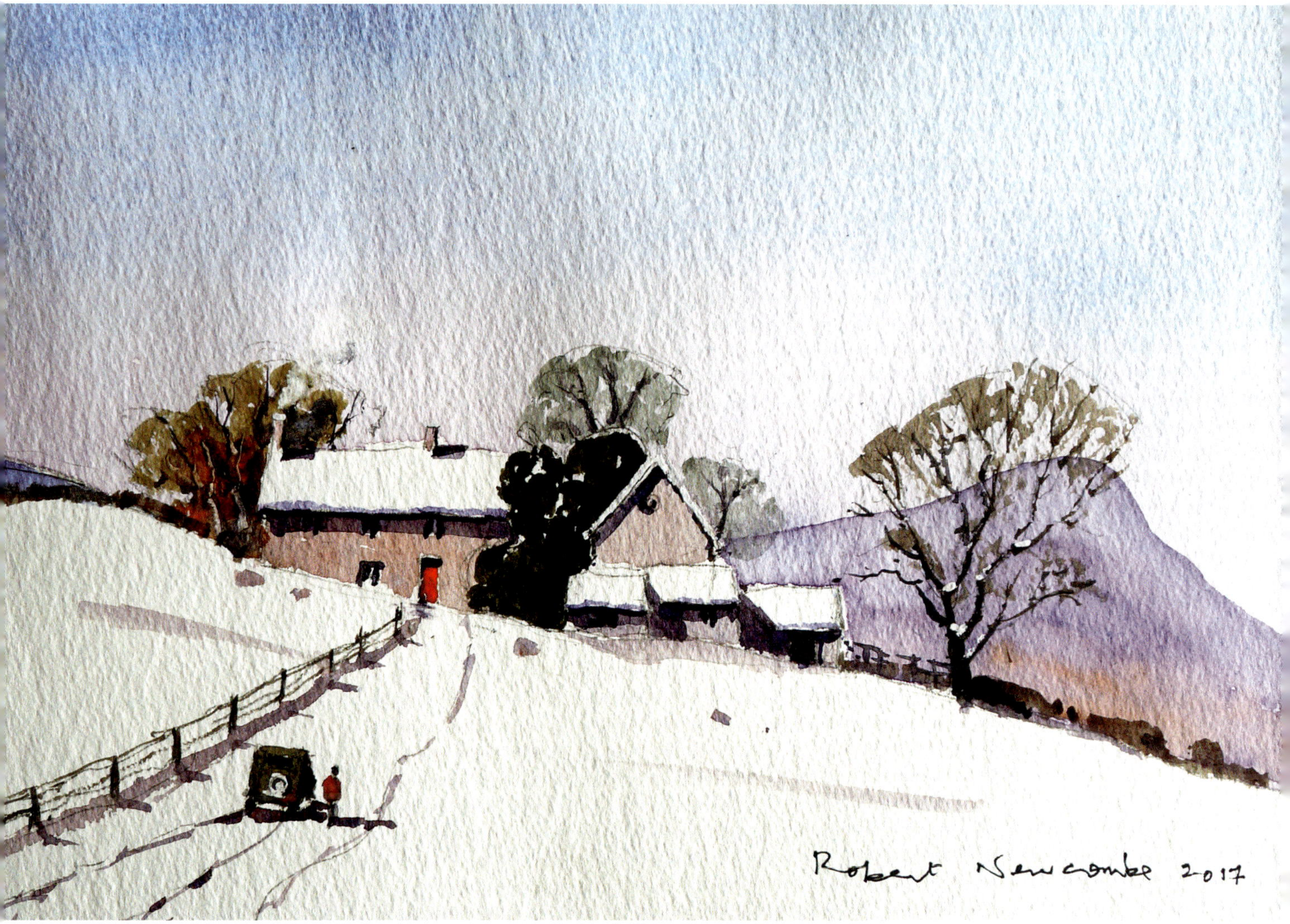

Working freely in watercolour

Jem Bowden used photos, plus a large helping of artistic licence and traditional techniques, to create a harmonious, impressionistic landscape

Mine is a fairly impressionistic style of watercolour, where detail is less important than a sound composition, good atmosphere and a bit of verve and directness in the painting process.

In this way, I try to capture the overall sense of a place, at the same time as allowing the medium itself to shine. I paint outdoors – 'en plein air' – as often as possible, as I like to interpret from life with the influences of the weather, sounds and smells, and the compulsion to work quickly. Working from photos, however, allows for a bit more reflection, with a different element of creativity and fun added to the process.

Although this scene was sunny, there was a strong wind that would have blown over my easel, so instead I walked all around the scene, snapping it from different angles, towards the light, away from the light, recording as many potential compositions as possible.

Taking a lot of photos will give you some facts about a place. From this you can take or leave whatever you need to create a painting that will work on its own terms. Use artistic licence to move or exclude items, change colours and so on. It's a fun process, and you'll see that even bad photos can be useful to you.

In the stages I follow, the brushwork is done swiftly, with regard for some important aspects of the photographic reference but not restricted by it. Don't worry about the result when painting, focus on the process! Enjoying your painting brings good results.

Follow these steps...

1 ◀ **The reference photo**

The photo has a nice atmosphere, typical of the beach at Aldeburgh. I like the composition in general because it has depth. The eye is led into and around the scene by a series of virtual zigzags, from foreground to distance. The sky is interesting, and will be fun to paint. There are some bright colours we can make the most of, and some things we can change... Have fun with artistic licence to improve on photos. Alter composition, contrast or colours to spice them up.

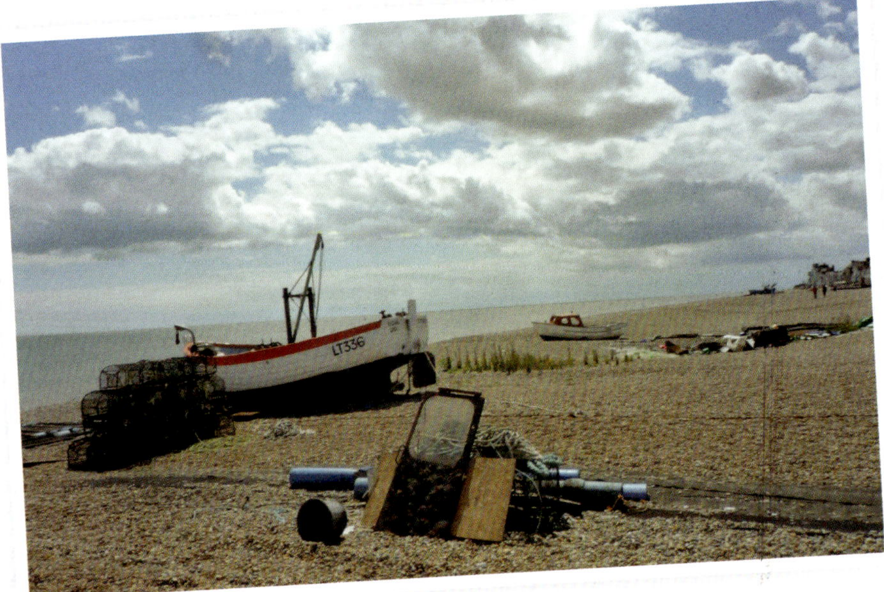

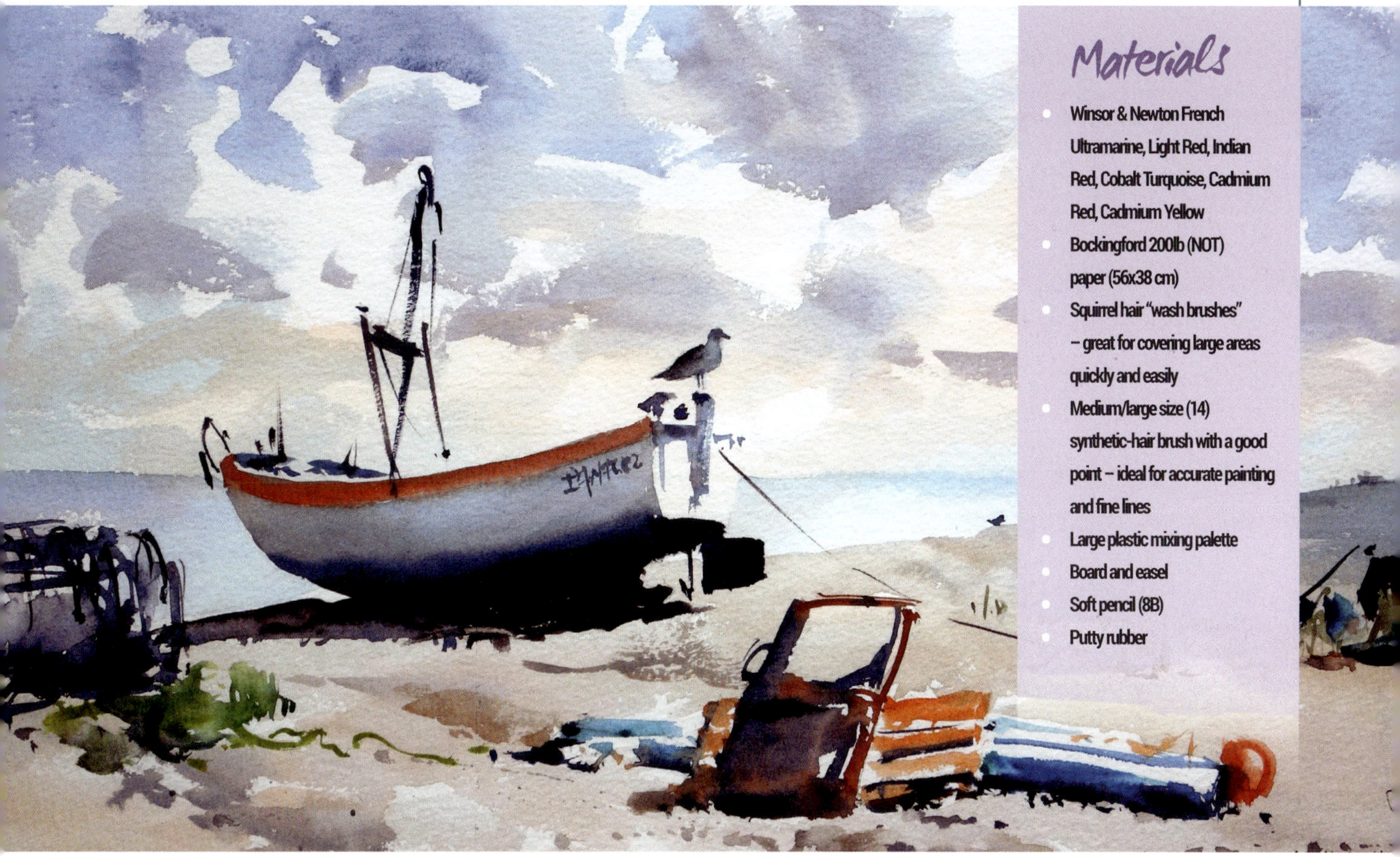

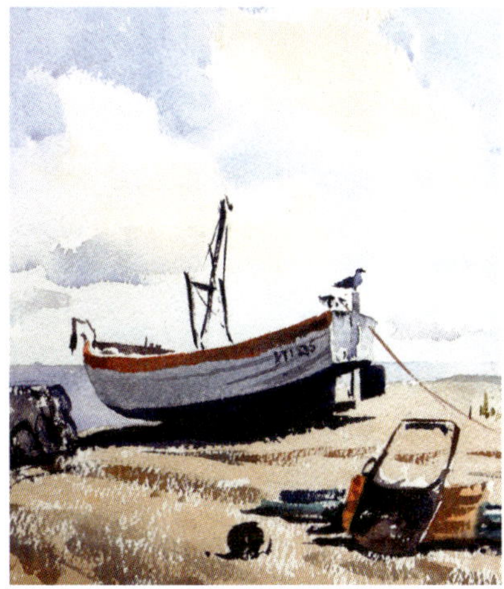

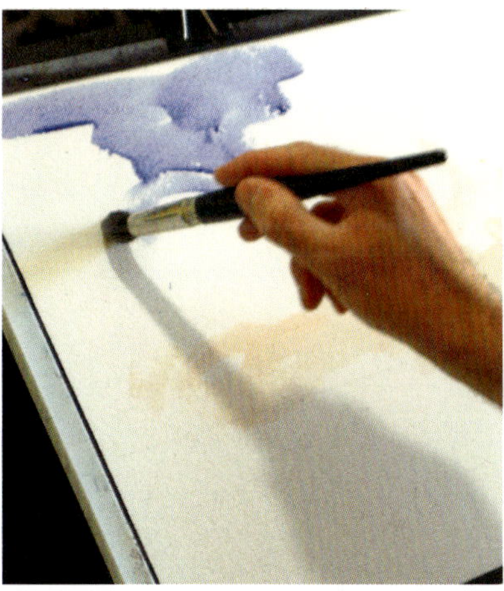

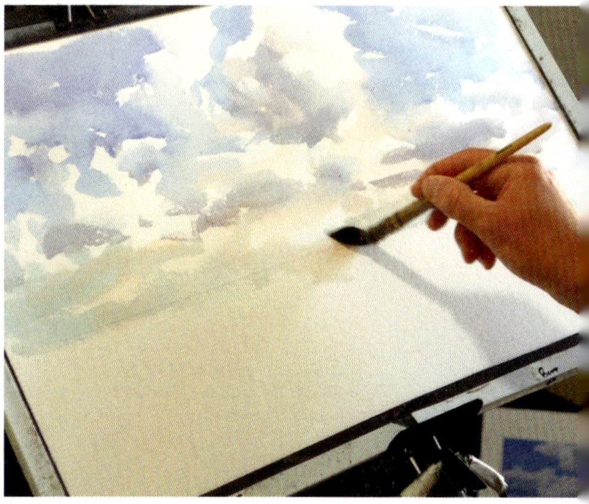

2 ▲ Creating an initial working sketch

First, I created a small watercolour sketch. To lighten up the scene, I tried out a sunnier sky. I also increased the size of the main boat, moved the crab baskets to the left, and added a couple of figures by the distant boat, to create more of a focal point. I also changed that boat to a dark one so it stands out. Finally, I put the whole background under the shade of a cloud. This could work, but the sky could contribute more. Let's go for it!

3 ▲ The exciting sky!

I draw out a horizon line with a soft 8B pencil. Having mixed plenty of paint for the sky colours, I dive straight in. First I wash on some Light Red near the bottom in a random fashion with the medium mop brush. Using my large mop brush loaded with French Ultramarine, I put in blue-sky sections. I move the brush fast to cover paper, looking at the photo for inspiration but not copying it closely. It's the general character we're aiming for.

4 ▲ Work fast with energy

Being careful to keep some white paper where sun is catching, I add in a greyish mix of Light Red, French Ultramarine and a bit of Indian Red (for variety) for shaded parts of clouds. This touches into the blue-sky areas wet in wet, so the two blend into soft edges. Where the blue or grey meet white paper there are hard edges. Moving downwards I work into the Light Red areas I did first, which are still damp, giving mainly soft edges.

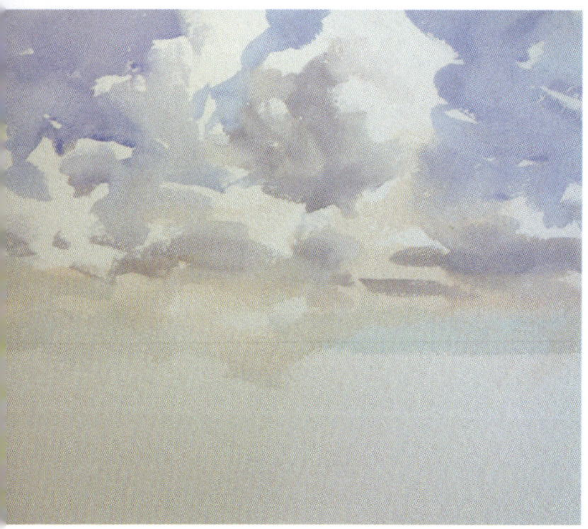

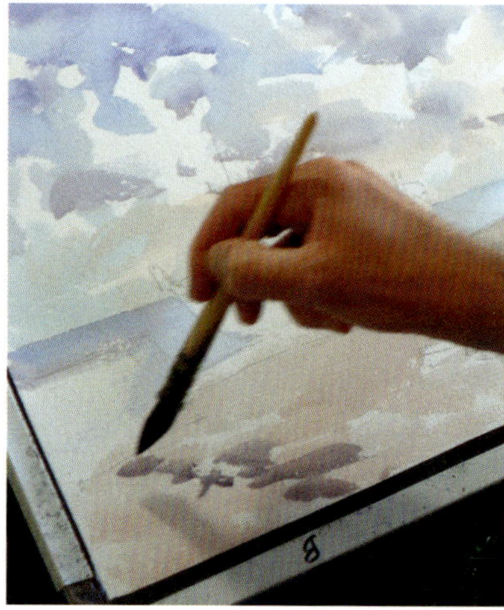

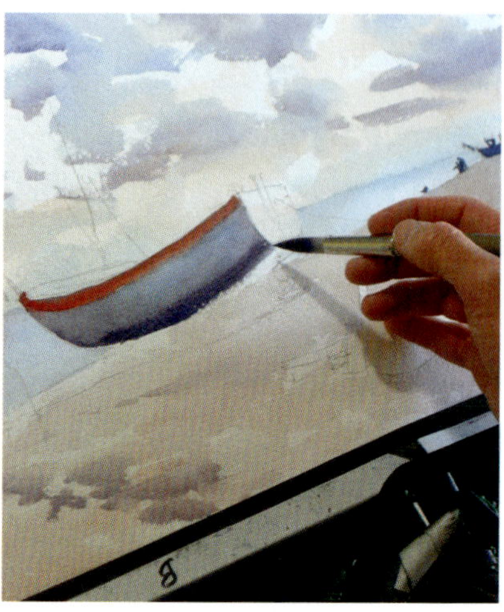

5 ▲ The completed sky

This mix of edges is key to an exciting watercolour technique. You need to work fast, so make sure to have plenty of paint mixed before starting. It's a good idea to practise on on scraps of watercolour paper. I wanted a couple of bold dark against light clouds near where the background boat will be, to help draw the eye. Some marks may look a little stark, but don't ever lose faith in a sky until you see it with land added.

6 ▲ Sea and beach washes

I draw in the main shapes loosely in pencil. Next I add the sea, in a similar blue to the sky and clouds, adding water to dilute the mix paler on the right. I let this dry before I paint the beach, starting in the distance and working down to the foreground, using first a mix of Light Red with a touch of blue, then pure Light Red towards the foreground. Before it's dry I add some darker patches, Indian Red with French Ultramarine.

7 ▲ The main boat

My techniques are very traditional, using the white of the paper and the transparency of the medium to capture the light. Using the synthetic brush I take thicker mixes of paint to get darker tones. Tube paints are essential for this. It's great fun using really thick paint! Don't be afraid to go dark first time. Watercolour looks fresher if you don't overlay more washes than necessary to build up tone.

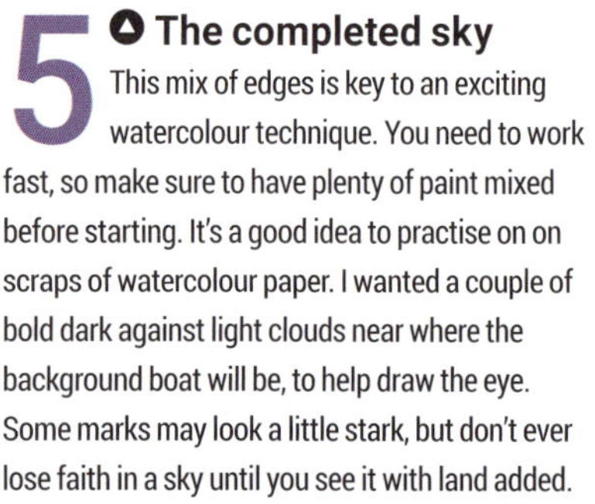

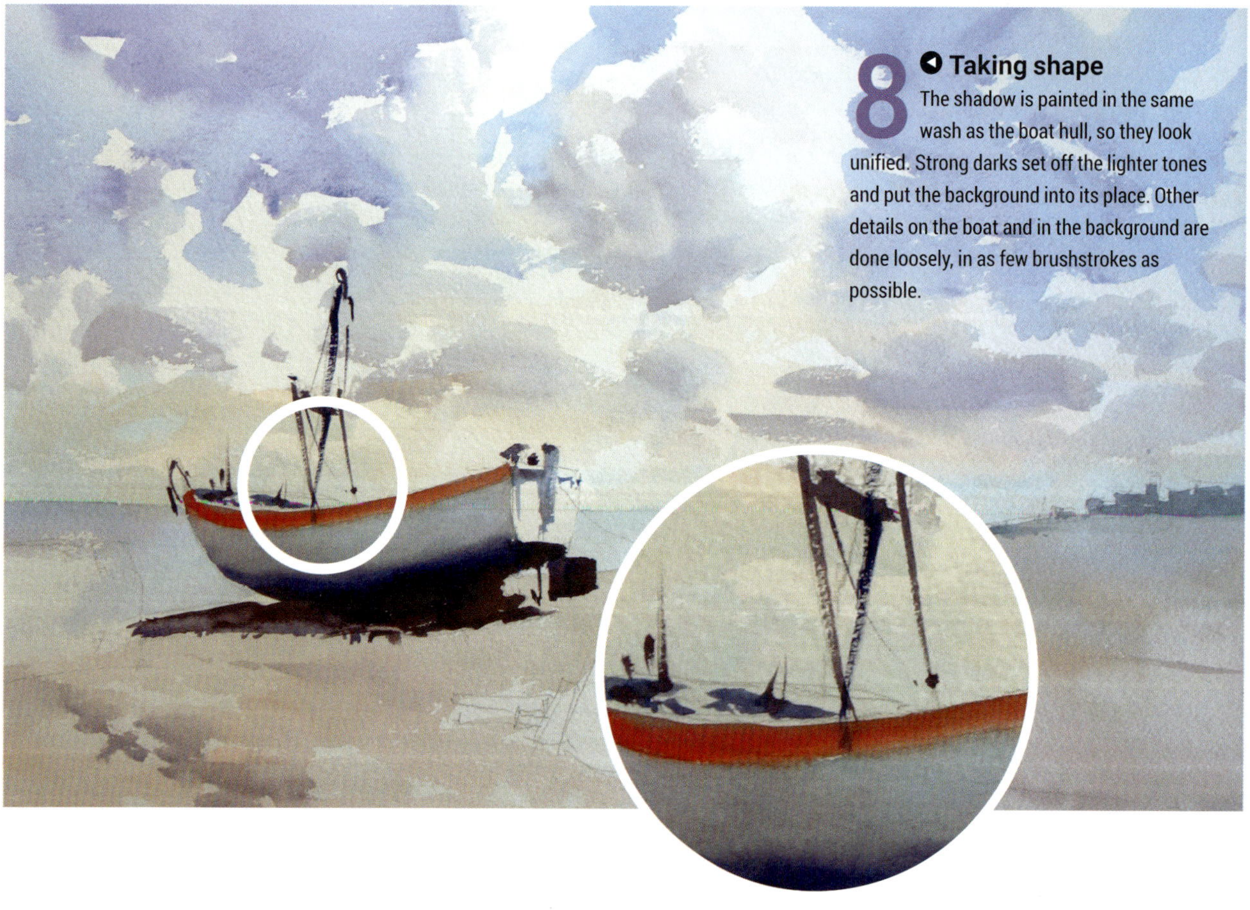

8 ◀ Taking shape

The shadow is painted in the same wash as the boat hull, so they look unified. Strong darks set off the lighter tones and put the background into its place. Other details on the boat and in the background are done loosely, in as few brushstrokes as possible.

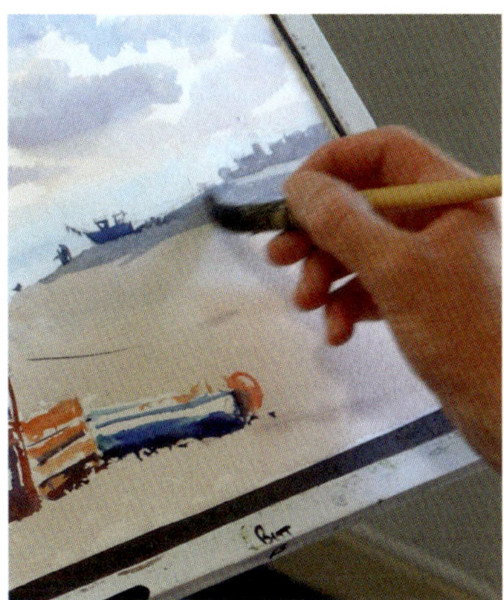

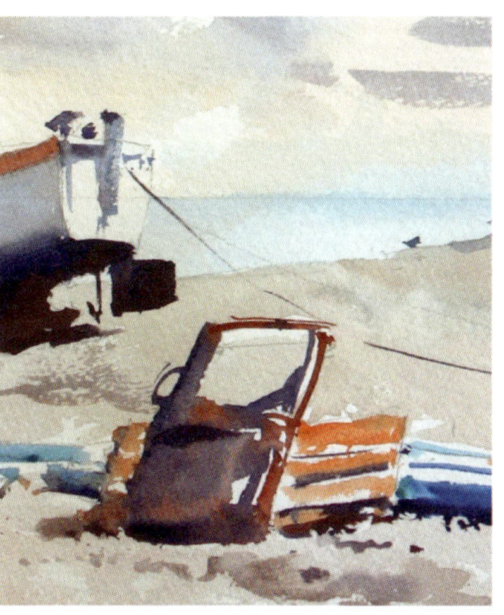

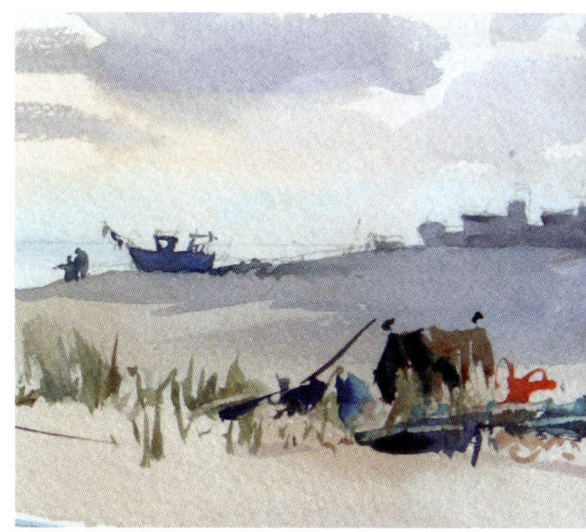

9 ⬤ Bits of stuff and background shadow

Next I paint the pile in the foreground, not worrying about what it actually is! What's important is the bright colours, which convey the notion of fishing gear. I put in a first wash for the baskets on the left, using free, fast and random brushwork to suggest their form. Next, a wash of grey goes over the whole background area, putting it into shade to draw the eye with added contrast.

10 ⬤ Adding in detail

Next I suggest detail – some dots, some dry-brush marks (by dragging a brush quickly on its side), and a bit of judicious spatter. Spattering is where you fling spots of paint from your brush by tapping it against your other hand while holding it over the paper. Less is more with this. I did the line from the boat using the pointed tip of the synthetic brush, held high up the handle and swiped from the wrist.

11 ⬤ Beach grasses and further stuff

I move the beach-grass section from the photo to where it best balances the composition in the painting. Again it is random shapes, allowing the key turquoise and orange colours to mix with the greenery. I swipe a couple of linear marks with a fingernail. This reveals the pale underlying paper and can be done in relatively thick paint, when it is just beginning to dry. Give it a go!

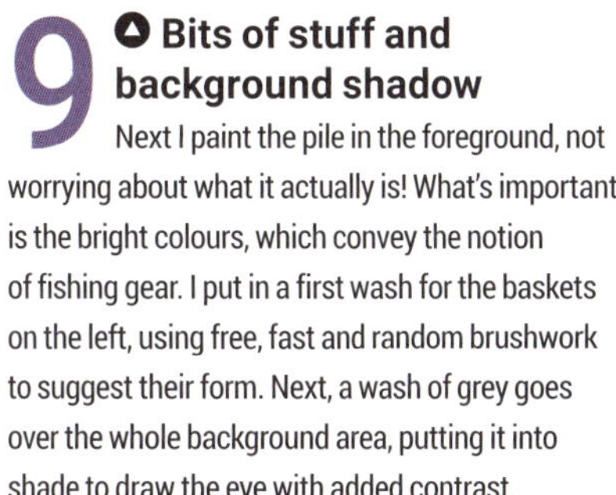

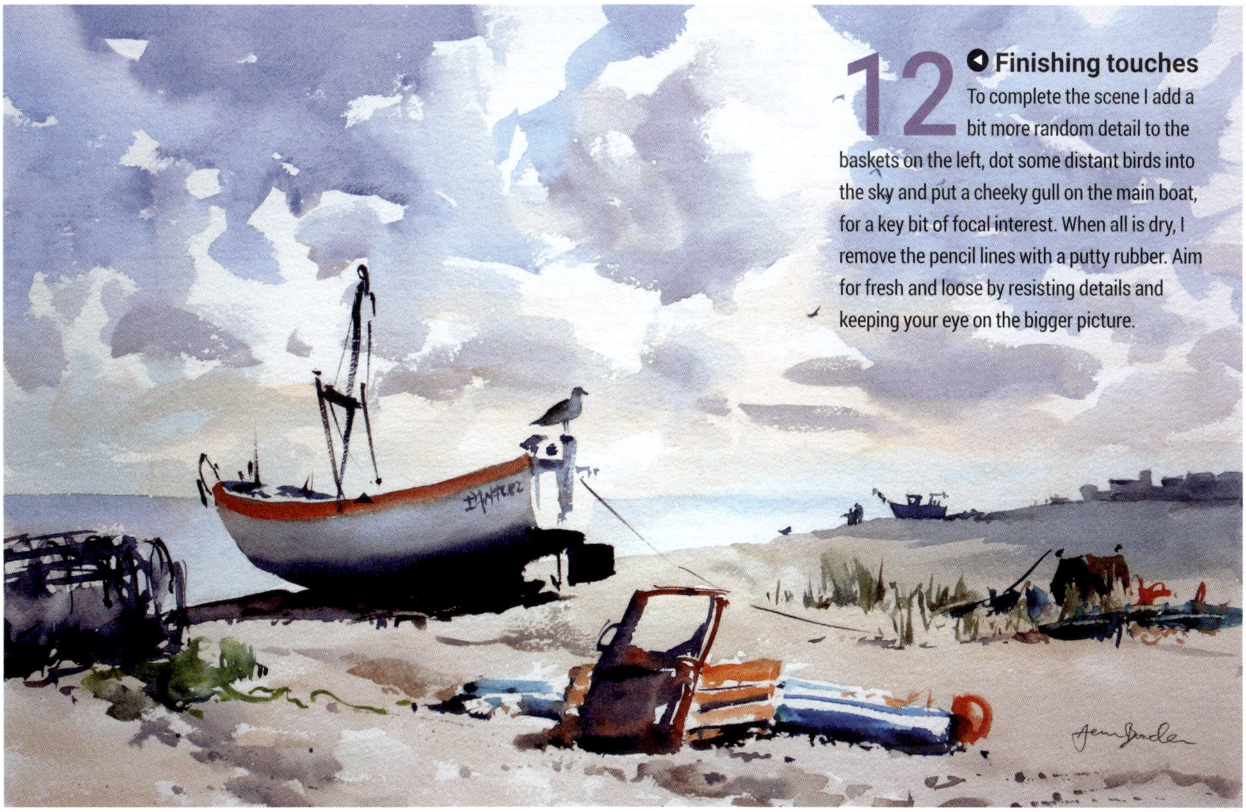

12 ◀ Finishing touches

To complete the scene I add a bit more random detail to the baskets on the left, dot some distant birds into the sky and put a cheeky gull on the main boat, for a key bit of focal interest. When all is dry, I remove the pencil lines with a putty rubber. Aim for fresh and loose by resisting details and keeping your eye on the bigger picture.

Paint beautiful blooms with wet-in-wet watercolour

Hazel Soan demonstrates how this technique can simplify a colourful array of flowers

Watercolour is wonderful. I discovered its appeal while I was still at art college, and used a tiny palette to make sketches when I was out on my bike in Leicestershire. I later discovered it was also the perfect medium for painting wildlife in the African bush. In both instances I had to work quickly, so I allowed my colours to blend into one another before they had dried.

The drifts and blends created when wet pigments merge on paper transfix me just as much now, as they did then. Along with transparency, this is also the appeal of this lovely medium. The pigments are so delicious in appearance when mixed in the palette and laid on the paper that painting in watercolour never fails to lift the spirits.

This wet-in-wet technique involves adding wet paint into wet washes, and allowing the added pigment to spread out unhindered – the ease with which it can suggest more with less is impressive! True, it is sometimes unpredictable, but that makes the challenge even more exciting.

Flowers and foliage offer the perfect excuse for practising wet-in-wet, because the organic forms and rich, deep colours lend themselves to a relaxed application. You can see from this workshop that, even though the paint is applied fairly freely, the overall appearance gives the impression you have painted more detail.

If you're new to watercolour, start with just one or two flowers on a leafy stem before you tackle a whole bouquet. In the worshop, you will see the variety of brushstrokes and applications that are possible with the technique, plus there's no need for a detailed pencil drawing. Let's get started!

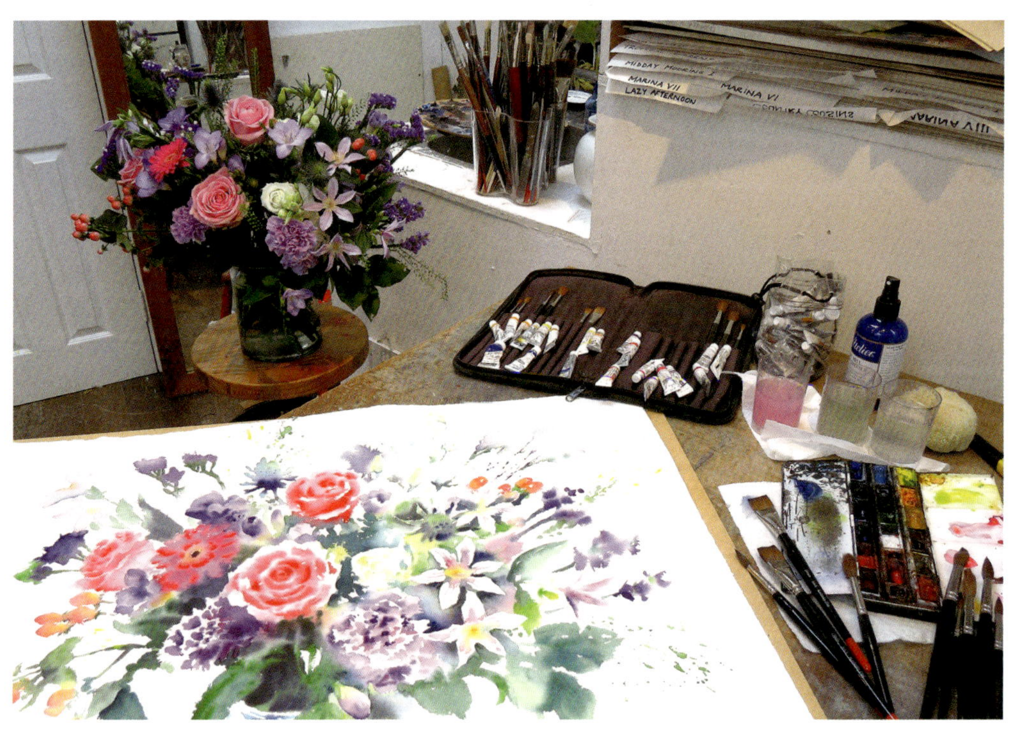

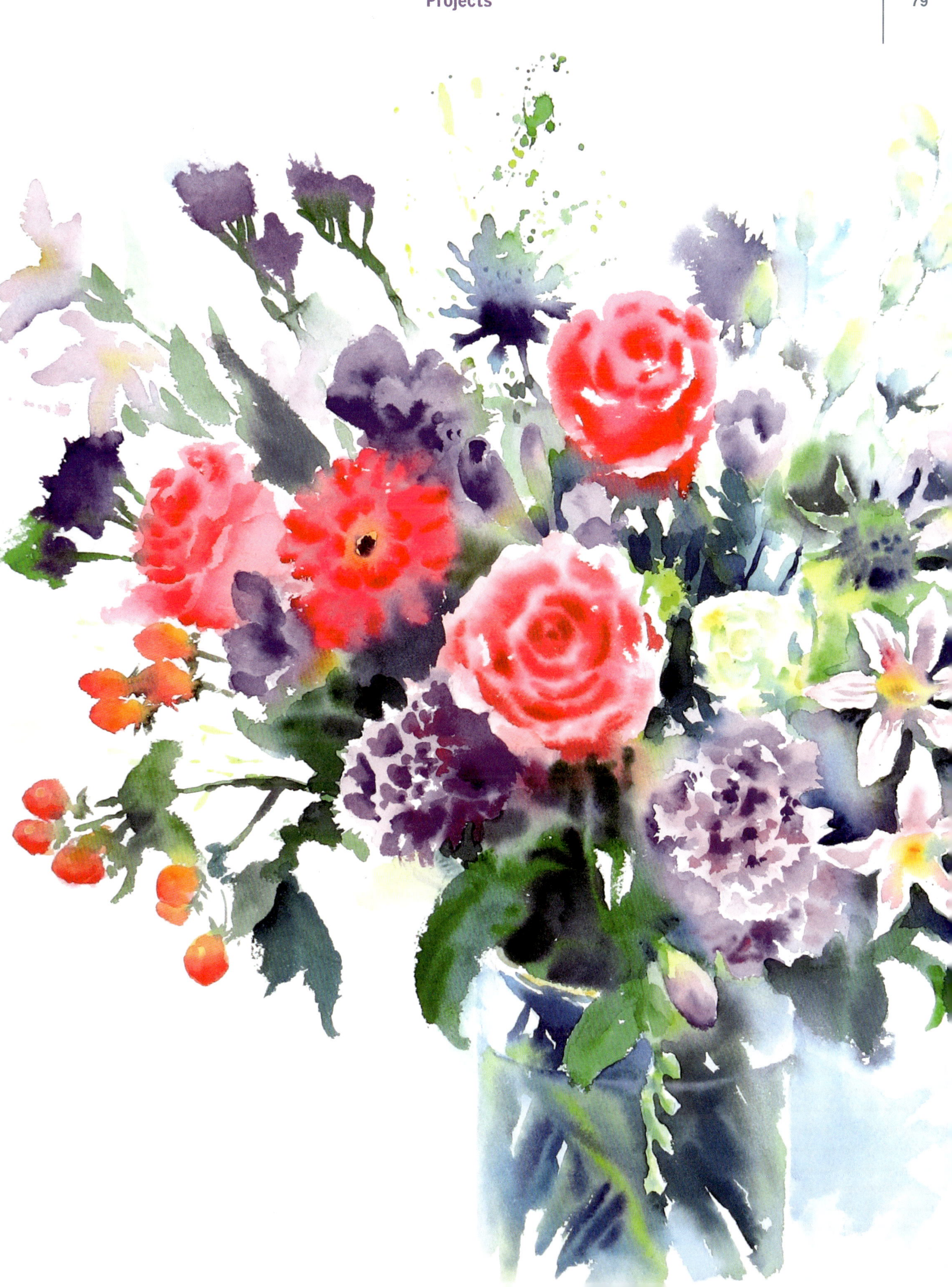

Follow these steps...

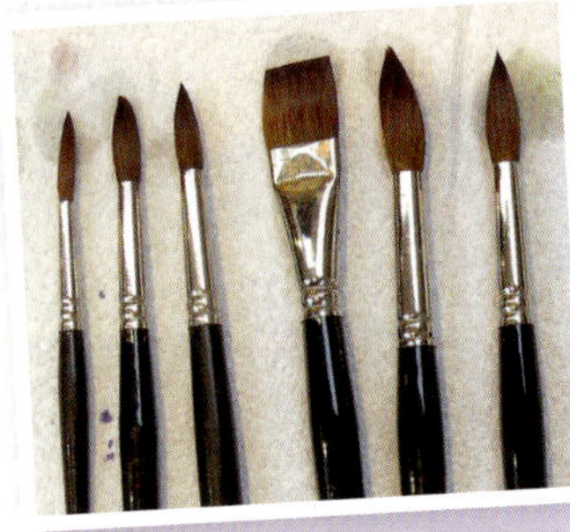

Materials

Hazel recommends using a round sable brush, as they have fine tips for detail and broad bodies that hold lots of paint. They release paint as you apply pressure, allowing full control.

- Schmincke Horadam Aquarell Watercolours
- Saunders Waterford watercolour paper, 300lb, rough pressed, 22x30in
- Round sable brushes, sizes 8, 10 and 12

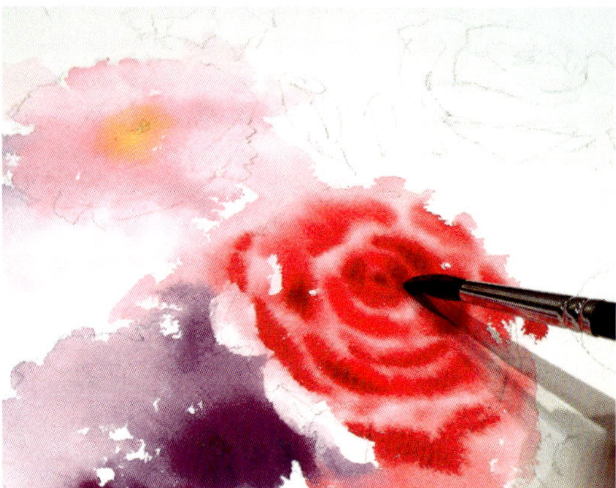

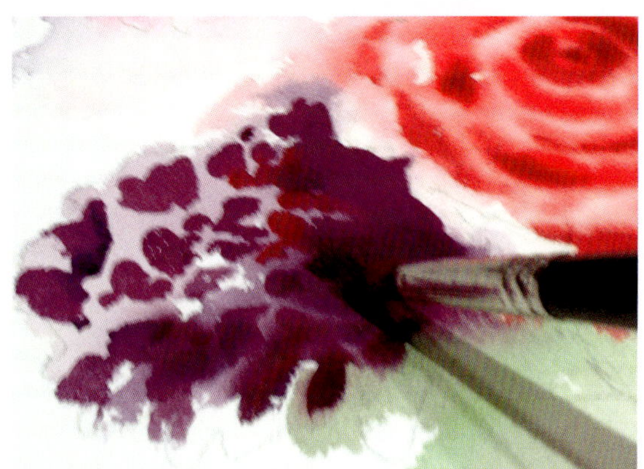

1 ◗ Start from the centre

After roughly sketching the bouquet, I paint the whole overall shape of the middle rose with a dilute wash of Permanent Rose. While the wash is still damp, I add more concentrated pigment of the same colour in thin concentric strokes to represent the shadow areas between the petals, enabling them to spread out into the wash to make gentle grades of colour. I darken the centre with a touch of neat pigment.

2 ◖ Use the carnation to bring out the rose

The carnation is darker than the rose, so I use this flower to shape the edge of the pale rose petal in front of it. I then add deeper violet wet-in-wet over the pale wash and in small triangular dabs to represent the shadows between the petals.

3 ◗ Add adjacent flowers

Adjacent flowers are added one by one, with a pale wash first and then more concentrated drier colour added into the wet wash. I use Opera Rose for the bright pink gerbera, adding the divisions between its radiating petals with short lines, like the spokes of a wheel to the centre of the flower.

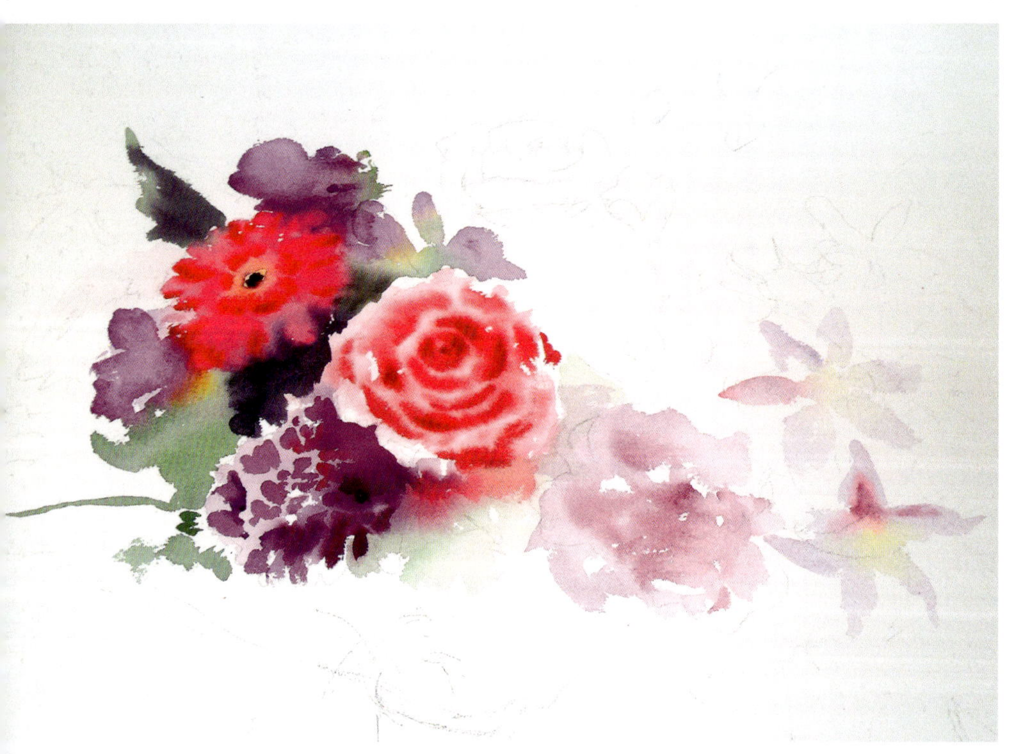

Palette design

Have you ever wondered why watercolour palettes are sloped? It's so that the paint can run down to show you how wet it is – if it runs into the gutter, it's probably too wet.

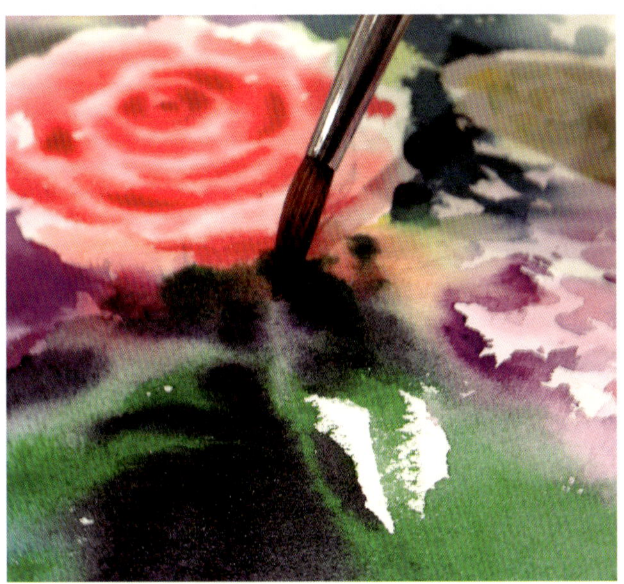

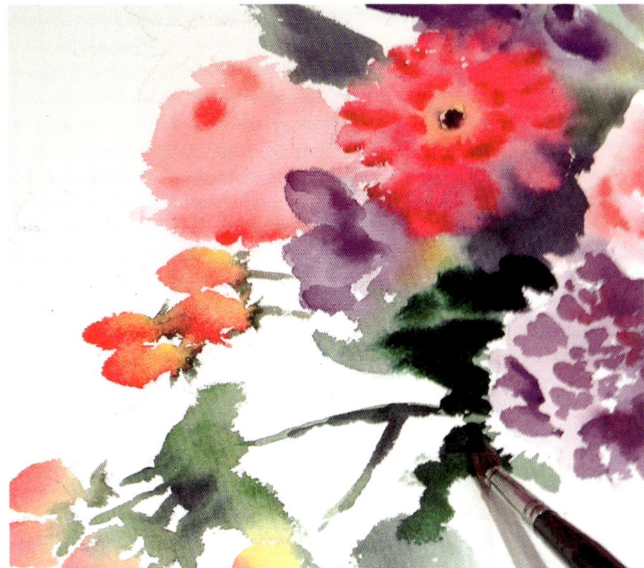

4 ⬤ Balance with dark foliage

Foliage acts as the darker counterfoil to the brighter flowers. I use pale Permanent Sap Green as the base colour, and sweeping strokes from a large brush, I add a really deep, dark mix of Prussian Blue and mauve into the wet wash and allow it to flow freely. The added colour needs to be much drier than the first wash, as there is already water on the paper. If it is too diluted it will cause a back run (a cauliflower-like drop or smudge).

5 ⬤ Keep it loose

I paint the rose hips with blends of Indian Yellow and Permanent Rose, and add their sepals beside them while they're still damp, so they blend freely. A few loose strokes for their leaves and stem, and they're quickly in position.

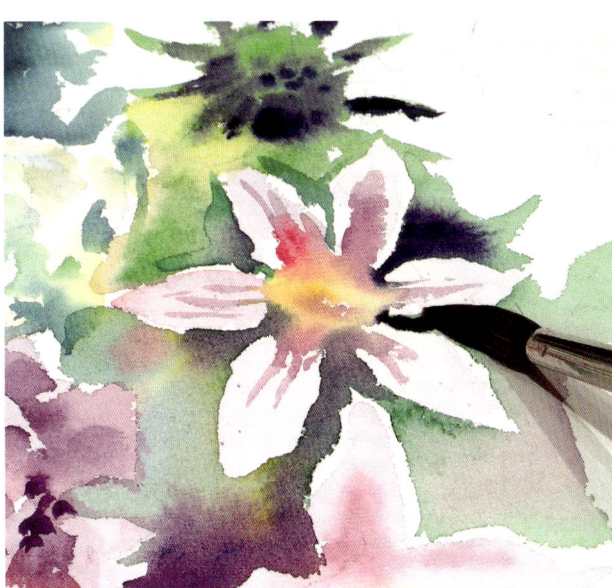

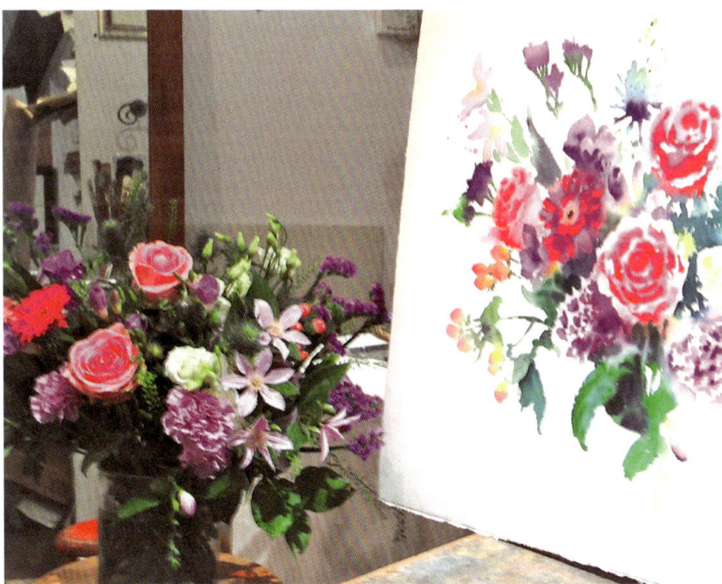

6 ⬤ Defining the petal shapes

A diluted wash of mauve tints the petals of the flower, then I touch Indian Yellow into the centre, blending wet into wet. I allow the flower to dry before painting the background foliage around the petals with a pale Permanent Sap Green and Aureolin. I then touch the tip of a size 8 brush into the triangular gap between the petals, wet-in-wet, to darken the foliage behind them.

7 ⬤ Check your progress

With the bouquet growing flower by flower from the centre of the painting, I finish each bloom as I go along. I work flat so I can control the direction of the flow of the paint as it diffuses into the damp washes. Occasionally, I place the board upright and step back to view my progress.

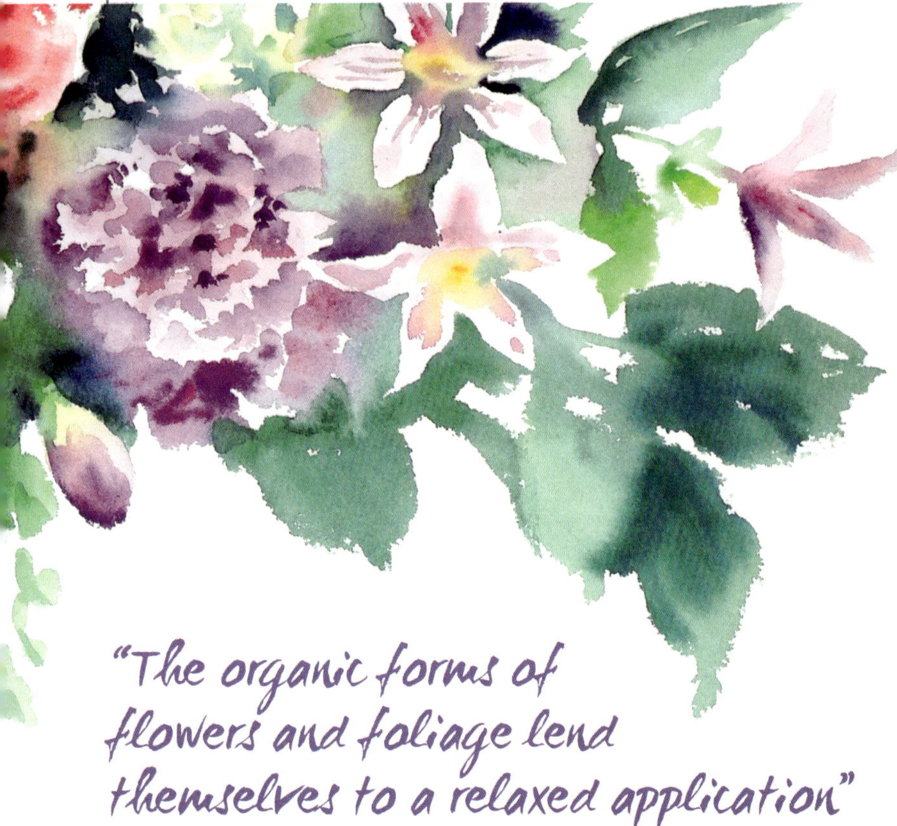

"The organic forms of flowers and foliage lend themselves to a relaxed application"

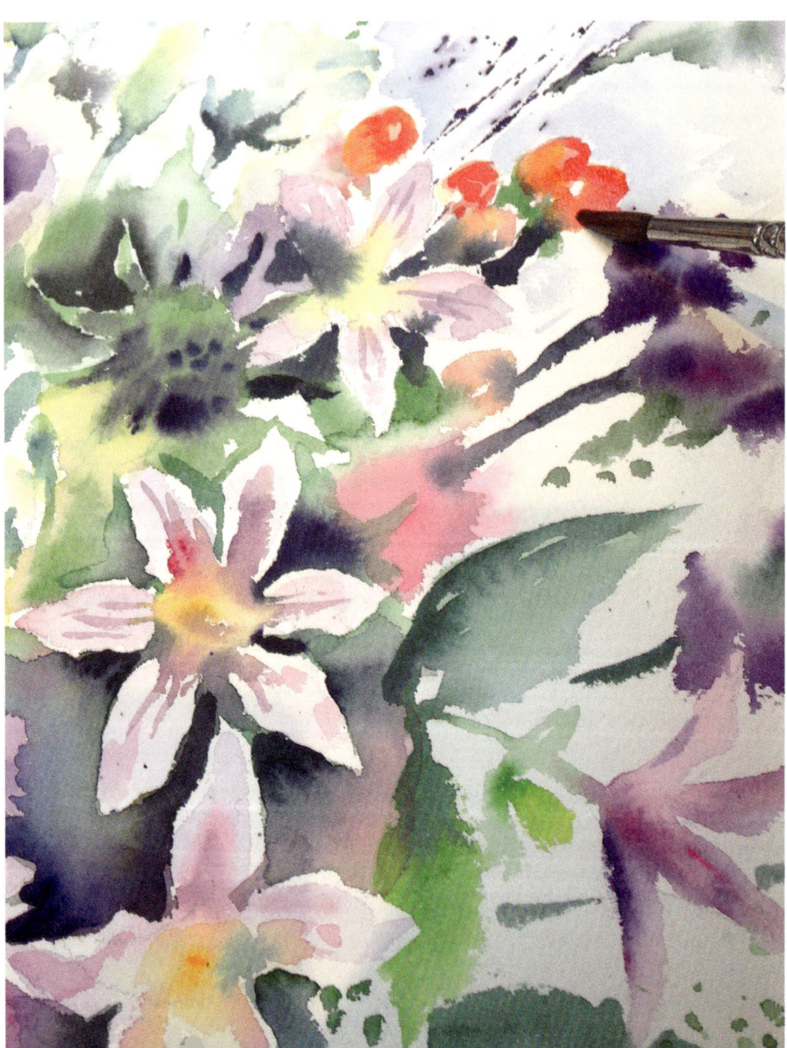

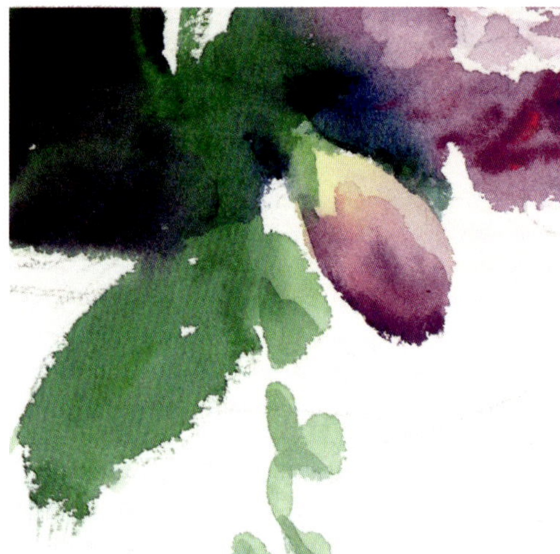

8 ◀ Shape the bud

I shape the freesia bud with pale mauve and Aureolin blended together, wet meeting wet. I create the roundness of the form by adding drier colour wet-in-wet on the side that's in shadow. I then add the sepal while the bud is damp, so the colours blend gently and give the organic appearance of the bud growing from the stem.

9 ▲ Use brushstrokes for leaves

For the lower leaves, I use a big brush to paint broad strokes, and deepen the shaded parts with wet-in-wet colour. By painting darker tones behind lighter ones, the lighter leaves and flowers appear to overlap the darker leaves and create a sense of depth under the bouquet.

10 ◀ Harness blending

The right-hand side of the bouquet looks quite detailed, but if you look closer you'll see the three pale flowers anchor the area. The rest is painted very quickly and loosely around them, leading away to the right, with brisk lines, blobs and brushstrokes representing approximate shapes. Such is the nature of the wet-in-wet technique that blending makes it appear that much more is represented.

colour therapy

Bright colours, especially pinks and reds, have a beneficial effect on the psyche – if ever you feel down, simply paint with warm, bright colours to lift you out of the blues!

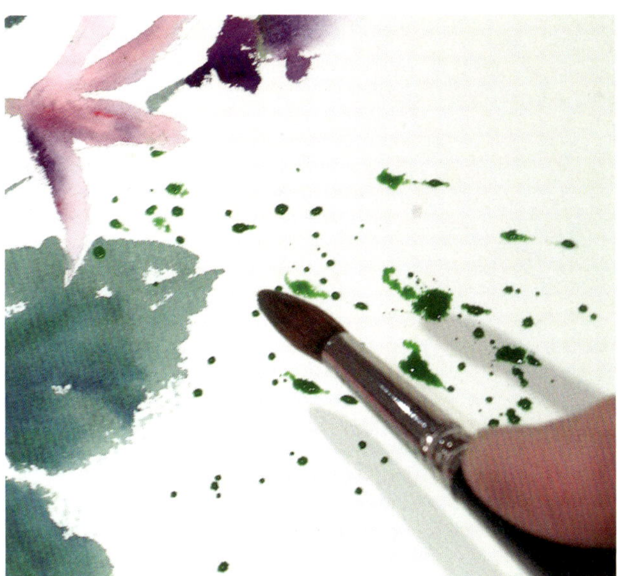

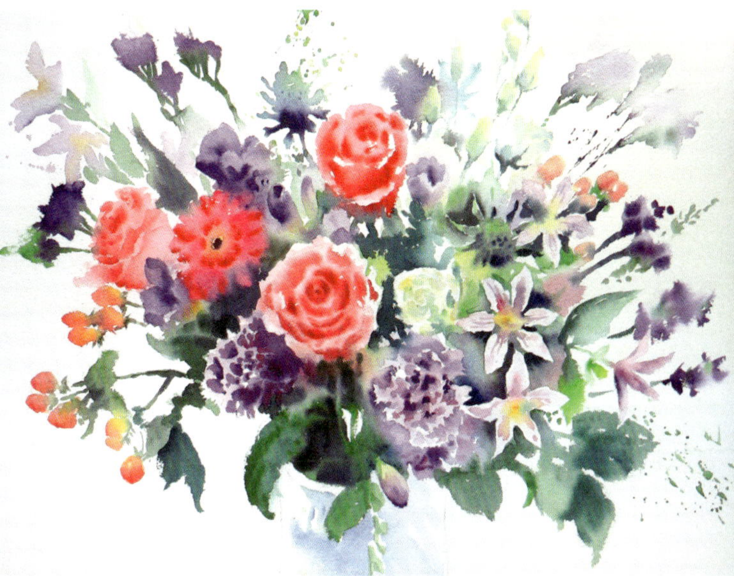

11 ⬢ Spatter

Using fairly wet diluted paint, I spatter the paper by lightly tapping on the handle above the ferrule (metal part of the brush). This lively spatter of paint aptly represents the feathery green foliage protruding from behind the bunch of flowers, without me having to paint a single mark.

12 ⬢ Balance the bouquet

I finish the bouquet with all of the blooms radiating from a central point to ensure they sit in the vase realistically. I am almost tempted to leave it like this with the ghostly impression of a vase that must exist in order to support the flowers, but I also love the angles of the stems below and the dark tones they bring in, so I relent.

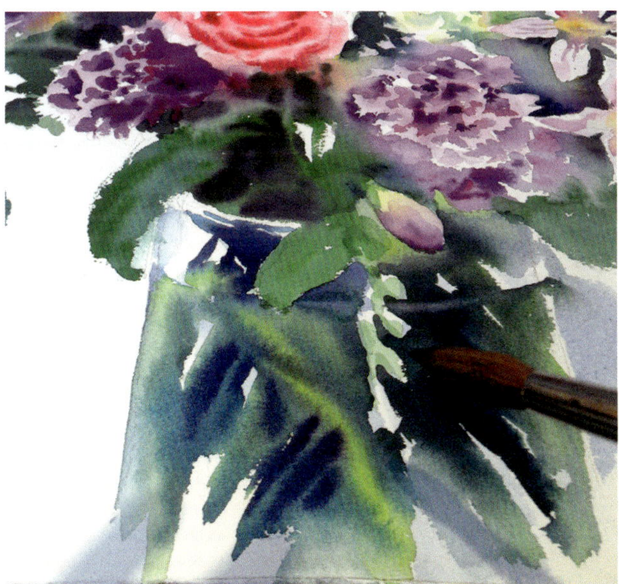

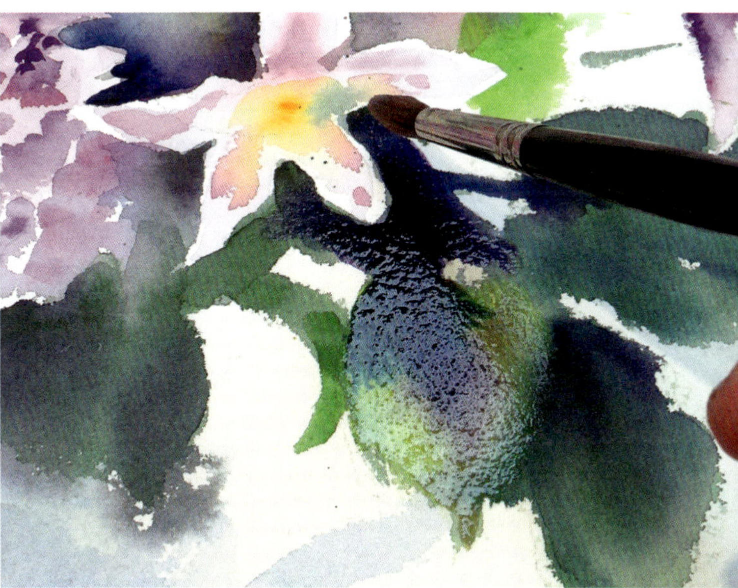

13 ⬢ Paint the stems

I create the stems in the vase with wet-in-wet washes, starting with the Permanent Sap Green (not too pale). I then add a deeply concentrated colour mix of Prussian Blue and mauve to follow the shadows along the line of each stem, leaving small lozenges of light between the criss-cross of the main ones.

14 ⬢ Make finishing touches

Final touches of deeper tone are needed in some areas of the foliage. To do this, I dampen the area with clean water then add in concentrated colour with the tip of the brush from the point of darkest shadow, allowing it to spread out into the damp wash.

Make spontaneous bees and butterflies

Kate Osborne reveals the secret to creating unique art with wet-in-wet watercolour, gouache and unusual printing techniques

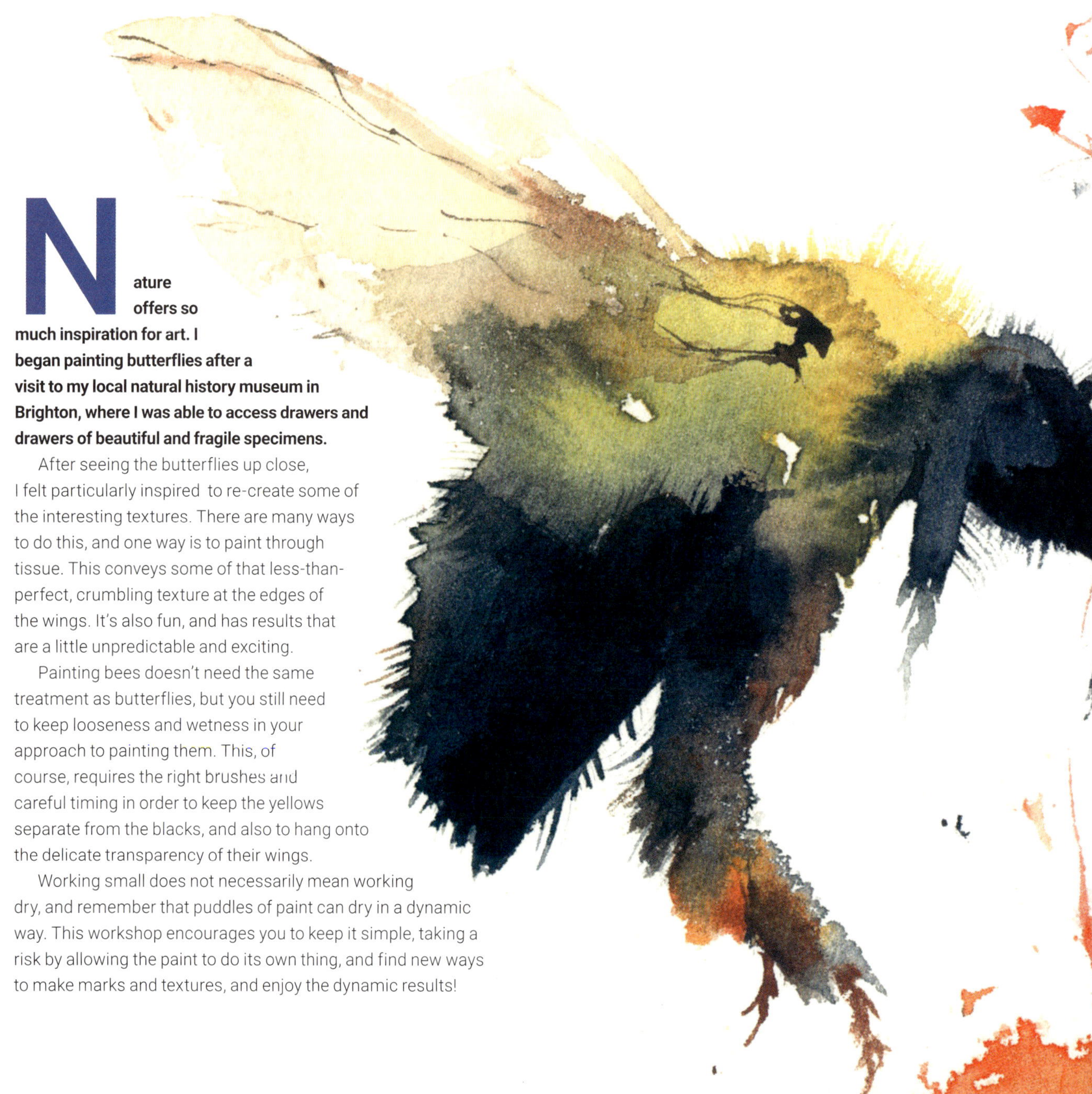

Nature offers so much inspiration for art. I began painting butterflies after a visit to my local natural history museum in Brighton, where I was able to access drawers and drawers of beautiful and fragile specimens.

After seeing the butterflies up close, I felt particularly inspired to re-create some of the interesting textures. There are many ways to do this, and one way is to paint through tissue. This conveys some of that less-than-perfect, crumbling texture at the edges of the wings. It's also fun, and has results that are a little unpredictable and exciting.

Painting bees doesn't need the same treatment as butterflies, but you still need to keep looseness and wetness in your approach to painting them. This, of course, requires the right brushes and careful timing in order to keep the yellows separate from the blacks, and also to hang onto the delicate transparency of their wings.

Working small does not necessarily mean working dry, and remember that puddles of paint can dry in a dynamic way. This workshop encourages you to keep it simple, taking a risk by allowing the paint to do its own thing, and find new ways to make marks and textures, and enjoy the dynamic results!

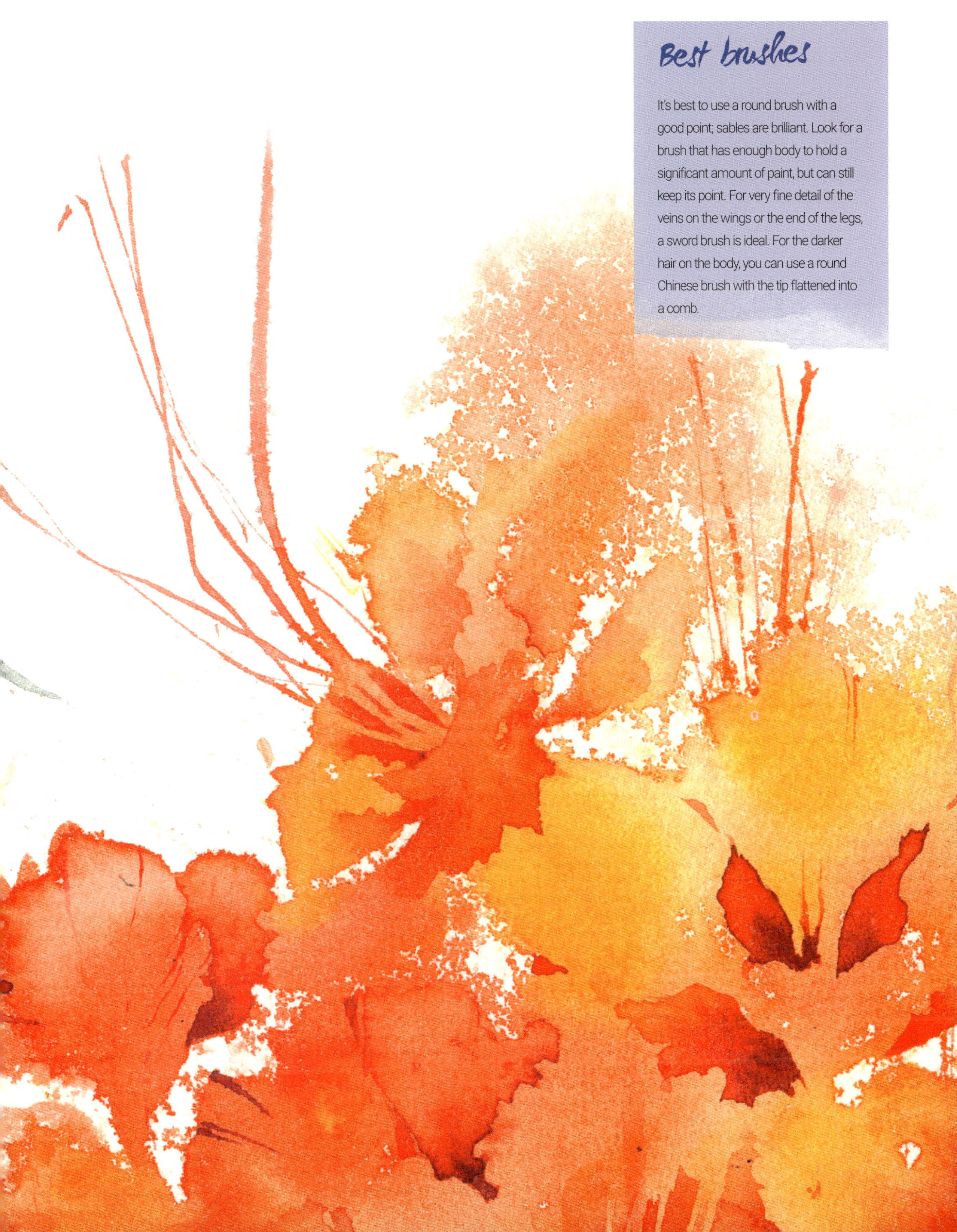

Best brushes

It's best to use a round brush with a good point; sables are brilliant. Look for a brush that has enough body to hold a significant amount of paint, but can still keep its point. For very fine detail of the veins on the wings or the end of the legs, a sword brush is ideal. For the darker hair on the body, you can use a round Chinese brush with the tip flattened into a comb.

Bee inspired

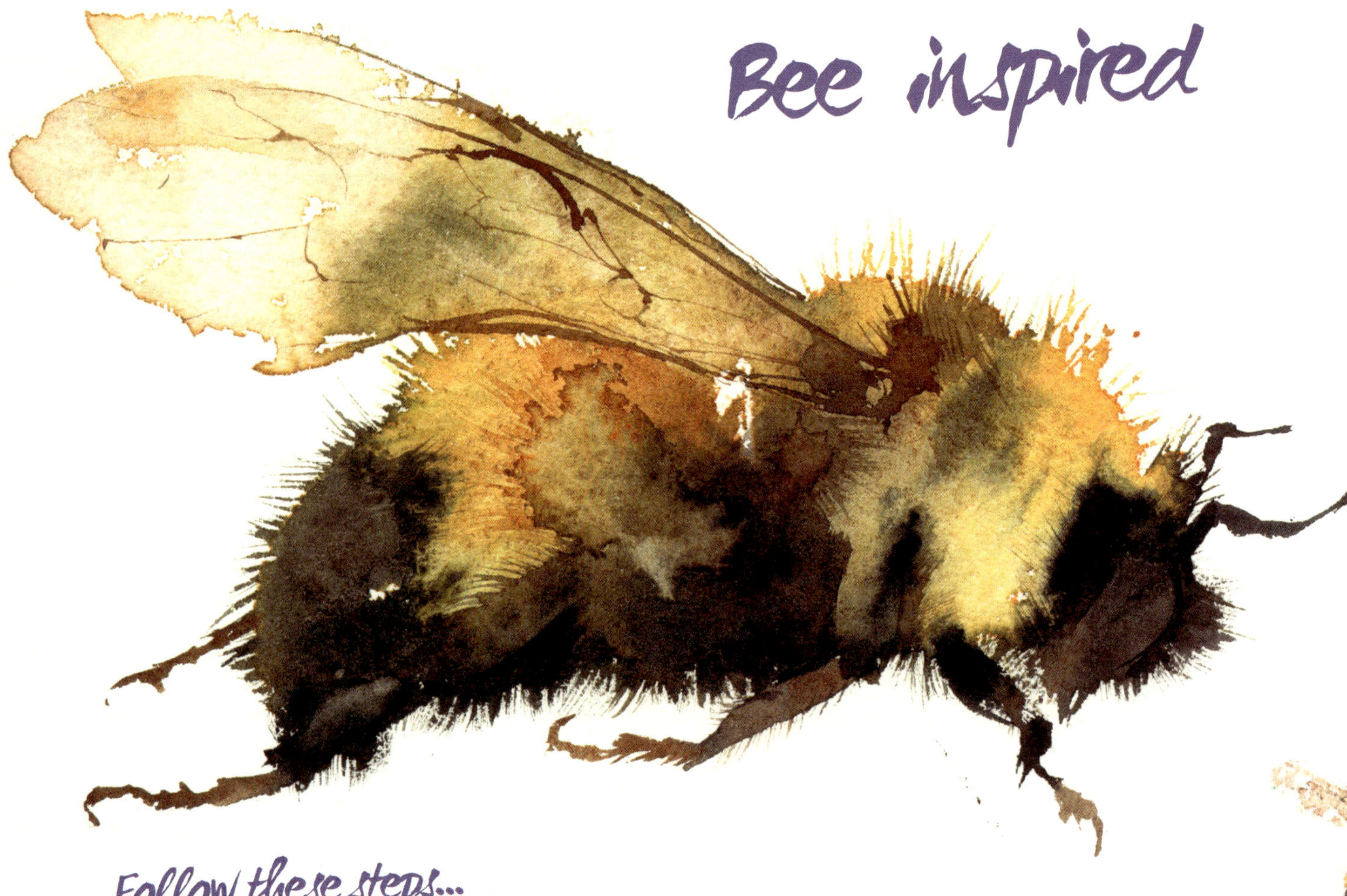

Follow these steps...

1 Begin with yellow

Start by mixing good puddles of Cadmium or Hansa Yellow, Burnt Umber and/or Burnt Sienna, and Paynes Grey. Now take the palest colour (the yellow), and paint the whole body and head, keeping everything wet by dropping in more paint, or adding clean water. Add the wings in a pale mix of brown, and if the yellow bleeds into them, mop it up and drop a little clean water into the area – this will 'push' the yellow away.

2 Try a bit of alchemy

Now drop in a rich shade of brown (or brown/grey mix) for the darker areas of the body furthest away from the yellow. Depending on how wet your paint is, how wet the area you are dropping it into, and how loaded your brush is, will dictate how much and how far this darker tone bleeds. Learning this bit of alchemy will take some practice and patience! Now let your painting dry completely.

3 Add the legs

With a darker mix of brown/black, find the negative shapes of the legs that are against the body, and paint the body around them. Try not to put in every detail – sometimes the smallest suggestion is enough and lets the viewer 'complete' the picture for themselves.

Say it with flowers

If you want to give your bees context, you can introduce flowers to the scene. Treat the flowers in much the same way as you would the bees, working loosely, keeping your paint flowing at the initial stage, not separating stalk from flower but allowing them to run into one another. It may be tempting to be exact and keep the petals apart from the green areas, but this blending echoes the organic nature of the subject. Once this first stage of the painting is dry, you can 'separate' the flower from the stalk or leaf with the next layer of tone. When painting with flowers, be more impressionistic with the bees and keep the detail down to a minimum. It's amazing how little information is required to describe these creatures!

Water ways

When you pull your brush through it, the paint in your palette should move like water. It should also have enough pigment in it so it doesn't merely look 'tinted' when it goes down on the paper.

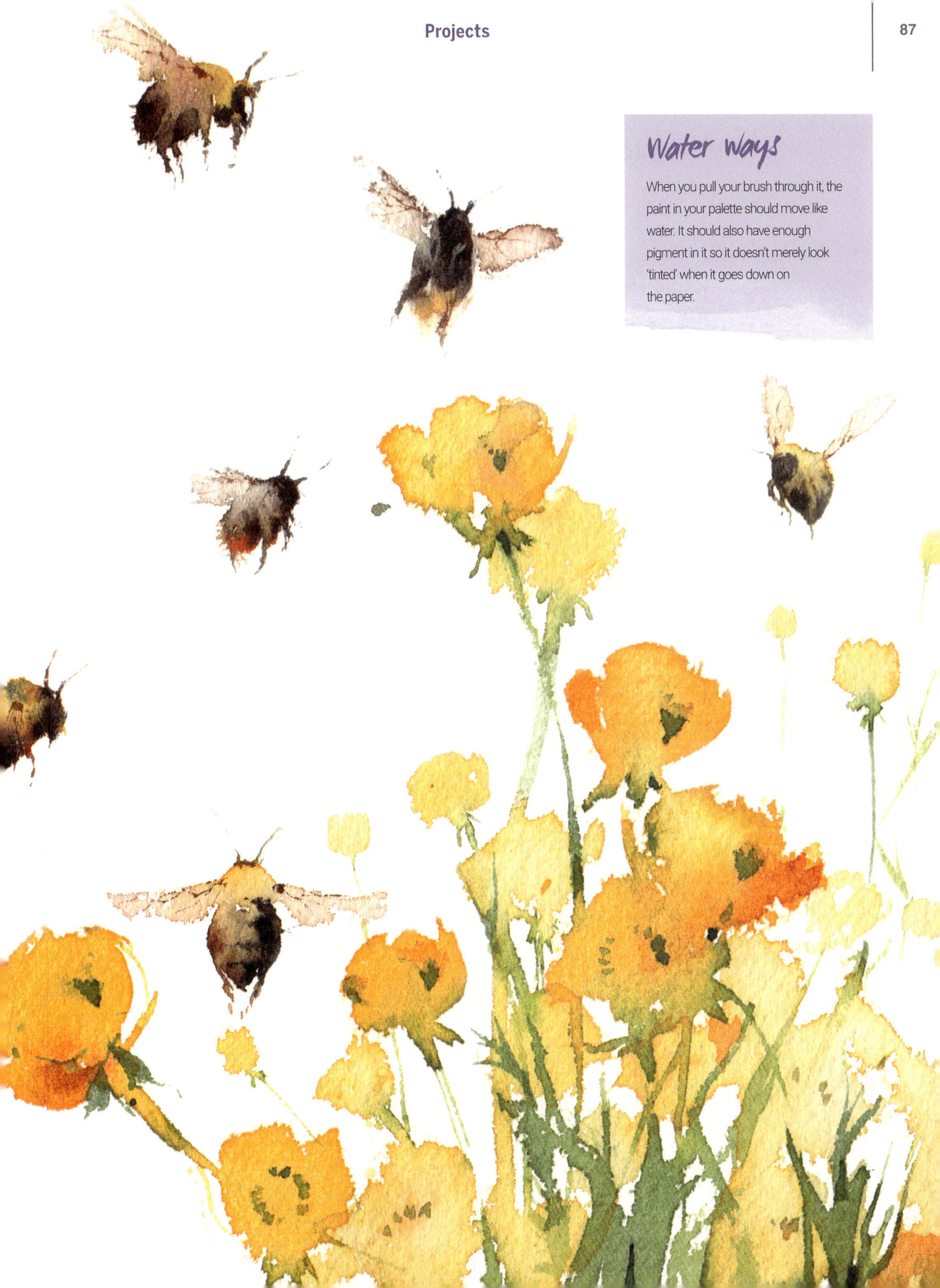

Better butterflies

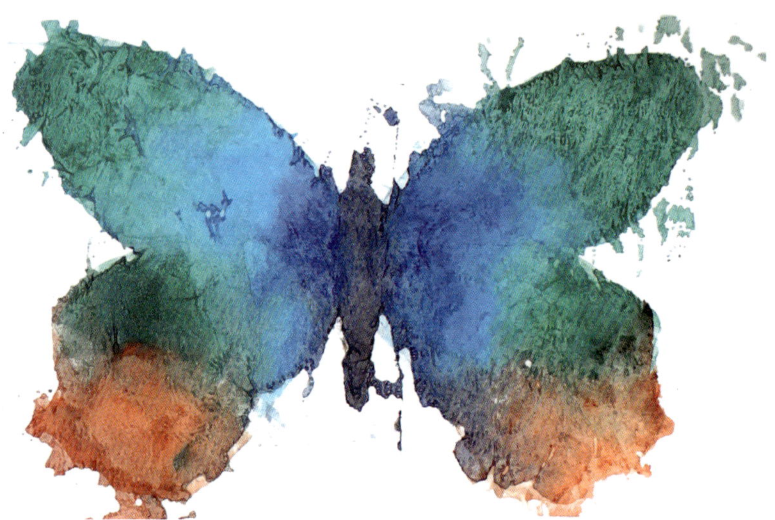

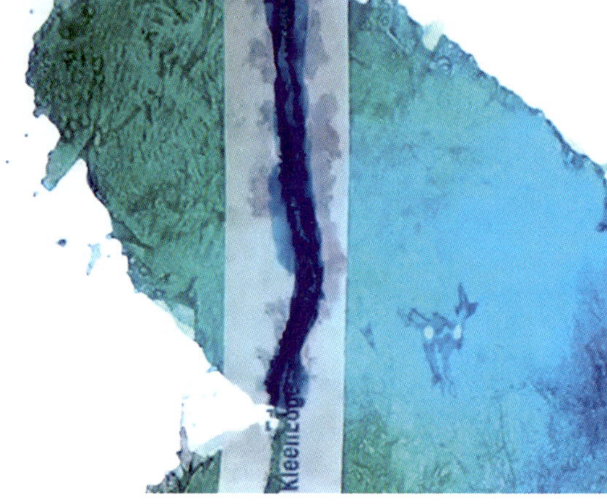

Follow these steps...

1 ⬕ Shape, colour and texture

Because butterflies are symmetrical, you can draw one half onto a folded sheet of tracing paper, turn it over and trace onto the other half. Once you've transferred the outline onto watercolour paper, create the initial stage of your painting, using some nice puddles of paint – make sure the whole area is covered. Before it has a chance to dry, place a layer of kitchen roll over the image and let it absorb the paint. You can now add rich, vibrant (and very wet!) colour on top. I've used mixes of Cobalt Teal, Perylene Red, Viridian and Indigo. Leave the tissue on until it is a little short of dry, before peeling it off for some lovely textures.

2 ⬕ Add in the detail

I take a strip of masking tape and tear it down the middle, before sticking it onto the image, leaving a small gap. I then paint over the gap with blue gouache. When the tape is removed, it will leave an irregular-edged blue stripe for detail on the wing. I then make another longer stripe, this time running the entire length of the wing. There are now two stripes on the top wing, and just one on the bottom wing. I repeat this on the other side.

3 ⬕ Add more detail

The hairs of the butterfly's body can now be painted on with a round brush flattened into a 'comb'. The wing veins are painted with a sword brush. For the red part of the wings, I've taken some Chinese/tissue paper and painted it with a rich mix of red paint. Once dried, I tear it into two circles. Next, I paint some textured craft paper with bright red gouache, and use this to print onto the tissue. The circles are then stuck onto the wings with glue. Finally, I print on the yellow gouache dots using my finger.

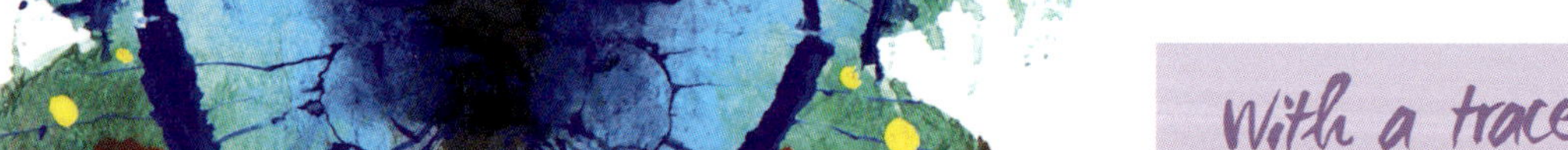

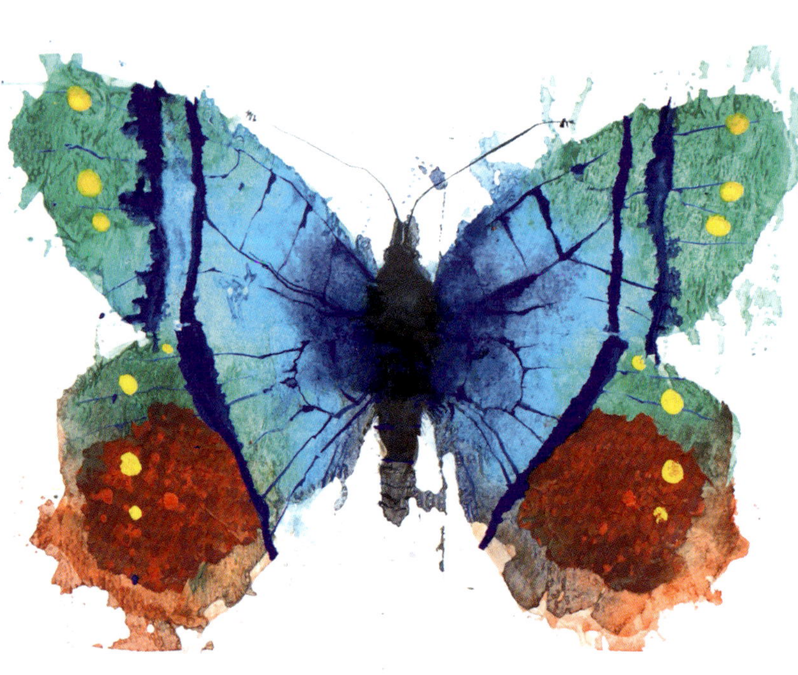

With a trace

You are looking to get the pattern as near symmetrical as possible, so it may be worth using your tracing paper again to ensure this if you're not confident doing it by eye.

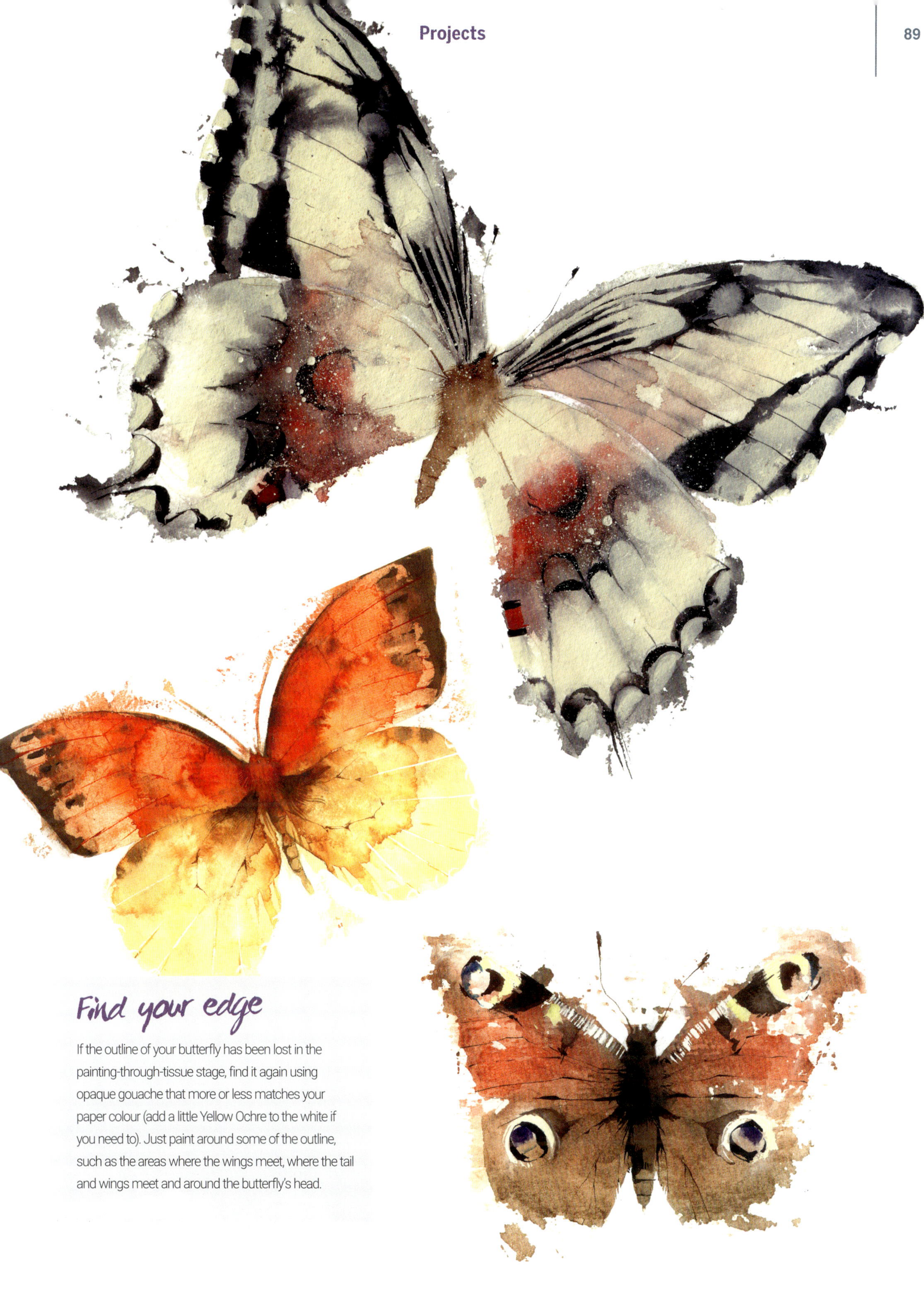

Find your edge

If the outline of your butterfly has been lost in the
painting-through-tissue stage, find it again using
opaque gouache that more or less matches your
paper colour (add a little Yellow Ochre to the white if
you need to). Just paint around some of the outline,
such as the areas where the wings meet, where the tail
and wings meet and around the butterfly's head.

Tips to paint a mischievous hare!

Hannah Dale is known globally for her beautiful wildlife illustrations. Here she shares her process for bringing a hare on the run to life

I've had to develop a different way of working over the last few years. Gone are the days when I could lock myself away in a studio for hours and immerse myself in a piece of work – I have three young children and take a very active role in our business so this has meant that painting time only comes here and there, often at the kitchen table where I can keep an eye on everyone while I paint (we even bought an extra long kitchen table so I can leave my paints out rather than having to pack them away each meal time!).

I found this pretty difficult at first but I've slowly adapted to being able to work in quite a fragmented way and it suits my lifestyle perfectly. It also means that if an idea pops into my head suddenly, I can quickly get to work with a sketch and put the ideas down on paper rather than having to wait until I can get some proper studio time.

Having studied zoology, animals and wildlife have always been a great passion for me and I never tire of painting them. We're lucky enough to live in the Lincolnshire countryside and have limitless inspiration right on the doorstep. In this tutorial, I'm going to give a step-by-step guide to painting a running hare. I must have painted hundreds of hares over the years and it's a real passion for me, but each painting always unveils a new character, which reveals itself as the painting progresses – I always find it an exciting process.

🔽 Capturing the essence of a spritely hare might seem a difficult task, but follow Hannah's approach and you will be sure to create something to be proud of.

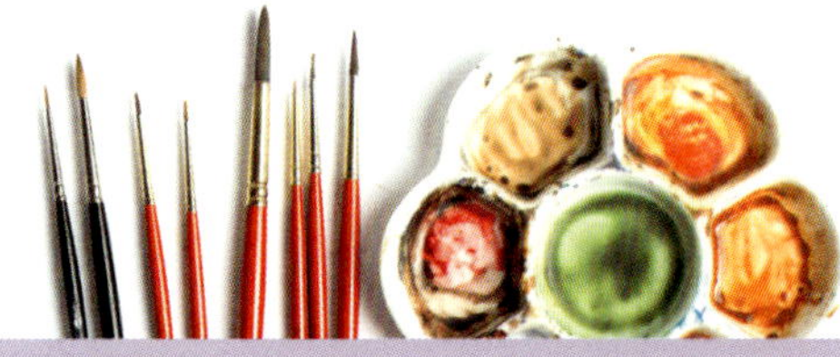

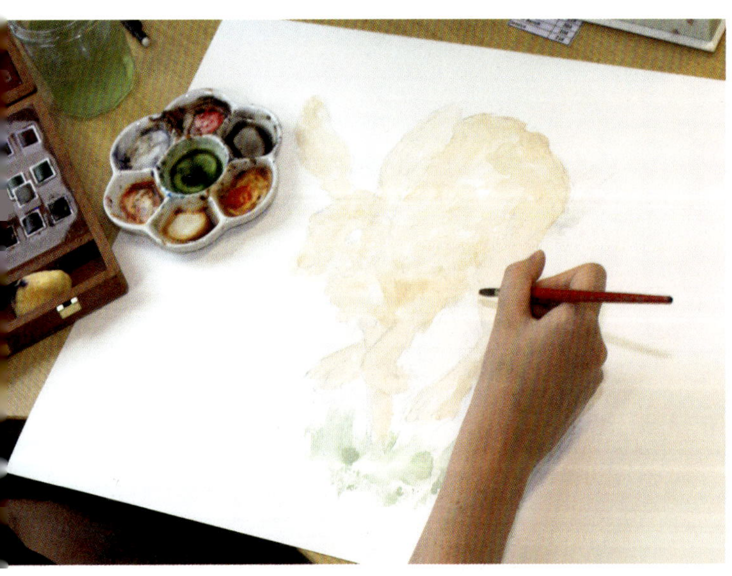

Materials

Hannah uses Winsor & Newton Professional Water Colour paints. She uses the pans rather than tubes because they offer more convenience.

The surface is Winsor & Newton Classic Water Colour paper, 300gsm cold press. The size is 16x20in, which she uses for a lot of her work. This paper has a nice toothy texture and handles the paints well.

The brushes Hannah uses are Winsor & Newton Sceptre Gold synthetic brushes and Series 16 sable brushes. The sizes range from 00 for the very fine details to 16 for the loose washes. Hannah gets through a lot of brushes, especially the finer grades, so she views the synthetic sable brushes as an excellent and less expensive alternative to the standard sable ones.

Hannah's initial sketch was created using an HB pencil.

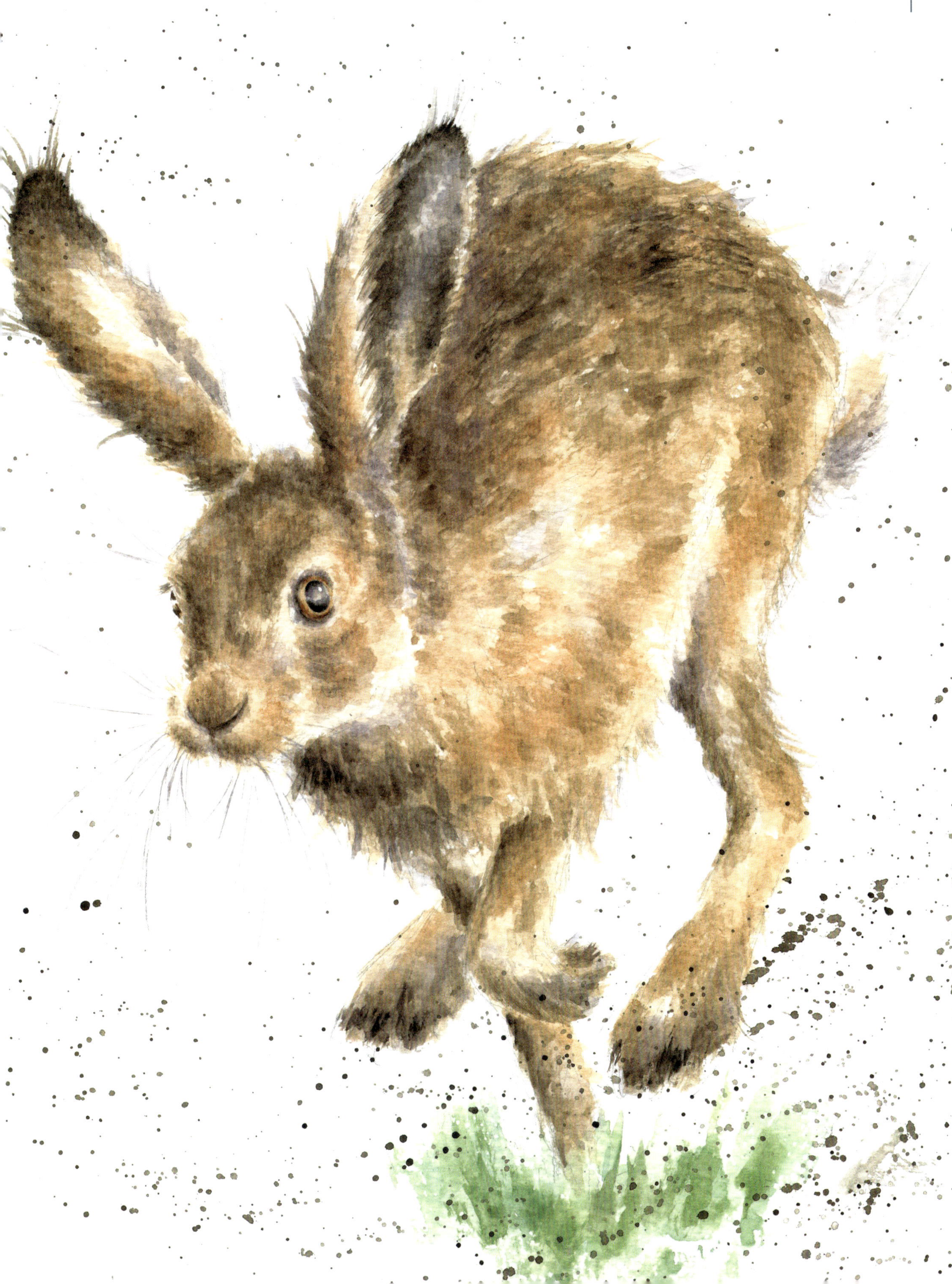

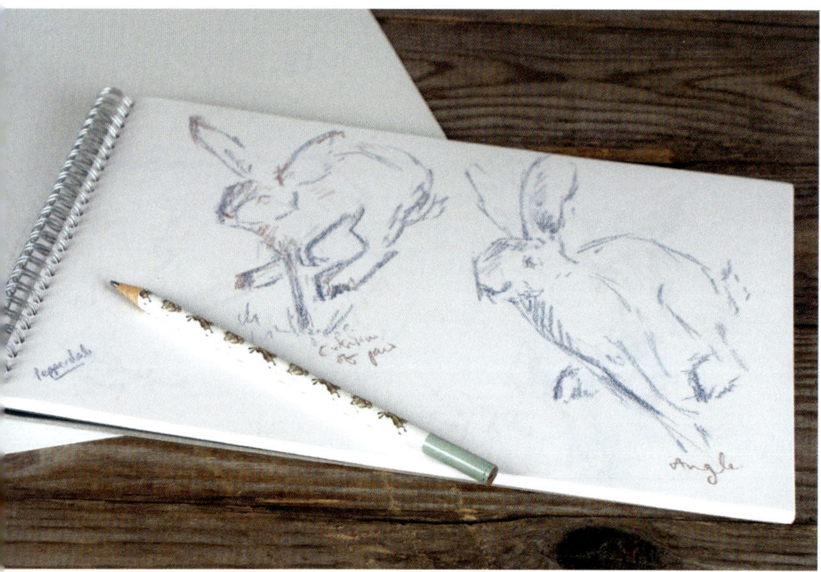

1 ▲ Create the sketch

Starting with a blank sheet of paper can seem pretty daunting, and the first marks can often feel the hardest. I want to paint a running hare and getting a sense movement and energy into a piece of work is quite challenging – I've started with some quick pastel sketches, which I find useful for experimenting with different compositions and poses. As a general rule, I want to avoid parallel lines and introduce as much contrast as possible in the lighting and colour palette to stop the final piece feeling too calm. It takes quite a while to complete this step – I keep changing things, and then leaving it for a few hours before coming back to reassess. For me, it's really crucial to get the elements right at this stage to save a lot of wasted time later on.

2 ▶ The first wash

I'm giving the painting its first wash using a mix consisting of Burnt Sienna and Yellow Ochre, along with a touch of red. I want the red to show through subsequent layers of paint and provide the painting with a warm base. One of the key points of this stage is to eliminate any white in the painting that will not remain white in the finished piece. In this case, the only white of the paper will be the glint in the hare's eye and a little dab on the tail.

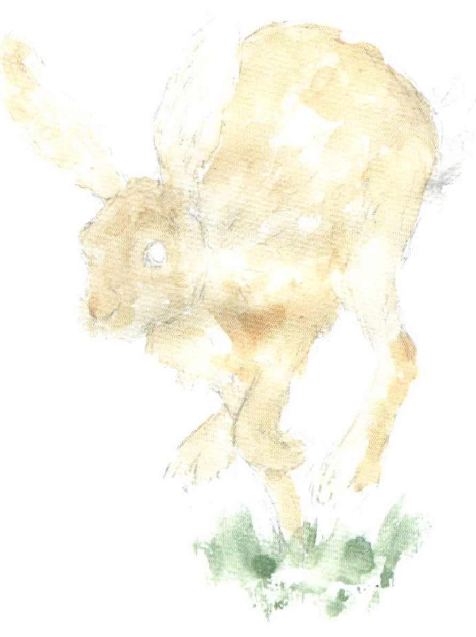

3 ▶ Add a contrast colour

The next stage is to establish the light source and work out where the shadows will fall. This instantly starts to give the hare some form and he begins to look three dimensional. I'm using violet, French Ultramarine and a tiny bit of Burnt Umber. This mix contrasts well with the warm wash and introduces a cooler element.

I look at my work through a mirror at regular intervals – it's like looking at it with fresh eyes and you immediately spot anything that's not working or that might be missing – it can save a lot of head scratching later on!

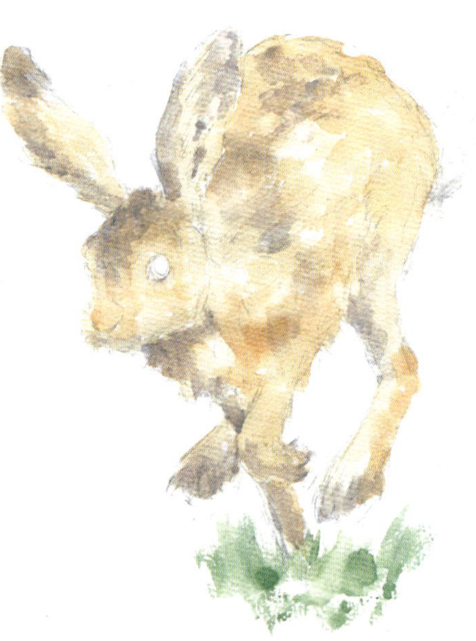

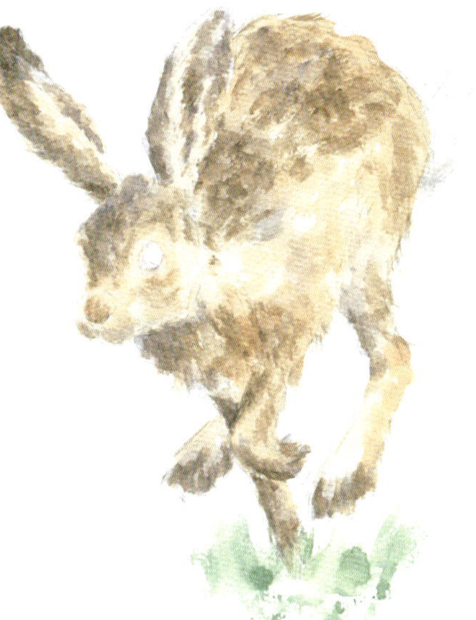 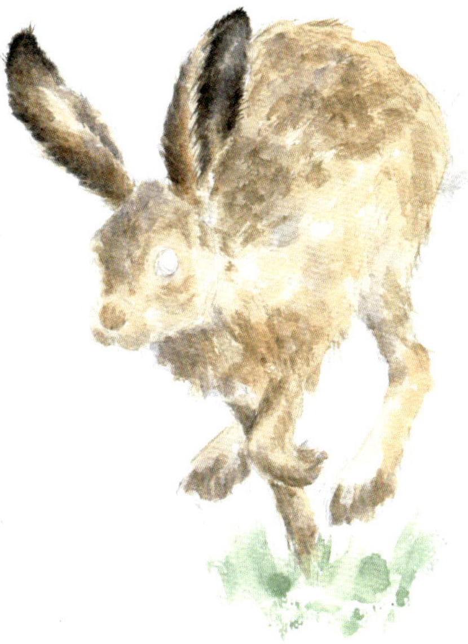 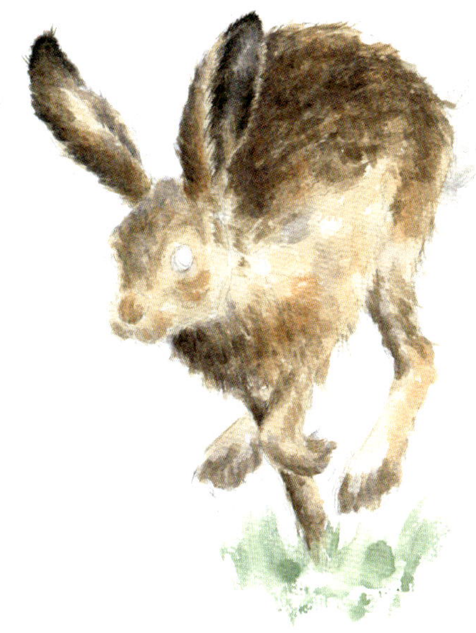

4 ⬧ Start work on the fur

Now I want to build up the areas of shadow while introducing the appearance of fur. With watercolour, I like to give the impression of fur rather than paint each individual hair, and it helps to work with more of a dry brush for this effect rather than the wet washes in the previous stages. I'm still working fairly quickly across the whole painting here, to build it up with consistency rather than focusing on a small area.

5 ⬧ Now for the ears

For some reason, when painting hares and rabbits, I always start with the ears when it comes to focusing on the detail. I think it's because you get a good range of colour and light contrast within the ears due to the way they fold, creating a deep shadow in the centre. Hares have a good range of colour variation in the ears with the black tips. This then becomes a good benchmark for the rest of the work and if you are constantly asking yourself 'is the shadow on the foot as dark as the shadow on the ear' etc, it helps to make the final piece coherent.

6 ⬧ Develop the fur

I'm now adding layer upon layer of fur – there is a huge variety of colour within fur and building up the layers help to make it look more realistic. I'm sticking with oranges, purples and browns and always being mindful of where the shadows are and where the light would be hitting the animal.

The 'it' factor

The most important ingredient in any artwork is a passion for what you are painting. I worry much less about the materials and paints than really engaging with the subject – for me it's about capturing a character and expressing that in watercolour. Even if it's not technically perfect, this will give the painting a kind of magic that is hard to define but is evident at a glance.

7 ▶ Time for reflection

The form is really starting to take shape now and I'm happy with the way the fur is looking. I like to take a bit of a break at this point and come back to the painting with fresh eyes – it's a good time to view it through a mirror, which reveals any areas needing a bit more attention.

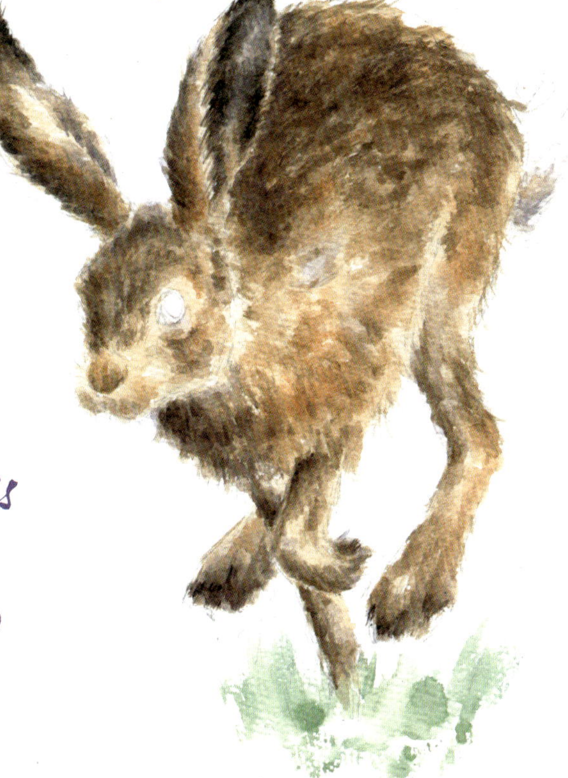

"I like to take a bit of a break at this point and come back to the painting with fresh eyes – it's a good time to view it through a mirror"

"I just need to make the final tweaks to the shading, add the whiskers and some splatters"

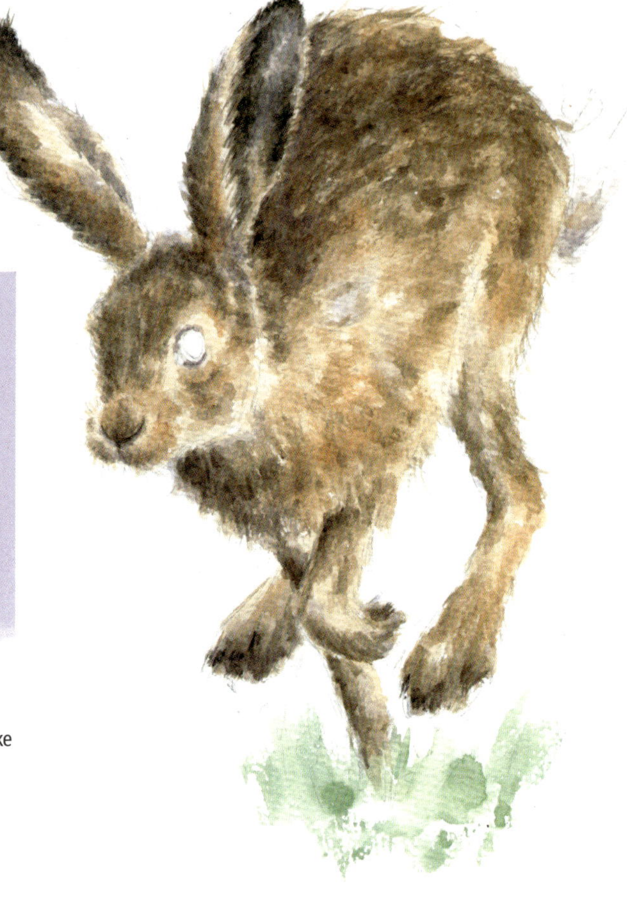

Have faith in yourself

I didn't study art beyond school and for a long time I felt I had to apologise for not being 'professional'. I had sold thousands of prints and still didn't have the confidence to call myself an artist or even to sell my original paintings as I was too embarrassed to put a value on them. I think as an artist you are your own worst critic and I am definitely no exception – it's so important to try and get past this and tell yourself 'I am an artist!'

8 ● Check the shading

This is a good time to check that the balance of the piece is working. I want to make sure that the darkest and lightest areas of shading are in the right place. It's really important to make the final piece coherent and ensure the whole range of shading, from white to black, has been used in all the right places. It's also a good time to adjust the warm and cool highlights to make sure there is good colour contrast as well.

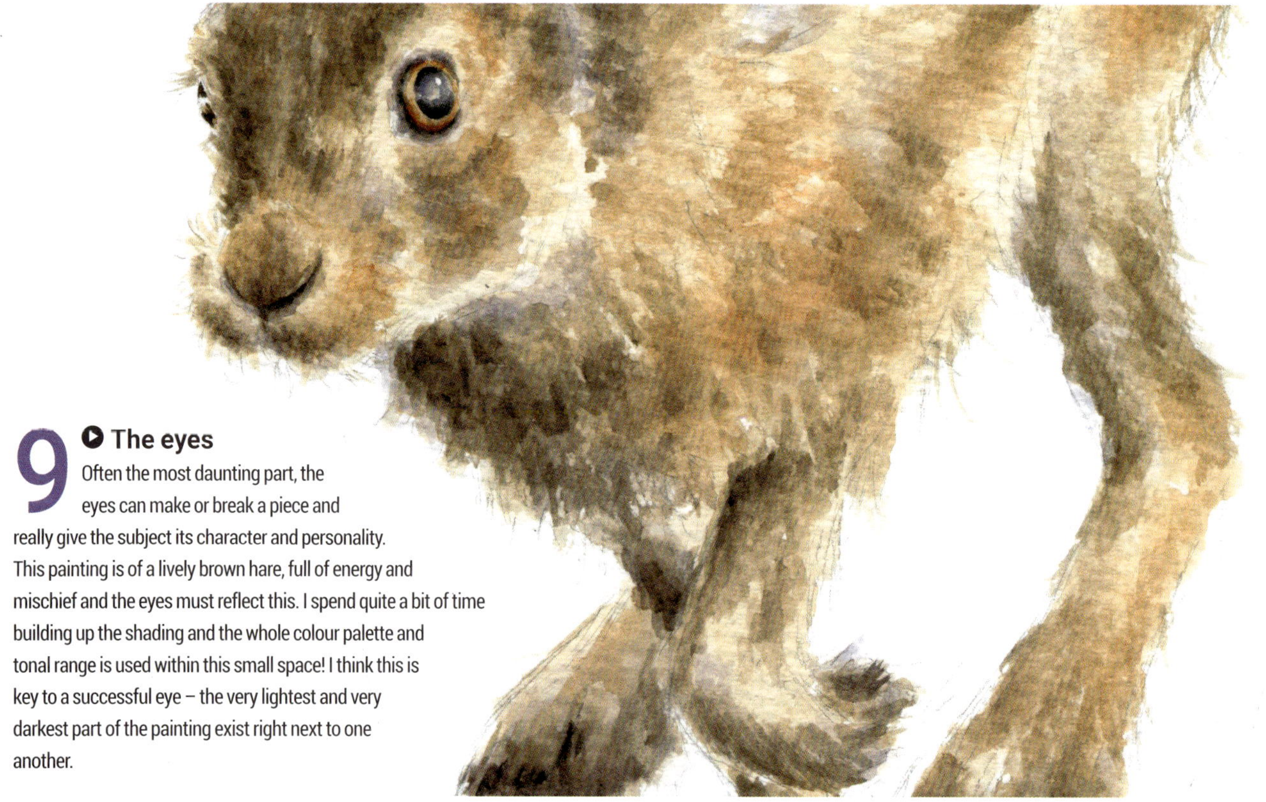

9 ● The eyes

Often the most daunting part, the eyes can make or break a piece and really give the subject its character and personality. This painting is of a lively brown hare, full of energy and mischief and the eyes must reflect this. I spend quite a bit of time building up the shading and the whole colour palette and tonal range is used within this small space! I think this is key to a successful eye – the very lightest and very darkest part of the painting exist right next to one another.

10 ⏷ Finishing touches

Nearly there now – I just need to make the final tweaks to the shading, add the whiskers and some splatters, which also help to add to the movement and energy of the piece. I'm focusing them around the back feet as if he is kicking up mud as he goes along! It was my original intention to paint more detail in the grass at the bottom but upon reflection I don't think it needs it. I like the way it sits there like a full stop at the end of the outstretched foot, anchoring the painting nicely.

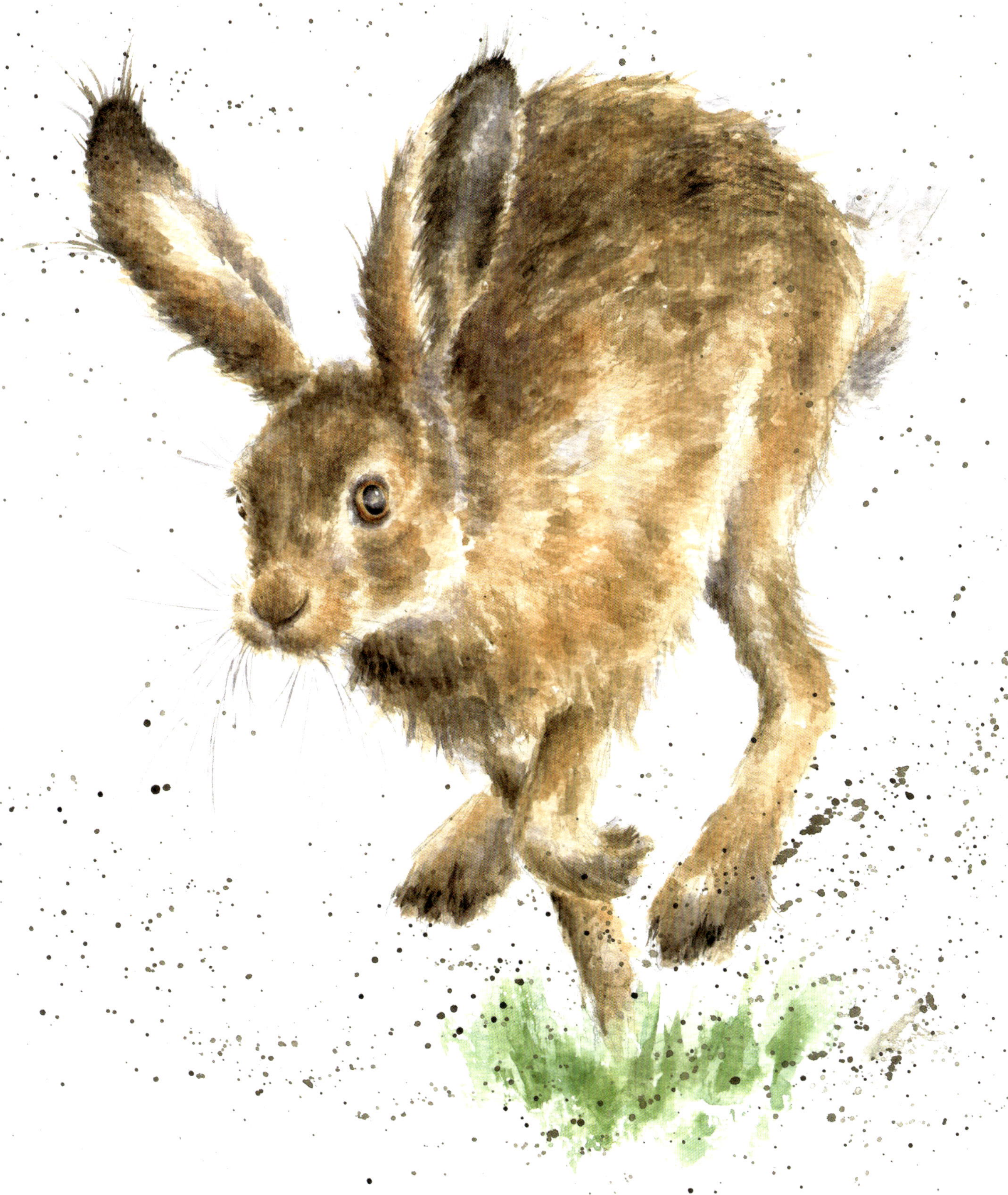

Paint your family in watercolours

Sue Sareen shares her methods for drawing and painting children using watercolour

With this workshop, I will explain the watercolour techniques I use to paint the young people in my family. It's important to practise drawing from real life – this way you'll soon find your own way of translating from three dimensions to two.

Children will sit still for a while when watching TV, or playing on their computers, for example, and this will give you the chance to make a fairly detailed sketch. But it's worth remembering that even unfinished drawings will fix knowledge in your mind, and also enable you to use photos more successfully.

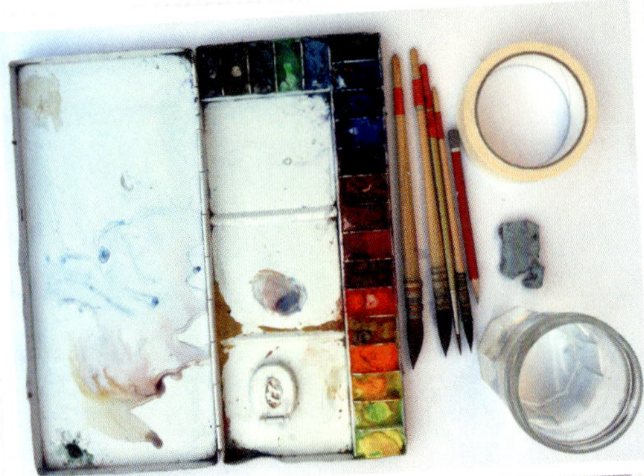

Materials

Sue uses Bockingford watercolour paper, 300g, NOT surface. She prefers this surface, as it's "not too smooth and not too rough". Bockingford is also more heavy than other papers, making it easier to sponge, and if necessary, remove paint. She uses squirrel-hair mop brushes in sizes 2, 8 and 11. These brushes hold a lot of water, enabling her to paint more freely, but at the same time "they keep terrific points". She also has a small synthetic brush, which can be useful when she needs drier, more precise marks.

Follow these steps...

1 ◀ Get the proportions

Note how the proportions of children differ from adults. An adult's body is roughly seven and a half times the length of its head, while a baby's body is roughly four times its head length. Note how the eyes of an adult are roughly situated halfway between the top of the head and the chin, and a child's eyes are lower. The eyes are large and the nose is small in comparison to the overall face.

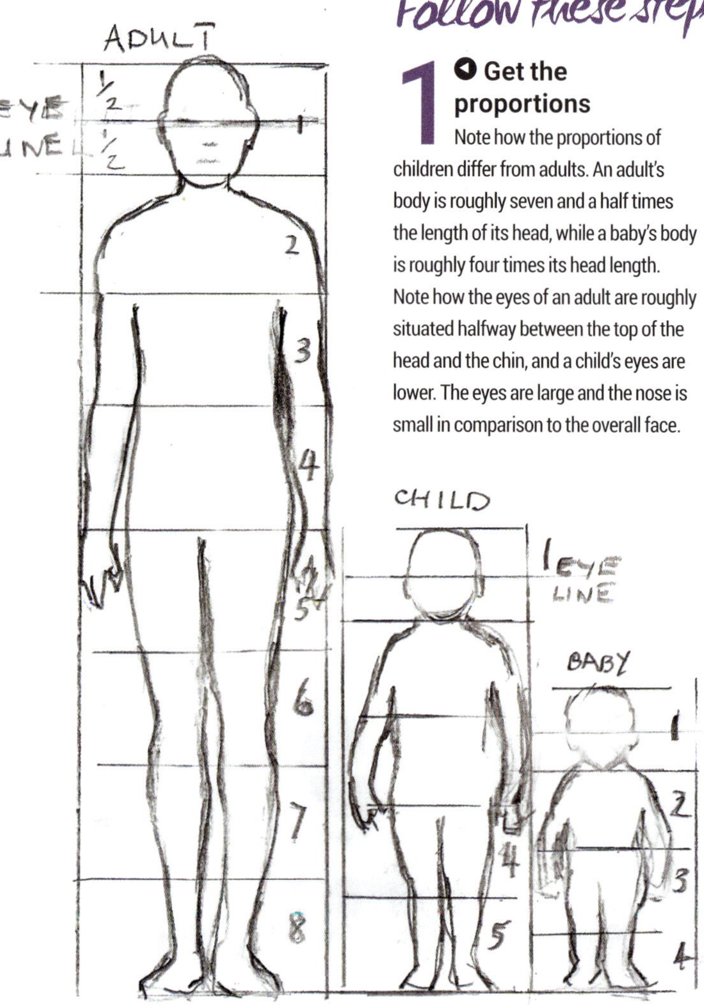

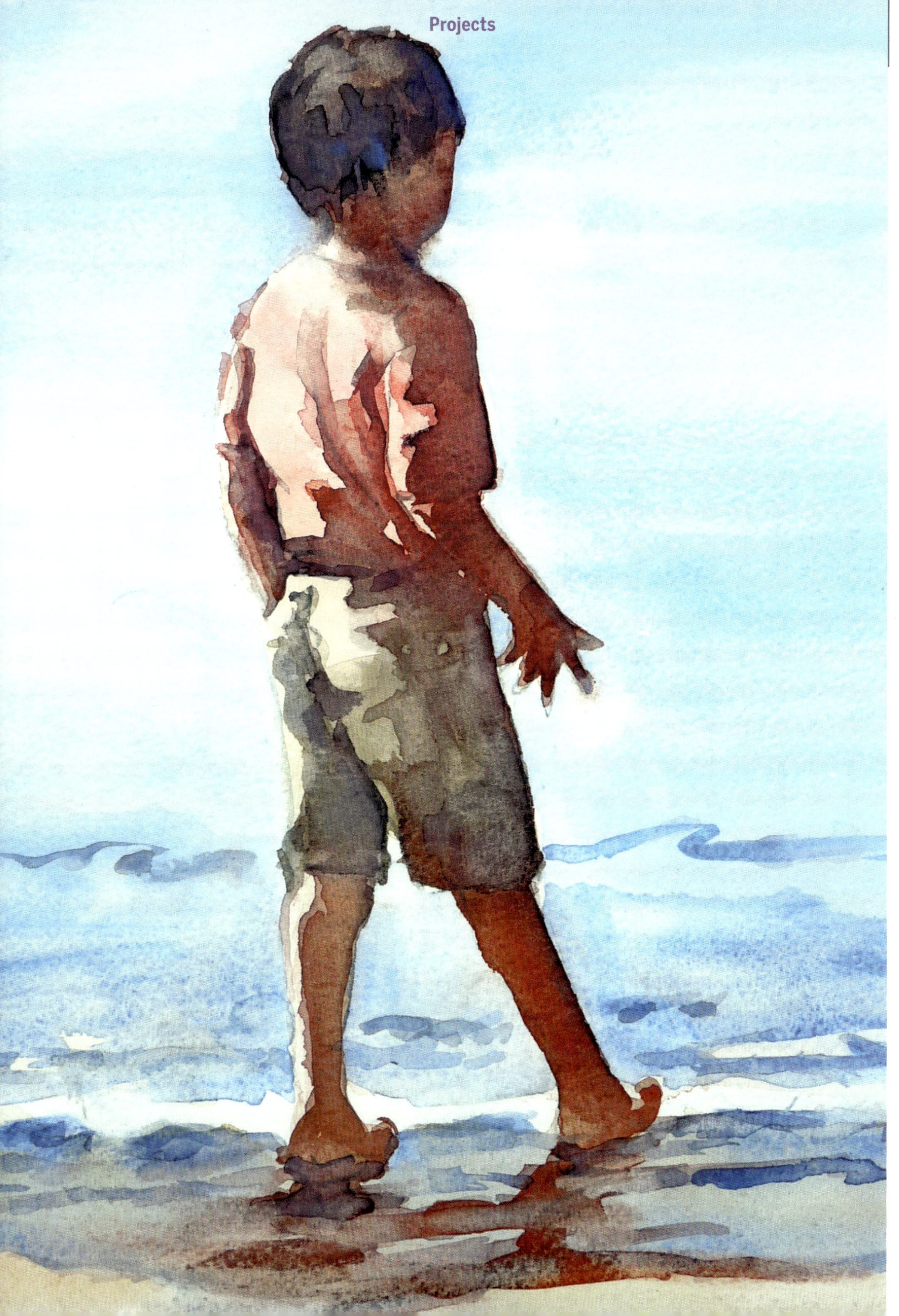

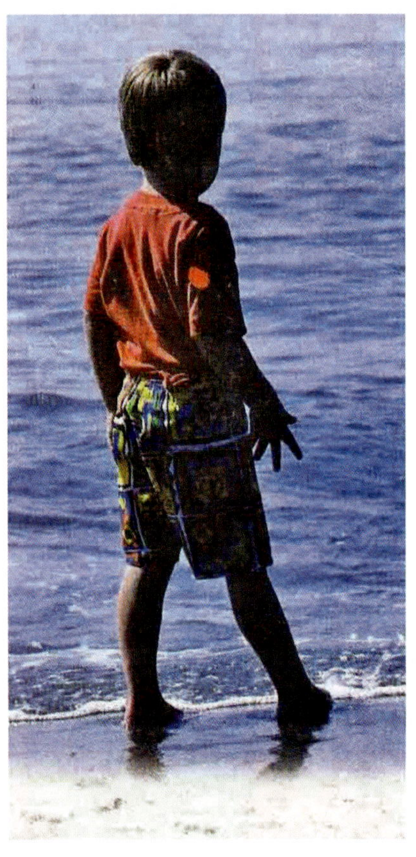

2 ◐ Start the sketch

Working from a photo, I lightly draw the figure onto the watercolour paper in pencil. I make sure I get the angle of the boy's legs, as well as his playfully splayed fingers. I leave extra space at the bottom of the paper to allow for the sea and sand, and notice how light comes from the left to create dark tones on the right of the figure. I will paint the picture working from light to dark, one layer at a time.

3 ▶ Paint in the tone

In this first tonal study, I aim to understand how the light affects the figure, creating highlights and dark tones. I use indigo for this – a clear, transparent inky blue. This is initially painted mainly as one layer, keeping the white of the paper to represent the lightest tones. Once this layer is dry, I add in darker tones. If necessary, I can add in even darker tones to create a third layer. You may need to increase the thickness of the paint to obtain a greater depth of tone for this.

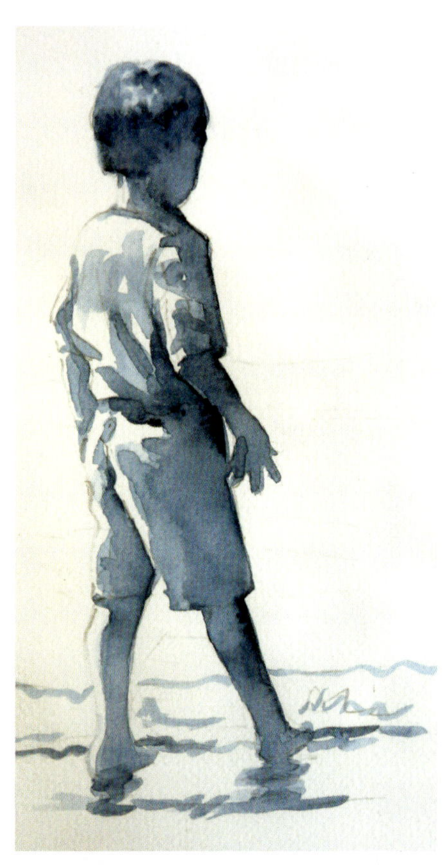

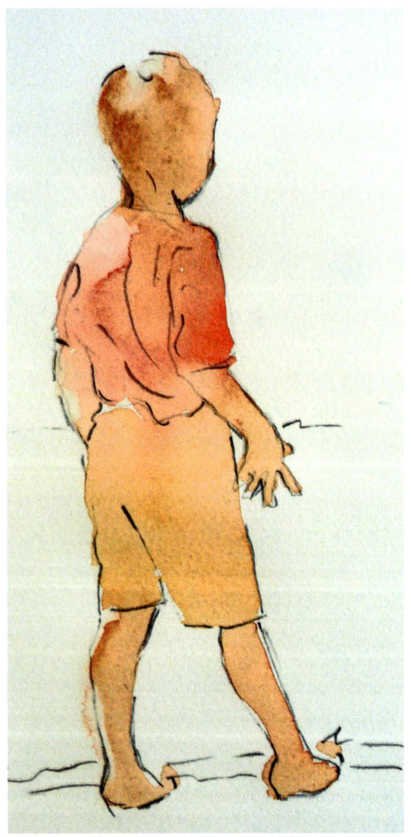

4 ◐ Adding in colour

With a pencil, I redraw the figure. Next, using a large brush filled with watery paint, I paint very light colours over it, changing the colours as I go. At this stage, I don't worry if the colours run into each other a little.

5 ◐ Blot to control

If you want to lighten any colours further, you can control the paint by blotting it with tissue. This both lightens, softens and dries the paper. Here, I'm keeping the colours light, so I can then paint in darker tones over the top of them.

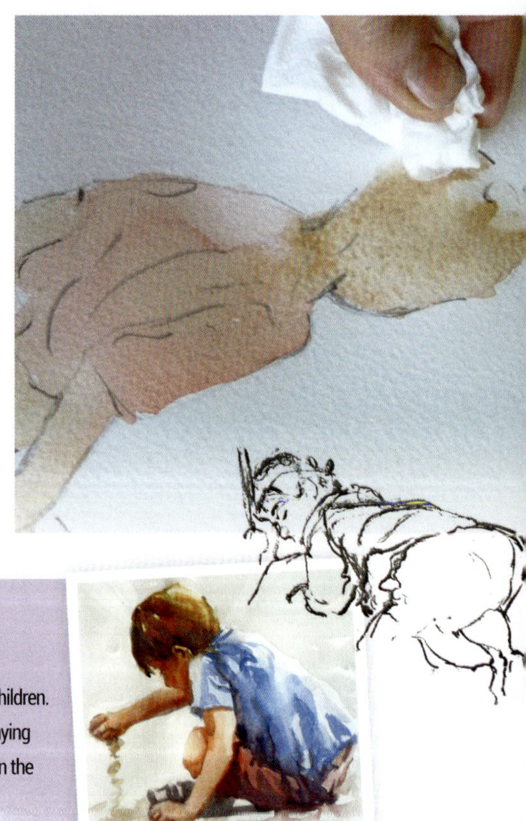

Sitting still lifes

Get into the habit of observing and sketching children. They sit still for longer while watching TV or playing quietly. Observe how they move when playing in the park, on the beach or wherever.

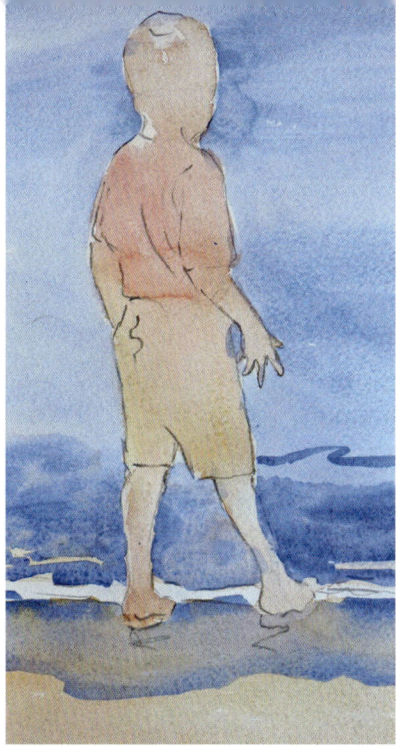

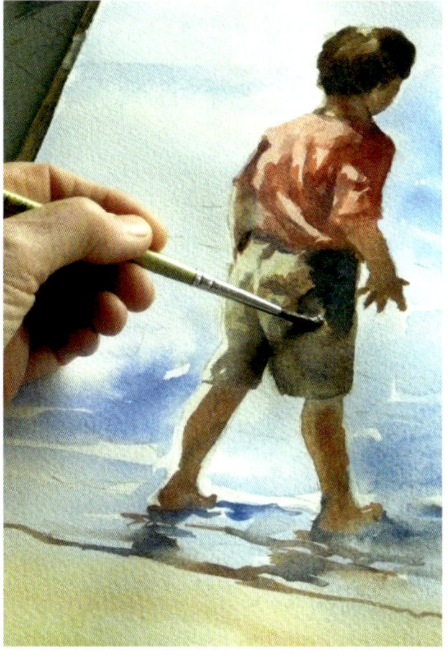

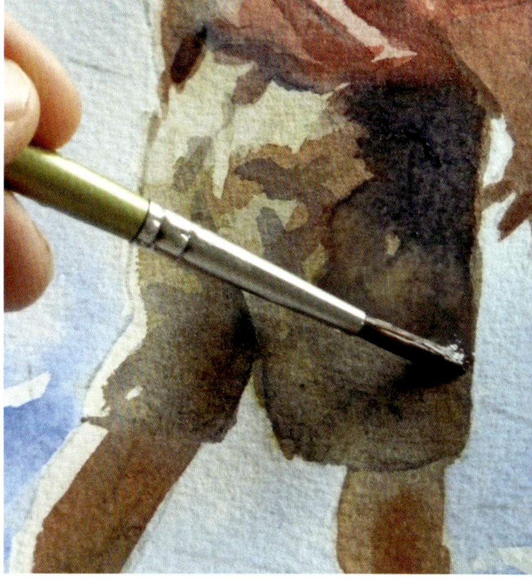

6 ⬟ Paint the sand and sea

I now add sand into the scene, using Yellow Ochre mixed with a little Burnt Sienna. I add water to dilute and lighten the paint – this will make it fade out as it recedes into the sea. When this part is dry, using a large brush, I paint light tones of Cobalt Blue around and behind the figure. Some of the paper is left unpainted to represent foam in the water. I wash blue over some of the foreground sand.

7 ⬟ Add darker tones

Now that the paper is dry, I paint in the darker tones and shadows on the figure. I use a mixture of the original colour with another to make it darker, making the paint slightly thicker than the first layer. I also add in the tones and colour in the water, aiming to keep the background simple.

8 ⬟ Add the darkest tones

I now add even darker tones where necessary, again making the paint slightly thicker. Increased contrast can really liven up a picture, making it more dramatic.

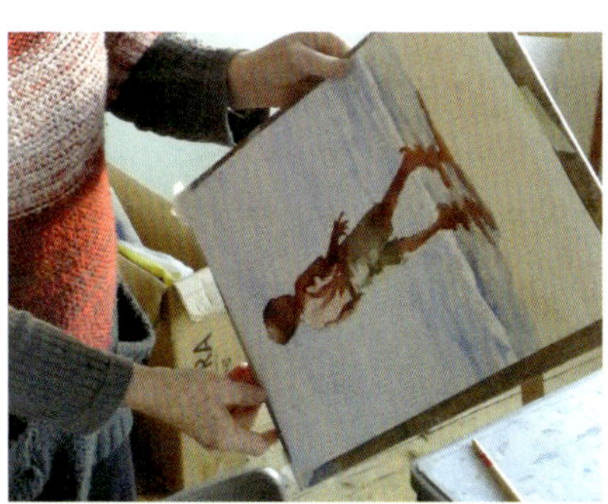

9 ⬟ Allow the colours to run

Occasionally, it's useful to tip the board and painting while the paint is wet. This allows the colours to run into one another and mix a little on the paper.

10 ▶ Move on

Having mastered one figure in watercolour, it's now possible to add an additional figure or two (or maybe a dog), and further develop the waves and beach. Painting the sea is another challenge, and would be another exercise in its own right!

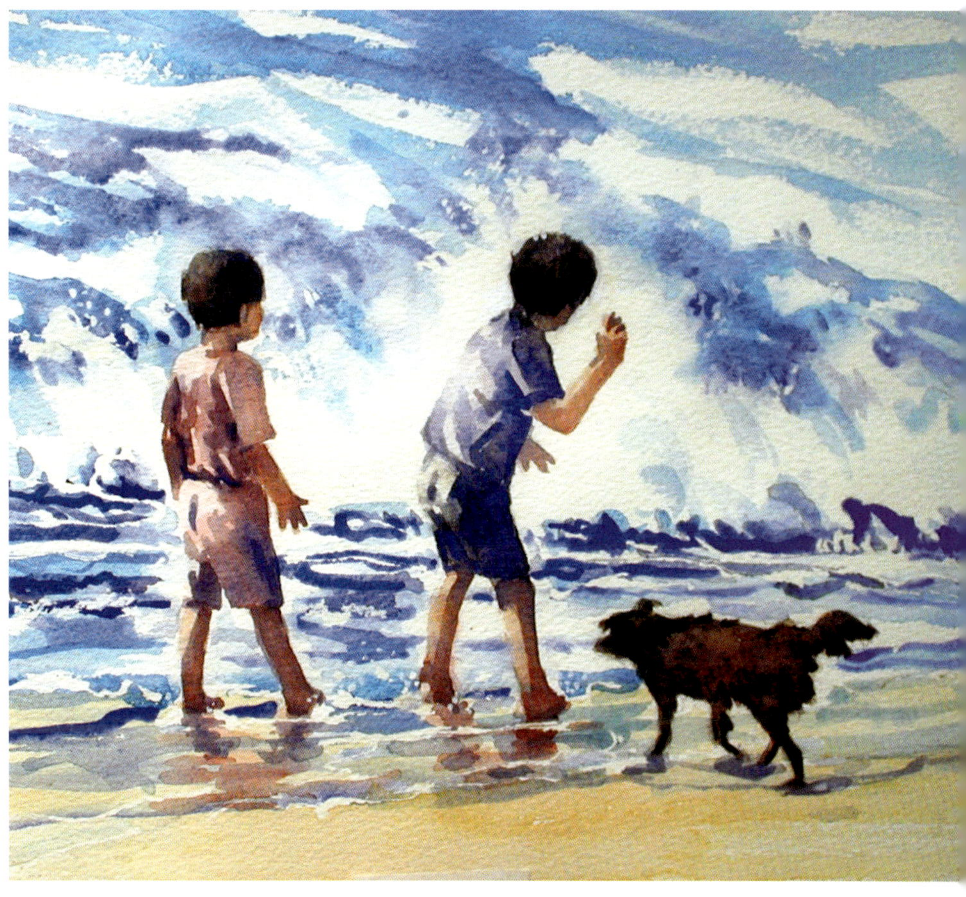

Emotive portraits in watercolour

Find out how to paint expressive portraits with **Stephie Butler**, using shape and colour to convey emotion

In this guide you will learn how to paint portraits in watercolour – full of colour, with an impressionistic feel that really makes your work stand out. The focus of this tutorial is the face, showing you how to portray feelings and emotions in your subject. Pay particular attention to the eyes, because they capture emotion, holding the story behind them.

Practising this technique will teach you how to paint instinctively. You can become comfortable painting with expressive colours that enhance the subject. Learn how to use your reference photo as a guide, rather than copying it slavishly. After this tutorial you may even go on to paint from black-and-white reference photos, allowing you to be braver and more confident with exploring colour.

Once you have mastered these skills you will be able to bring life to your portrait using shapes of colour to bring form. I'll show you that painting bigger portraits using bigger brushes, creates the freedom to paint without being confined. One of the most important factors in painting a portrait that shows an emotion is in choosing the right reference photo. Step one: learn the techniques. Step two: find a photo that engages you and makes you want to reach for your paints. Step three: Practise what you have learnt in this tutorial.

Mastering these techniques will enable you to go on to paint portraits of people who interest you, inspire you and engage you.

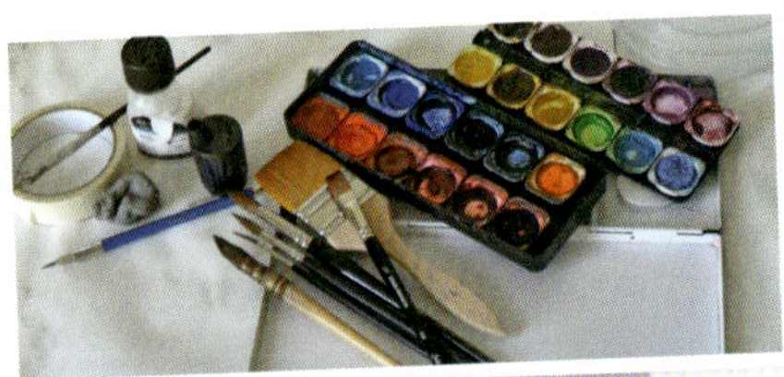

Materials

- 1/2 sheet Arches 140lb paper, NOT (CP)
- Winsor & Newton colourless masking fluid
- Mixing palette
- Winsor & Newton Artist quality paints; Aureolin / Permanent Rose / Cerulean Blue / Cobalt Blue / French Ultramarine / Cadmium Red
- Brush; Large Mop / Sable Round Size 14 / Pointed Round Size 8 / Rigger Size 3 / Large & small flat

Follow these steps...

1 ▸ Save the light

Draw the face, leaving plenty of space around it to allow for freedom of movement when painting, along with the added choice to crop when finished. Only add minimal suggestion lines for the direction of the hair. It's important to save the highlights in the eyes using masking fluid. This will enhance the focal point, engaging the viewer and telling the story. The main highlight should start just inside the pupil, carrying through the iris to the eyeball. Be sure that this is dry before adding any water or paint.

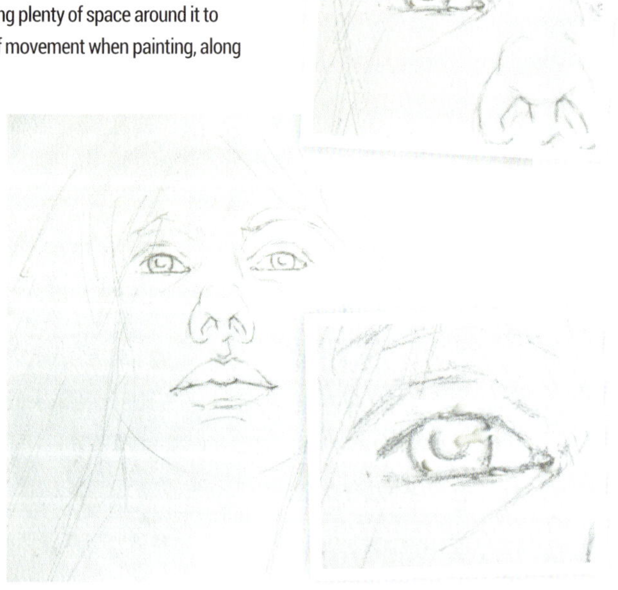

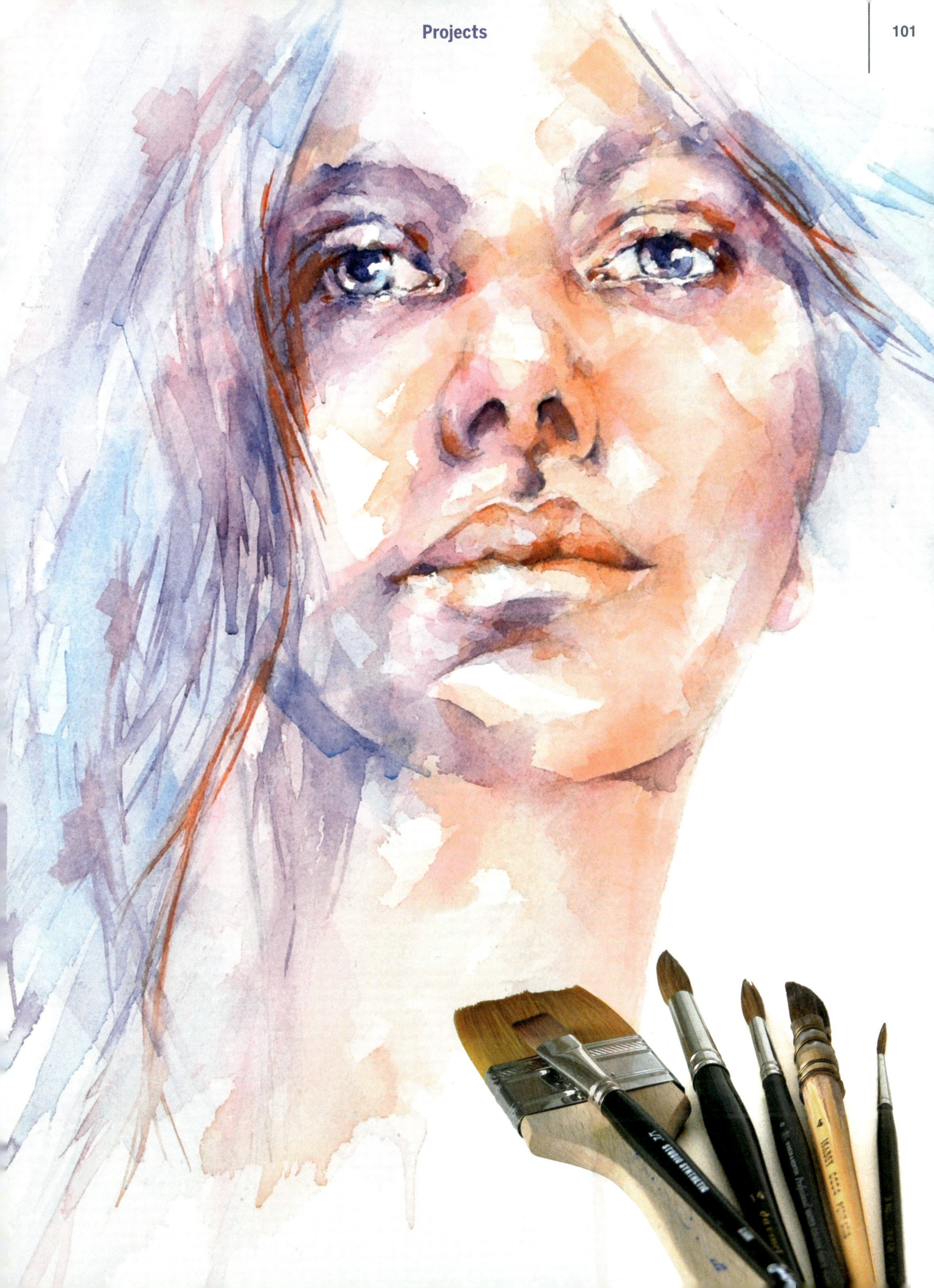

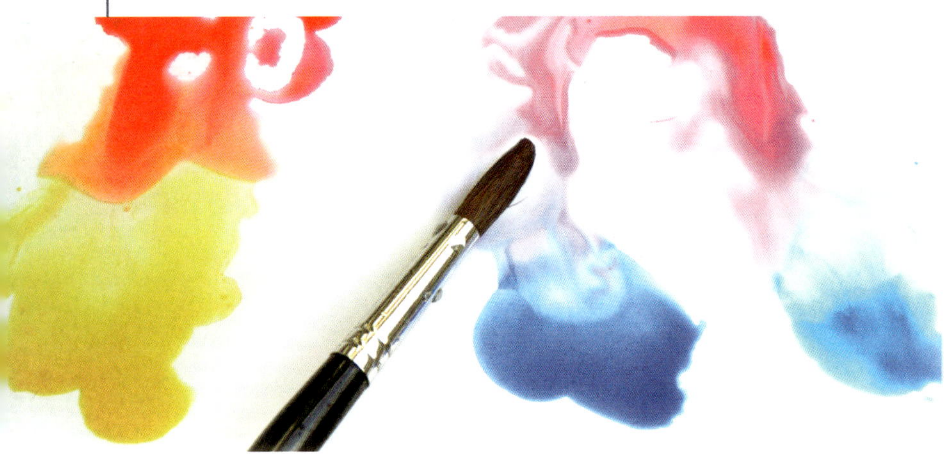

2 ⬆ Basic colour mix

At one end of the palette put out mixes of Aureolin and Permanent Rose. This will form your flesh tones, keeping these at one end of the palette away from the blues. At the other end mix some Cerulean, Cobalt plus another mix of Permanent Rose. Using a wet brush gently bring the colours together making sure you also leave some colour pure. To keep your colours bright and transparent, never introduce a third colour when wet – this would form a neutral grey. Keep two pots of water, one for the reds and one for the blues.

3 ▶ Limit your palette

Limit your palette of colours and learn how to mix them. Try it and see how many shades you can make from just two colours. Working this way will also help the colours unite with each other in your subject and keep a freshness to your work.

4 ▶ Paint it with water

Use a squirrel mop for this stage as it holds lots of water and allows you to use the point when needed. Treat this part as though you were sketching. Run the wet brush around concentrating mostly in the mid and dark-tone areas. Make sure you connect all the features as you go. Keep your subject and background as one and carry this on throughout. Move your brush more freely and abstractly from the face to the hair. This is a foundation for you to build on so resist the urge to paint with detail.

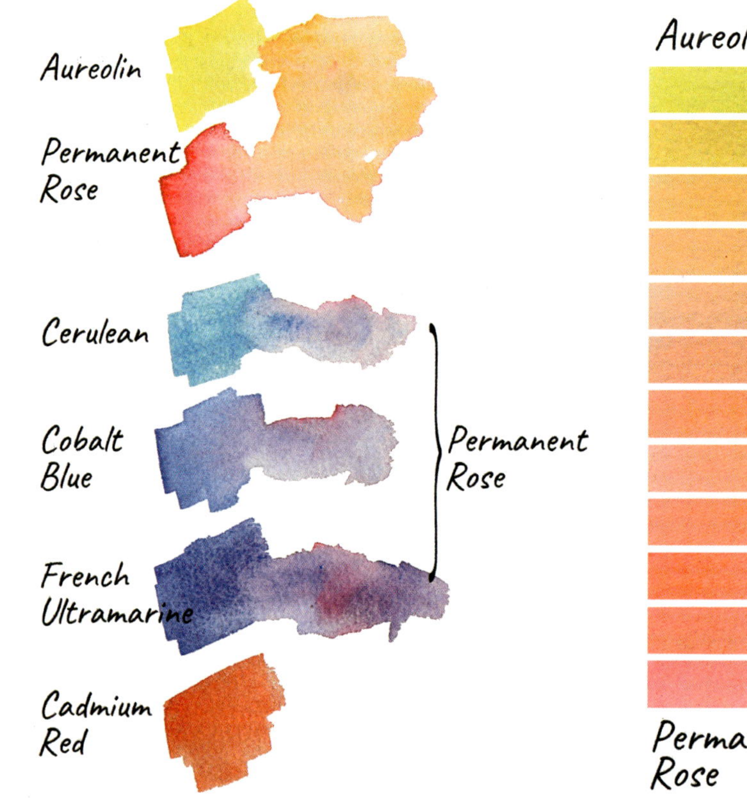

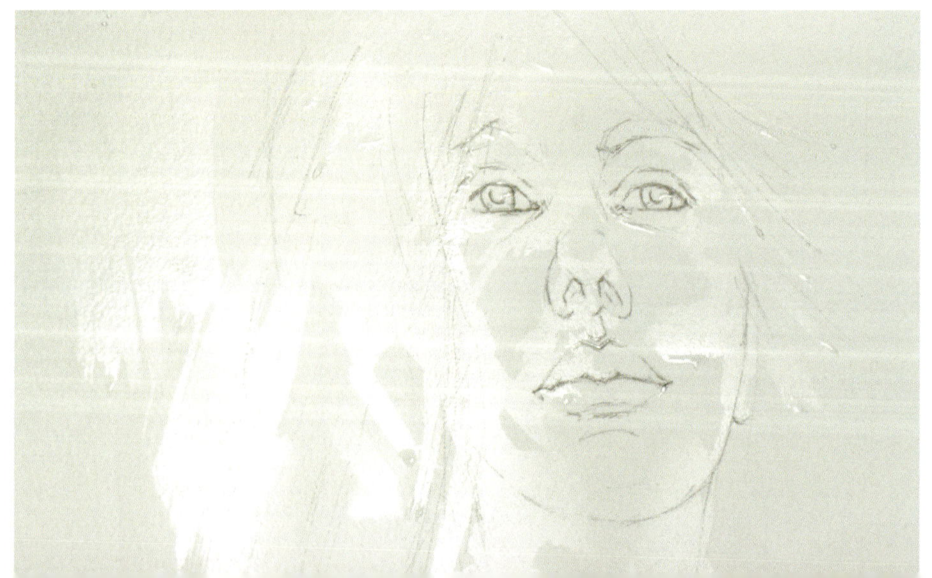

5 ◀ The first wash

Begin dropping in the flesh tone colour on the right and middle of the face. Vary the mix as you go to create more interest. Add more Rose towards the hair and shadow areas. You can now start to bring in the blues, as the Rose creates a barrier, stopping the yellow (the third colour) from mixing with the other two colours. Use Cerulean on top of the hair left to catch the light and the Cobalt to the right, letting the colours mix on the paper. Watch for hard edges forming, soften some, but not all of these edges.

6 ◀ Windows to the soul

The eyes are the soul of the subject and are the focal point of your portrait. They will be painted using many layers, using slightly different mixes each time. With a mix of Ultramarine and Rose and a pointed round, start by adding some darks to the pupil. Soften this and anchor it to the top lid. Placing some darks at this stage will help you see where to change your tones around the rest of the painting.

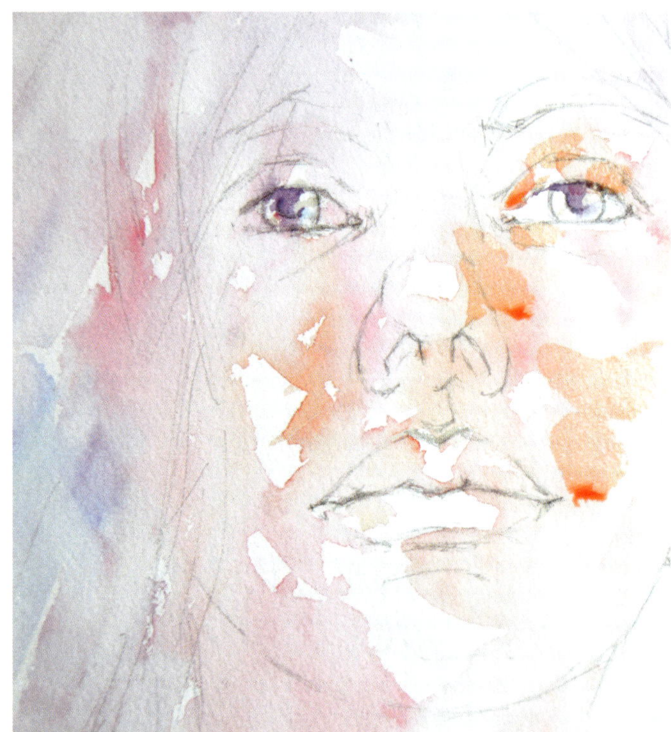

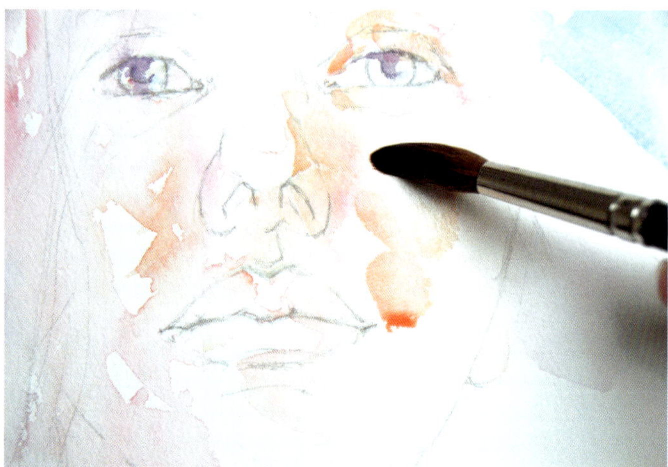

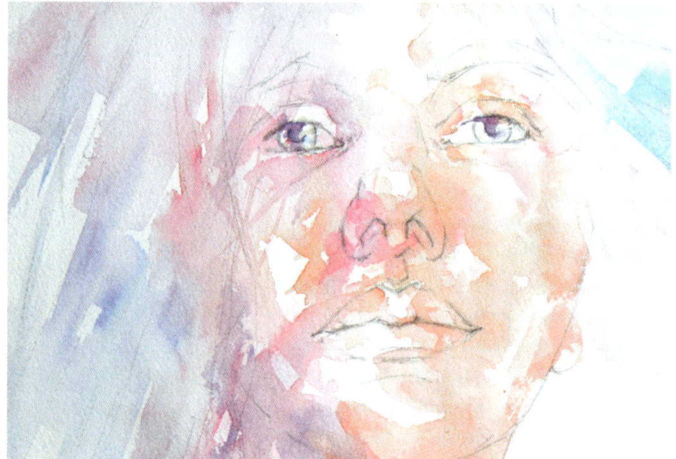

7 ▶ Shapes of colour

The painting is built with shape and colour. Keep changing the shapes, size and colour. After the first wash is dry, start by placing more flesh tones. With a large round wet brush, move between the colours touching the edges, allowing them to soften and pick up some pigment. It is important that when you soften an edge, you carry the remaining pigment into another shape. Do this across the face and hair changing colour as you go.

8 ▶ Build the shapes

Go back to the pupil each time you add more layers, pushing your tone deeper and keeping you engaged with your subject. Strengthen the pupil with a blue mix, then soften out to the side of the eye and down into the hair. As you go into the hair think about the shapes you are forming, using your reference photo continuously as a guide, but don't try to copy it exactly. Use abstract shapes to create some dynamic areas of shadow and light in the hair.

Make time to practise

Practising techniques enables you to play and experiment. Becoming familiar with picking the right colour, a brush and how to control it, how much water to add, all leaves you more relaxed with a sense of freedom. Allowing you time to engage more with your subject, focussing on the emotions, concentrating on your interpretation of it.

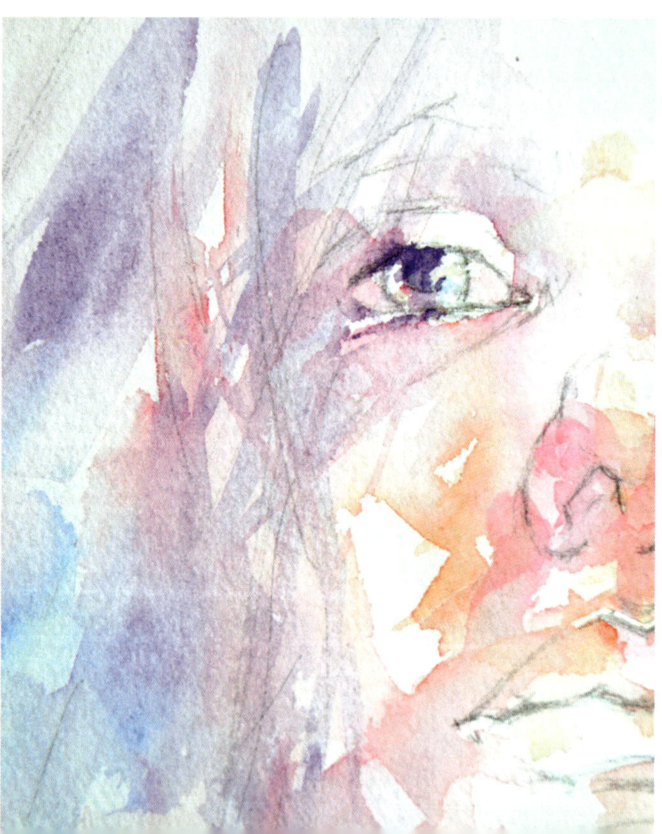

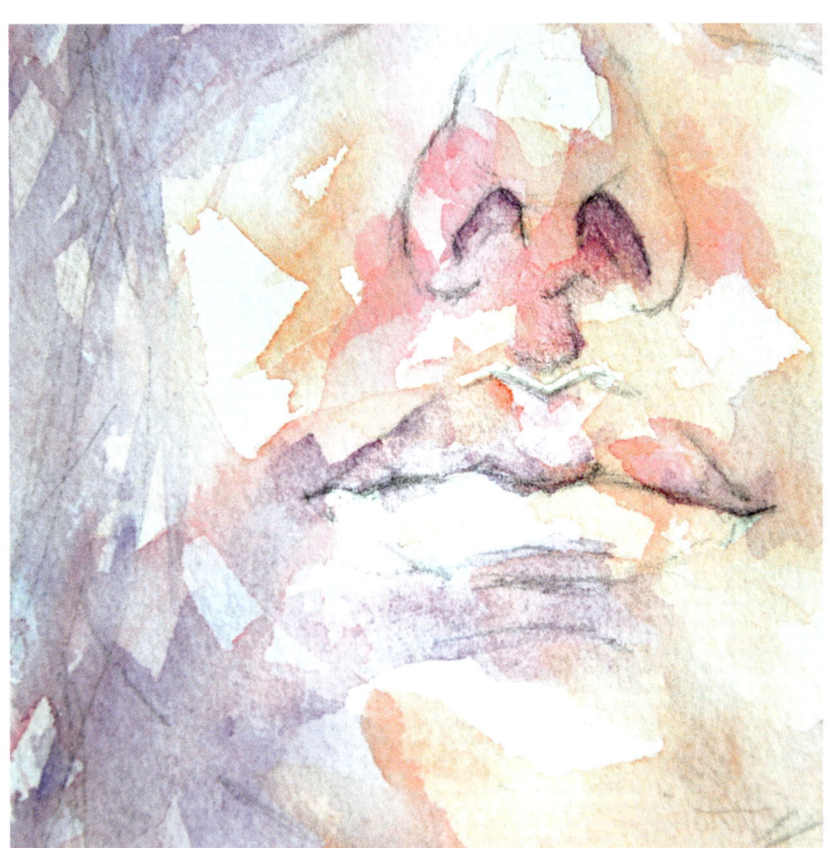

Know your subject

Take time to learn about your subject, doing sketches of features and the placement of them. Learning the planes of these will benefit your painting greatly, as you will know instinctively where to add tone and colour.

9 ◐ Create form

This stage of the painting becomes more detailed to build up the shapes of the eyes, nose and mouth. Darken the nostril area taking it down under the bottom lip, around the chin and over to the left, into the hair. Joining these areas of the face creates a unity in the portrait and connects the features. This is a warm area so I started with Permanent Rose, gradually adding more Cobalt to it for variation as I went across towards the hair.

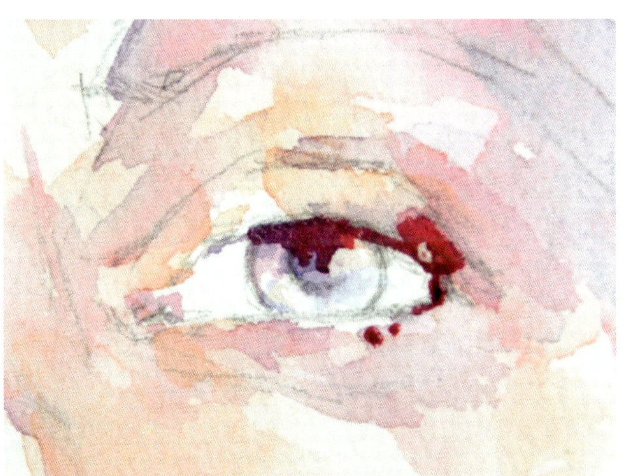

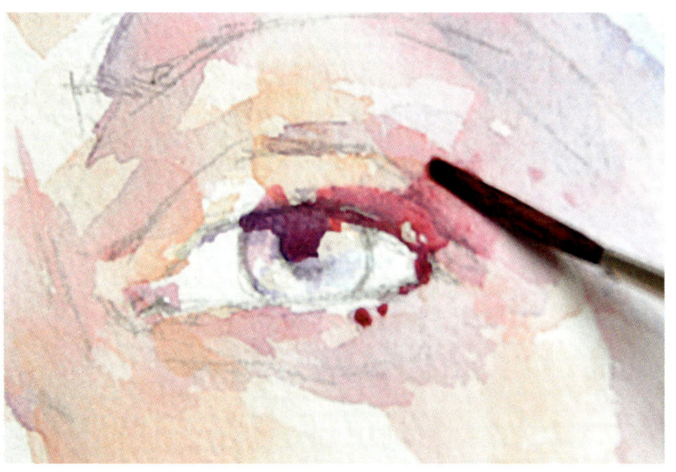

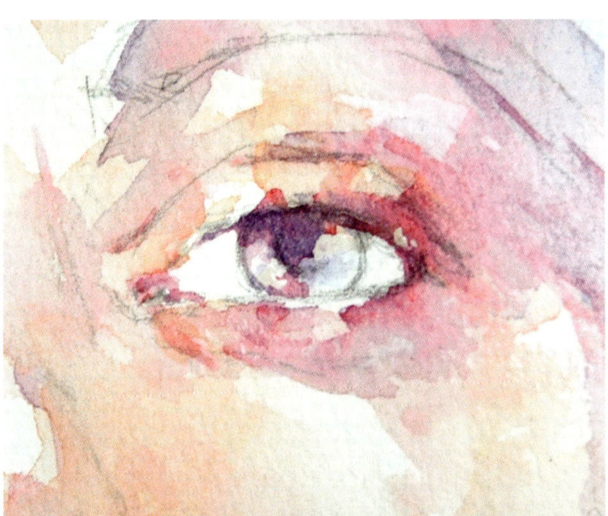

10 ◐ Add drama to the eyes

Once again, add colour to the pupil area, this time with more Permanent Rose. With a wet rigger, using the side of the brush, pick up the pigment taking it into other areas around the eye and out to form some of the hair. Using smaller brushes will help keep your shapes smaller where needed. The level of detail at this stage of the painting puts the expression into the eyes. While the area is still damp, drop in a touch more pigment to deepen the tone.

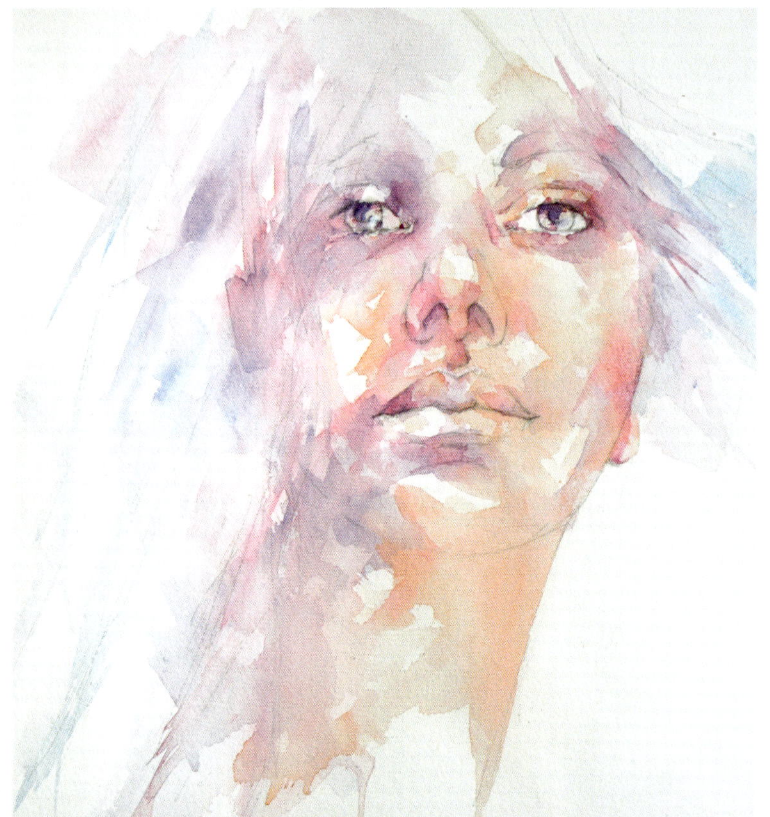

11 ◐ Forming the features

Carry on throughout the face, building on the mid-tones to form the features. Where there are areas of light retain this by creating fewer layers. You can see on the upper lip that I've added many small shapes, avoid painting this in one go. This helps to provide interest as you build layers to form the shape of the lips. Pay attention to the darker areas in shadow and away from the light. These should have more layers than the lighter areas.

12 ◑ Bringing in detail

Once you have a foundation of shapes you can start to add more detail. Go back to the eye, this time with the darker blue mix, start with the pupil, bring it out to form more of the upper lid and to represent eyelashes. Soften up to form the outer areas of the lid and crease, and over to start building the hair. Keep it soft at this stage, remembering you can always add more later.

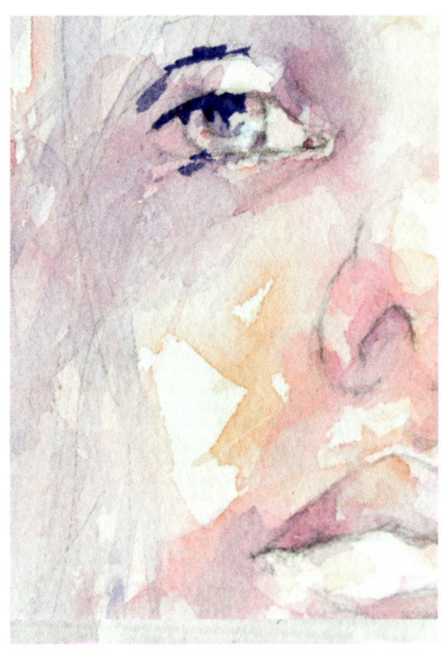

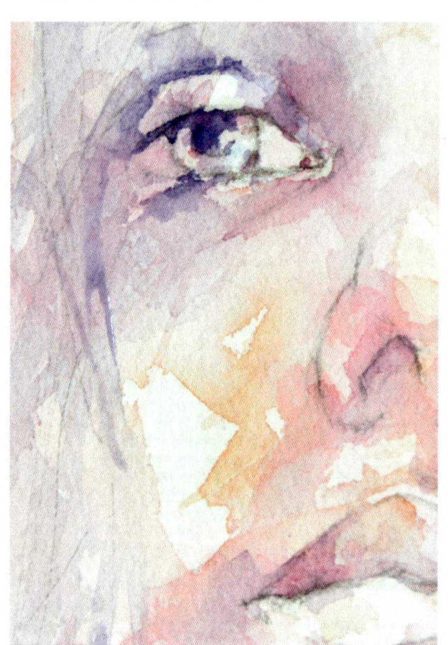

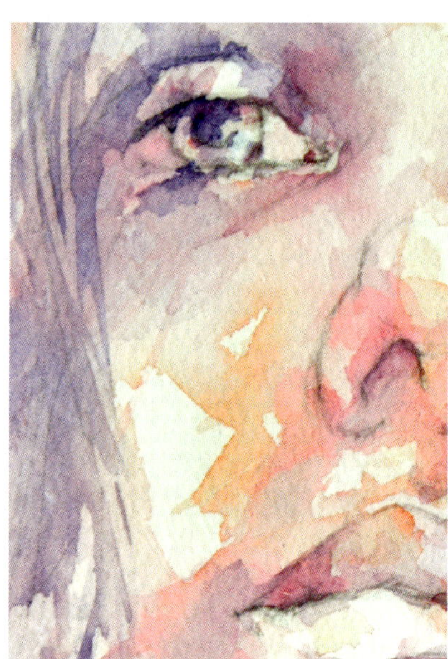

13 ▶ Positive and negative

While adding further shapes around the face, start to form the edge of the face. This is done by placing a positive shape on the chin directly under the bottom lip, and taking it under the chin (negative) onto the neck, creating a shadow between the side of the face and the hair at the neck line. The lighter, left side of the face will appear to come slightly forward, in contrast. This is a very useful technique that can be used in many places.

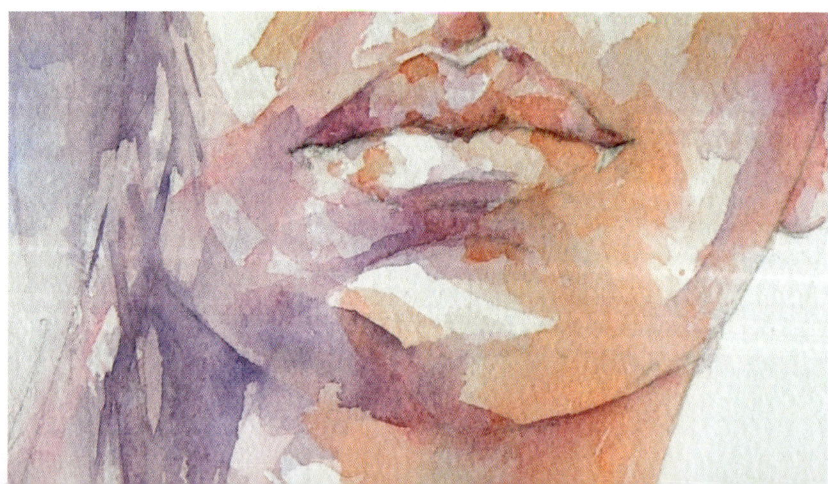

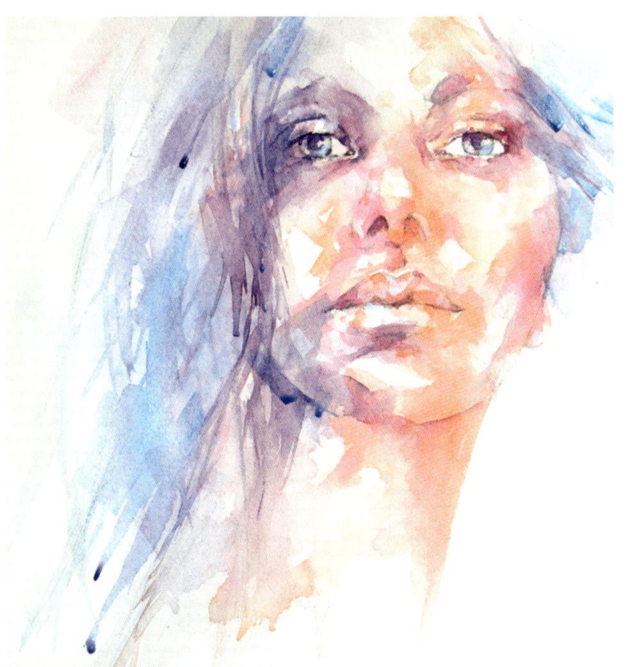

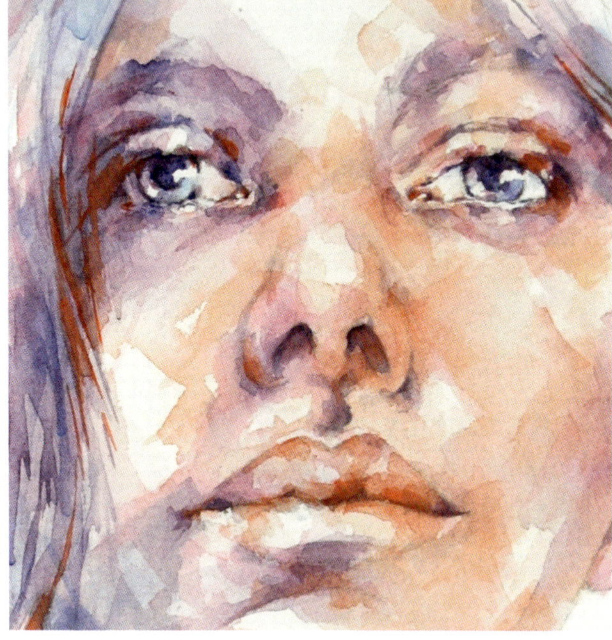

14 ⬢ Abstracting

Use pure blues add random shapes and abstract marks, keeping the lighter blues in the light. This will add more drama and looseness to your subject. This step can be quite daunting at times, but learn to step back form your work to see how all the areas work together.Remember that watercolour becomes much lighter when dry so what may look too dark when still wet will actually be exciting and dramatic once it is dry.

15 ⬢ Accent colour

I call this my go-to colour. I often find nearing the finish, the painting needs a colour to lift it. For me, that colour is red, but this will depend on the emotion you are feeling in your work. Do this slowly, adding a bit at a time. It is very easy to overdo it. I've also used it in very diluted form washes to add warmth to the face. Cadmium Red will be very bright when wet but darkens as it dries.

Your reference

You should instinctively know when you see a photo that you want to paint. Painting portraits is a passion, a feeling, wanting to capture a moment, to explore the story behind the eyes. Use the photo to guide you, don't be a slave to it and stop when the story is told.

"Do this slowly, adding a bit at a time. It is very easy to overdo it"

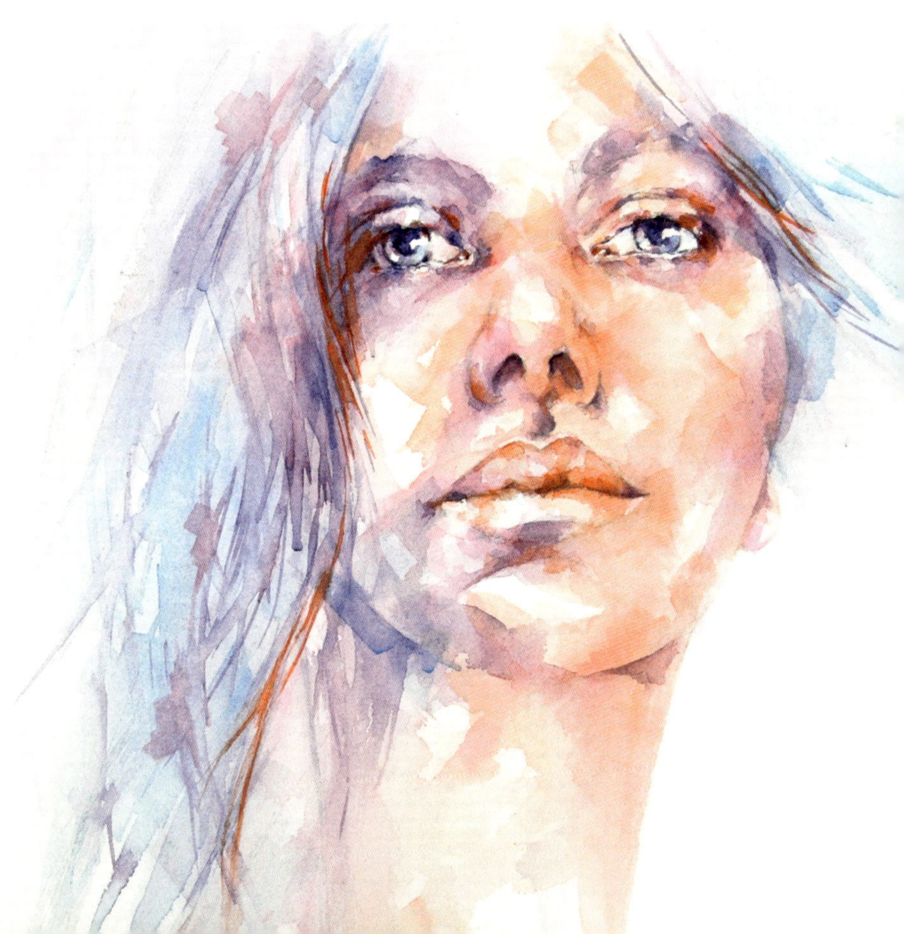

Create a painted scene from an outdoors sketch

Liam O'Farrell takes you through a pencil-and-watercolour workshop, based on a quick watercolour sketch painted on a chilly Hampshire beach

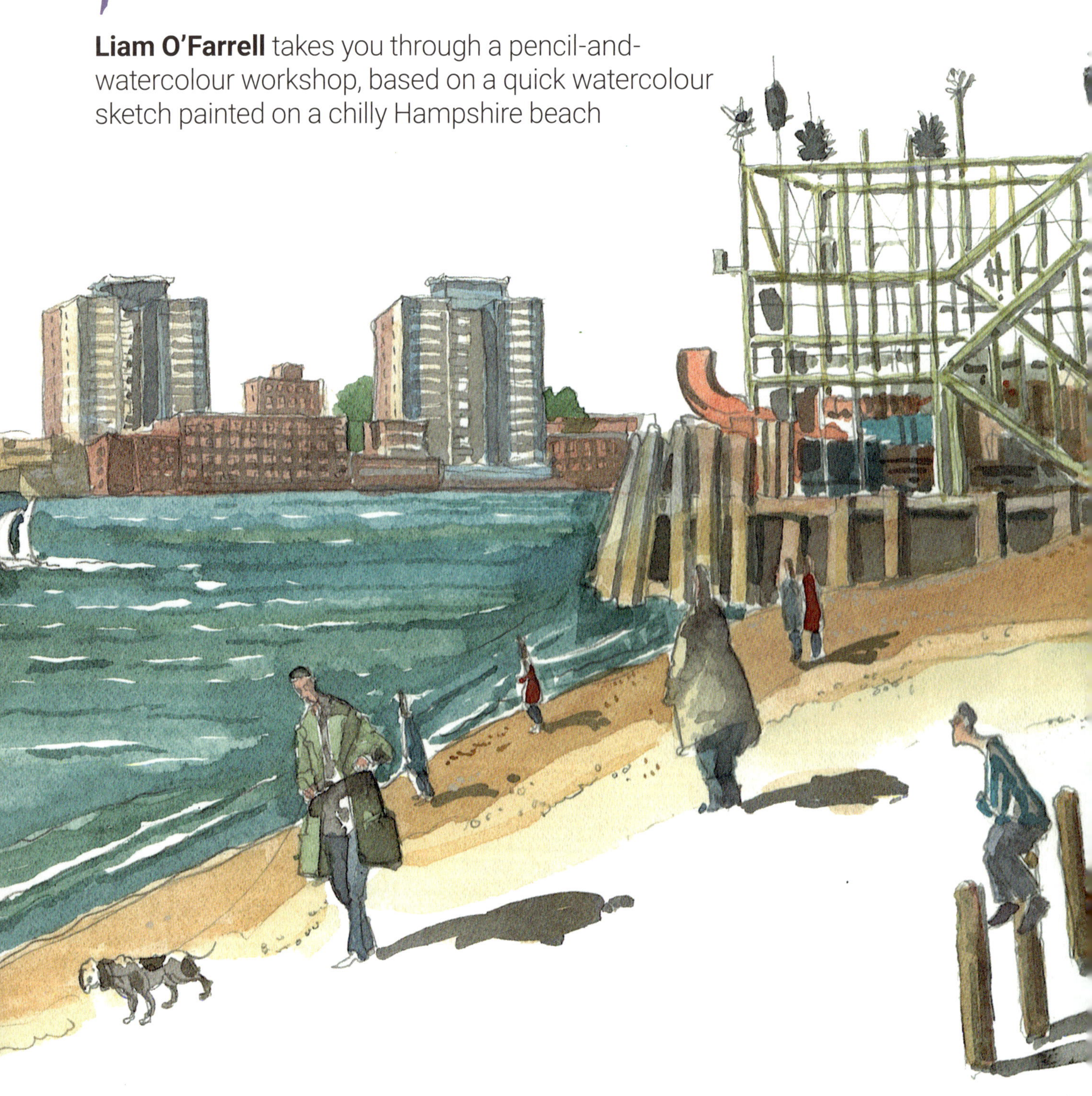

During February, I visited my old home town of Portsmouth. While walking along the beach I came across Clarence Pier. It looked an ideal painting subject to me, because it's in a state of disrepair – a bit of dilapidated glory always stirs me! The pier also holds some fine memories from when I was a child. Added to that, along the beach there were a few locals taking a walk with their bouncing dogs.

People who walk on beaches in winter tend not to be the same people who sunbathe on them in summer. I was enthused, and decided to paint the scene. I would use it a basis for a studio painting. I always travel very light. I pulled out a small watercolour box, a sketchbook, some pencils and brushes.

I sheltered from the wind behind a café, got myself cosy, pulled my hat down and, wearing my fingerless gloves, I began...

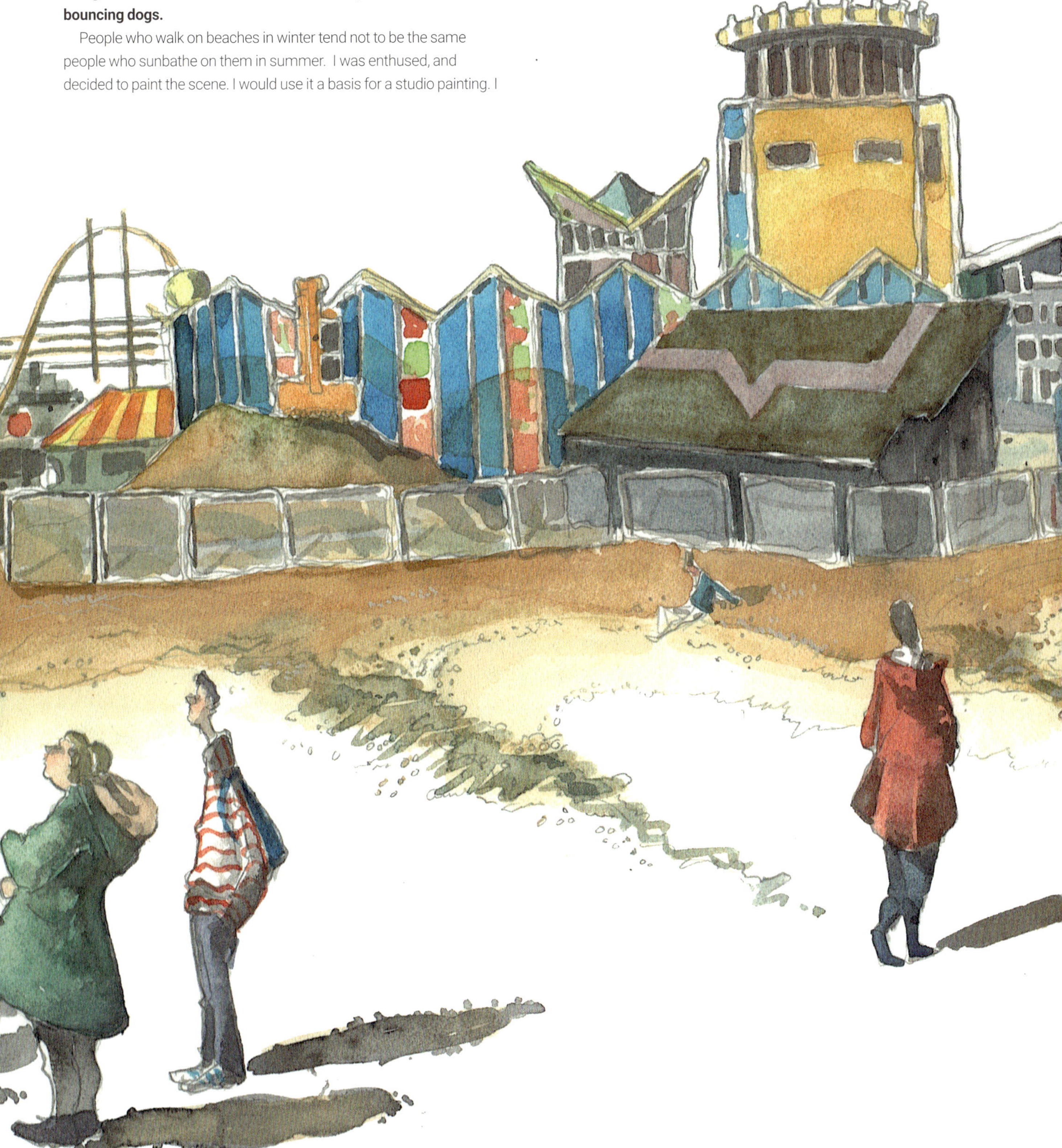

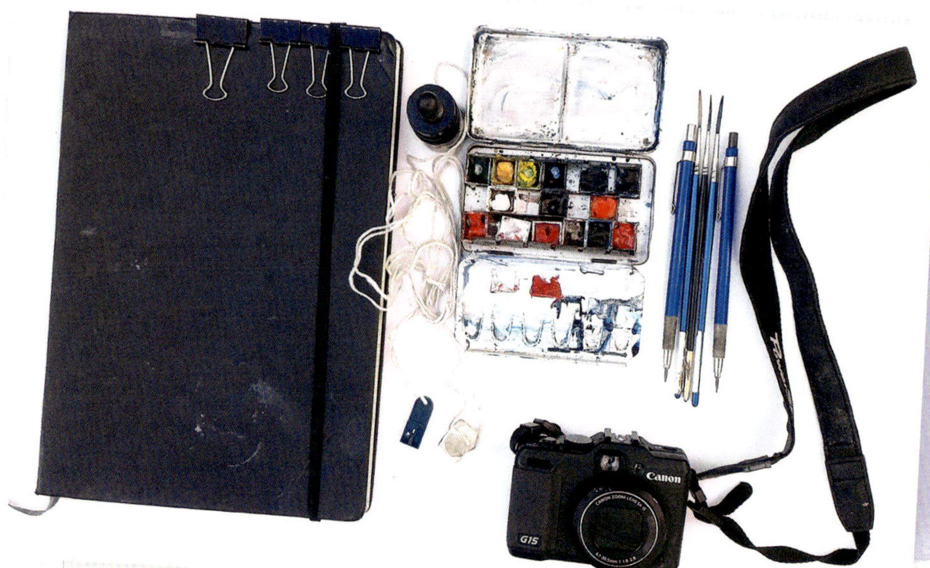

I paint on Fabriano Hot Pressed, 300g paper, because it's very smooth and gives great blooming effects, helping me to deliver a loose feel. As you can see in this photograph, I use a simple watercolour palette with sable brushes in Sizes 6 and 8, as well as no. 1 rigger for those finer details. And I'm never without my trusty HB and 2B pencils, which are perfect for quick sketching when I'm out and about.

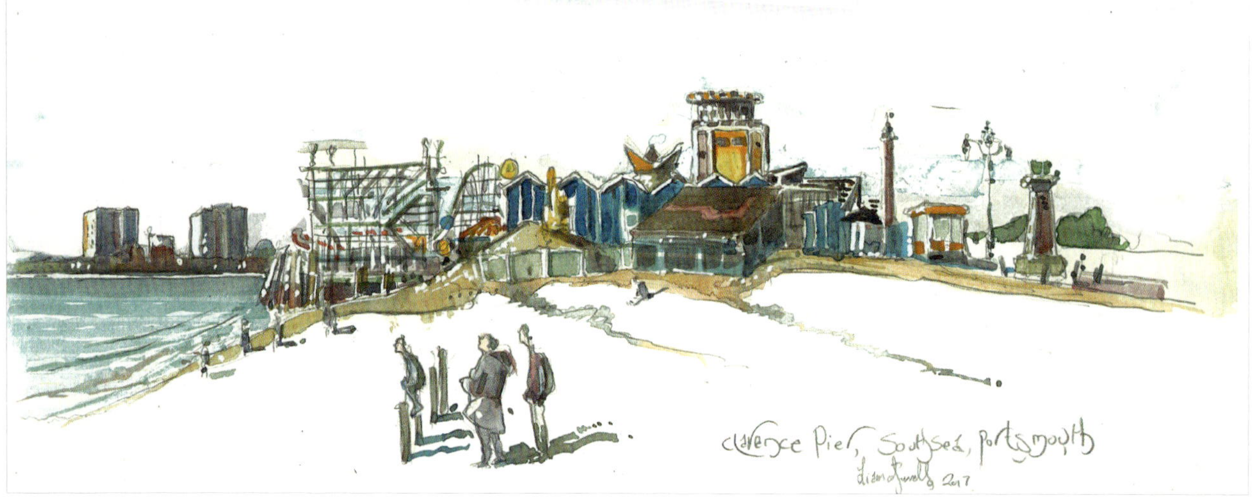

Follow these steps...

1 ⬥ Loosely colour sketch the scene

First I get the loose idea of the whole scene. It's cold so I'm going to have to work fast. The light doesn't hang about for long either. After working for about an hour and a half, I get all the bare bones I need. I also note the local people who are taking a brisk winter's walk.

2 ⬥ Work up characters

In the cosiness of a warm studio I begin by working up some characters I noted on the beach. Here I saw a family of three; the child was playing on some exposed logs poking out of the shingles. His chilly parents watched on, hoping he would get fed up soon. I also enjoy drawing dogs and their owners. While I was working a good few dashed merrily into the freezing water.

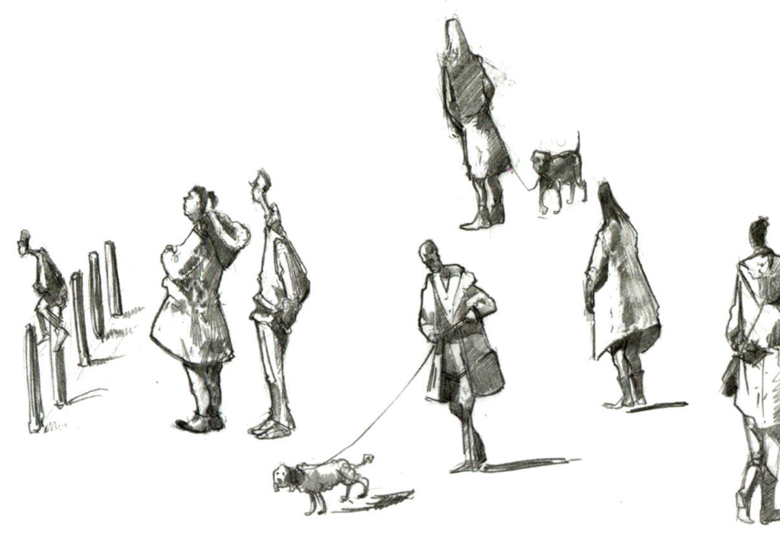

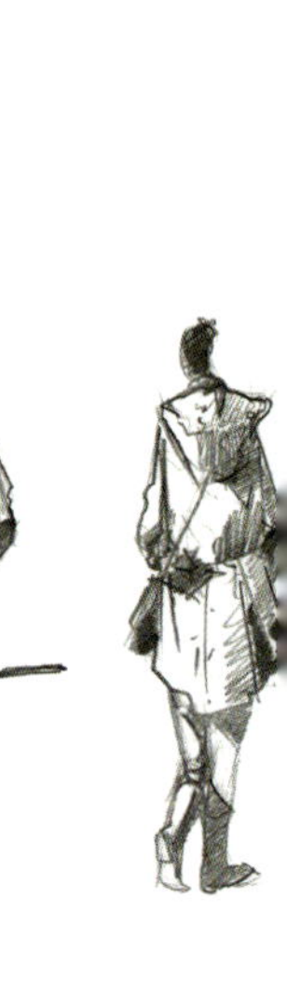

I've spent years dropping erasers and sharpeners, watching them head towards drains or be crushed under cars. The problem is now solved as I hang both around my neck on some string.

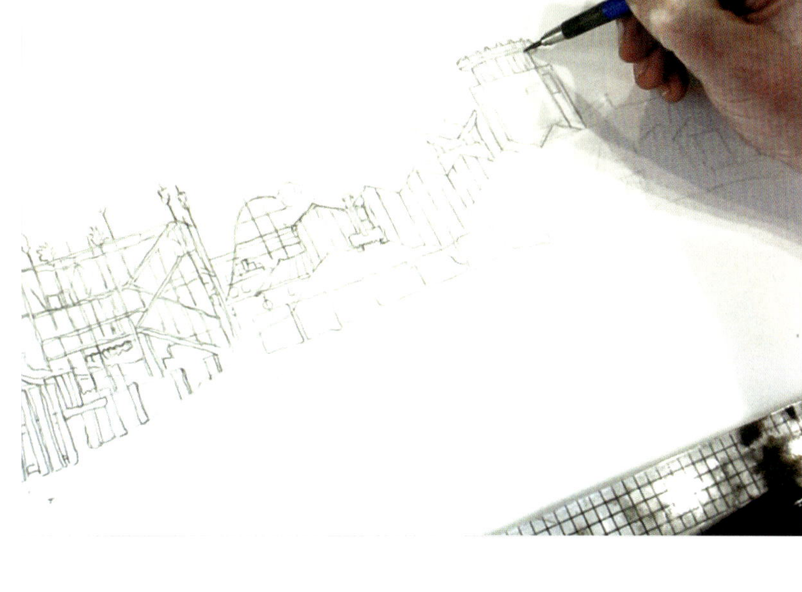

3 ▶ Laying down the pencil work

I'm now going to do the pencil work for the final painting. This is kept loose and I almost never use a ruler. It has to maintain the same spontaneity as the initial sketch. I work from left to right so I don't smudge what I've already done.

4 ▶ Adding people

Using my drawings as reference, I line in the characters. My years spent practising figure drawing has been a long road, but it's well worth it. In my opinion, all architectural art is enhanced by figures to populate it. I really enjoy doing this bit – there are some real characters in Portsmouth!

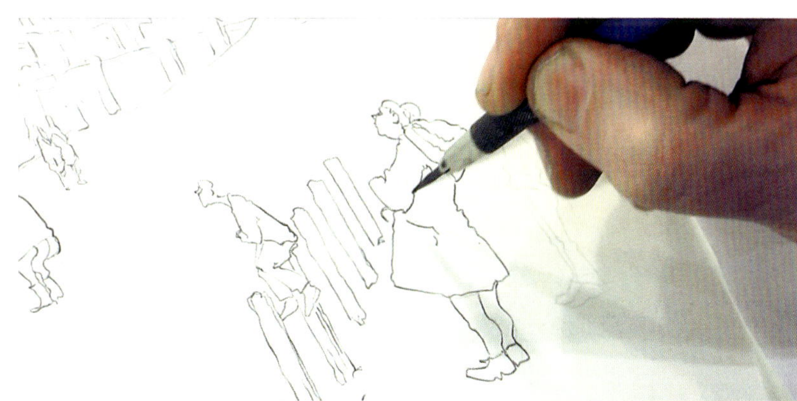

5 ▼ Adding tone to the architecture

I ink in the tonal values with Indian ink or dark watercolours. This is a good way of avoiding a weak and flat finish to the final piece. It breaks the picture down into more stages, but it's worth it in the end. opinion, all architectural art is enhanced by figures to populate it. I really enjoy doing this bit – there are some real characters in Portsmouth!

My subjects are generally architecture that has been amended, bodged and changed over the years to suit the current times. They're often a bit dilapidated.

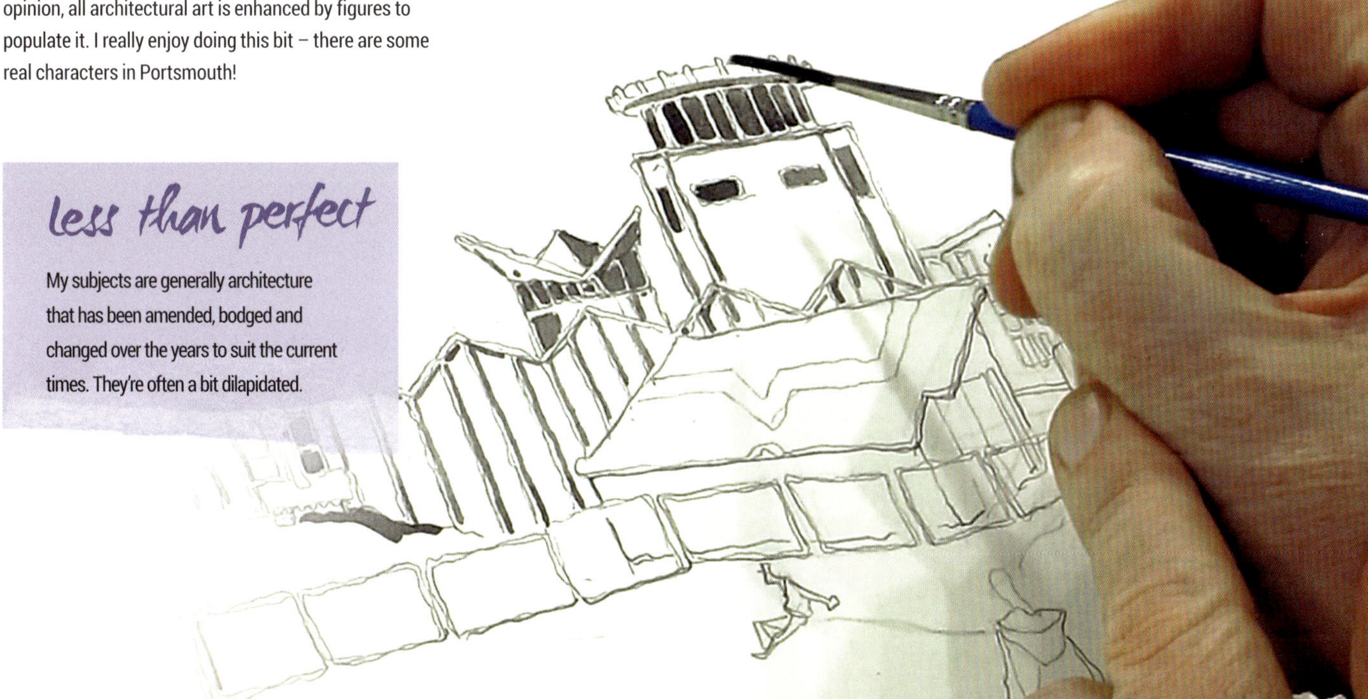

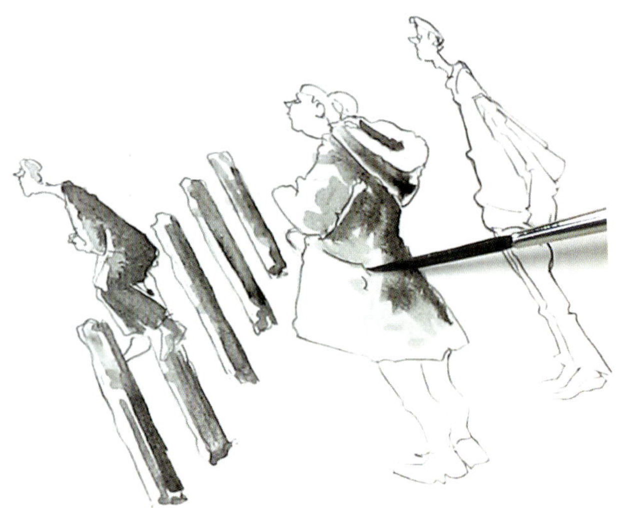

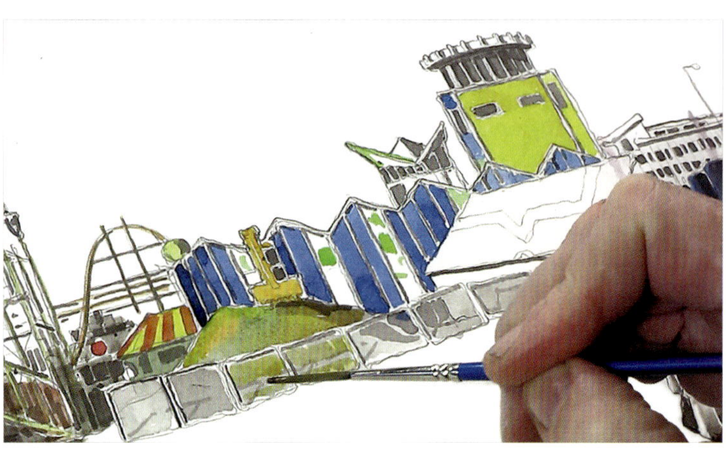

6 ⬖ Adding tone to characters

Putting tonal values on characters is slightly different. I need to keep in mind that I'm painting fabric and humans! I keep the brush moving about in little flicks to give the feeling of cloth, while all the time dabbing extra water and ink here and there. The looser you are, the more life they have in the end.

7 ⬖ Add colour to the pier

Using my rigger, I mix up the colours to paint the pier, working over the top of the tonal values that I've already established. This is where all the preparation starts to pay off: you can sweep the brush right over the top without worrying about the tonal values. Simple!

Enjoy it

I always wanted to be an artist. And because I like to do my best on everything, it's as hard now as it was when I was ten. However, the results are just a bit better... So find your own way of enjoying it. If you love it you will carry on for life.

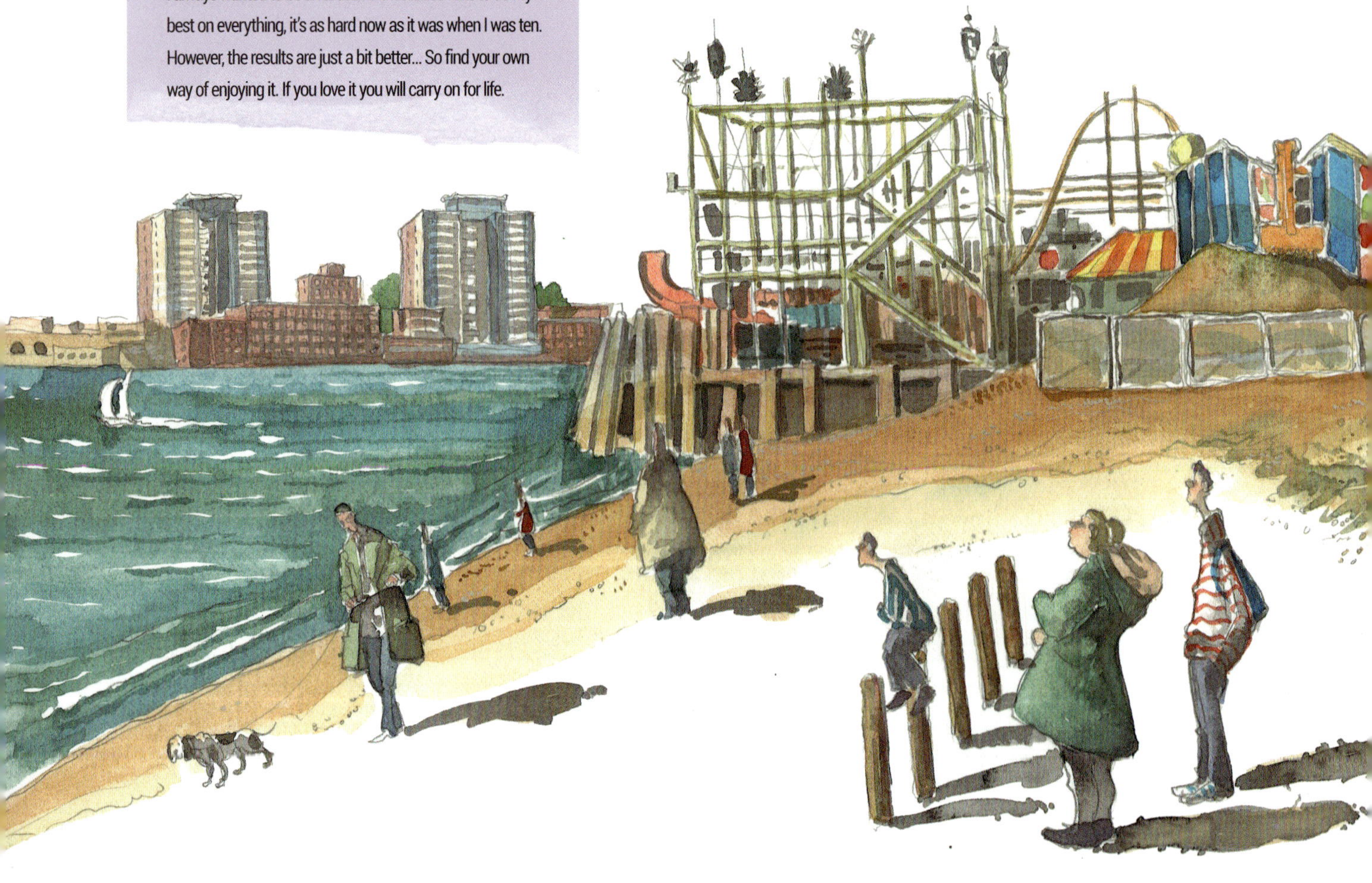

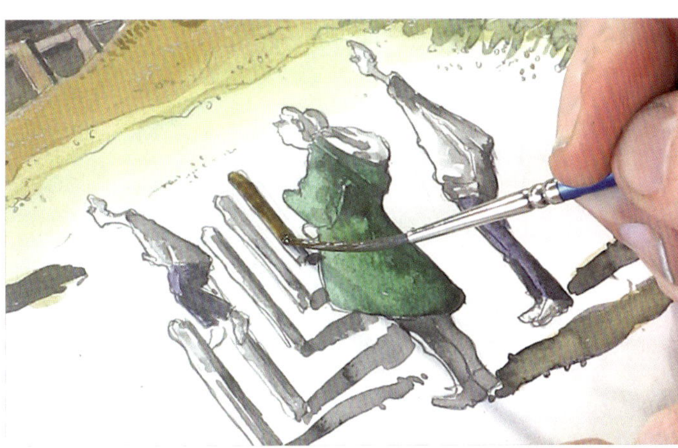

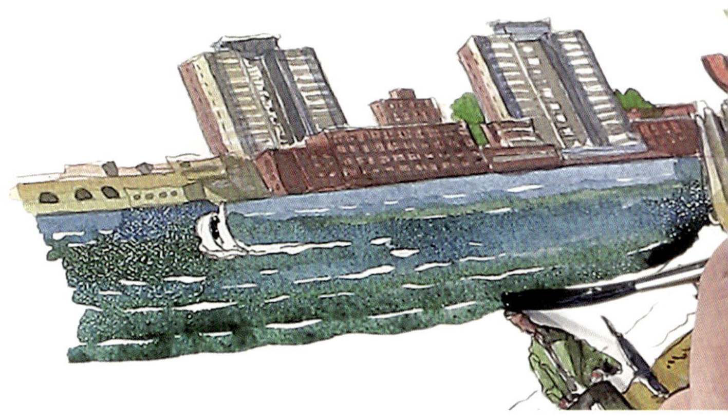

8 ⬤ **Paint the people**

When painting the people, again all our initial work is paying off. I sweep on the green of the parka, then just before it dries I add a very watery Winsor Yellow on the side facing the sun, and a bit of dark green or red on the shady side. Occasionally, I'll drop bits of water here and there to get some blooming going on.

9 ⬤ **The sea**

Finally I paint the sea. I'm using two colours – a blue and a green. I take up one colour and move left to right. When one colour has run dry I pick up the next, maintaining a wobble so the white paper gives the effect of waves. I continue like this. Finally, I nip the shoreline in with a wet brush.

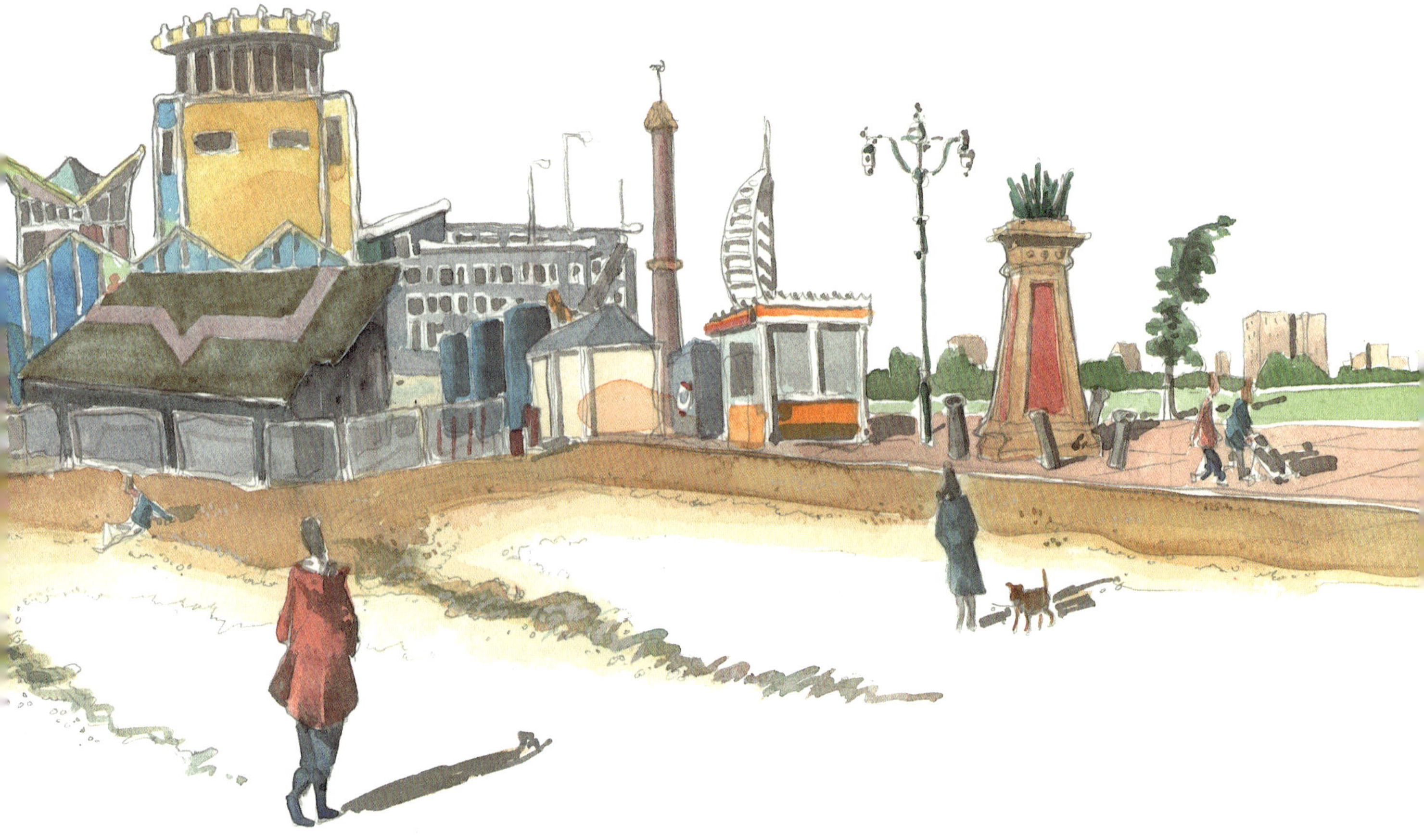

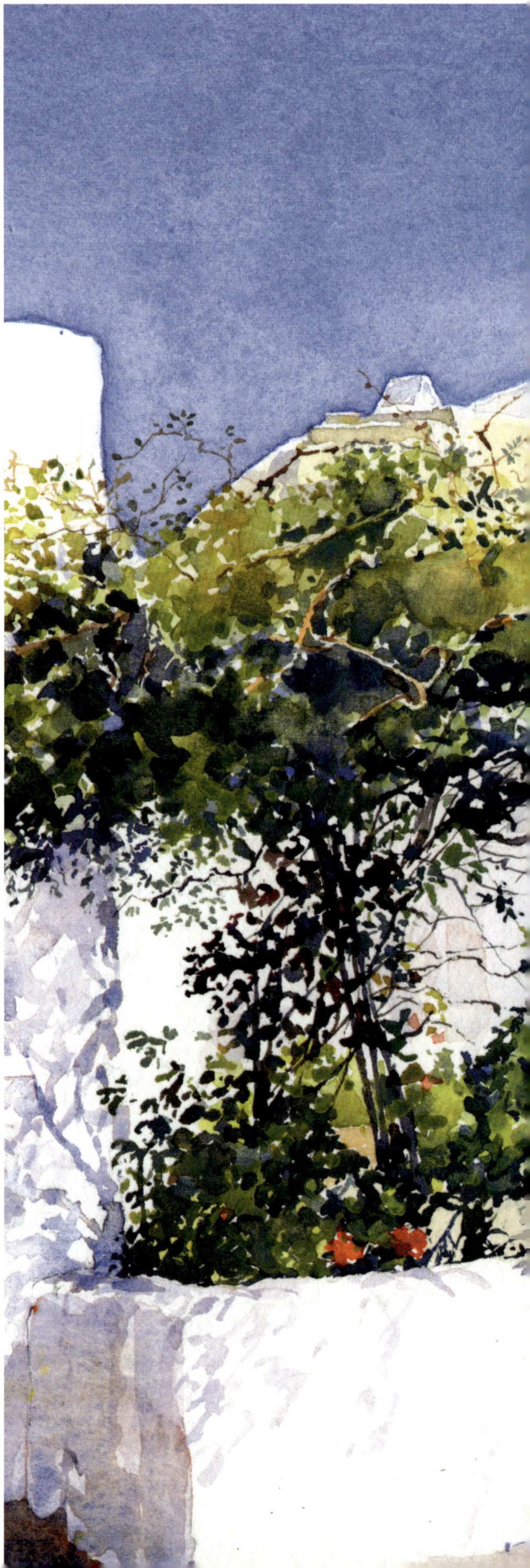

Capture light and shadow

Margaret Merry demonstrates how to depict light and shadow using a limited palette

I was attracted to this subject by the contrast of the dazzling white walls of the cave dwelling against the intense blue of the sky. I liked the way in which this blue was repeated in the shirt on the washing line and the bucket on the terrace. The shadows on the walls also reflect the strong, blue light and the painting itself is an exercise in how to paint shadows while retaining transparency.

The principle of watercolour painting is to reveal the brightness of the paper through transparent washes of pigment, and to achieve this I always use a limited palette. Water is a vital ingredient and in order to avoid muddy colours it must be kept as clean as possible while the painting is in progress. I use a separate container of water to rinse brushes. I never use black or any colour that contains black pigment because it contaminates the purity of other pigments and destroys the transparency. The temptation to use black or grey pigments for painting shadows should be resisted.

The painting demonstrates the use of loose brushwork contrasted with detailed brushwork. I used a #2 brush for the latter because I find this is the best size for drawing with watercolour; anything finer doesn't hold enough water. When painting, I leave detailed work 'til last, when all the main work has been completed.

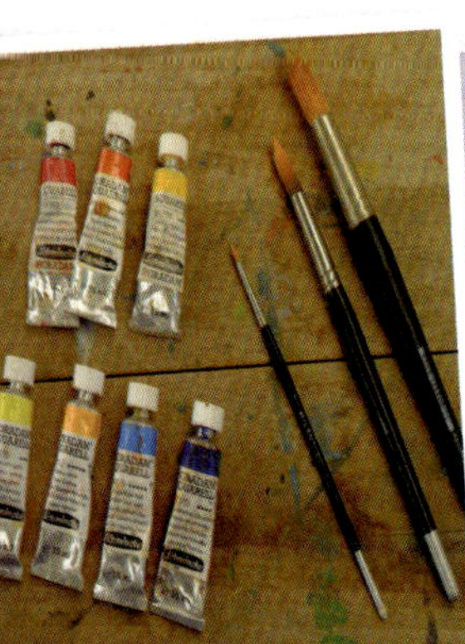

Materials

- Arches Aquarelle 300gsm Not watercolour paper
- Schmincke Horadam watercolours: Raw Sienna, Burnt Sienna, French Ultramarine, Cobalt Blue, Alizarin Crimson, Cadmium Yellow, Lemon Yellow, Cadmium Red
- Milan watercolour brushes sizes 2, 12 and 24
- Pencils 2B and 3B

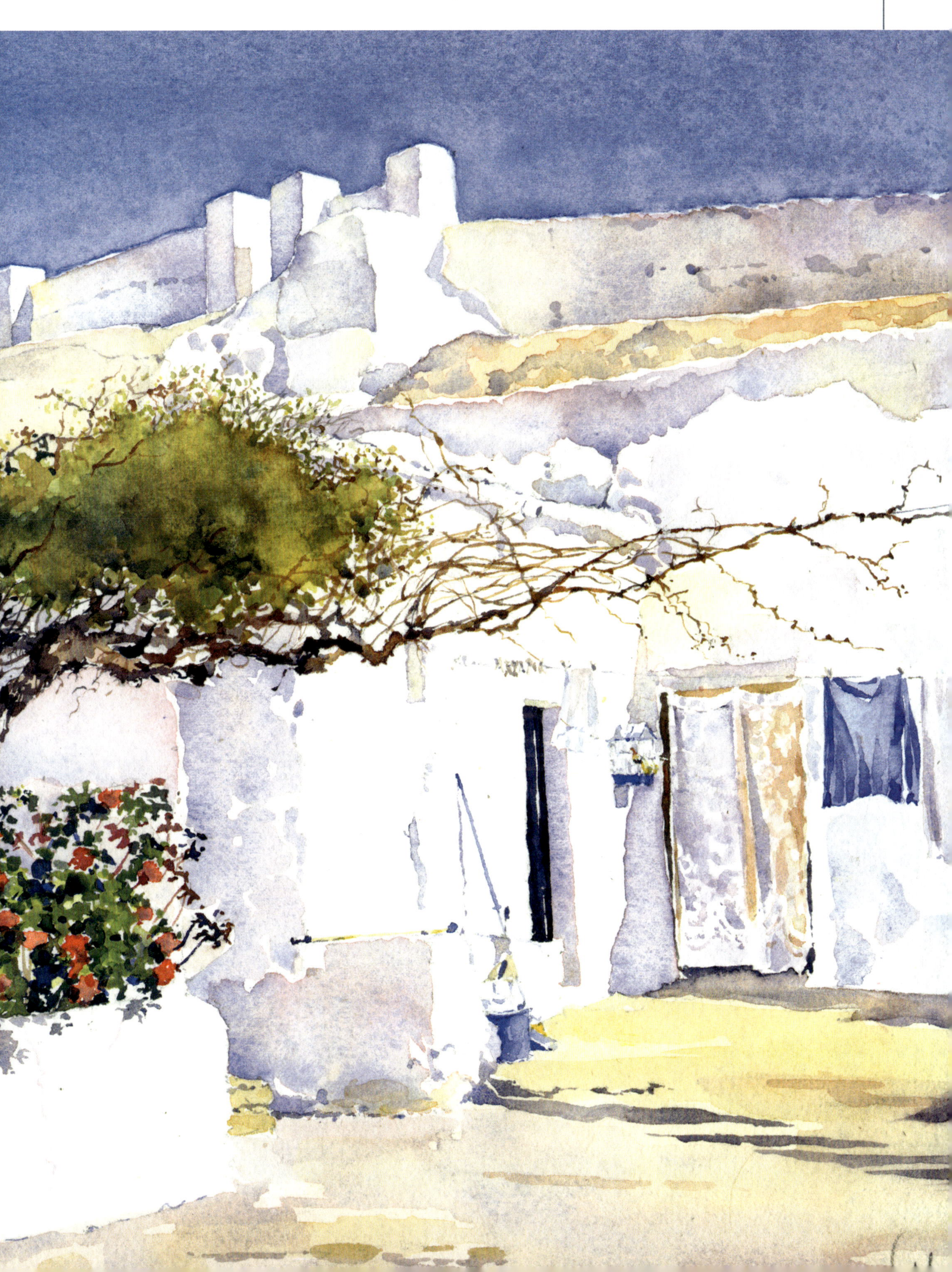

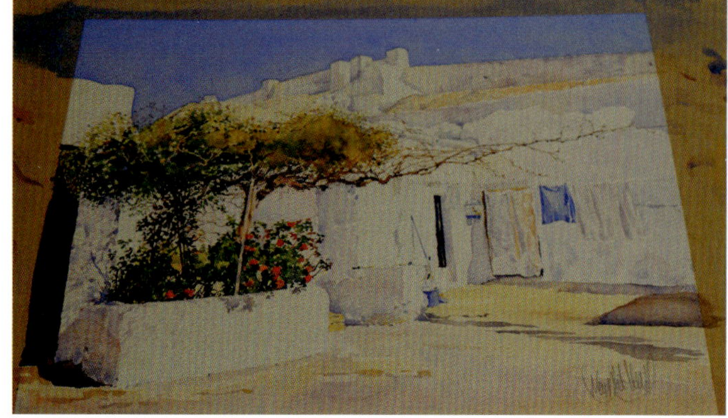

Follow these steps...

1 ▶ Compose the painting

My preliminary drawing is quite detailed and I've emphasised the outline where the building meets the sky because this will act as a barrier when I apply the paint. I'll rub it out when the paint is dry. Never use a rubber before painting as it can damage the surface of the paper and result in uneven colour. Next, I soak the paper for about five minutes and then attach it to a board with gummed paper. I allow the paper to dry naturally. I always work on stretched paper as the ground for watercolour painting needs to be as flat as possible.

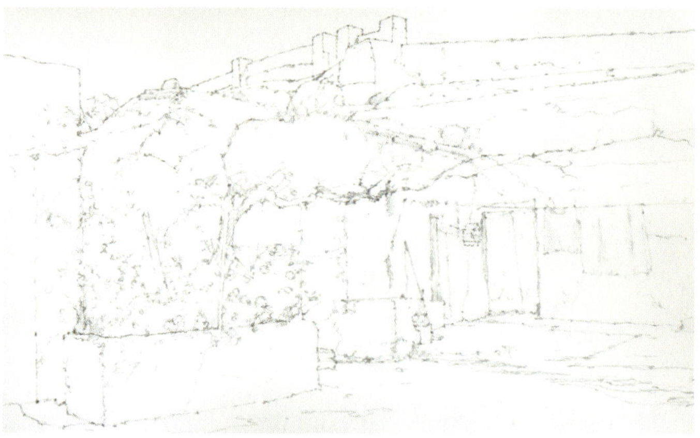

2 ▶ Preliminary washes

I invariably begin a landscape painting with the sky and Cobalt is my preferred pigment. Painting a typically cloudless Andalusian sky is quite tricky as it requires a flawless wash of blue. To facilitate this, I apply clean water over the area to be covered, taking care not to go over the outline of the drawing. I dilute the Cobalt to the desired intensity then quickly paint the sky with my #24 brush. I tilt the board so the paint runs upwards. When it's dry, I add a very diluted wash of Raw Sienna to the lower part of the painting in order to 'kill' the white where it isn't needed.

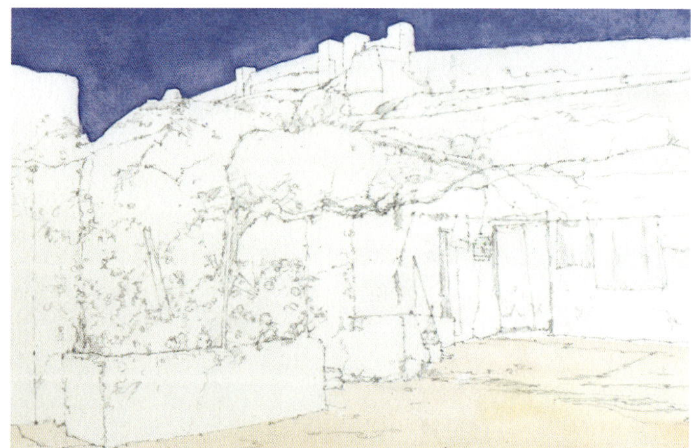

3 ▶ Paint the shadows

For the blue shadows, I mix a good quantity of diluted French Ultramarine with Cadmium Red. Working quickly and keeping the mixture as fluid as I can, I begin painting the uppermost parts of the building and, in order to illuminate the places where the light is reflected on the walls, I add a touch of very diluted Cadmium Yellow onto a clean brush and drop it into the wet paint. I tilt the board so the yellow runs into the blue mixture, giving the illusion of light.

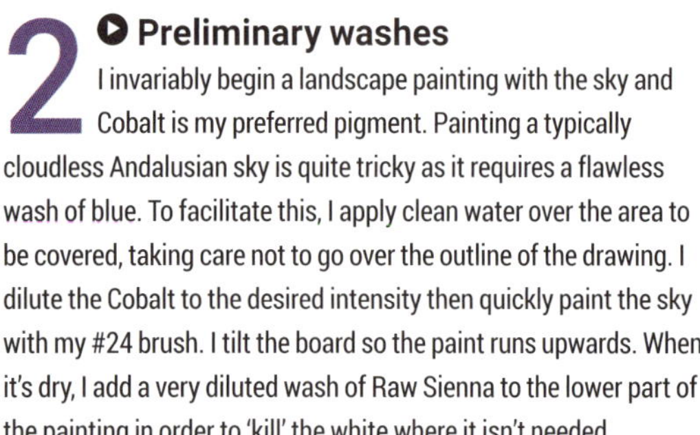

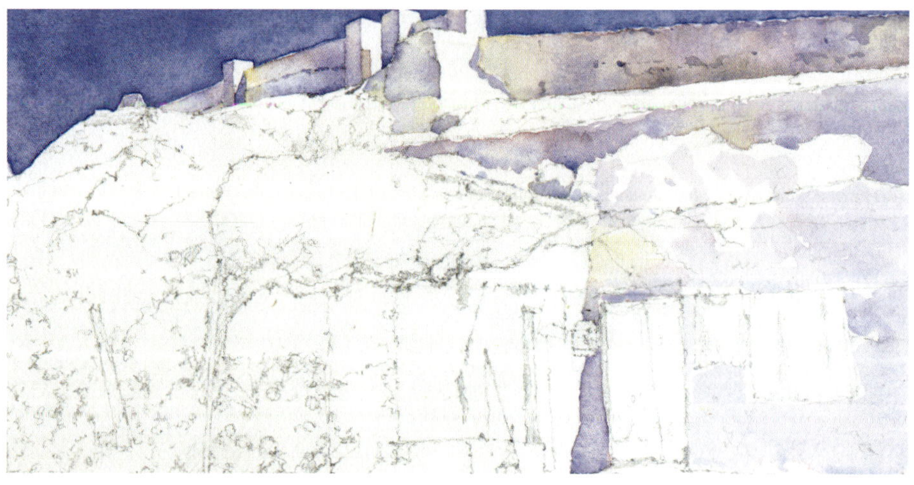

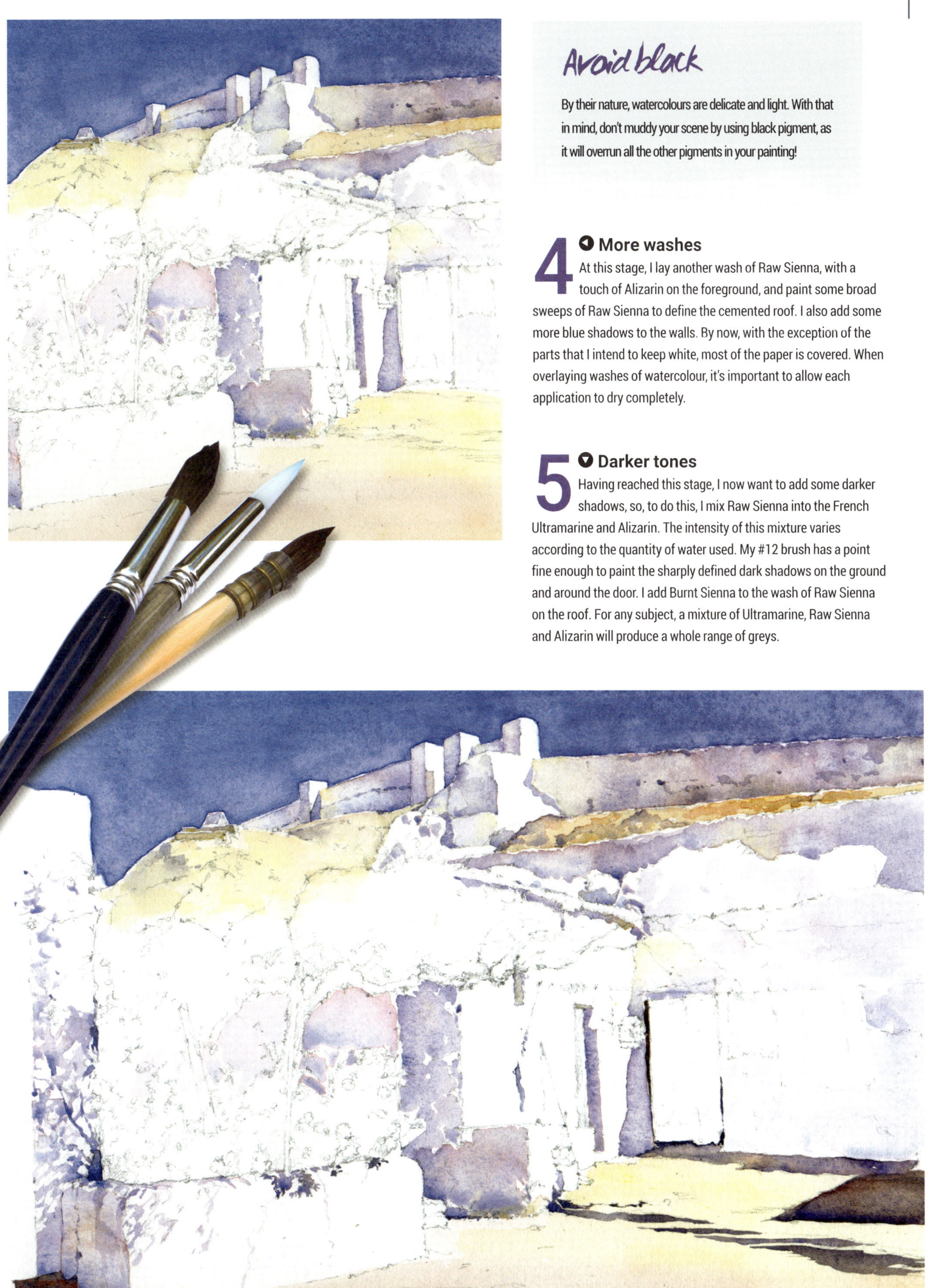

Avoid black

By their nature, watercolours are delicate and light. With that in mind, don't muddy your scene by using black pigment, as it will overrun all the other pigments in your painting!

4 ◐ More washes

At this stage, I lay another wash of Raw Sienna, with a touch of Alizarin on the foreground, and paint some broad sweeps of Raw Sienna to define the cemented roof. I also add some more blue shadows to the walls. By now, with the exception of the parts that I intend to keep white, most of the paper is covered. When overlaying washes of watercolour, it's important to allow each application to dry completely.

5 ◐ Darker tones

Having reached this stage, I now want to add some darker shadows, so, to do this, I mix Raw Sienna into the French Ultramarine and Alizarin. The intensity of this mixture varies according to the quantity of water used. My #12 brush has a point fine enough to paint the sharply defined dark shadows on the ground and around the door. I add Burnt Sienna to the wash of Raw Sienna on the roof. For any subject, a mixture of Ultramarine, Raw Sienna and Alizarin will produce a whole range of greys.

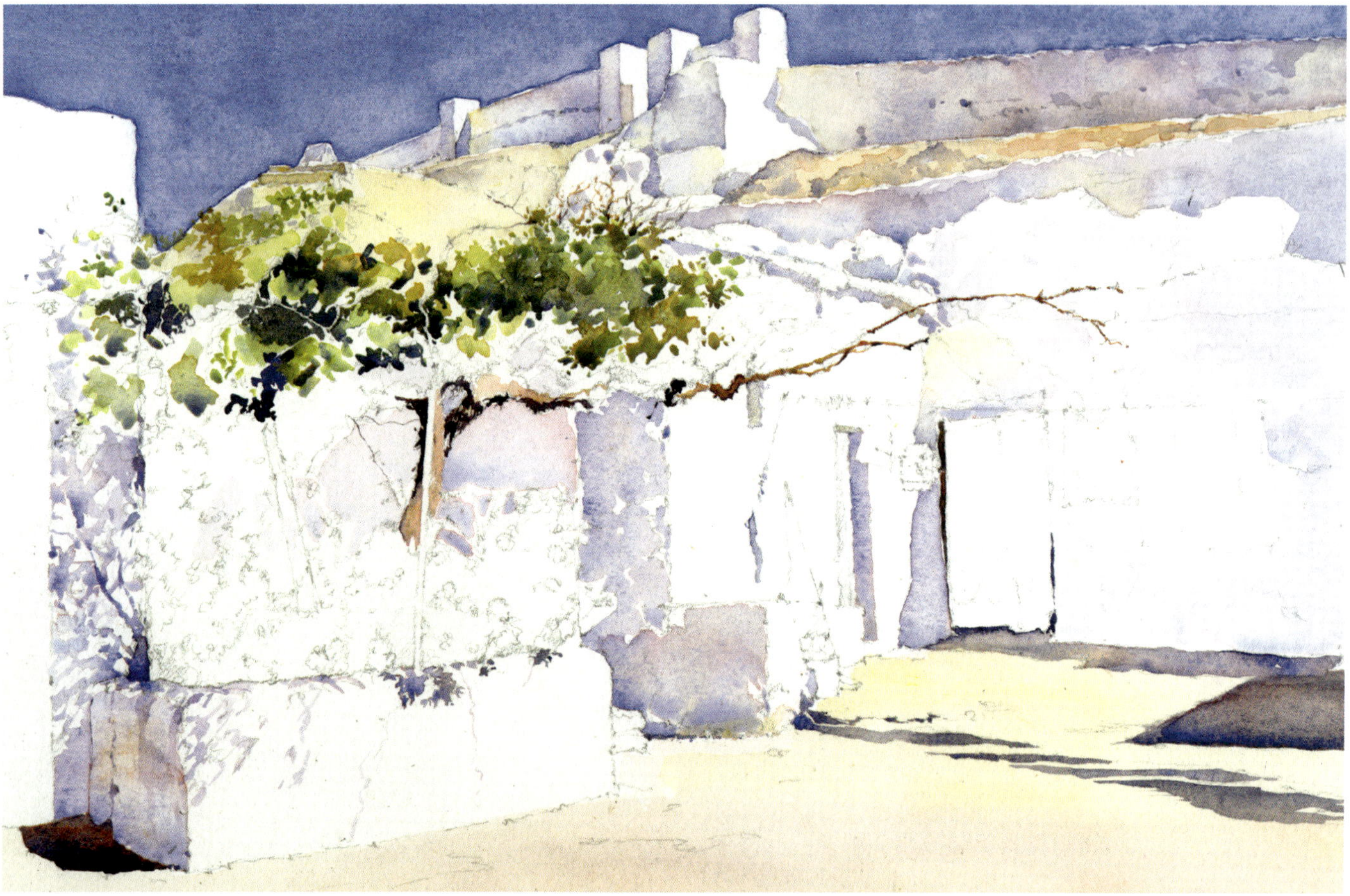

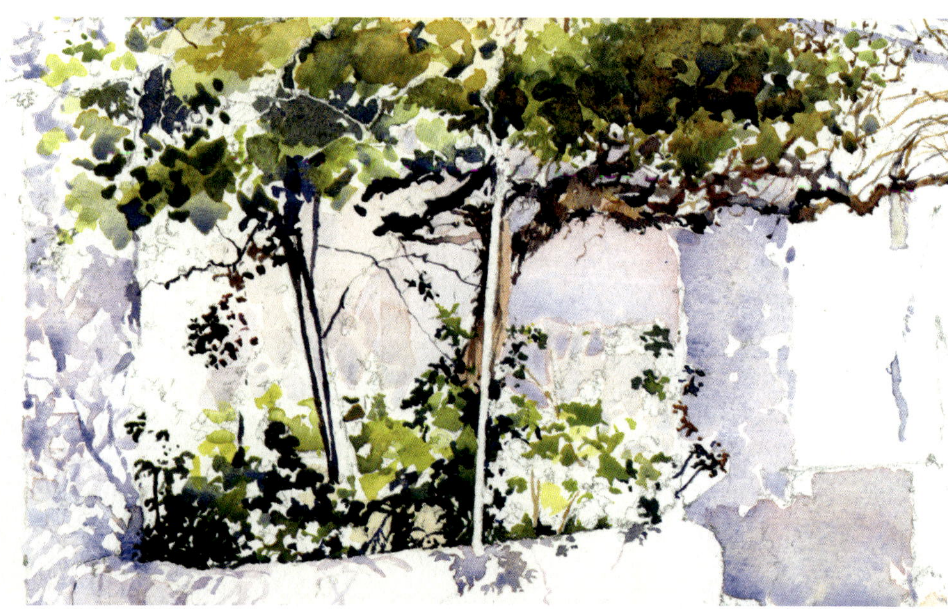

6 ▲ Introduce colour

Having separated the light areas from the shadowed parts, now is the time to introduce colour in the form of green. Apart from Hooker's Green, which I occasionally use, I dislike ready-made greens, much preferring to mix my own. For the jasmine tree, I use Ultramarine, Lemon Yellow and a little Raw Sienna. This is a preliminary wash, to be manipulated at a later stage with water and a clean brush. The advantage of this combination of pigments is that it can be moved about, unlike some greens that tend to stain the paper and don't mix well with other pigments. I use a fine #2 brush to begin drawing the vine extending across the front of the house.

7 ▶ Down to detail

Next, I tackle the bed of geraniums under the jasmine and the vine using the same green mixture but adding a little Burnt Sienna to darken the colour where necessary. I also use Burnt and Raw Sienna to outline the trunk and to paint more of the slender twigs of the vine. A useful trick when painting foliage is to drag a fine brush out of pooled wet paint, as I do in this instance. The lightest parts of the trunk and branches are painted with Raw Sienna and Alizarin.

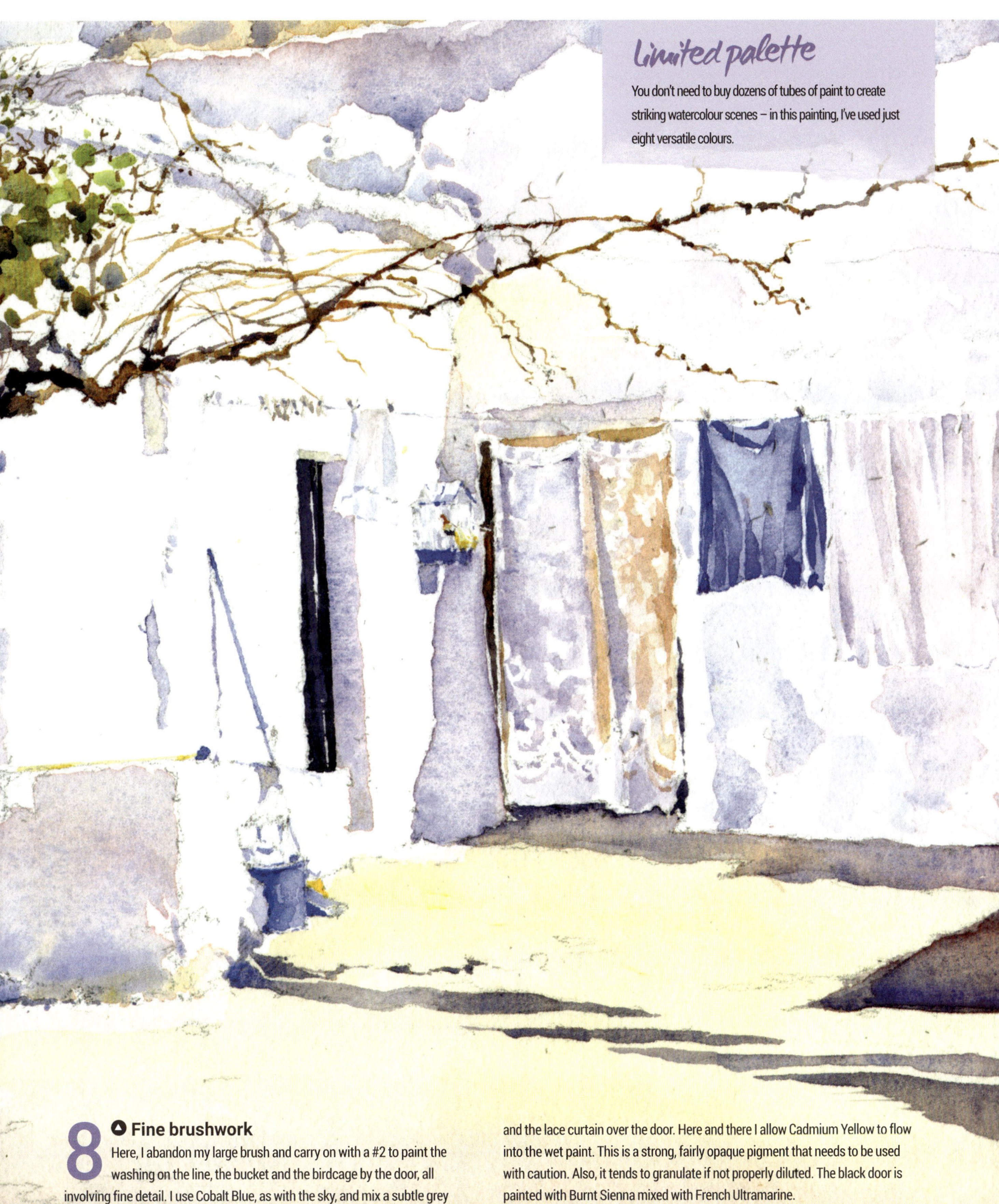

8 ⬥ **Fine brushwork**

Here, I abandon my large brush and carry on with a #2 to paint the washing on the line, the bucket and the birdcage by the door, all involving fine detail. I use Cobalt Blue, as with the sky, and mix a subtle grey using the same pigment and adding Alizarin and Raw Sienna to paint the towel and the lace curtain over the door. Here and there I allow Cadmium Yellow to flow into the wet paint. This is a strong, fairly opaque pigment that needs to be used with caution. Also, it tends to granulate if not properly diluted. The black door is painted with Burnt Sienna mixed with French Ultramarine.

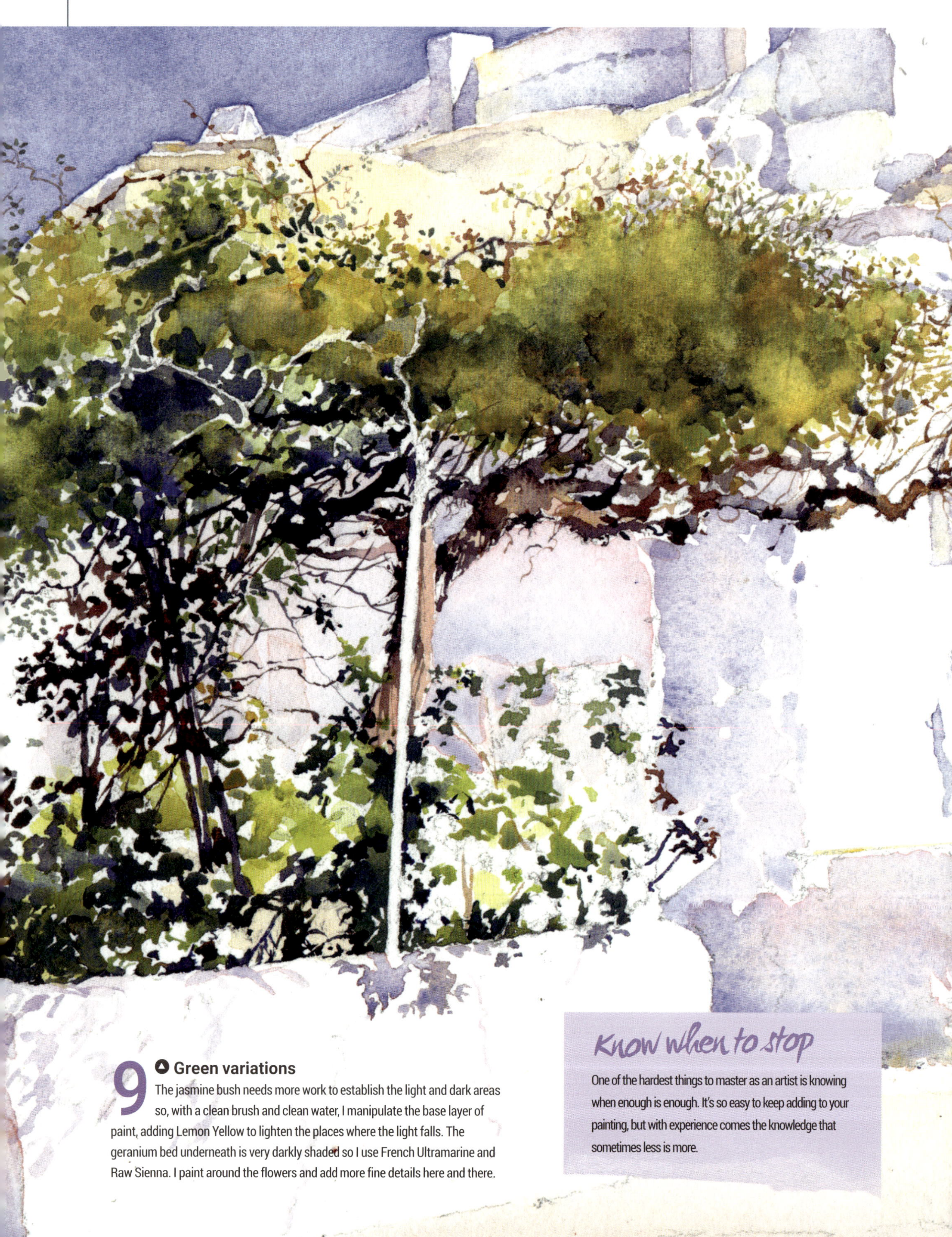

9 ⬤ **Green variations**
The jasmine bush needs more work to establish the light and dark areas so, with a clean brush and clean water, I manipulate the base layer of paint, adding Lemon Yellow to lighten the places where the light falls. The geranium bed underneath is very darkly shaded so I use French Ultramarine and Raw Sienna. I paint around the flowers and add more fine details here and there.

Know when to stop

One of the hardest things to master as an artist is knowing when enough is enough. It's so easy to keep adding to your painting, but with experience comes the knowledge that sometimes less is more.

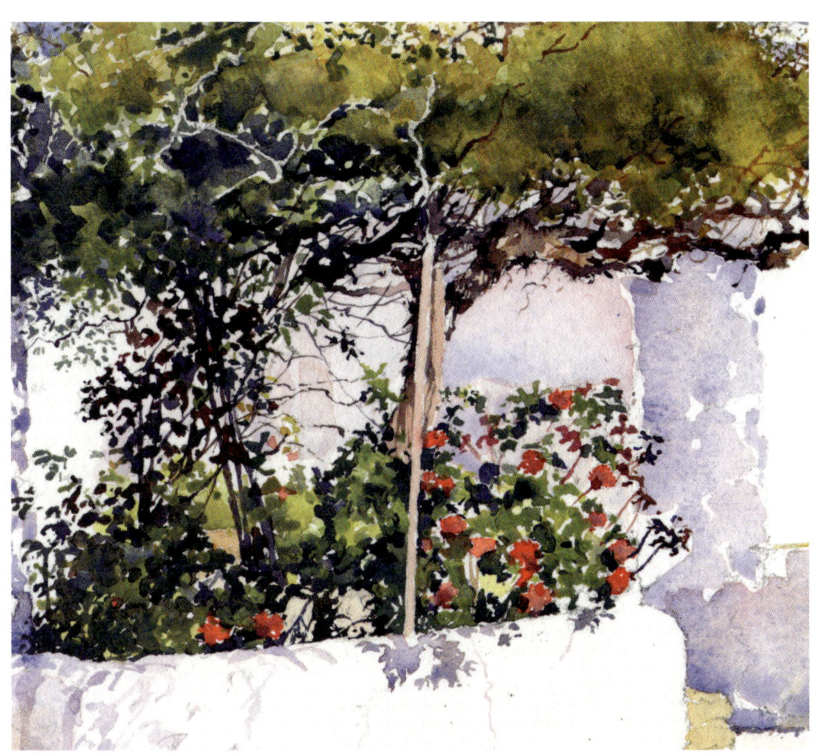

10 ◐ Contrasting colours

When the green paint has dried, I fill in the spaces left empty for the flowers with Cadmium Red, darkened at the shadowed edges with Ultramarine and Alizarin. When painting flowers, the pigment needs to be as clean and pure as possible so the brilliance of the white paper can show through. Overworking will have disastrous results. Because the subject of the painting comprises mostly cool colours, the warm red of the geraniums complements the composition nicely.

11 ▼ Final details

For the finishing touches, I add some more details here and there and, to give warmth and substance to the foreground, I lay a thin wash of Alizarin and Raw Sienna over the original layer of paint, with streaks of Raw and Burnt Sienna in places to break the monotony. I could carry on adding even more details but there comes a point in a painting where experience tells you it's time to down brushes. There's really nothing more to say about the composition so I decide that the painting is finished.

"The pigment needs to be as pure as possible so the brilliance of the white paper can show through"

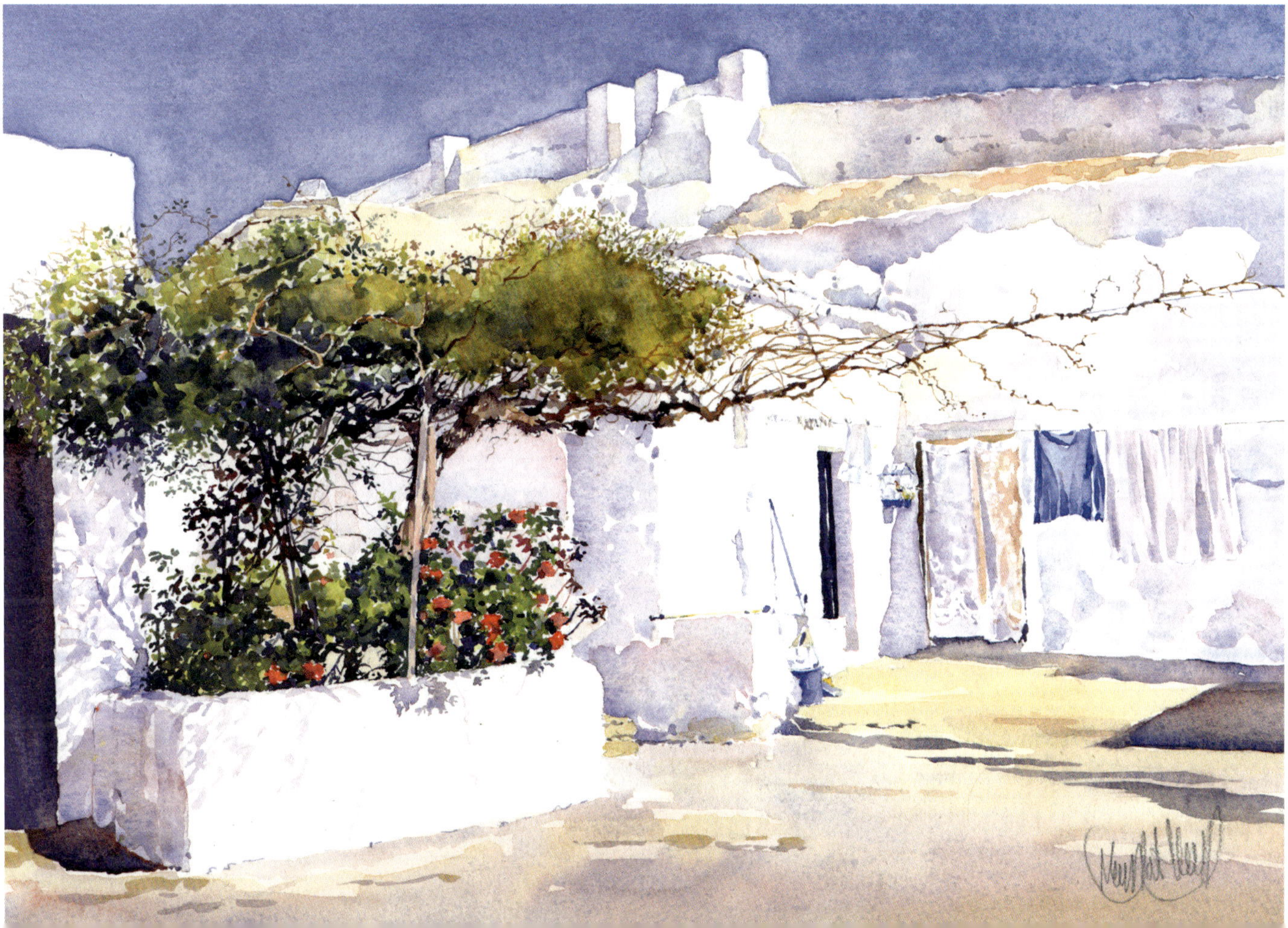

Find beauty in a fading flower

Julia Trickey creates a translucent watercolour featuring minute detail

For this workshop I still adhere to the basic principle of botanical art – to represent my subject accurately and in detail – but have chosen to capture it at this fading stage for its aesthetic appeal. I've also enlarged and cropped the flower somewhat, to focus in on the detail and to give the viewer a different perspective.

When starting any new painting I'll think through the stages and techniques I need to accurately capture my subject's key natural characteristics. This may include looking at more complicated parts or textures of the plant, or having a trial run.

Here, you'll see how I work in layers of watercolour to capture the light, shadow and form of the petals, how to use masking fluid to deal with the arrangement of stamens in the centre of the flower, and how to build up details towards the end of the painting process.

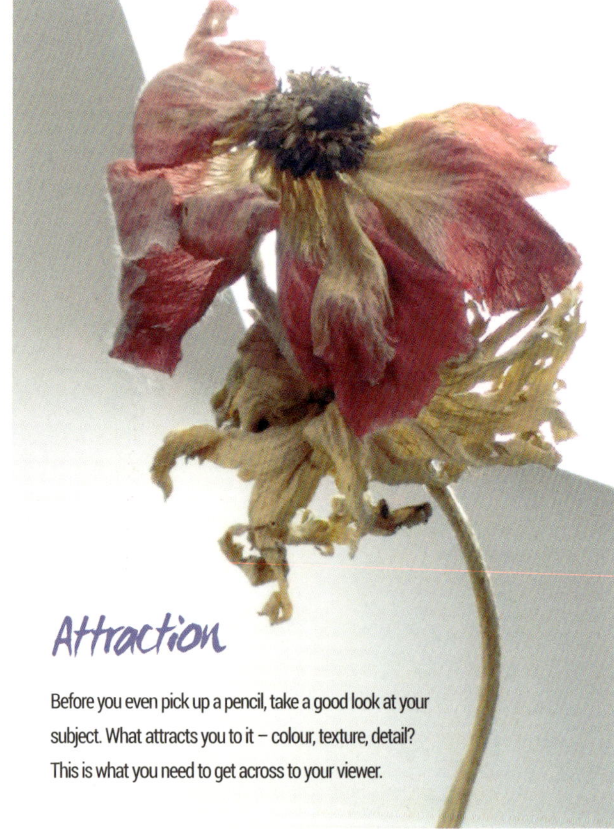

Attraction

Before you even pick up a pencil, take a good look at your subject. What attracts you to it – colour, texture, detail? This is what you need to get across to your viewer.

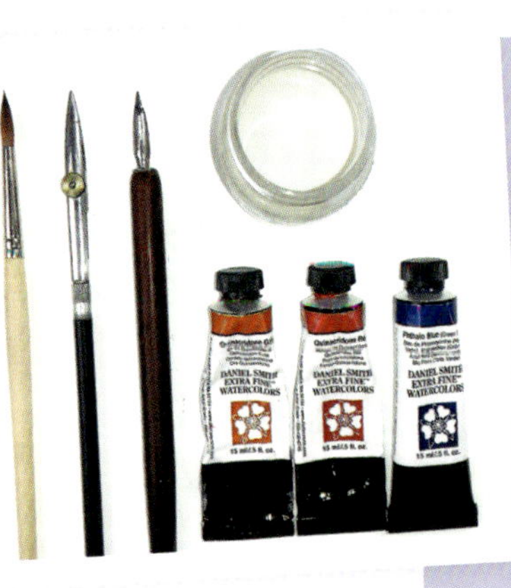

Materials

- **Daniel Smith Extra Fine Watercolours**
- **Fabriano Artistico HP 140lb extra white watercolour paper (old stock) 21x21cm**
- **Jackson's One Pound Sable paint brush, size 4 (no longer available)**
- **Ruling pen**
- **Drawing nib**
- **SAA white masking fluid**

Follow these steps...

1 ⬤ Establish your lighting scheme

By working from the real plant material, as well as carefully taken photographs, you can keep checking structure and detail as your painting progresses. Set your subject up, lighting it from one side (traditionally the left) to give yourself a good range of lights and shadows. A little extra, optional back light will help to emphasise the translucence nature of the petals.

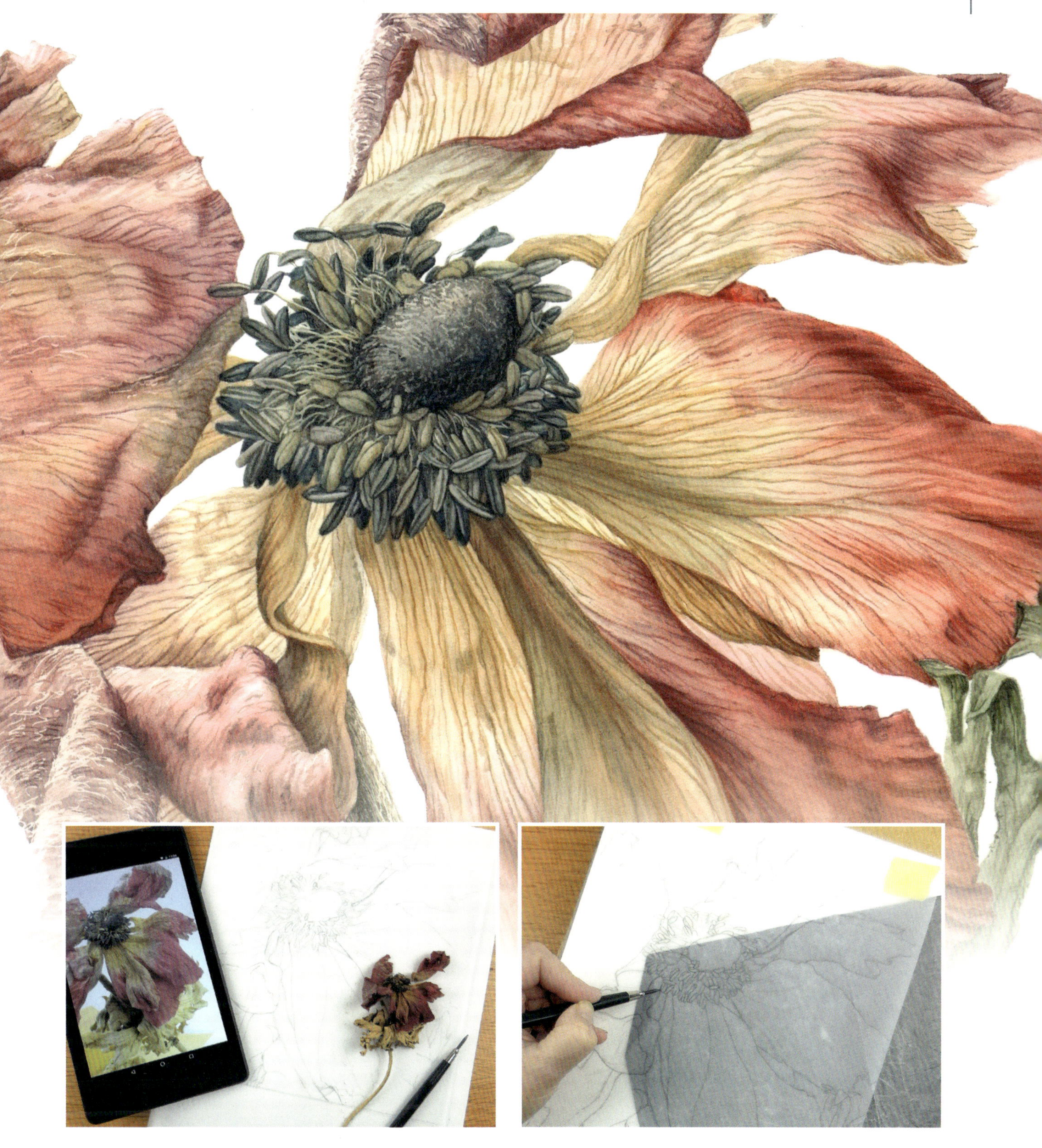

2 ⬤ Observational drawing

Start with a carefully observed drawing, referring to the photos that you've taken and the real flower. Draw this on tracing or inexpensive paper – this way you don't need to worry about making mistakes and spoiling the surface of the watercolour paper. Scale up your subject if you like.

3 ⬤ Transfer the drawing

To transfer the drawing to the watercolour paper I use graphite transfer paper. This is sandwiched between the drawing and the watercolour paper, and works just like carbon paper. However, you may prefer to use a traditional lightbox and trace the image, or use a bright window in the same way.

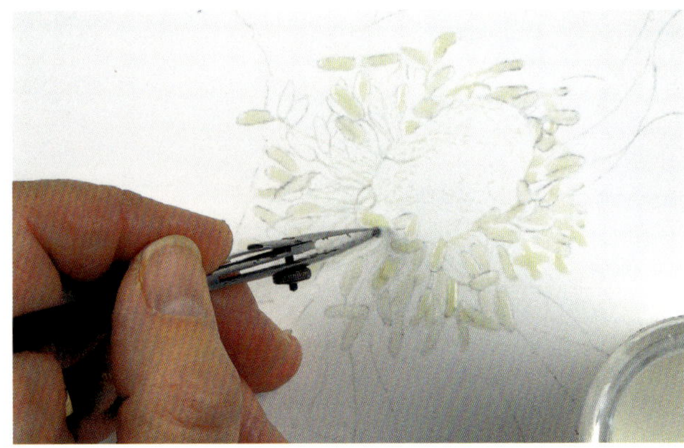

4 ⬆ Masking fluid

Before starting to paint, decide if any of your image needs masking out. This means you can protect parts of your painting while you work on background colours or other areas of the picture. Here, I've decided to mask out the stamens in the centre of the flower.

5 ▶ Wet-in-wet petals

Working on one petal at a time, aim to create its form using wet-in-wet watercolour techniques. Wet the area until thoroughly and evenly wet. Wait for a surface sheen (rather than lots of surface water) before dabbing in colour, adding stronger colours where you see darks or shadows. Stop once the paper starts to dry, even if you haven't quite finished.

6 ⬇ Working in layers

If you don't manage to capture all the colour or form of a petal in one wet-in-wet layer, don't worry. Botanical watercolours are built up over several layers and so you can revisit areas as many times as needed. However, the absolute golden rules are never fiddle with drying paint, and allow each layer to dry completely before working on the next.

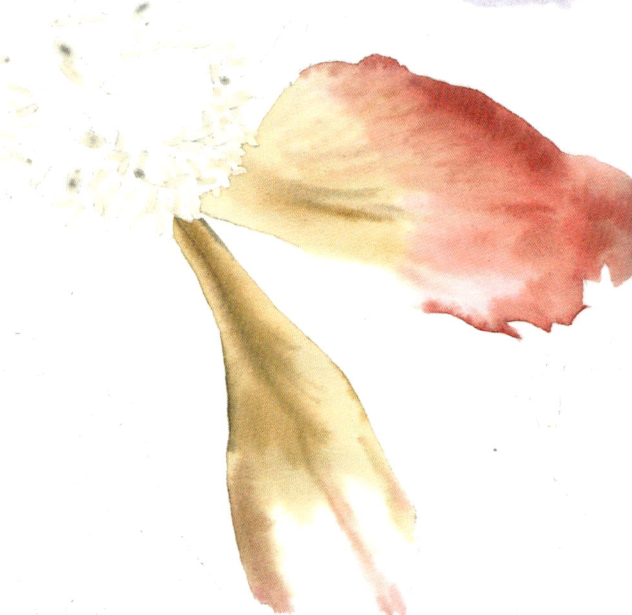

7 ⬇ Building up shape and form

Work on each petal, building up the form using wet-in-wet techniques. On subsequent layers carefully retrace your steps when applying the water to avoid developing a double edge to the shape, which would need correcting later. Add new colours and strengthen shadows as needed. Compare the tonal value of each petal and then adjust them accordingly.

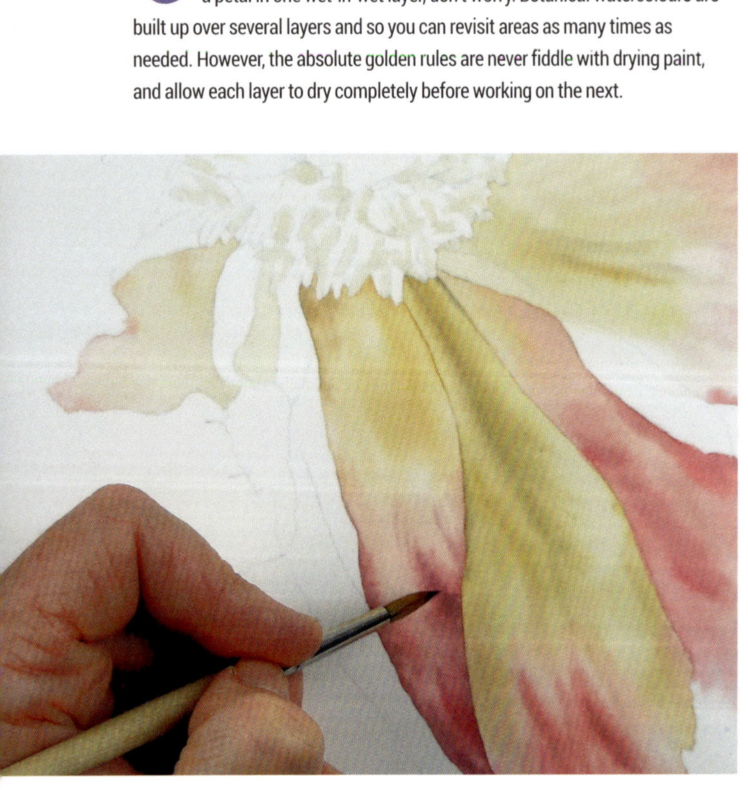

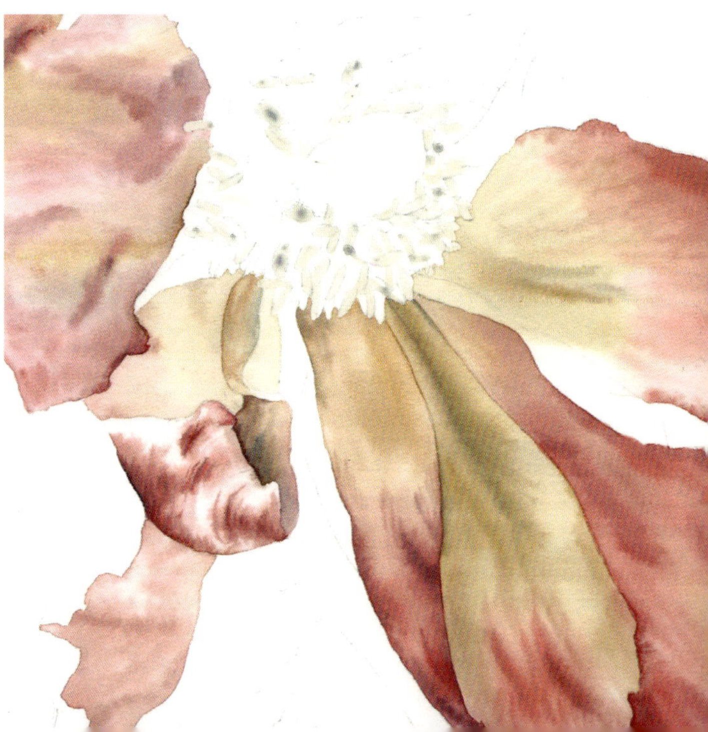

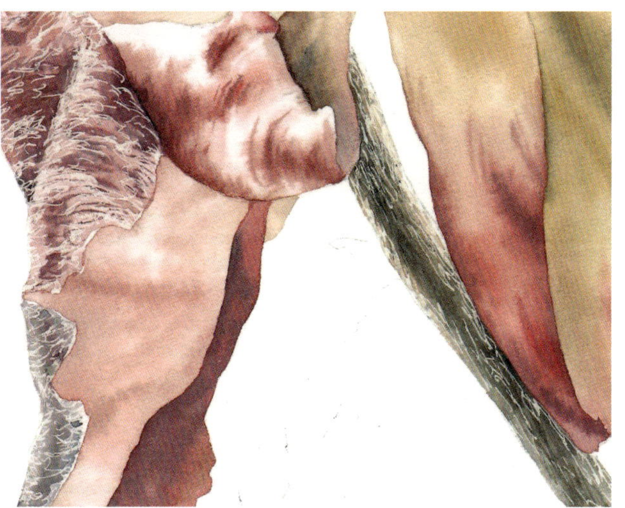

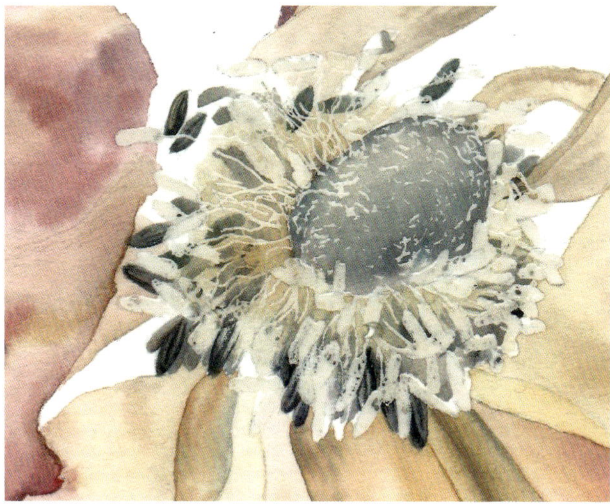

8 ⬢ Dealing with hairs

The back of the anemone petals and stem have quite a hairy texture. These hairs can be applied with a fine drawing nib and masking fluid. This enables you to continue with wet-in-wet techniques over these areas, while ignoring the hairs for now. You'll see that the paper remains white where the hairs have been masked out.

9 ⬢ Tackling the flower centre

Now that you've got some shape and form on each petal, it's a good time to look at the centre of the flower. Wash greys and other neutral colours over the masked area – try to create some form on the central 'mound' and background colours behind the masked stamens and filaments. You can

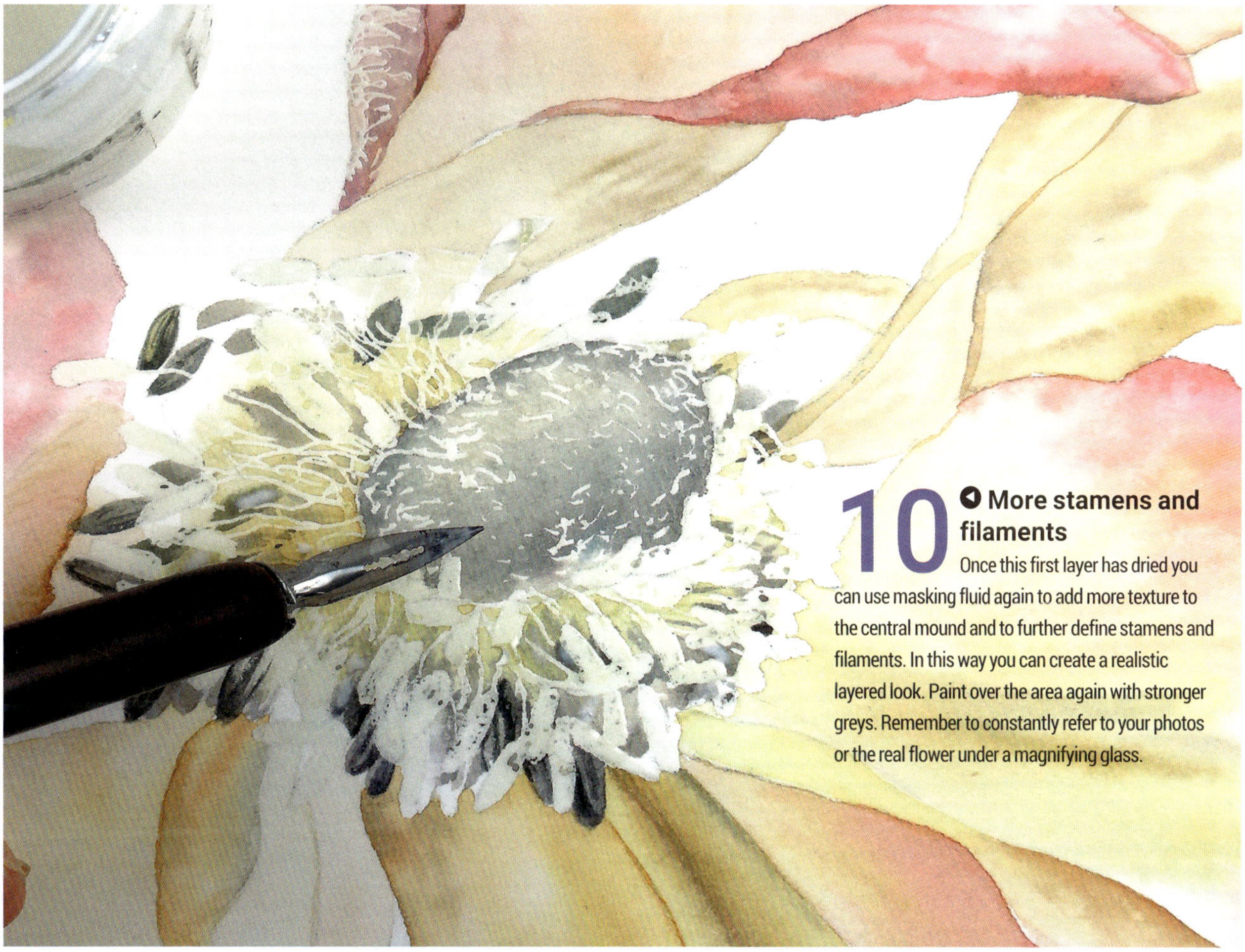

10 ◗ More stamens and filaments

Once this first layer has dried you can use masking fluid again to add more texture to the central mound and to further define stamens and filaments. In this way you can create a realistic layered look. Paint over the area again with stronger greys. Remember to constantly refer to your photos or the real flower under a magnifying glass.

Worth the risk?

The first time I exhibited a set of larger-than-life, faded flower paintings was a nail-biting experience. I wasn't sure how they would be received. However the judges loved them and they were awarded a gold medal. Sometimes it's worth taking a risk.

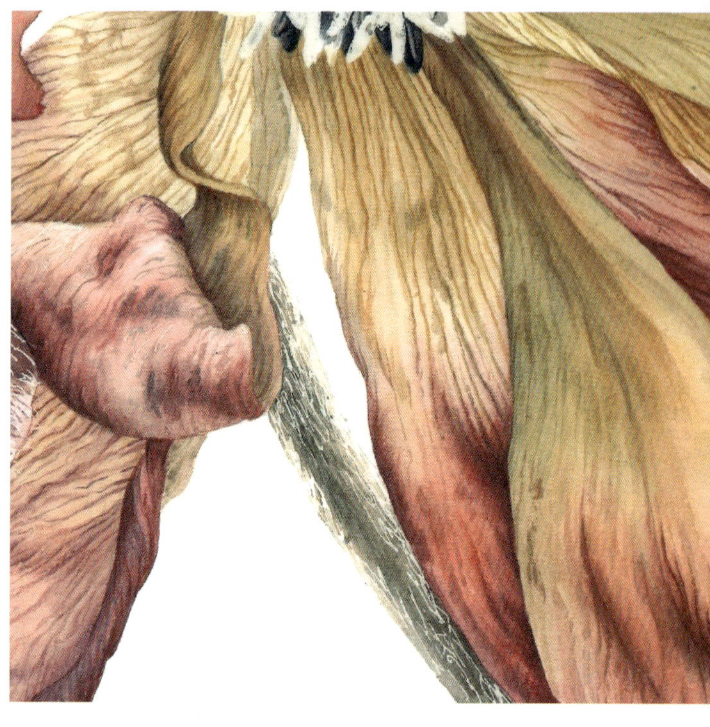

11 ▶ Add detail

While the centre of the flower is drying, you can start adding detail to the petals. This is done with small amounts of stronger paint on the brush. The veins are then drawn on, following the undulations of the petals. Don't make these marks too strong initially because they need to blend into the background. You can strengthen them later as you see fit.

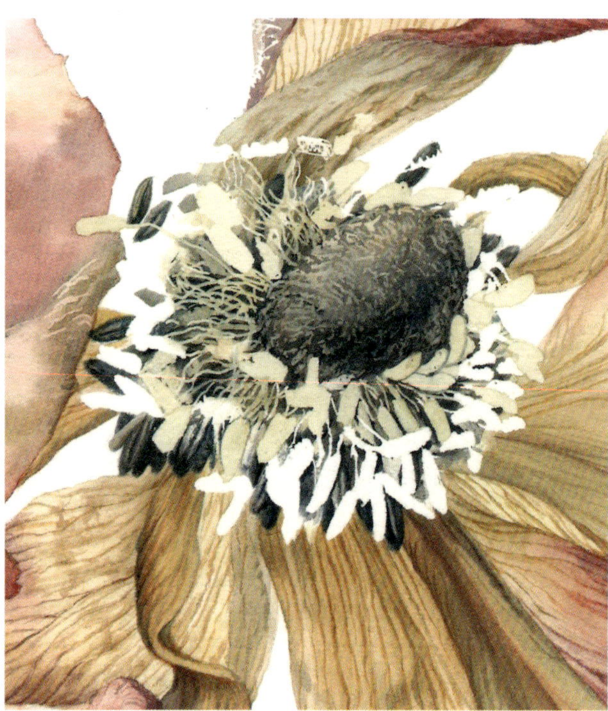

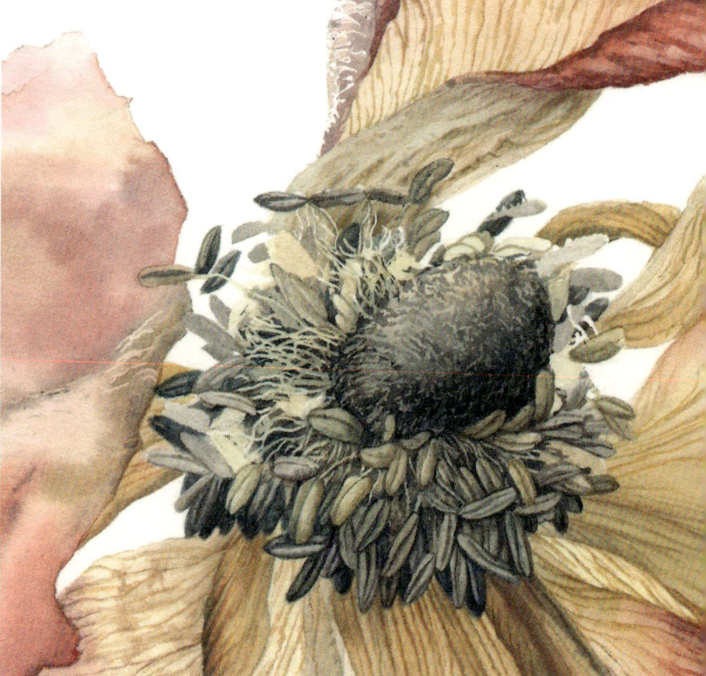

12 ▲ Back to the middle

Once you're happy with the depth of colour behind the masked stamens and this area is thoroughly dry, you can remove the masking fluid. Rub it off carefully with a clean finger. The white shapes left by the masking fluid will seem quite stark and will need refining. Start this by washing greys and beiges over the white shapes.

13 ▲ Refine the centre

The centre of the flower is where the eye is drawn to, so take time studying the detail before attempting to recreate it on your painting. Consider each shape and decide if it's darker or lighter than the one next to it. If you find this too complicated, focus on getting the main stamens right, then hint at the ones behind.

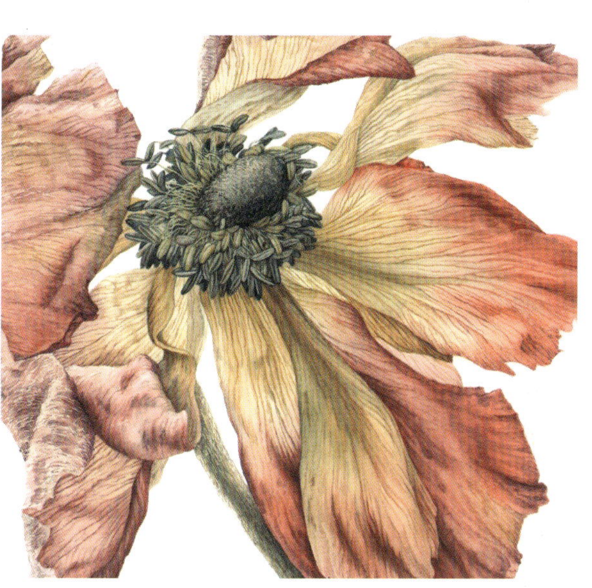

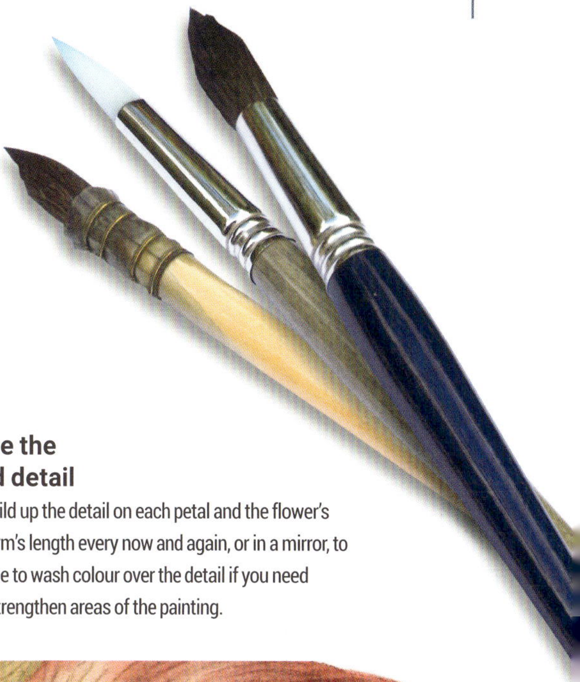

14 ◖ Balance the tones and detail

Continue to build up the detail on each petal and the flower's centre. Look at your picture at arm's length every now and again, or in a mirror, to check the overall balance. It's fine to wash colour over the detail if you need to either soften the detail or to strengthen areas of the painting.

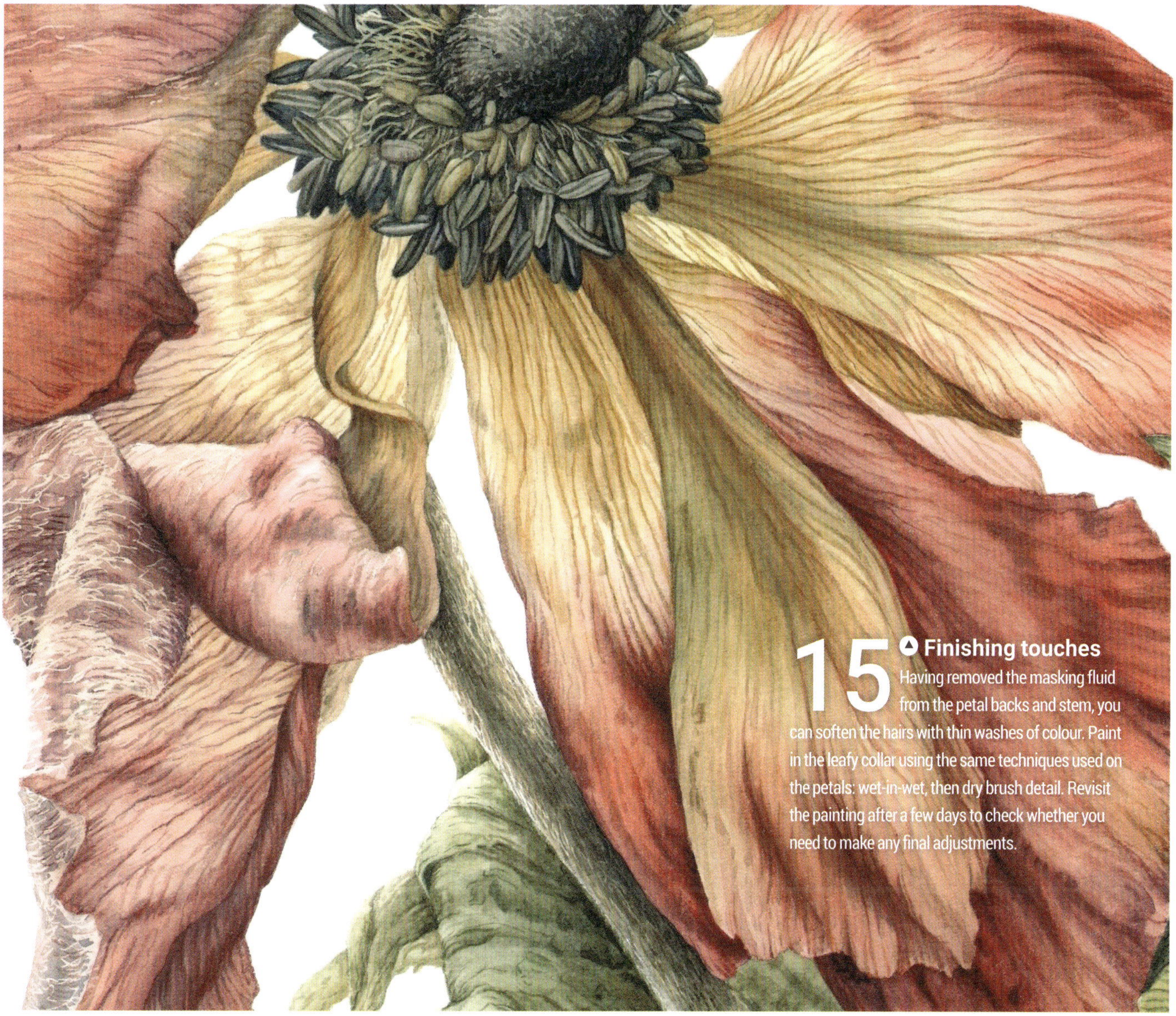

15 ◖ Finishing touches

Having removed the masking fluid from the petal backs and stem, you can soften the hairs with thin washes of colour. Paint in the leafy collar using the same techniques used on the petals: wet-in-wet, then dry brush detail. Revisit the painting after a few days to check whether you need to make any final adjustments.

Painting in watercolour & gouache

In this summer landscape demonstration, **Lancelot Richardson** shows one painting process that combines watercolour and gouache

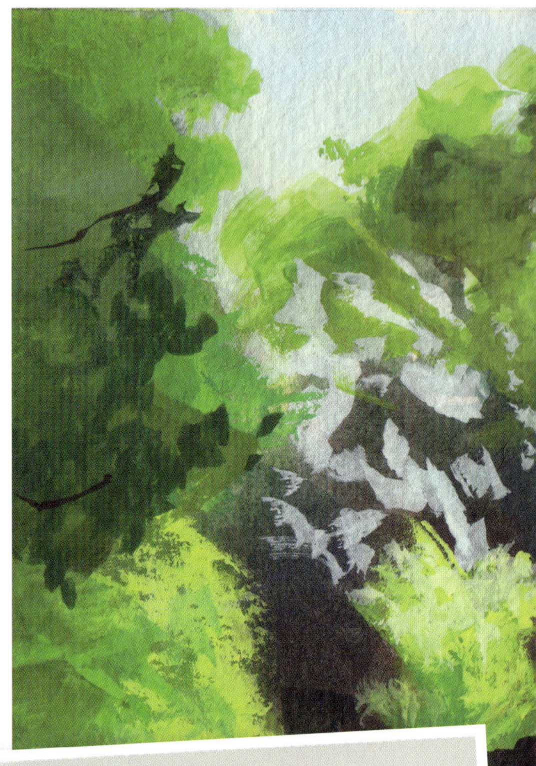

Watercolour and gouache are two complementary, water-soluble materials that each have distinct properties. Watercolours are more familiar to most, providing vivid, translucent colour. Gouache is a little different, as it tends to be thicker and more opaque than its watercolour counterpart. It also has the ability to reactivate, meaning that gouache applied to paper will become malleable again once wetted.

This demonstration shows how to make the most of the strengths of each, utilising the intense colours and translucency of watercolour to create a vivid base on which to work with the opaque and more textural gouache. As they're both water-soluble, they can be intermixed, where watercolour mixes are added to gouache to create opaque, light colours.

This process will cover the creation of a sustained studio landscape painting, but the techniques can be carried directly into plein air sketching, where a watercolour kit and sketchbook make for an excellent portable set-up for taking colour notes. These techniques can be applied to many other subjects, and the textural qualities of gouache are especially well suited for animal and still life subjects.

When using gouache, haphazard mixing can lead to chalky colours as the gouache contaminates other mixtures. In particular, white gouache can 'deaden' shadows. Reactivation can make it challenging to paint on top of gouache, as layers of wet paint reactivate the gouache and combine with it. To avoid these issues, leave the gouache to the later stages of the process, and work with clean water. Gouache is more forgiving than watercolour, allowing for small mistakes to be painted over with opaque paint, and reactivation means gouache can be blended at the edges.

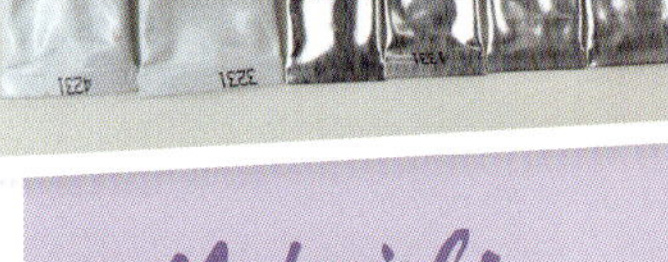

Materials

- 350gsm watercolour paper
- Brushes - #8 round sable, 3/8 inch synthetic flat, 1 inch synthetic flat
- Winsor and Newton Professional tube watercolours: Winsor Lemon, Cadmium Yellow Deep, Yellow Ochre, Winsor Red, Permanent Alizarin Crimson, French Ultramarine, Winsor Blue (green shade) Winsor Green (yellow shade) Venetian Red
- Winsor and Newton gouache: Permanent White, Lemon Yellow
- Faber Castel Watercolour Pencils: Deep Scarlett
- Masking tape
- Jars
- Water spray bottle
- Plastic palette
- Cardboard or drawing board mount
- Paper towel
- Pencils, Conté sticks and cartridge paper for planning sketches

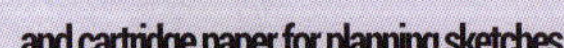

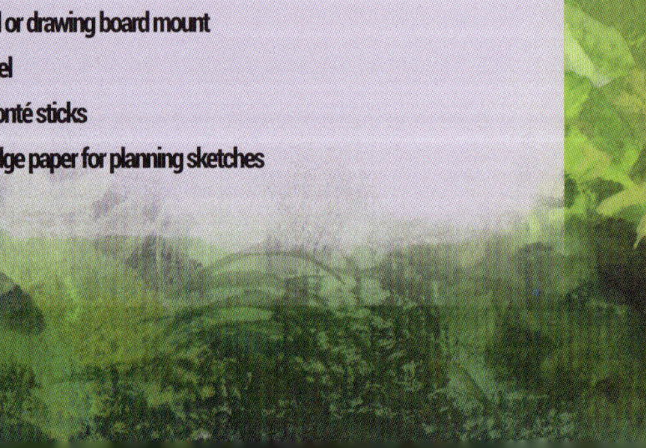

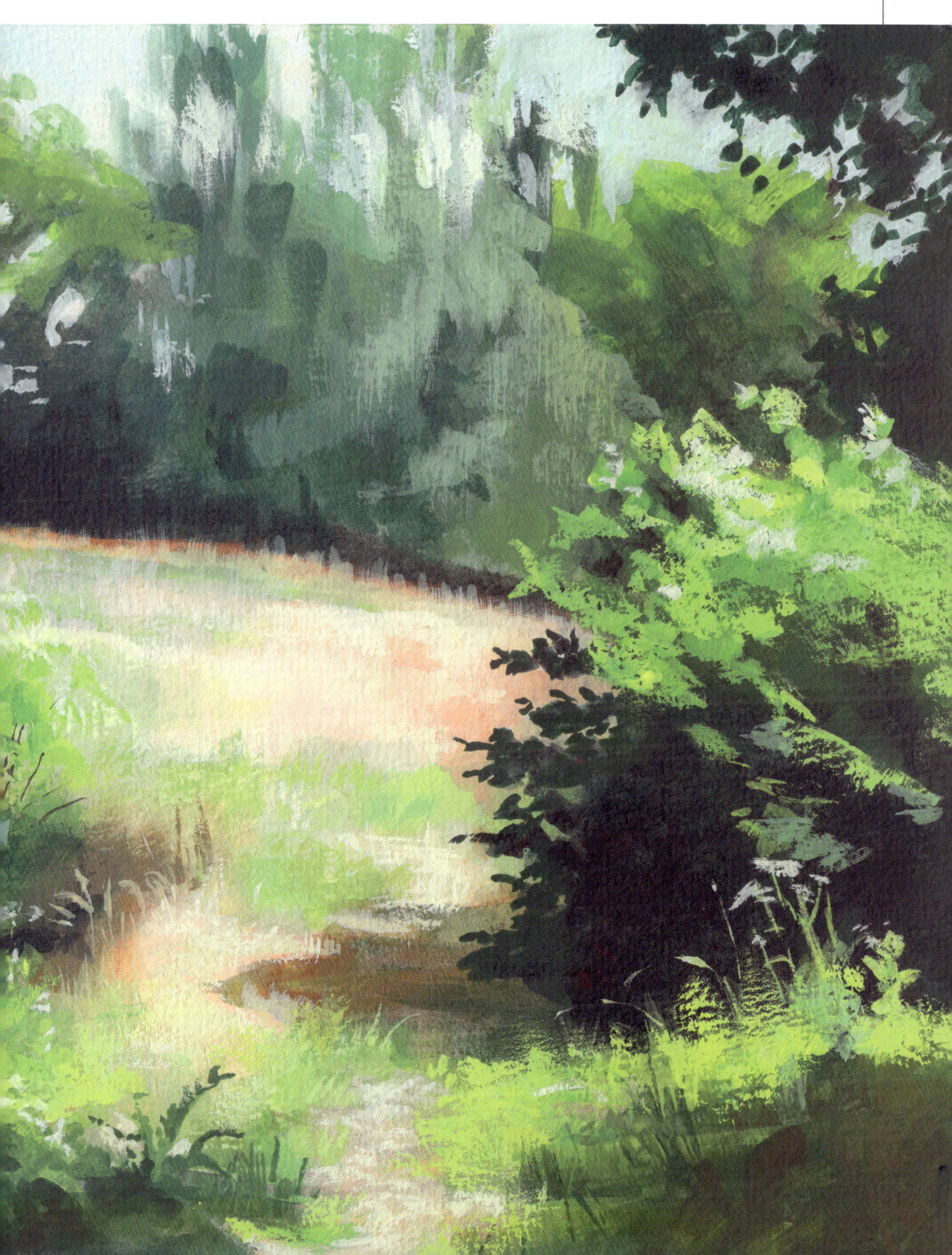

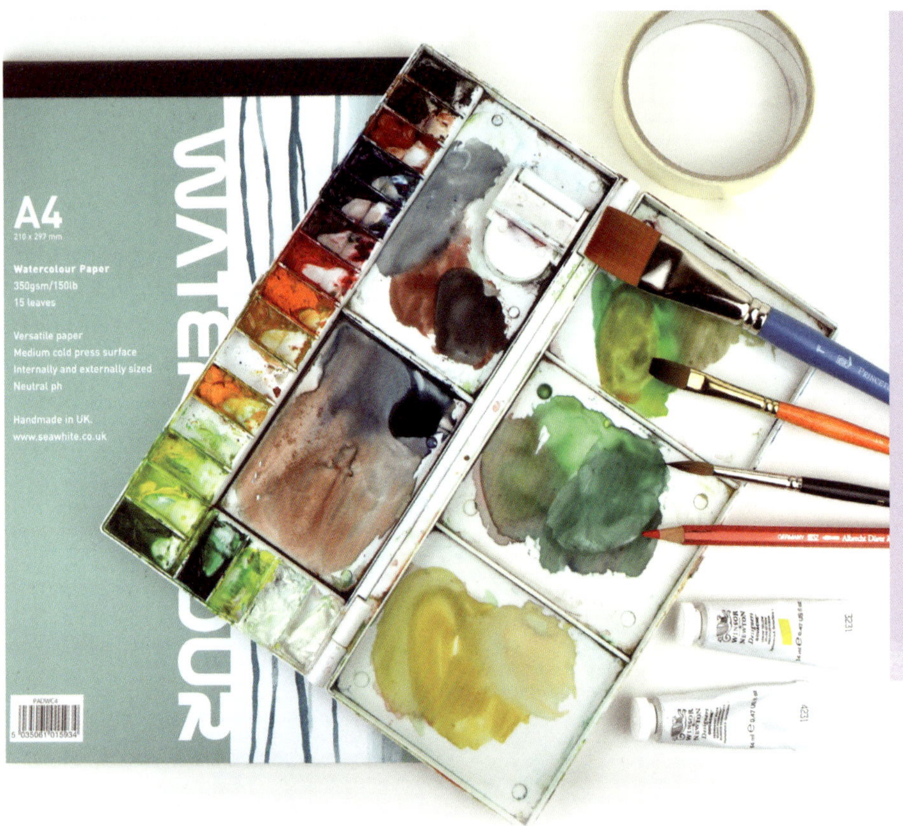

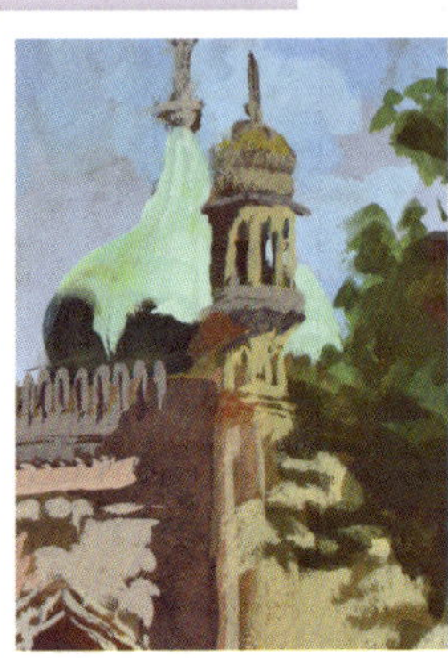

Opaque lights, translucent darks

When working with watercolour and gouache, be mindful of the layers of paint that need applying. In this approach, I work from translucent, darker lower layers to more opaque, lighter upper layers. To keep light areas fresh, try to save them to the end and avoid painting over them.

Follow these steps...

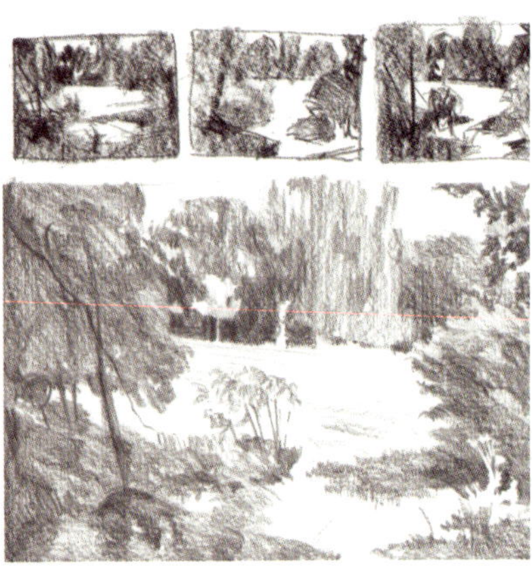

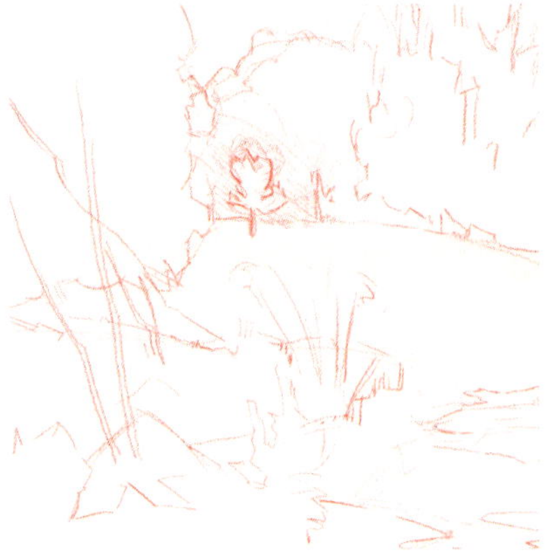

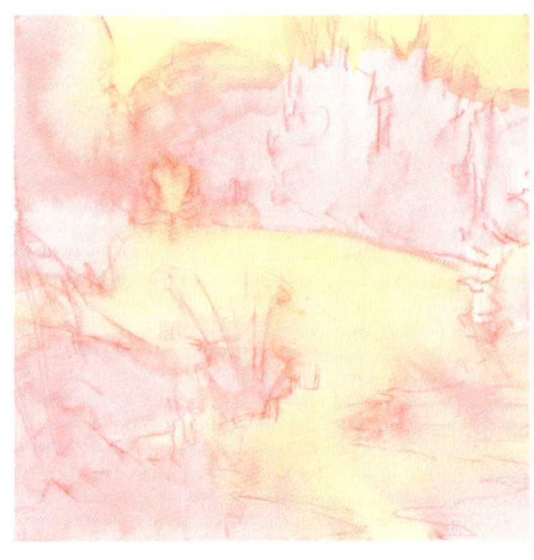

1 ▲ Plan the image

Sketching out a plan is a worthwhile investment of time when starting a painting. Here I explore the major tonal shapes in a series of loose thumbnails using Conté sticks, discovering how the light and dark tones interchange. Despite deciding from the start that I want a landscape format, I experiment with different crops to see how they split up the image between the sky, trees and ground. Once I'm happy with this rough idea, I sketch it out in pencil to resolve some of the details, and give myself something to refer to during the painting process.

2 ▲ Sketch the layout

With the idea resolved, I draw a rough sketch on the watercolour paper using a water-soluble pencil. This will either dissolve or get covered up before any details are added, so keep this under-drawing simple. I mostly work from the pencil sketch, rather than the original reference, roughly indicating simple masses of colour and tone – these big shapes should indicate where later washes go. If you don't have water-soluble pencils, a firm graphite pencil will do fine – avoid softer B pencils, which can muddy watercolours.

3 ▲ Add a contrasting wash

In this stage I create dilute washes of red and yellow watercolour to cover the page. They're intentionally saturated, and will cover the white of the paper to create a vividness that will peek through later layers. For this image, I picked red because it is the complementary of green; the overall colour scheme sits between yellows and greens, so having the red underneath adds a little colour contrast. For a more varied colour scheme, it might work better to match the later layers by using similar colours as opposed to contrasting ones.

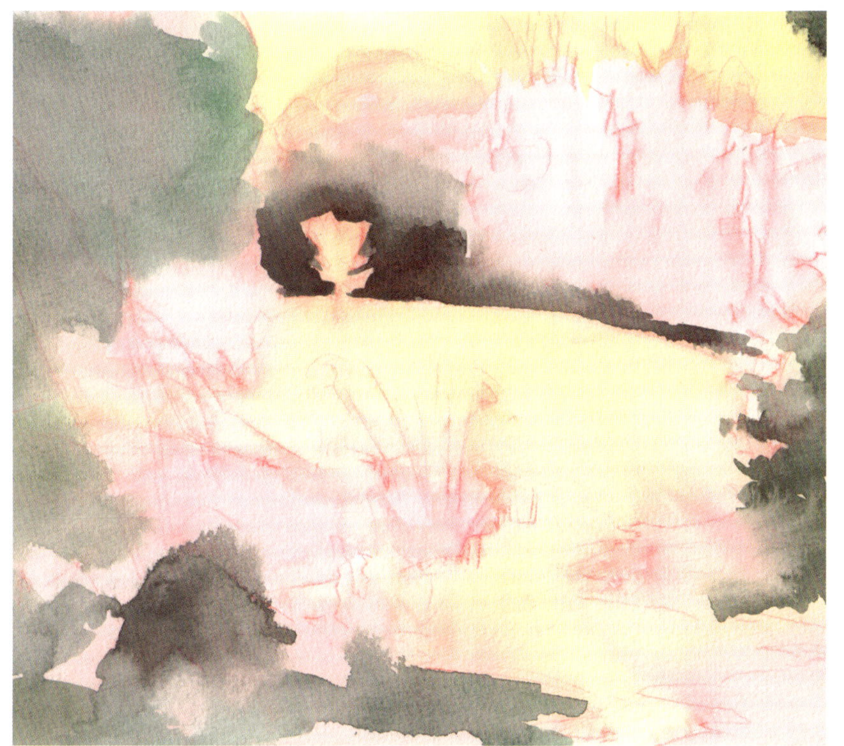

4 ● Place the darker shades
For the shadow areas, I mix some greenish chromatic blacks using varying mixtures of greens and reds. Chromatic blacks are mixed using colours rather than tube black, as the latter can make shadows appear dull. This is done by mixing a black using Winsor Red and Winsor Green, and then adjusting it with other colours in my palette to create a little variety – mostly either Winsor Lemon or Yellow Ochre to create both vivid and dull greens. These early washes are all done in transparent watercolour – this helps them contrast with the opaque lights added later on.

5 ● Add greens
Here more colours are added to cover all of the greenery. The shapes are kept loose and simple, with just a suggestion of leaves, and I'm trying to maintain the tonal shapes from the initial sketch. The most vivid greens appear in the mid-tone and lighter areas, with Winsor Green and Winsor Lemon being used to make the brightest colours. To make duller greens, I add a bit of French Ultramarine or Yellow Ochre. A variety of greens helps the vivid areas 'pop', so don't be afraid to mix some dull or 'ugly' greens.

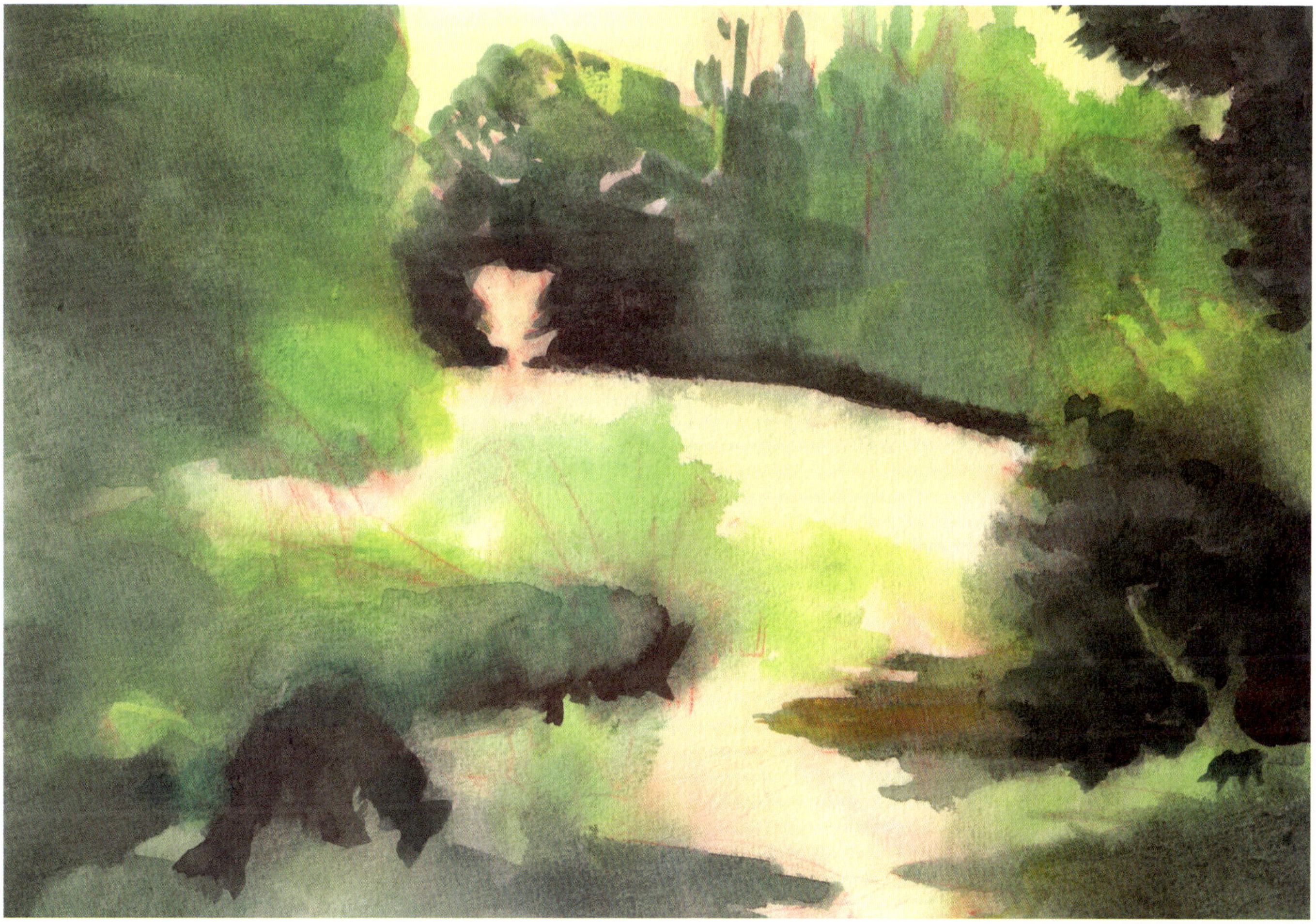

Brushes: quality over quantity

While brush choices change with individual styles, with watercolours it is often best to opt for a few good-quality brushes rather than lots of different sizes. Consider including a larger flat brush for washes, and a good-quality round brush – even one of medium size – will handle most fine details.

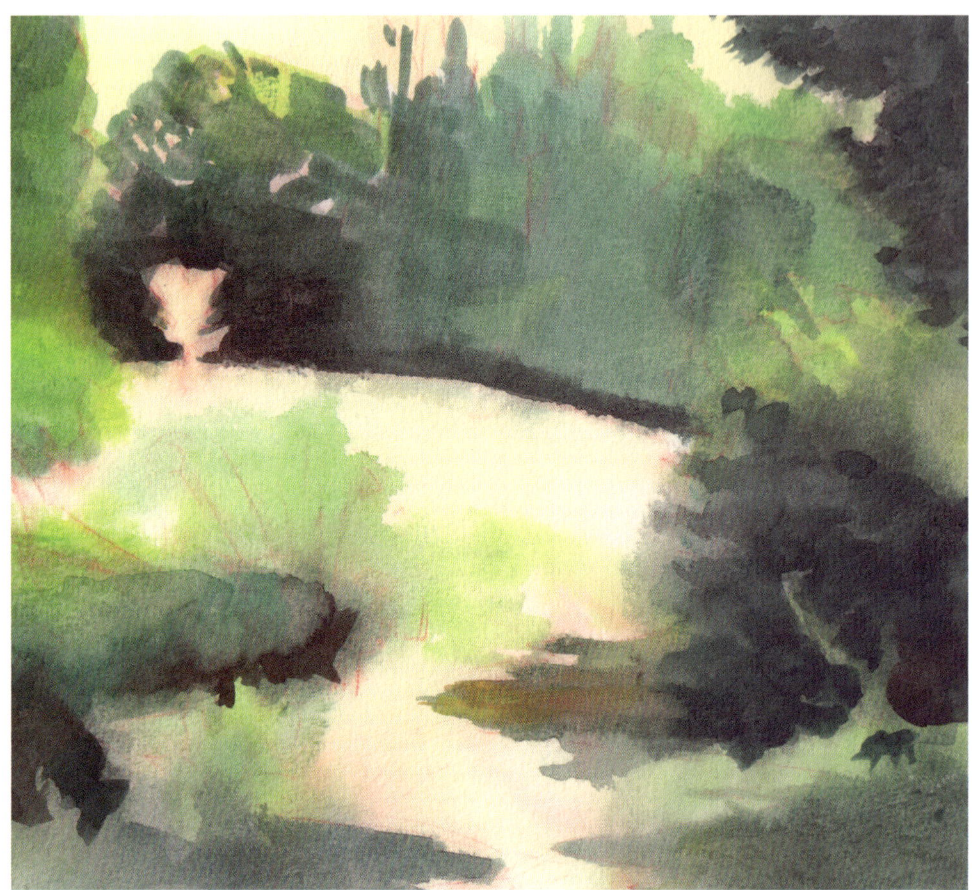

6 ▶ Add the deepest shadows

In this stage I mix some more intense dark greens from the Winsor Green and Winsor Red to define some of the deepest shadows. Because watercolour is so translucent, shadows need a bit more pigment to appear dark enough. – mixing from tube colours will help with this. Here, the shadow greens are bluer to contrast the yellowy light greens. At this point I start to define the silhouette of the foliage, but still leave the tight detail for later stages.

7 ▶ Push the colour

The colours seem to go a little crazy in this stage, but don't worry – most of this will be covered up by gouache later! The red on the dry grass is Winsor Red with a little Cadmium Yellow, and the greens are Winsor Lemon and Green with a little French Ultramarine. These colours will peek through the gouache in places, and are restricted to the lightest areas of the painting. White gouache can appear a little blue and chalky, so having this layer of vivid colour underneath helps to enliven it.

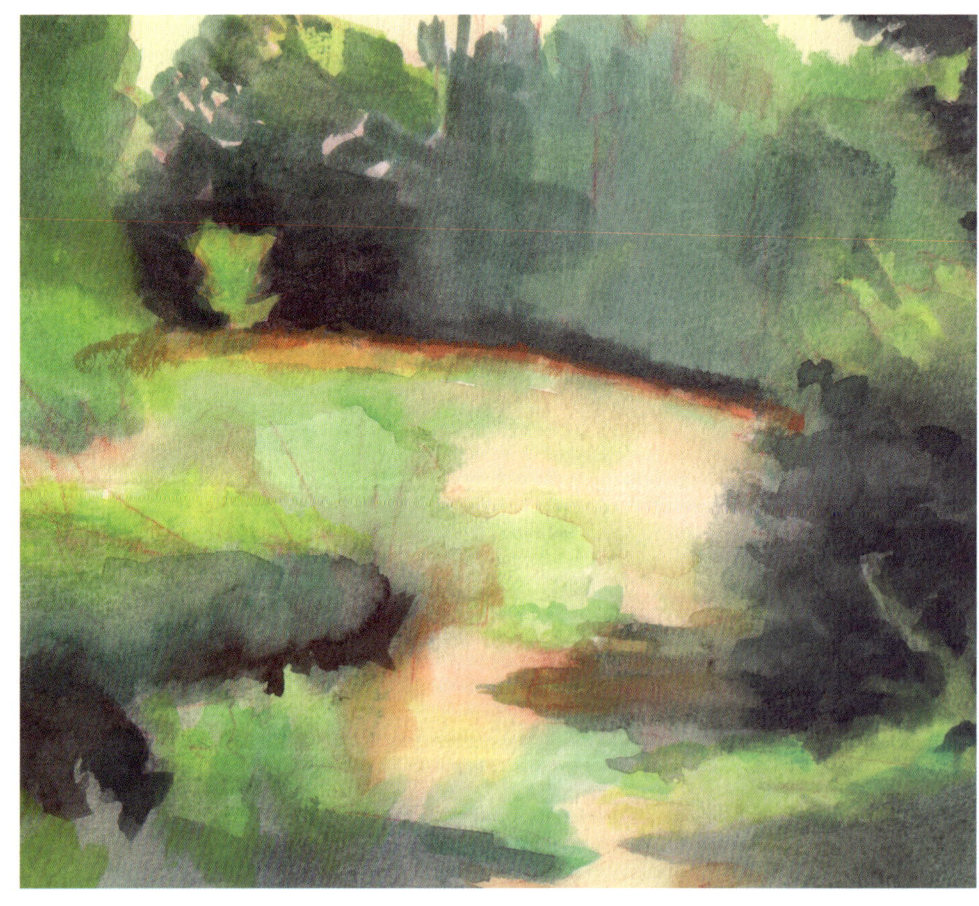

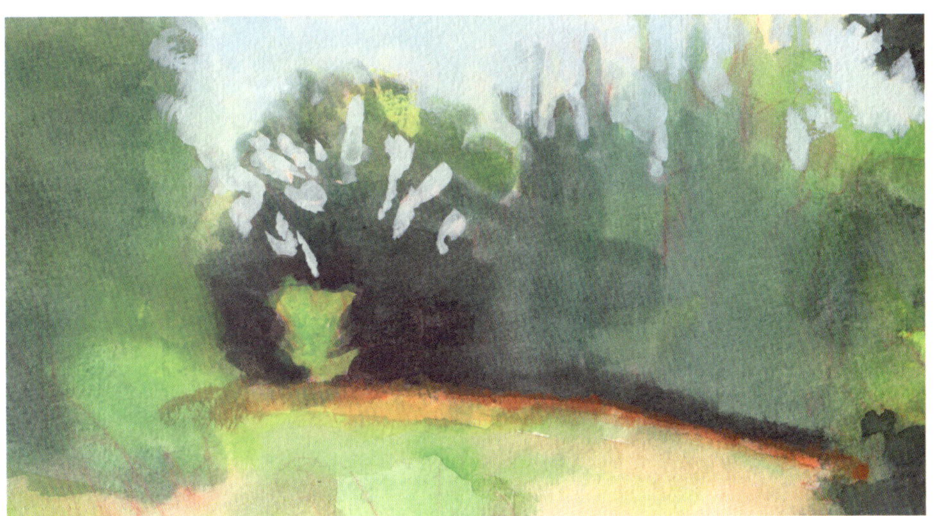

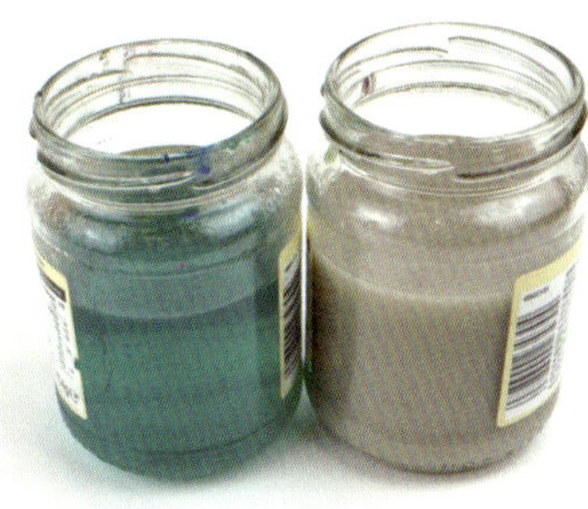

8 ▲ Add the sky

It is finally time to break out the gouache, starting by mixing white gouache with a little Ultramarine watercolour for a light-blue sky. As a general rule, light gouache dries darker than it first appears, while dark gouache dries lighter. To combat this, I make sure my mixture is very light, as the sky is one of the lightest parts of this image. All of the sky goes down in this stage, even the bits between the tree branches. This helps to ensure it has a consistent tone and colour.

9 ▼ Create opaque greens

The opaque greens in this stage are created by mixing the Lemon Yellow gouache with different combinations of watercolours – Winsor Blue, Ultramarine Blue and possibly a bit of white gouache for the blue-greens of the tree on the centre right. Using Lemon Yellow gouache helps keep the greens vivid, but still opaque – white gouache can be used, but it isn't as good for mixing vivid yellowy greens. When painting trees, try to look for the basic shapes and rhythms, and avoid focusing on details like leaves.

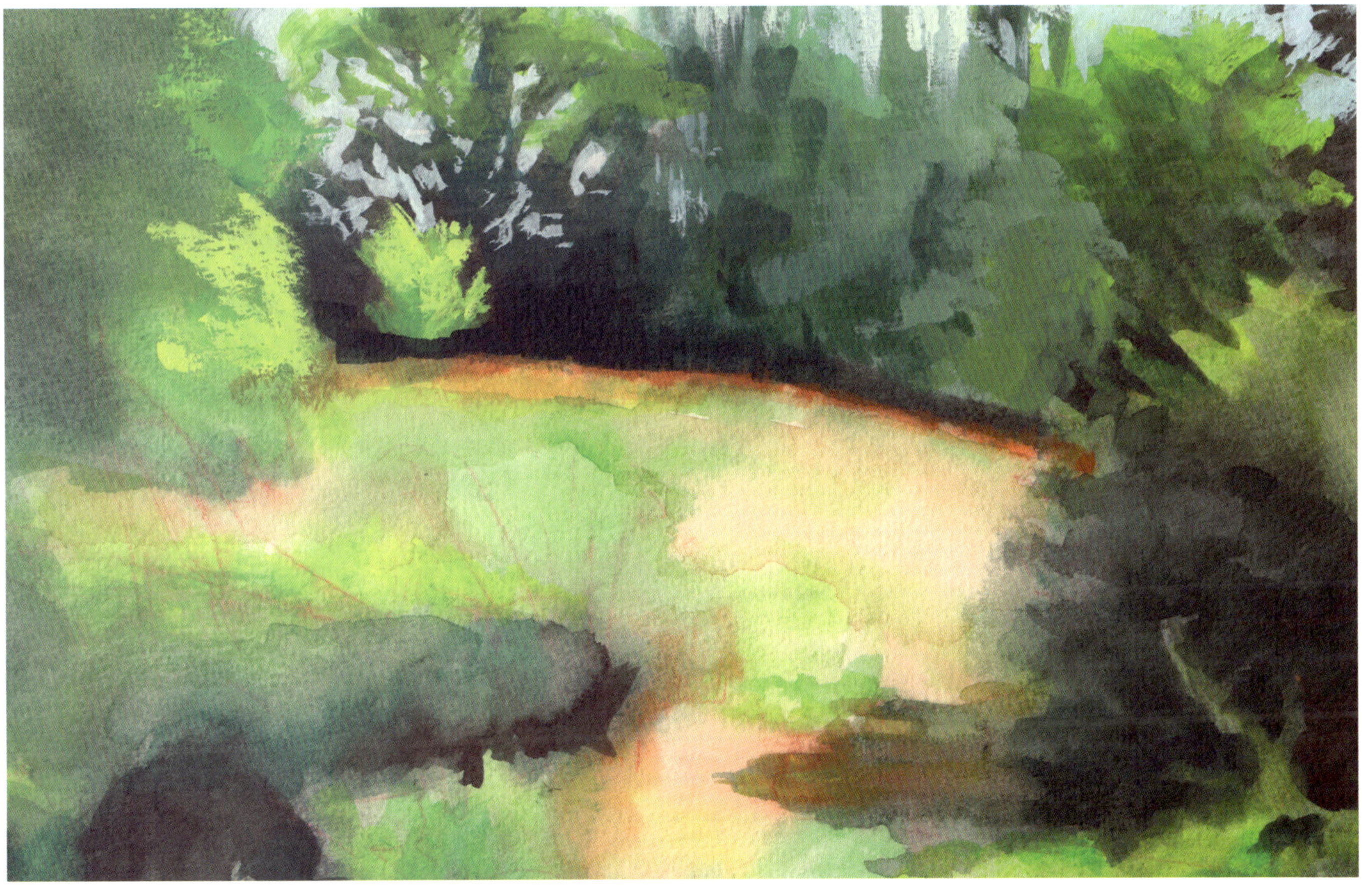

Work clean

Regular changes of water are important to avoid muddying watercolours, and even more so when adding gouache. Where possible, I set up a second jar for washing gouache out of my brushes, and keep it separate to the watercolour jar. This prevents the white gouache from contaminating darker mixes.

10 ▶ Translucent gouache textures

Gouache can be watered down a little to make a translucent, chalky layer, which is ideal for the texture of the dry grass in this scene. The translucency hints at the underlying vivid colours, and fragments of the original colours peek through around the edges. Here I'm mixing combinations of watercolours with the gouache to create a little variety – there are browns, reds and greens in their respective areas. Only tiny amounts of watercolour are needed for this – when mixing, I tend to add them with the corner or tip of a brush.

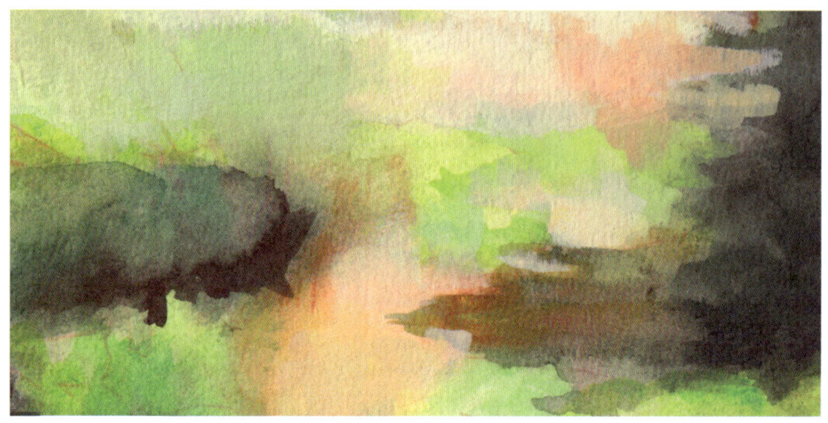

11 ▶ Build up foliage

A lot more definition is added to the foliage in this stage. I work from the background areas towards the foreground, as this helps with avoiding repainting any areas that overlap. Focus on capturing the silhouettes of clumps of leaves, with maybe a few loose ones on the edges. Again, I mix chromatic blacks and dark greens with the watercolours, this time adding a little Lemon Yellow gouache to them to make them more opaque so they sit on top of previous layers. Try to avoid using white gouache for shadowy areas.

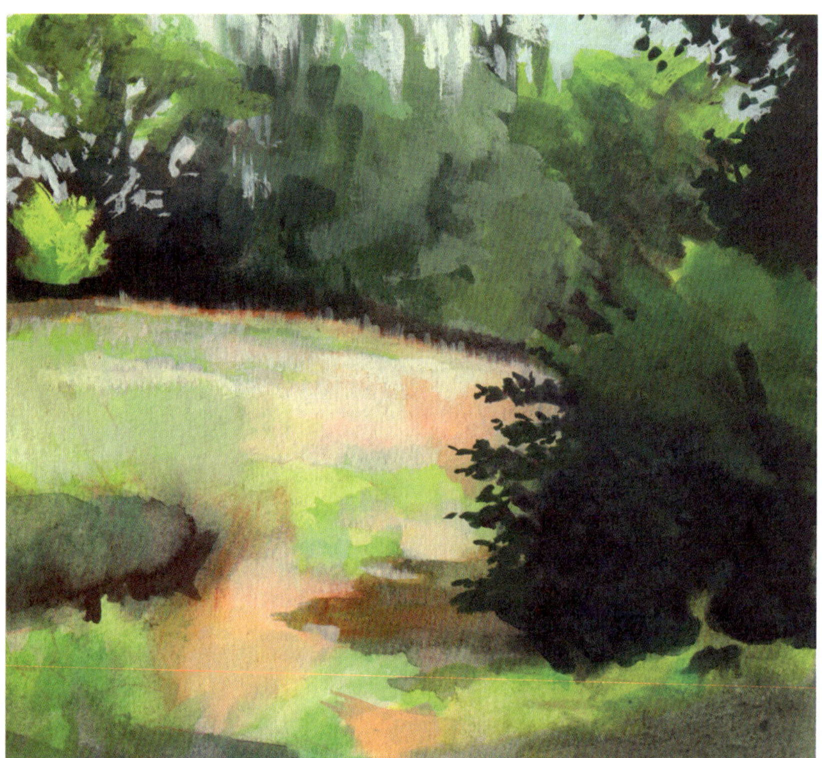

12 ▼ Dry brush textures

I add more opaque greens in this stage, continuing with working from the more distant foliage to the nearest areas. Textural effects tend to be added in the well-lit areas where they are most visible, using Lemon Yellow gouache mixed with greens, and occasionally a little white gouache, with a fairly dry brush. I dab moisture out of the brush using a paper towel and lightly drag it over the paper. Gouache has a 'drier' feel than watercolour and lends itself well to these grittier textures.

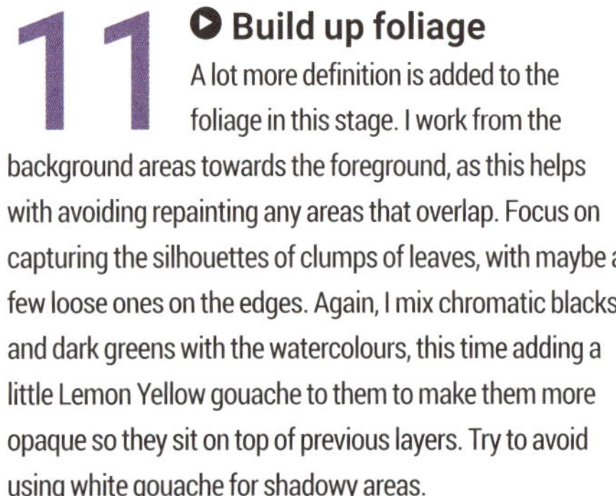

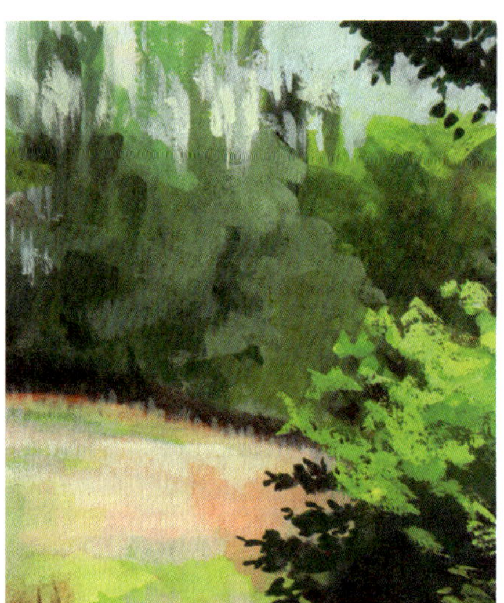

Reactivating gouache

One unique and useful property of gouache that I have not used much in this particular process is its ability to 'reactivate' – when dry gouache gets wet, it becomes malleable again. This is useful for softening edges and creating interesting textures, as wet gouache can bleed into its surroundings.

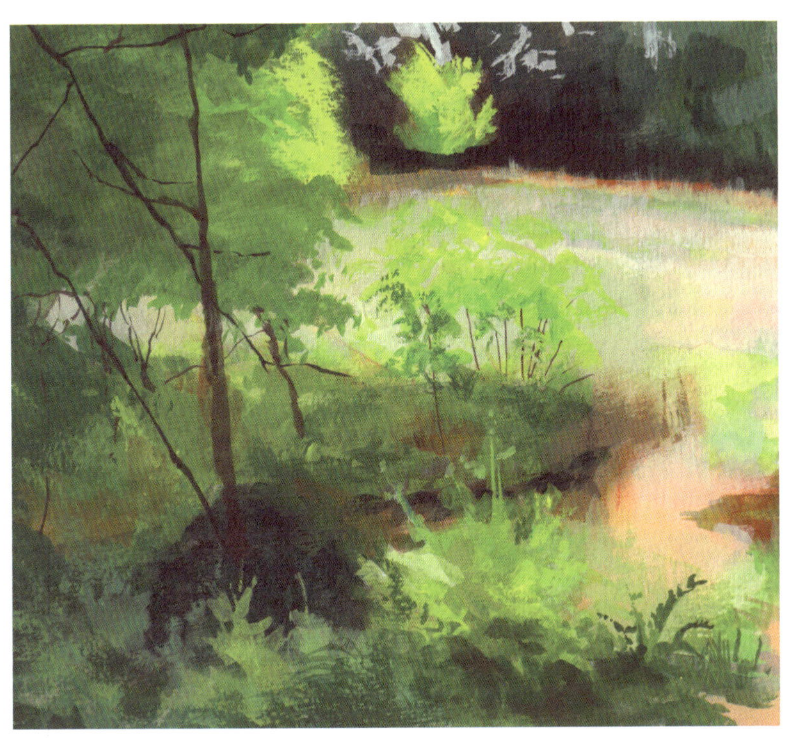

13 ◀ Foreground details

This final layer of foreground details is applied in an opaque layer of dark paint – again created using Lemon Yellow gouache mixed with watercolour pigments. The finer details, such as the grass, branches and ferns are added in using the round #8 sable, while the larger blocks of colour are applied with the 3/8 inch flat brush. There is a lot of noisy detail in the undergrowth areas here, so I simplify it by focusing on the details at the edge of the colour masses, where their edges are most contrasted.

14 ▼ Final touches and highlights

To finalise the details, I add a scattering of small highlights across the painting, and brighten the lit area in the band of dappled light in the foreground. This has been done using yellow gouache mixed with watercolour and applying it with a dry flat brush to add extra texture. Then the final touches are added with the round brush, picking out highlights on the foliage, in the grass, and on the branches, as well as brightening the path to emphasise the lead into the centre of the composition.

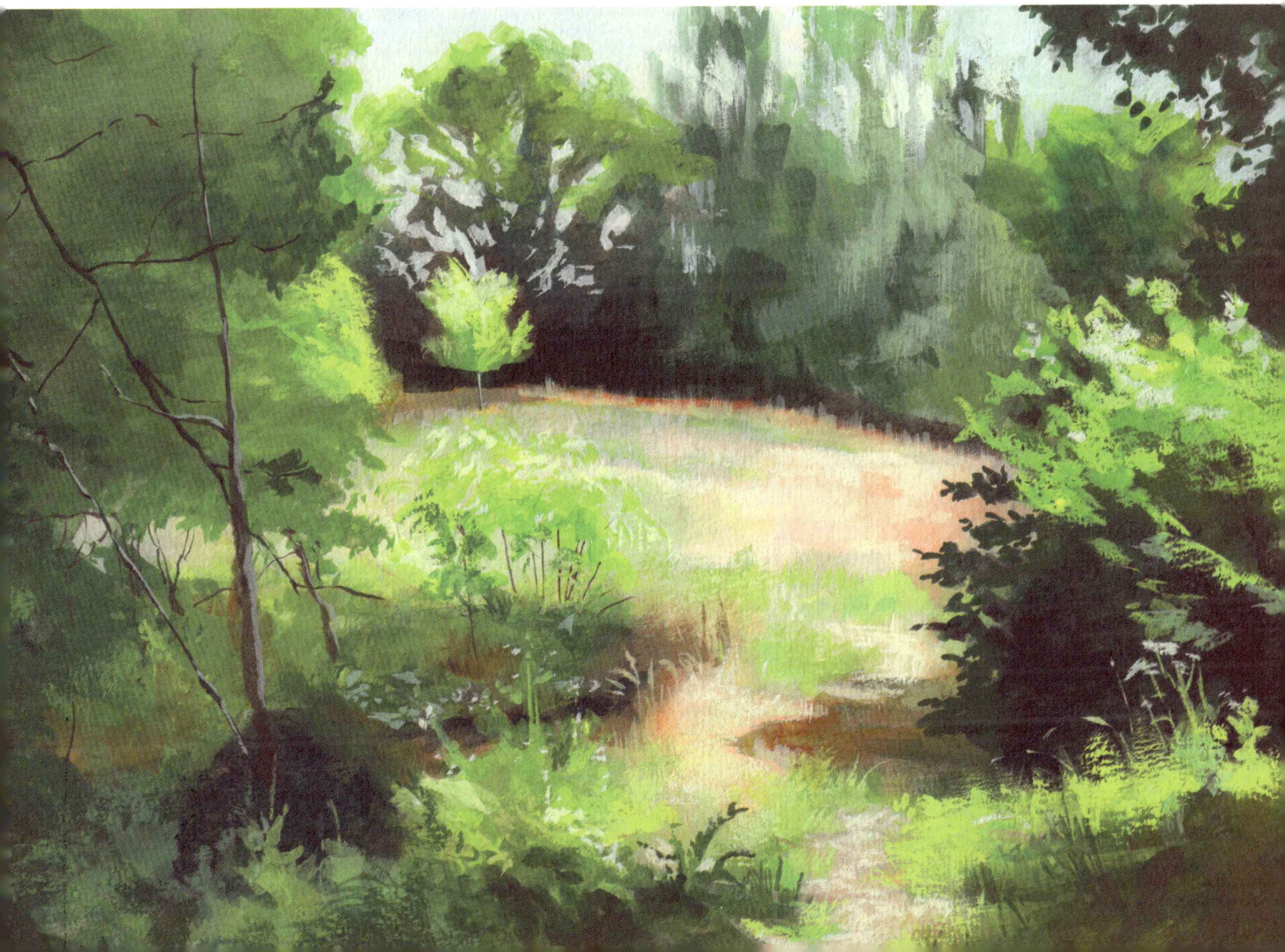

Create artwork that shines

Discover how **Sophie Klesen** (aka SoMK) brings her watercolour painting Estones to life through the application of gold and sterling silver leaf

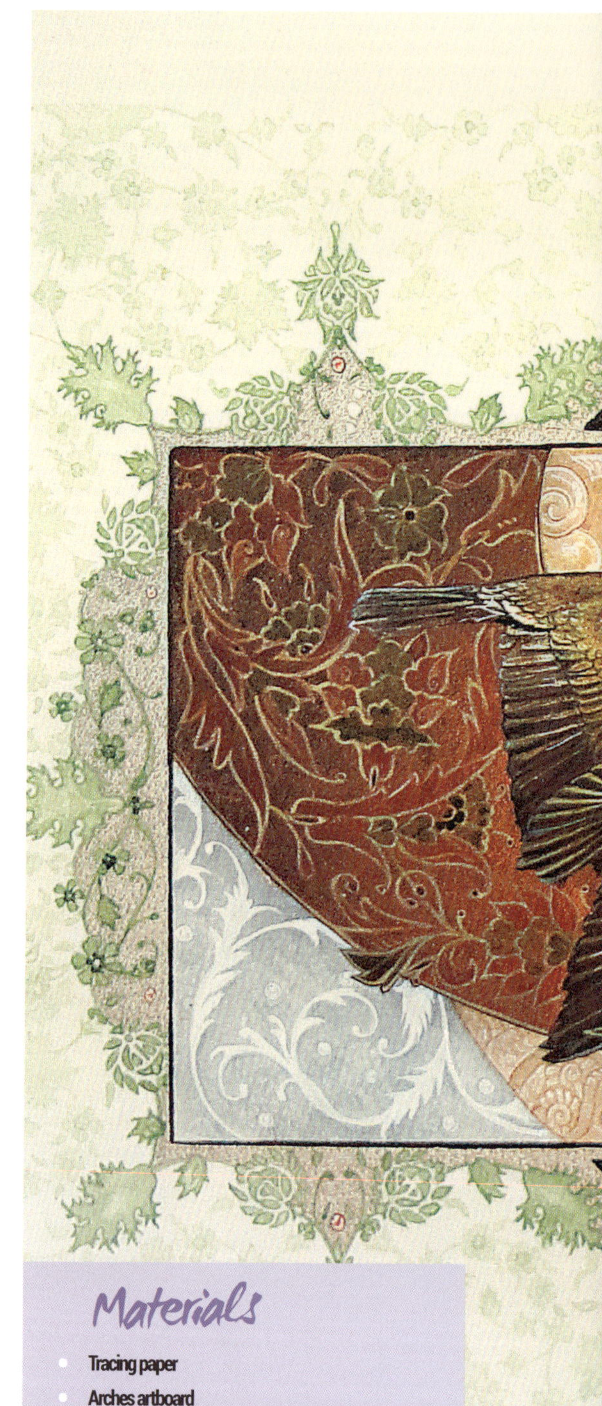

Planning is key to my creative workflow. In this workshop you'll see how I consider every stage beforehand: from creating sketches and thumbnails, to transferring the design to paper, to gilding and painting the piece.

My studio comprises two big tables with several lighting sources and a swivel chair. I use table easels, too – mainly because of wandering cats, but also because I need to change position once in a while. Sometimes work flat on the table (mostly when gilding) or at an angle on the easel, for when I'm painting. My approach to illumination gilding techniques goes hand in hand with the hoarding of art supplies. Pigments of all sorts, brushes, watercolours, papers, vellum have a tendency to quickly accumulate, so I've had to make space among the cupboards and shelves in my studio.

Once you start, gilding is an art with little leeway for improvisation. Yet as you'll see in my workshop, it's possible to change course right in the middle of the creative process!

Even skilled artists can learn something new when they work in an unfamiliar medium. When exploring the possibilities of gilding, don't rush into things. You'll need plenty of practice to feel confident around the various sizes, leaves and burnishing tools, as well as additives, mediums and sometimes historical pigments, papers and vellum. It's a whole new world for you to explore. You'll learn something new every day for the rest of your life, as you lose yourself in history books and museums. I can guarantee it!

This painting was an enjoyable experience for me. As you'll soon see, even if you think you're prepared for everything, what sometimes feels like a good idea in your head and even in thumbnail form, doesn't perfectly translate at a larger size. Sometimes, gold and silver don't shine the way you want them to!

Still, it makes for an interesting journey. And who wants to travel on a smooth road anyway...?

Materials

- Tracing paper
- Arches artboard
- Canson artboard
- Princeton series 3050 brushes
- David Jackson brushes
- Daniel Smith Watercolours
- Transfer champagne gold metallic leaf
- Loose oxidised sterling silver leaf by Gold Leaf Supplies
- Copper leaf
- Gilding media Ormoline by Roberson & Co
- Oil-based gold size
- Burnishers, Tape, Ox gall, Claret (egg whites)

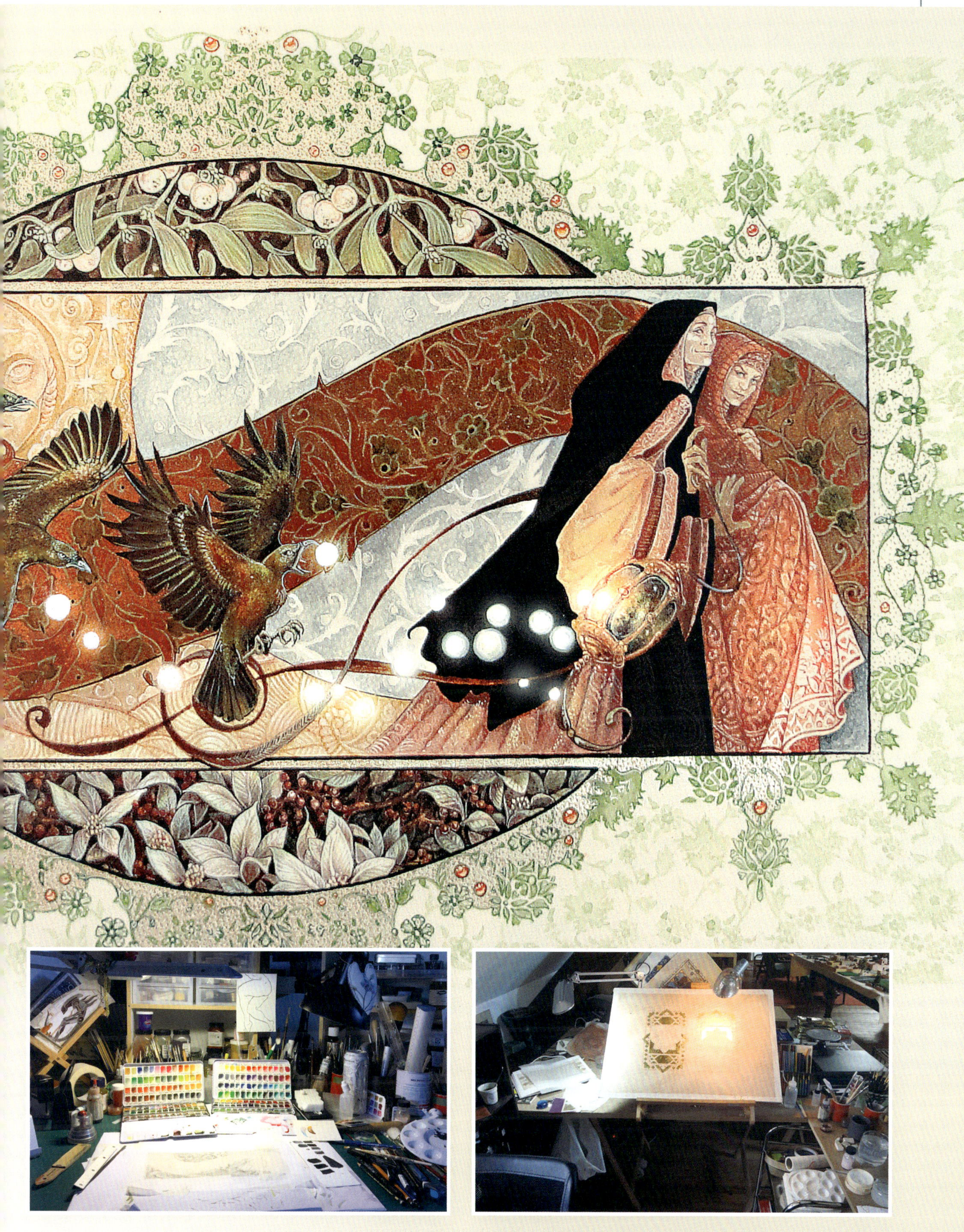

Prepare your surfaces

When gilding on paper, use 200lbs/300g and think about stretching it first. I often prepare my boards this way, even stretching 400lbs paper. This will be useful when gilding large areas and even more so when gilding with illuminator gesso, which is a mix of plaster and glue, and can buckle the paper.

Think about your paint requirements

When dealing with historical pigments and a homemade binding medium, try to work out the exact quantity of paint you'll need. If you make too much paint, it will more or less be lost and some pigments are quite expensive. If you run short, there's a good chance you'll never be able to produce a new mix of the same colour.

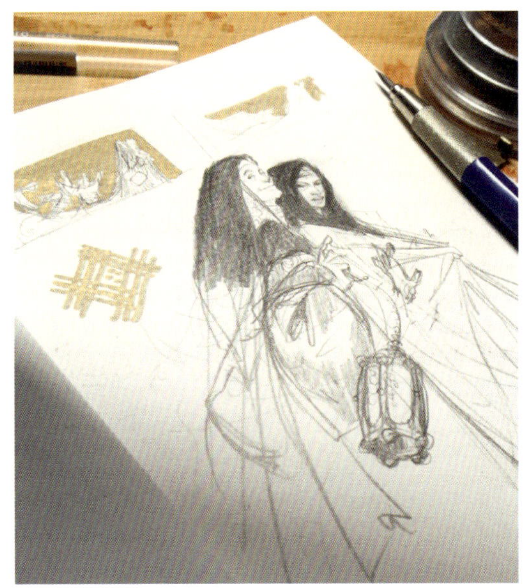

1 ⬠ Sketches galore!

Everything starts from a small sketch. I steadily fill blank books or loose sheets of paper every day, drawing whatever comes to mind. Sometimes a small sketch turns into a bigger painting. The aim, of course, is to sketch a lot, all the time. First, because the results can be funny; and second, because it makes us better artists.

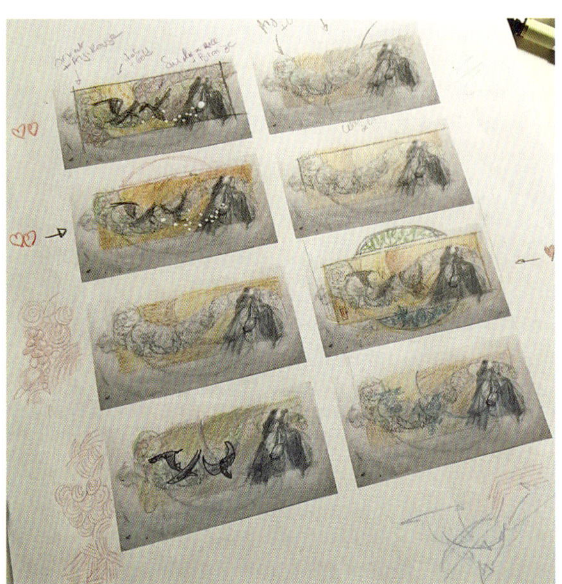

2 ⬠ Turn a sketch into useful thumbnails

Ah, thumbnails! Now this is an especially important stage. It's when you decide what the painting will roughly look like, its layout, the atmosphere you want to convey and any colour choices. It's the first time you can translate what's in your head into tangible mini-images on paper. So many possibilities... it's hard to pick just one.

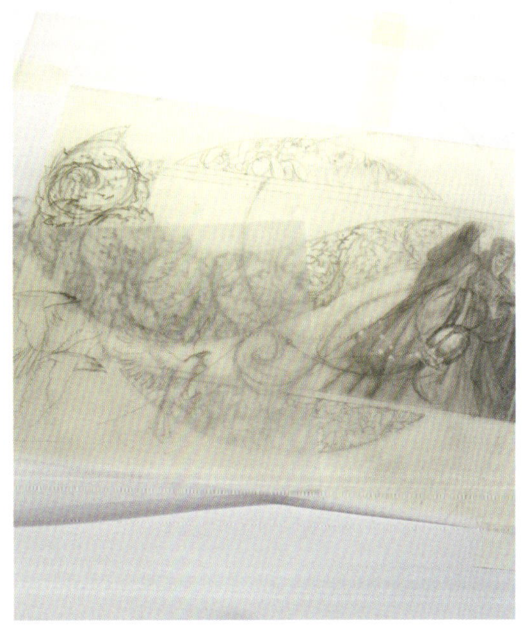

3 ⬠ The power of tracing paper

Tracing paper enables you to sketch different elements, arrange them and finalise the composition of your painting. Not all tracing papers are made equally. I prefer to use thin sheets for sketching and layout decisions. To finalise the design before transferring it, I prefer a thick tracing paper that I'll keep for reference.

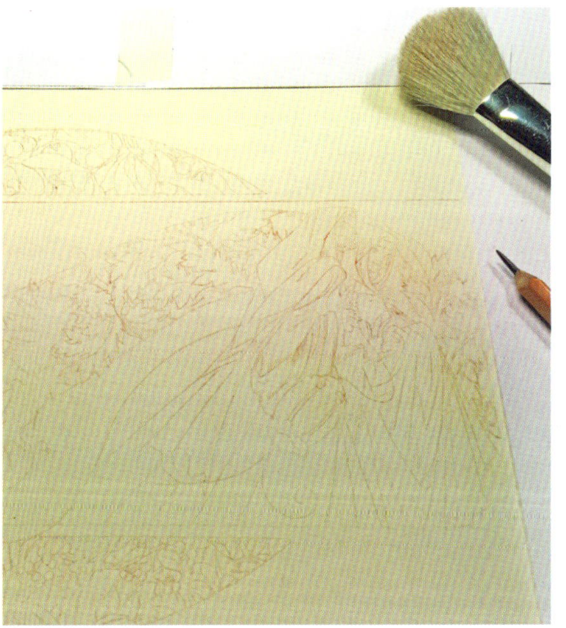

4 ⬠ Transfer the design

I transfer the art on to a very thick and smooth Canson artboard. When you work on vellum you might choose to use sanguine (red chalk) instead of graphite powder, which can become stuck in the pores of vellum. Its greasiness won't help watercolours, either. I prefer to use sanguine, even when working on paper.

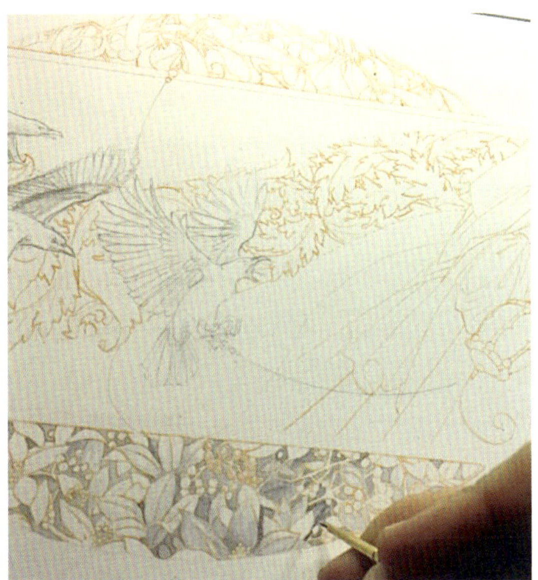

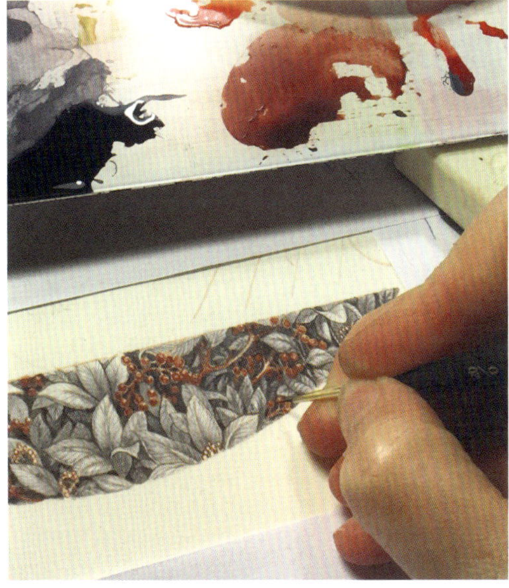

If you're using different metal leaves, gild with gold first! Gold adheres to gold, but will leave sparkles elsewhere.

5 ⬤ Set the design

Because I'll take a long time working on the design, I don't want it to disappear too quickly. So I go over it with a thin brush, applying a light wash of iron oxide. I pick up the remaining sanguine powder with a kneaded eraser so as not to smudge it on the areas that I want to stay white.

6 ⬤ Add grisaille in the leaves

Before working with grisaille you need to decide where the values will be. I start by brushing a few layers of very transparent colours on top. The basic grey is a neutral grey, and the layers of colours have some egg white in the mix to provide a good base for the glaze.

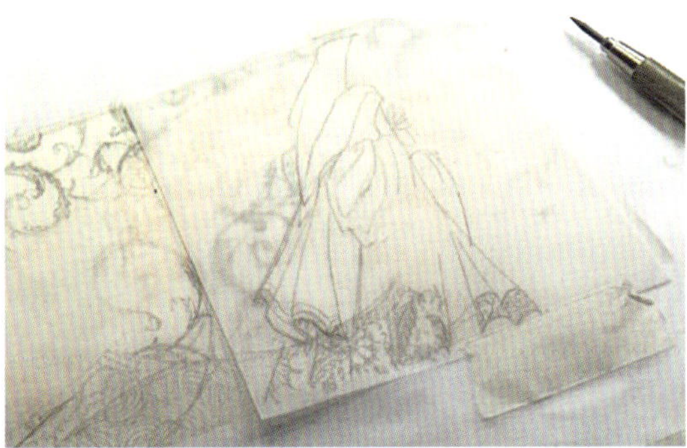

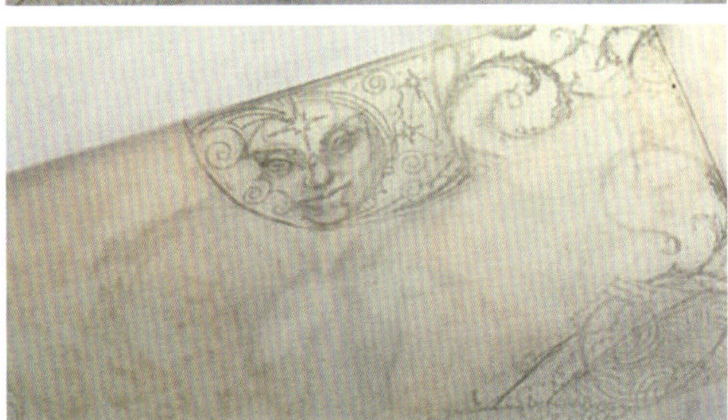

7 ⬤ Protect and refine

Because this is a lengthy project, I need to maintain my interest, so I jump from one part to another to keep the work varied and let the various paints dry. I cut and rearrange a lot of papers throughout the process. It's now time to bring some details to the central area.

8 ⬤ Gold and silver leaves

Now I brush in gold size (tinted with iron oxide for readability) and apply transfer gold leaf and loose sterling silver leaf. I'm not aiming for a shiny rendering, but rather a more weathered, powdery look. All the details on the various leaves will have to be painted afterwards.

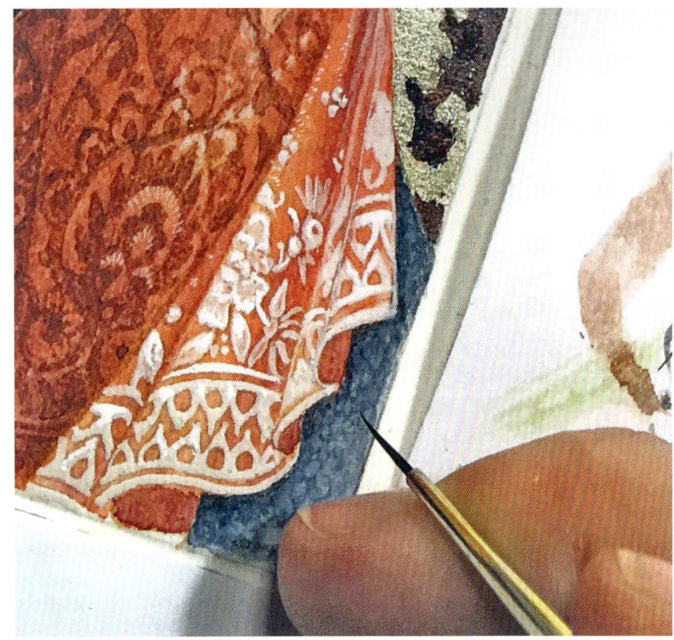

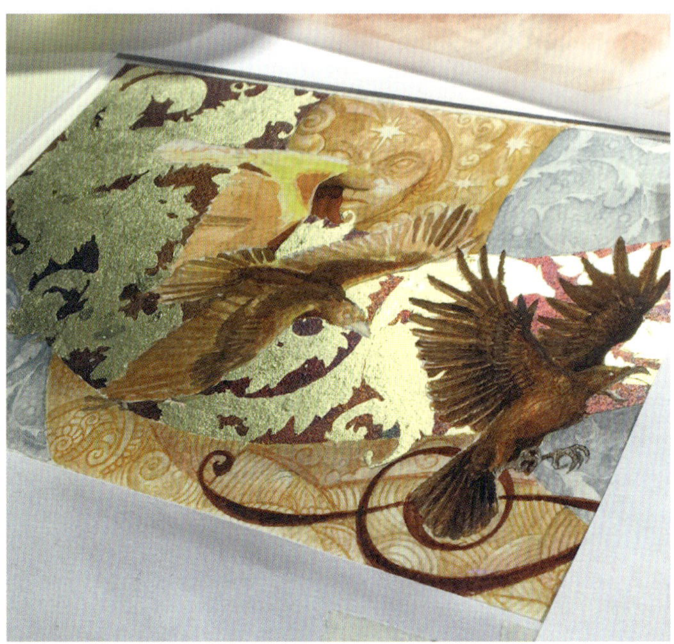

9 ▲ Tackle the details in the cloth elements

I find painting details such as the embroidery on the cloak very relaxing. The main colours are three Quinacridone watercolours: Yellow, Sienna, and a deeper Burnt Scarlet for the shadows. The details are painted in translucent Eggshell White and Titanium White. I use a Princeton Monogram series 3050 brush: the tip is thin and precise, and perfect for the task.

10 ▲ The birds fail to take flight

Something is bugging me. The gold and red background looks overpowering. The birds are lost in that complex shiny design – and if I follow through with my intention of painting all the details of the Acanthus leaves, things will look even worse. I carry on painting the background and the birds while thinking about this…

11 ▶ Illustrate an Iranian-style vine element

I decide to use a very light Sap Green wash, which helps to knock back the complex design of the border. I sketch one of the corners and mirror it four times all around the painting. I then design the middle sections to complete the painting's border. I want to keep the monochrome fabric looking vibrant.

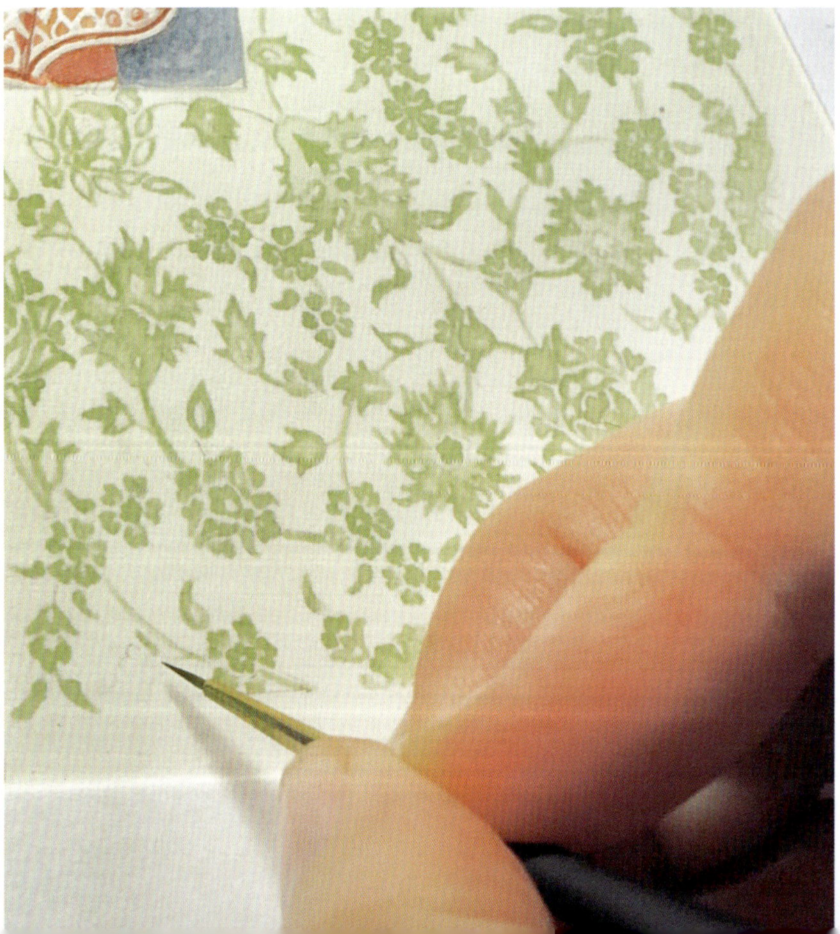

Painting on gold

When you've finished gilding and you want to paint something on the gold, bear in mind that the metal leaf will do everything it can to shake off the wet paint. The answer is to either add a wetting, dispersant agent to the mix, or to paint the area first with, for example, ox gall.

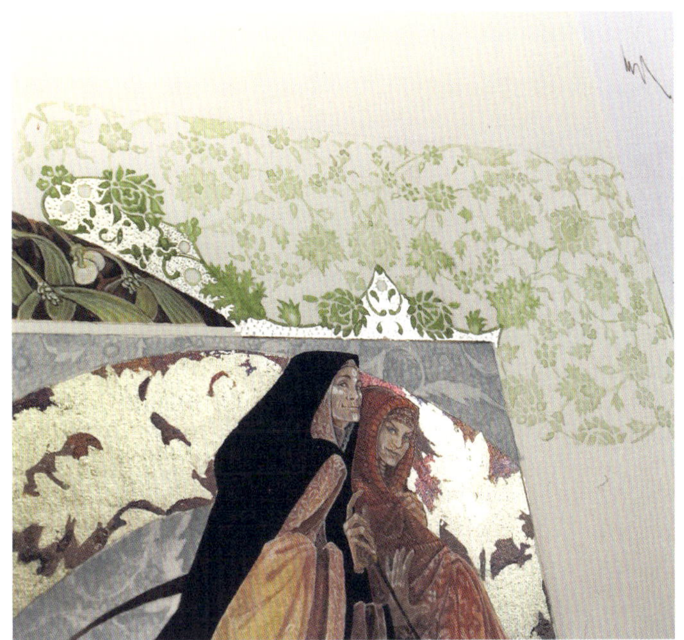

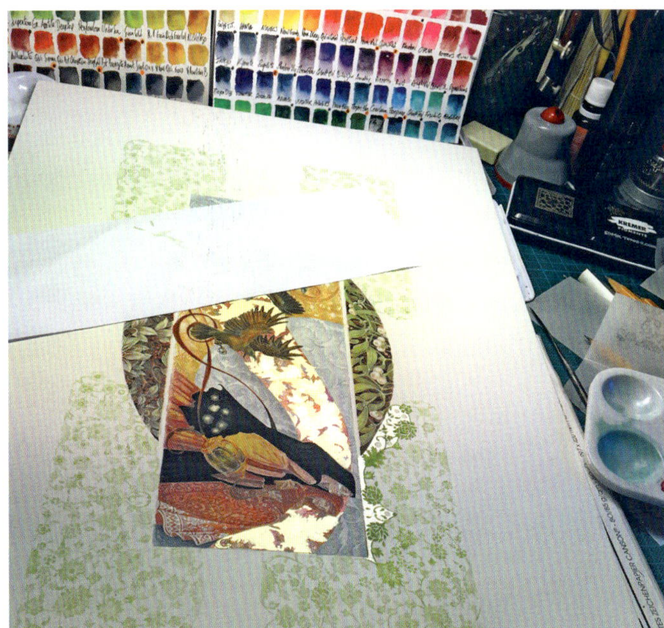

12 ⬥ Add Champagne gold

I apply Champagne gold leaf on the inner side of the border. I work it to generate an interesting texture to the gold and make it a little less shiny. I really want to keep a subdued look to that border. A strong colour and shiny gold could make it look unsubtle and off-putting.

13 ⬥ Finally, a big change of heart

No, no, no – those gold and red leaves are just too loud! I'm losing my birds in there, because all I can see are just see the shiny parts! But I know that using oil gold size will enable me to correct this with another layer of copper leaf! A pentimento if I ever saw one, but I'm sure the piece will look so much better for it.

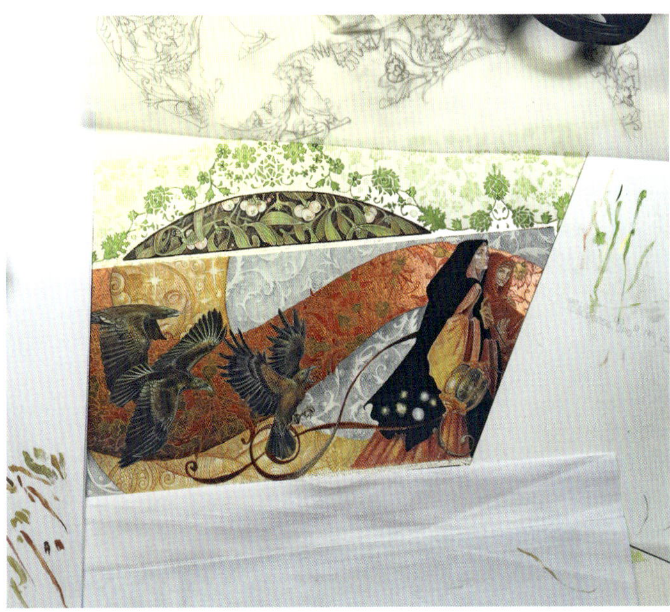

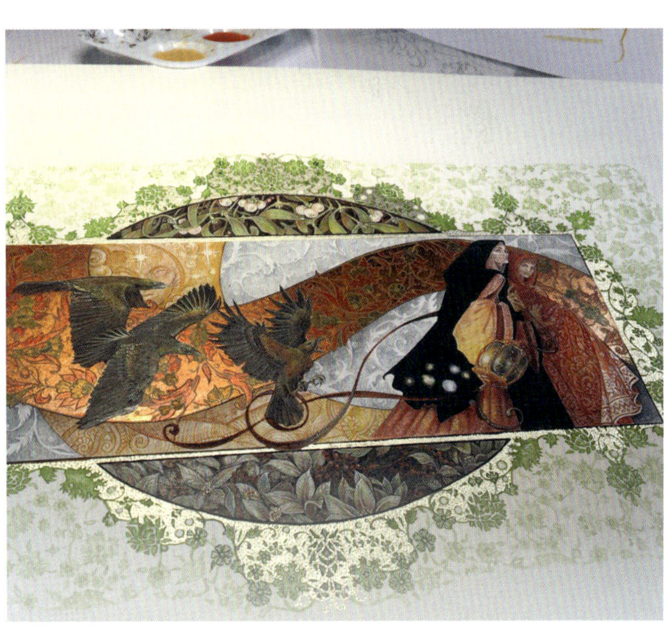

14 ⬥ Copper to the rescue!

The surrounding details are now much clearer: they're warm and blend in when I add a layer of translucent red and green flowery designs on top. The paint adheres to the leaf thanks to the added ox gall. I like the result of this move. It shows you can always change your mind, if you have the confidence to act on your ideas.

15 ⬥ On to the finish line!

From here it's just a case of putting cherries on top! I refine, add details and straight lines to tidy things up. I play with the white fireflies and the very deep black on the cloak, then tweak the colours and, because I could keep on painting in there for hours, declare it done! Now let's start something new…

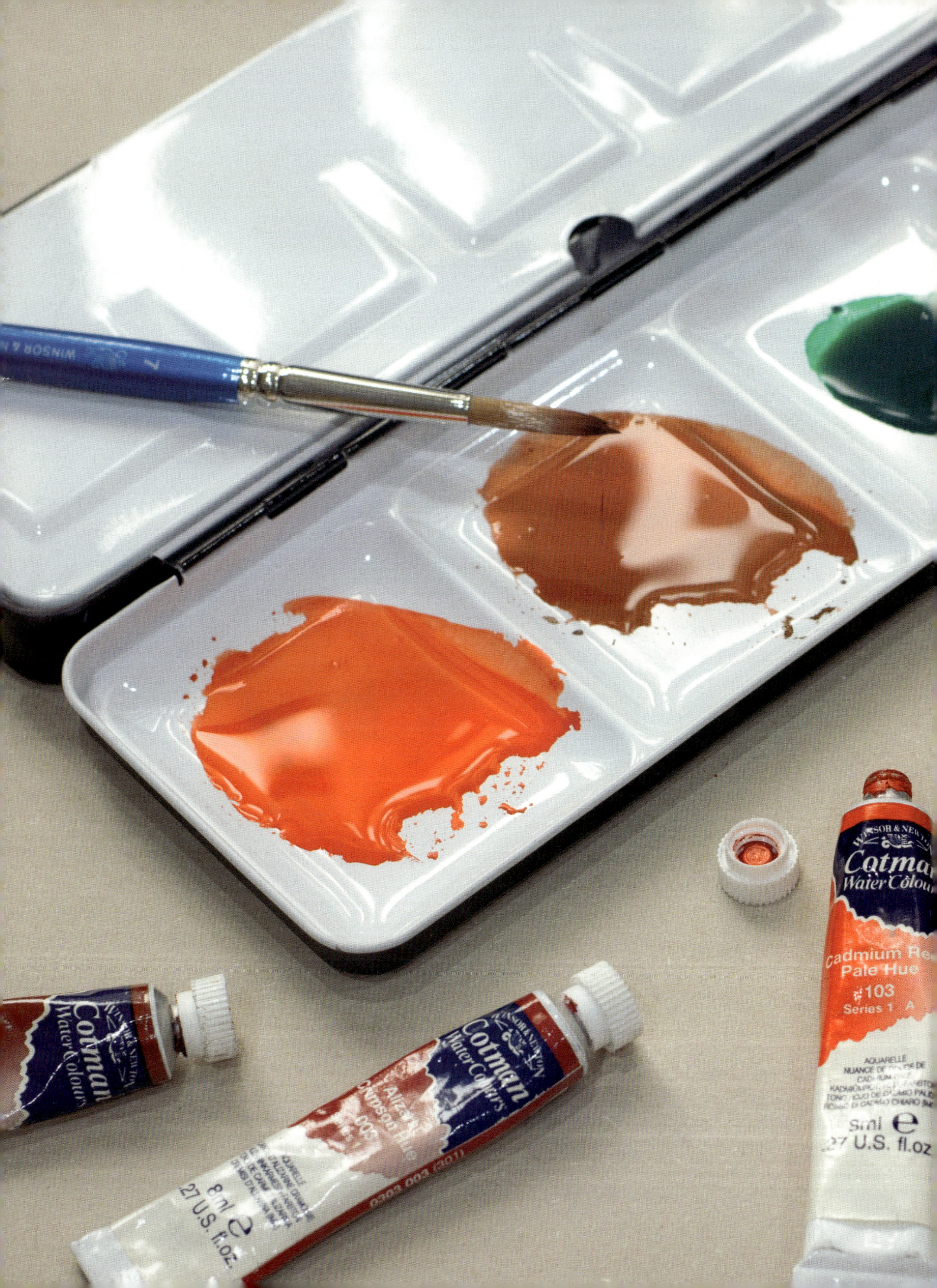